AUTHORS SERIES · VOLUME III

THE NORWEGIAN-AMERICAN HISTORICAL ASSOCIATION

ARTHUR O. DAVIDSON, *President*

Board of Publications:

KENNETH O. BJORK, *Editor*

ARLOW W. ANDERSEN

C. A. CLAUSEN

ERIK J. FRIIS

CLARENCE A. GLASRUD

EINAR HAUGEN

ODD S. LOVOLL

PETER A. MUNCH

CARLTON C. QUALEY

Kristofer Janson (*c.* 1865)

AUTHORS SERIES · VOLUME III

Kristofer Janson in America

by NINA DRAXTEN

1976

Published for the
Norwegian-American Historical Association
by Twayne Publishers
A Division of G. K. Hall & Co., Boston

Library of Congress Cataloging in Publication Data

Draxten, Nina.
  Kristofer Janson in America.

  (Authors series ; v. 3)
  Bibliography: pp. 387–94.
  Includes index.
  1. Janson, Kristofer Nagel, 1841–1917—Biography. I. Title. II. Series:
Norwegian-American Historical Association. Authors series ; v. 3.
PT8902.Z5D7   839.8'2'16 [B]   75–42198
ISBN 0–8057–9000–4

The figure that appears on the cover and title page of this book is one of the twenty-four letters in the older Germanic runic alphabet used in the Scandinavian countries from about 200 to 800 A.D. In addition to representing the sound "m," approximately as in modern English, it also has a name, meaning "man" or "mankind." It thus serves here as a symbol for the humanities.

IN MEMORY OF

BERSVEND O. DRAXTEN

Foreword

WITH NINA Draxten's *Kristofer Janson in America,* the Association presents the third volume in its Authors Series. Clarence A. Glasrud, in *Hjalmar Hjorth Boyesen,* gave us not only a vivid description of a career that touched the boundaries of immigrant life, but also analyzed the forces at work during a transitional period in American cultural history. Lloyd Hustvedt's *Rasmus Bjørn Anderson,* by contrast, is a realistic study of a person who—as teacher and editor—for decades was at the very heart of Norwegian-American life, but whose literary skills hardly matched those of Boyesen. We look forward to issuing in the next few years a volume recounting the activity of Marcus Thrane in the New World to include his America-based plays and skits, and a biography of Waldemar Ager, creative writer and social reformer.

Kristofer Janson was unique in that, although a recognized poet in Norway at the time of his first visit to America in 1879 and a prolific writer in the following decades, he devoted the better part of his time in the 1880s and 1890s as a minister, furthering the cause of Unitarianism among the Scandinavians of the Upper Midwest. To this difficult task, he gave unsparingly of his abundant energy and used both pen and pulpit to advance his liberal cause. None of his congregations was large, and even his central church in Minneapolis failed to survive to the present; but the Nora Free Christian Church, which he organized near Hanska, Minnesota, continues as a vigorous memorial to his teachings.

Janson's influence cannot, however, be measured by the formal membership of his congregations. Great numbers of immigrants, many of them passing through the Twin Cities en route to points farther west and north, crowded his Minneapolis church to hear his sermons and readings; others read his publications; even more heard his lectures when he toured the Norwegian settlements. Most were spellbound by Janson's platform performances, and many found in his messages—religious, historical, social, and literary in content—their first introduction to the world of American thought in a period of vigorous agitation for reform. Janson was, perhaps first and last, a champion of the social gospel and of the oppressed.

The author of this exciting biography was born in Minneapolis, and she has spent the greater part of her life in that city. A graduate of the University of Minnesota, where she also earned a master's degree, she taught English in the General College of her alma mater from the late 1940s to her retirement in 1969. She devoted many years to researching, planning, and writing the biography. It has been a pleasure to work with her and to witness her dedication to truth, remarkable even among scholars. I have been impressed, too, by the understanding and sympathy she brought to her discussions of family life, especially to Janson's relations with Drude, his cultured and talented wife.

I wish to acknowledge the invaluable assistance given me by Ralph L. Henry, retired professor of English at Carleton College, in the task of editing this volume, and by Charlotte M. Jacobson, curator of the Association's archives, who prepared the index.

KENNETH O. BJORK

St. Olaf College

Preface

THIS BOOK germinated in the winter of 1888 or 1889. At that time my grandfather was farming in Brooklyn Center, an area lying north of Minneapolis. He was a Norwegian Synod man, never fanatically partisan, but zealous enough to be one of the organizers of a "mission congegation" among the farmers in his neighborhood.

Life on the farm was hard and lonely. What leisure time the family had was best spent in reading, but books and other printed materials were scarce. Thus when sample copies of Kristofer Janson's magazine *Saamanden* made their way to the farmhouse, they were read by everyone in the family old enough to do so, and—like every other newspaper or periodical—they were carefully put away to be taken out again when pickings were few.

My father, then in his early twenties, more than once read and pondered over what he had found in *Saamanden*. One day while he and my grandfather were at work in the fields, my father mentioned his interest in Janson, saying, "There is much to what that man says." My grandfather smiled indulgently, commenting that it might seem that way, but, from what he had heard, Kristofer Janson was just another troublemaker.

That winter my grandfather's cousin Nels came for a visit. His family had homesteaded in Meeker County, and Nels was known to be an enterprising man, if a little eccentric. On this occasion he revealed that he, too, had been reading *Saamanden*, and he declared that the one thing he must be sure to do before he left the area was to hear Kristofer Janson. My grandfather hospitably offered to drive him over to Janson's Minneapolis church the following Sunday evening if the weather was at all favorable.

Kristofer Janson in America

That night my father waited up to give the men a hand with the horses on their return. The church was seventeen or eighteen miles away and, even on a mild winter night, a ride home in an open sleigh could be chilling. Yet when the two got back home, they said nothing about being cold. Nels had been very deeply impressed by what he had heard, and the change in my grandfather was phenomenal. Years later my father told me that my grandfather "came home a different man." He declared that "he had never heard anything like it." As my father reported it, thereafter my grandfather couldn't get enough of Kristofer Janson.

This was how I first learned about Janson. The story has always had an electrifying effect on me, for I understood from the first what my grandfather had experienced—something that lighted up a world that he had been unaware of before. With the passage of time, I came to see that my father's estimate of Janson had remained with him and was part of the bond he felt for such men as Ivar Odegaard, Siver Serumgaard, John C. Huseby, and especially for Lauritz Stavnheim, who lived a remarkably disciplined life in adherence to Kristofer Janson's principles.

It is commonly said that a biographer must have a thorough knowledge of his subject, a sympathy for it, and a willingness to tell the whole truth. I have tried to keep these criteria in mind. Fairly early in my research, I was able to open a correspondence with the Jansons' second son, Dr. Eilev Janson, a dermatologist in Seattle, then eighty-eight years old but still continuing his practice on a limited scale. After an exchange of several letters, I spent a week as a guest in his house. At first Dr. Janson felt that it would be best not to make a full disclosure of the circumstances leading to Janson's departure from America. I assured him that I would respect his wishes, even though I felt that a complete account of what had actually happened would be the wiser course. As we discussed the matter, taking into consideration such factors as the passage of time and the earlier publication of *Mira,* Dr. Janson came to agree with me.

While I was in Seattle, I came to know Mrs. Dina Behr Kolderup and Miss Borghild Lee, both of whom have given me invaluable help. At Mrs. Kolderup's suggestion, I wrote to Fru Signe Forchhammer in Copenhagen, then the Jansons' only living daughter. As a result, I exchanged several letters with her and received a photograph of the Janson family taken in the early years of their stay in America. I have also had help from Mrs. Eilev Janson, my hostess in Seattle. After the publication of my first article on Janson's lecture tour of 1879–80 in *Norwegian-American Studies,* I heard from Mrs. Elinor Janson Hudson, a daughter of Arne Janson, who has supplied me with considerable pertinent information.

Of the many other persons who have assisted me, I must first mention the Reverend Carl W. Schevenius, pastor emeritus of Asbury Methodist Church in Minneapolis. At the time I began this investigation, I did not know him, but he shortly became a friend and counselor, lending me books and helping me obtain information. It was he—when all my other efforts had failed—who located the daughter of Oscar Gundersen, Mrs. Gudrun Rom.

I am also grateful to the late Dean Theodore C. Blegen for the encouragement he gave me in the early stages of this investigation. Professor Einar Haugen allowed me to use his files of the Janson-Bjørnson correspondence. Through the courtesy of Mr. Erling Grønland, head librarian of the Norwegian department of the University Library in Oslo, I had access to source materials otherwise unobtainable. Professor Lloyd Hustvedt, archivist of the Norwegian-American Historical Association, gave me useful leads, and the late Beulah Folkedahl, custodian of its archives, called my attention to the Peder Ydstie letter. Professor Harald Naess of the University of Wisconsin made available to me various articles on and by Hamsun, in particular the unsigned piece, "Kristofer Janson i Amerika," which appeared in *Verdens Gang* (Kristiania) on January 22, 1885. Through the courtesy of Mr. Thor Ohme, I received several of Janson's books from Oslo Lodge, No. 2, Sons of Norway. Mr. Sigvald Stoylen gave me access to his extensive collection of Norwegian immigrant material.

I have had very generous treatment from people associated with Nora Free Christian Church in Hanska, Minnesota. I am especially grateful to Miss Julia Becken, foster daughter of Dr. Amandus Norman, for books, photographs, and material on both Janson and Norman. Miss Minnie Running and Miss Jessie Haugen supplied me with information on the Jansons' days in Brown County. I have had help from the late Revered Peter J. Hanson and Mrs. Hanson, and I am especially in debt to V. Emil Gudmundson, who came from the Icelandic Unitarian colony in Canada in which Janson was interested many years ago, and who is now interdistrict representative of the Unitarian-Universalist Association with headquarters in Minneapolis. I also owe thanks to Dr. Charles H. Lyttle, James Freeman Clarke professor emeritus of church history at Meadville Theological School. In Underwood, Minnesota, I had the valuable assistance of Mr. Halvor Moen and Miss Gunda Hansen. I have had help from Mrs. Marie

Stoep of Minneapolis, who had been a member of Nazareth Church, and Mrs. Petra Wallace, who, as Mrs. Hagbarth Jorgensen, had been a member of Janson's St. Paul congregation.

I am grateful to my colleagues at the General College of the University of Minnesota for many kindnesses. I have used the manuscript and newspaper departments of both the State Historical Society of Wisconsin and the Minnesota Historical Society. I am greatly indebted to the University of Minnesota Library and to the libraries of Luther Seminary, St. Paul, Augsburg College, Minneapolis, and Meadville Theological School, now affiliated with Lombard College and located in Chicago. In particular, I should like to acknowledge the many courtesies of Mr. John Jensen, Mr. Karlis Ozolins, and Miss Agnes Tangjerd at Augsburg College, and the great assistance I had from Dr. Margaret Boell, then librarian at the Meadville Theological School.

My brother, Chester T. Draxten, has helped me in ways too numerous to detail. It has been my good fortune to have as editor Professor Kenneth O. Bjork, whose sympathetic guidance has helped me over many a hurdle.

NINA DRAXTEN

Minneapolis

Contents

Illustrations between pages 216 and 217.

KRISTOFER JANSON IN AMERICA

1

American
Lecture Tour

FEW VISITORS are so warmly welcomed as was Kristofer Janson when he reached the United States in September, 1879. The first announcement of his coming had been made by Professor Rasmus B. Anderson, five months in advance, in *Skandinaven* (Chicago); and this notice was followed by a second that listed thirty-eight lectures Janson was prepared to deliver.[1] As the news was channeled through the Middle West by such papers as *Fædrelandet og Emigranten* in La Crosse, *Budstikken* in Minneapolis, *Red River Posten* in Fargo, and *Decorah-Posten* in Iowa, immigrant settlers felt drawn to Janson by the accounts they read of his long career as *den djærve maalstræver* (the staunch champion of the peasant vernacular).

The epithet indicated more than an interest in linguistics. In Norway, as in other countries that have known foreign rule, there were two languages: the official Dano-Norwegian, used by church and state and mastered by all educated people, and the spoken dialects used in the country at large. Dano-Norwegian, or *riksmaal,* was the accepted literary medium. Ivar Aasen had developed, from the spoken dialects, a language called *landsmaal* (New Norse), linking it with Old Norse. That *landsmaal* had a valid claim as a bona fide language was a central issue in Norway's nationalist movement; but, up to the advent of Janson, the cause had been espoused largely by peasants—among them, besides Aasen, the newspaper editor, A. O. Vinje. In the mid-1860s, young Kristofer Janson, himself a member of a distinguished Bergen family, deliberately chose to write his stories of peasant life in New Norse. By doing this he demonstrated that *landsmaal,* generally de-

3

spised by the cultivated classes as a crude patois, had a beauty and eloquence peculiarly its own and was suited to the production of a literature. For years Janson met with ridicule and abuse; yet, though his stories were caustically reviewed by many critics, they became popular all over Scandinavia. In Janson's efforts to popularize New Norse, he used it on the lecture platform, frequently telling Bjørnson's peasant stories in *landsmaal* and achieving such effects that even die-hards were forced to acknowledge that his versions gave the tales an added poignancy.[2]

Thus Janson was described as a man who had fought for his ideals and had, through dogged persistence and high courage, forced all Norway to recognize his talent. In 1876, when the Storting (parliament) inaugurated the *digtegage* (a pension for poets), Janson was among the first four to be honored, the others being Ibsen, Bjørnson, and Lie. Janson knew the *bonde* or small farmer at first hand: For nine years he had been a teacher in Christopher Bruun's folk high school in Gausdal.[3]

When Janson arrived in the United States, people realized that, just as he had fought for the common folk in Norway, so he was now their spokesman in America. Audiences found themselves fighting back tears as Janson pictured the privations and injustices the humble people of Norway had endured in the past; and then his listeners would feel a surge of pride as he told them that the *bonde,* in spite of his lack of privilege, had been the guardian of Norway's native culture, its legends and fairy tales—which Janson called *en arvesølv* (a silver heritage) and a vast storehouse of folk wisdom. In a historical lecture—even on so well-known a subject as the events that clustered about the Eidsvold convention in 1814—Janson would bring the whole milieu to life, and his listeners would realize how much of the story they had been missing.[4]

For six months Janson traveled through the cities and settlements of the Middle West. Here and there were heard mutterings that his ideas were "liberal and false" or that his talks on folklore were better suited to children than to adults, but these were no more than stray, discordant notes. All along his route he was met by enthusiastic audiences —some people traveled thirty or forty miles to hear him. There were banquets and receptions; he was serenaded and cheered; and even in communities where money was scarce, he was shown some token of affection and gratitude. It was only at the conclusion of the trip—after his final lecture—that some persons came to see a bitter travesty in the whole tour. Many who had applauded Janson's liberal

4

ideas of social reform had not realized how thoroughgoing his "break with tradition" had been—that it included a radical view of religion. From many quarters came outraged cries that Janson had acted in bad faith, and there was even the insinuation that he was a money-grubbing opportunist.

Reports of Janson's reception along his tour are to be found in the weekly newspapers of the period. Not all the lectures can be accounted for, nor were they, except in isolated instances, printed in full. The sampling is large enough to be more than adequate, however, and newspaper reviews of the talks are sufficiently comprehensive to indicate their content.

For Janson's report of what he saw in America we have a few letters but otherwise must rely largely on his book, *Amerikanske forholde*, which contains five lectures he delivered on his return to Norway. This volume, as much as anything Janson ever wrote, reveals him as a romantic idealist who, as is generally characteristic of such a person, does not so much search for the truth as carry it in his own heart and look about in the exterior world for confirmation of his beliefs. Throughout *Amerikanske forholde* one sees Janson's heightened enthusiasm for the American republic. He found precisely what he had expected, as he remarked early in his opening chapter: "I will admit I was favorably disposed to America before I went there. As one who favors a republican form of government, I have great faith in the power of democratic institutions to teach, develop, and ennoble a people. As a republican, I longed to see that land whose basic laws expressly declare that all men are equal, and whose government strives to put the theory into practice."[5]

Janson was strongly influenced by Walt Whitman, whose work he knew and whom he most admired among new-world writers. In Whitman he recognized a great creative talent, one uniquely native. Throughout *Amerikanske forholde* Janson quoted from Whitman, reserving his greatest admiration for *Democratic Vistas*, saying, "I have rarely encountered so noble a work." It was this book, Janson declared, that led him to the United States and brought him to look upon it as the land of the future. In Whitman Janson found the voice of new-world conscience. "No one else," he went on to say, "has drawn such a devastating picture of American society in its unadorned nakedness."[6]

Janson accepted Whitman's strictures, freely admitting that political corruption, crudity, a taste for luxury, and an aversion to physical labor existed in America; but he shared Whitman's exuberant faith that these were transient evils, bound to give way before the "en-

5

lightened might of a democratic people." What concerned Janson far more was this country's continued practice of absorbing immigrants. He pointed out that the kind of citizenship offered so generously by the United States demanded a level of education that most immigrants did not have. Year after year, he remarked, Europe thrust not only the outcasts of its prisons and poorhouses upon America but also a seemingly endless stream of others, people drawn from the lowest stratum of society with virtually no learning beyond the ability to read and write. In time, Janson feared, the United States might find the assimilation of the newcomers so difficult that it would be forced to enact more stringent regulations.[7] Thus, as Janson surveyed the scene, he found the ignorance of the immigrants posed the big problem, and this was true of the Norwegians as well as of people of other national groups. Later, when Janson came to censure the Norwegian Evangelical Lutheran Church (the Norwegian Synod), his chief criticism was that it fostered ignorance by keeping the immigrants hermetically sealed off from society.

When Janson made his tour, he was thirty-eight years old, married to the former Drude Krog, and the father of seven children. He had been trained in theology at the university in Kristiania, but not ordained. He wholeheartedly endorsed Grundtvig's folk-school philosophy but apparently never took any interest in Grundtvig's theology, one centered about the Danish bishop's "marvelous discovery" that redemption was possible after death. Nor was Janson, when he came to America in 1879, an orthodox Lutheran. His break with the state church resulted from his having read Viktor Rydberg, a liberal Swedish theologian, and the sermons, as well as the biography, of Theodore Parker. When Janson made it known that he could no longer accept such beliefs as those involving the divinity of Jesus, verbal inspiration of the Bible, and the existence of an everlasting hell, he was forced to sever his connection with Bruun's folk school. This event, in fact, precipitated his lecture tour. Professor Anderson had long been urging him to come. As Janson remarked in his autobiography, he felt that the tour would give him an opportunity to see how his countrymen were faring and to study liberal religious movements here at close range.[8]

Kristofer Janson, from all accounts, was a good-looking man—tall, of slender build, with blue eyes and reddish-brown hair and beard. Rasmus B. Anderson has described him as having the appearance of an evangelist, adding that he "had a great resemblance to the conventional portraits of our Saviour." Profile pictures of the period do

6

not in any striking way justify this comparison, but front-view portraits of a few years later reveal a high forehead, regular features,
and an unusually serene, even compassionate gaze—and make Anderson's description something more than plausible. Many persons found
a spiritual quality in Janson. Others beside the professor were to say
that he put them in mind of the man of Galilee. People in Minneapolis
who remembered Janson (although their memories did not go back to
the lecture tour) spoke of him as having an unusually gentle nature,
one incapable of malice.[9]

The Norwegian immigrants whom Janson visited in 1879–80, attached to Norway by ties with beloved kin left there and by their own
childhood memories, were not yet fully assimilated into the main stream
of American life. They were torn by bitter internecine theological strife.
In the late 1870s the chief disputants were leaders of the Norwegian
Synod and of the Conference of the Norwegian-Danish Evangelical
Lutheran Church in America, each having its cadre of able dialec-
ticians—men trained, for the most part, at the university in Kristiania.
The ill will engendered by these dissensions was often so pervasive as
to divide local communities, making social relations between members of rival synods difficult, if not impossible. As such differences
generally do, they tended to make the participants rigidly doctrinaire,
in this case much more so than the Lutherans in Scandinavia or
Germany.[10]

In Janson's homeland, on the other hand, barriers were breaking down. Norway had already felt the first tremors of the democratic
ground swell that had resulted in the emergence of the Venstre (the
Liberal party), in growing tension between the Norwegians and the
Swedish crown, and in an increasing demand for social and political
reform. In the folk schools, themselves a manifestation of revolt against
the old order, social and political issues were commonly explored,
as Janson relates in his autobiography. He speaks of gatherings in
his home at which such issues were debated, the meetings sometimes
moving outdoors when the quarters became too small to accommodate
the assembly. He mentions mass meetings at Lillehammer where,
among other things, politics and republicanism were discussed; his
description of the period concludes with the comment, "Indeed, there
was life in Gausdal."[11]

2

Late in August, 1879, Janson went to Kristiania to begin his long
journey to America. His last days there were somewhat frustrating.

He had planned to have a brief holiday in the city with Drude, to attend the theater and have long talks about what the tour "might mean for the future."[12] But a crisis in the Krog family kept the Jansons apart much of the time. Apparently the only encouraging event during this interval was the appearance of an article about Janson's forthcoming tour in *Dagbladet* (Kristiania), September 1, so strategically timed that it reached America early enough to be reprinted well in advanced of his opening lecture:

"Kristofer Janson is in town on his way to America, where he is awaited by Norsemen and other Scandinavians. This is the first time one of our scalds has gone to visit our countrymen across the sea to refresh their thoughts of their homeland's saga lore, history, and present-day life. Janson is one of the outstanding lecturers of the North (as a narrator of our lyric-epic tales undoubtedly our very best). He will awaken cherished memories and a nostalgia for Norway and endear himself to his audiences.

"Our people do not have a better ambassador to send to our distant kinsmen; the majority are or have been peasants, and certainly after Janson has spoken to them in *landsmaal,* they will have an understanding of how much has been done in their old home to honor the peasant who, in their time, was treated with contempt. From his presentation of our struggle, they will have greater faith in us and in our future.

"His attractive personality and his mild engaging manner will reconcile many whose lot here was not of the best and whose memories are therefore by no means entirely pleasant. He goes, we feel free to say, with our best wishes, and we hope he will be well received and bring back good reports of that great nation in which our emigrants now play no small part."[13]

The article in *Dagbladet,* though unsigned, was apparently written by Bjørnson. In a fragment of a letter that survives, Janson wrote to thank his friend: "I feel the need to send you a last greeting and thank you for what you wrote in *Dagbladet.* People do not realize that you are the author. Actually they imagine that someone here has taken an interest in me—and thus the main purpose has been accomplished. If only our brethren in America will imagine the same, all will be well."[14]

Janson arrived in New York on the "Arizona" on September 20. He may have stopped briefly with Hjalmar Hjorth Boyesen. No record of such a visit exists, but in Boyesen's letters to Professor Anderson in the late summer of 1879, he mentions repeatedly having extended such an invitation. It is not clear whether the two men were acquainted, but Boyesen had for some years been bringing Janson's work to the attention of the American reading public. As early as October, 1872, Boyesen published an article entitled, "Kristofer Janson and the Reform of the Norwegian Language," in the *North American Review,* and that same month he briefly reviewed *Sigmund Bresteson* for the *Atlantic.*[15] In April, 1879, five months before Janson came to this country, Boyesen translated his short story, "Ein tulling," for *Scribner's,* giving it the title "Half-witted Guttorm."

Boyesen was doubtless aware that a translation of *Den bergtekne* was in process, although he was not personally involved. Early in 1879, Miss Aubertine Woodward, a friend and collaborator of Rasmus B. Anderson who wrote under the pseudonym Auber Forestier, had begun a translation of the book. This venture, undertaken long before Miss Woodward had any intimation of Janson's coming, apparently was an attempt to capitalize on the popularity of Ole Bull, who was a prominent character (though not the central one) in the book. On May 10, 1879, Miss Woodward wrote Anderson, "So Janson is coming to this country. We must have the 'Bergtekne' ready when he comes."[16] Her translation, entitled *The Spellbound Fiddler,* appeared early in 1880, and while Janson was less than delighted with the result (Boyesen, in his review, also deprecated the translator's work), he made use of the book in introducing himself to Henry C. Lea, the historian, during his later sojourn in the East.

Throughout the tour, Janson remained in close touch with Boyesen, a fact which may have been significant in the light of Janson's later criticism of the Norwegian Synod. Early in 1879 Boyesen published *Falconberg,* a novel dealing with the machinations of a tyrannical minister in a small Minnesota community, a figure whom Clarence Glasrud has recently characterized as "the blackest villain Boyesen ever introduced into his fiction." The book was an attack on the Norwegian Synod, as Boyesen himself admitted somewhat later. Critics of that day, as well as more recent ones, thought the book so overdrawn as to be a caricature. Yet, whether *Falconberg* was an unfair picture or not, it clearly reflected Boyesen's views at the time, and he could not have failed to communicate them to Janson.[17]

Janson was scheduled to arrive about October 1 in Madison, where he and Professor Anderson were to plot the strategy of the trip. From Janson's account we can follow him imaginatively as he boarded a train headed westward. Friendly toward the scene before his eyes, he was quick to observe features that demonstrated the benefits of life in a republic. Although he described in detail the comforts of American trains, with their facilities for sleeping and dining, he was more impressed by the fact that they had only one class. "The official and the laborer sit side by side," he remarked. "The silk dress is next to the linsey-woolsey." He admired the informal manner of the conductor as he strolled through the train, stopping for small talk with passengers. "It is all so natural and pleasant," Janson said, at once seeing a causal relationship between all this and the conduct of Americans generally. "The fact that the humble get just as good treatment as the better classes and are shown the same concern and courtesy has caused the common people to develop poise and good manners."

He was amused by American advertising, which fascinated him all during his stay. As he sped along toward Chicago, he could hardly glance out the window without seeing, on the sides of barns and on rocks, signs glorifying Rising Sun Stove Polish. Somewhat naïvely, he speculated on how it could be profitable to spend vast sums of money promoting such a small article as stove polish. On billboards he saw "before and after" pictures displaying everything from shoes to washing machines, each product brashly proclaiming to be "the best in the world."

In Madison Janson found not only Professor Anderson but also Ole Bull, with whom he renewed an acquaintance. Plotting the strategy of his tour by no means absorbed all his time; shortly he was going about, exploring Madison. He listened to campaign speeches for the coming fall election. He told of being amused and slightly nettled at the antics of a lively Irishman, who, referring to the candidate of the opposing party, said, "He is a Norwegian. Nothing more need be said," accompanying the statement with a grimace. "He was born across the sea with his eyes closed, and he hasn't opened them yet."

Janson went to meettings of the Association for the Advancement of Women, which was holding its seventh congress in Madison, October 8–10. In describing the sessions, he said, "I consider those three days among the most interesting I spent in America." The congress, which received front-page coverage in the Chicago papers, was attended by women from all over the country, some of them professional people but many of them housewives. Six lectures were given each day, all by women, the subjects ranging from "Occupations Suitable for Women" to "The Physiological Basis of Thought." According to Janson, the talks were excellently delivered and showed considerable research and scholarship.

After each lecture a general discussion was held, something Janson found as remarkable as the addresses. The women, knowledgeable and self-assured, discussed issues with a frankness and liveliness Janson found amazing. He commented that young women in Norway would turn crimson in embarrassment merely listening to the bold talk, for, as he added deprecatingly, there they were hardly expected to have opinions worth listening to, let alone encouraged to speak in public. He learned, however, that the delegates were a comparatively conservative group; he ventured to ask some of them about Mrs. Victoria Woodhull, who among other things had been campaigning for a single standard in sexual mores, only to find that these women held her in great abhorrence.[18]

3

Meanwhile Chicago awaited Janson. For weeks *Norden* had been reporting his movements, and it reminded readers, as the date of his open lecture neared, that the capacity of Aurora Hall was limited and that Ole Bull might come from Madison for the event. Prominent Scandinavians busied themselves with preparations for a banquet. When Janson arrived in the city on the evening of October 11, he became the guest of Hallvard Hande, editor of *Norden*.[19]

Hande, according to Johs. B. Wist, was extraordinarily gifted; he had educated himself for the ministry in Norway through independent study, passing his theological examinations with distinction. Here he had served a Norwegian Synod pastorate in Iowa, where the rigors of the life—visiting several congregations and traveling great distances through swamps and over roadless terrain to visit parishioners—had caused him to contract tuberculosis, and after this misfortune he became embittered. Possibly Hande gave his guest a graphic account of his experience, for, as Janson moved westward, he seemed to grow increasingly sensitive to the privations of pioneer pastors, coming to feel that as individuals they were kindly, self-sacrificing men and that the repressive tactics they practiced on parishioners were forced upon them by the arbitrary synods.[20]

Hande, whose paper, *Norden,* was generally considered favorable to the Norwegian Synod, was later accused of hypocrisy when he expressed his shock at the tone Janson's final lecture took. There is strong evidence, however, that the charge was unjust. Hande must have assumed his guest to be an orthodox Lutheran, for he apparently confided to Janson his own resentment against the synod, a revelation not likely to be made to an outsider. Janson reported that Hande was reprimanded by the synod for publishing an article in *Norden* on the cretaceous period which stated that the era lasted several thousand years; the synod had condemned it as freethinking because it conflicted with Scripture. The article had been reprinted from *Folkevennen* of Norway.[21]

Three days after Janson's arrival in Chicago, a banquet was held for him, attended by prominent Swedes and Danes as well as Norwegians. The tables were tastefully decorated, a special musical program was provided, and a verse written by H. J. Blegen was sung by the entire assembly as the festivities began:

> Welcome to you, our Norseman brother,
> To this, our new-found home.
> You come, we know, from our dear mother
> With greetings from the ancient North,
> With mem'ries of our cradle days,
> Our spring, our dream, our roundelays.[22]

Toasts and speeches followed, as representatives of various organizations welcomed the guest, Pastor Vilhelm Koren speaking for *Norden*. Janson, in his response, characterized the time as an age of ideals, in which people were no longer content with dreaming of utopias and coining fine phrases but insisted on transforming their visions into reality. Aboard ship, he said, he had seen many wretched people bound for a new life—adding parenthetically that he was glad to report that the Scandinavians looked better than most of the rest—and he was grateful to America for giving them a home. The affair lasted until midnight. In reporting it on October 22, 1879, *Norden* concluded: "We have never been at a banquet where the mood was so cordial. The speakers seemed inspired. We consider this a sign that Janson will have good luck on his tour."

Two days later, on October 17, Janson gave his opening lecture at Aurora Hall. In the audience of five hundred were Ole Bull and representatives from the Swedish- as well as the Norwegian-language papers of Chicago. A review in *Fædrelandet og Emigranten* indicated that F. A. Husher, its editor, had attended from La Crosse. The lecture had been advertised as having three sections: greetings to the Scandinavians, greetings to America, and the main address.

After a men's chorus had sung, Janson, addressing his audience as "Scandinavian Friends," began: "I greet you, my countrymen. First you, the earliest to come, whose deeds are now legendary. With the valor of your Viking forefathers you made your way through the forest

12

with ox teams. Tireless, ever vigilant, you conquered the wilderness in which you now live as secure and fortunate men. Under your watchful eyes, the wilderness has been transformed to acres of waving grain. You have seen the Indians, with their war cries and bloody tomahawks, supplanted by the locomotive, with its cheerful clang; you have seen cities rise, as if by magic, out of the wilderness. . . .

"And you, the later arrivals, who came to the open arms of your friends, to the warm rooms of relatives, to the work pioneered by your earlier kinsmen, to the dearly bought experience and advice which has gone like a snowplow before you."

In much the same vein he addressed the courageous women, the young people born in America, even the young girls, who, Janson said, were so far removed from Norway that Bjørnson's *Synnøve Solbakken* must seem to them as antiquated as grandmother's brooch, packed away in the chest she had brought with her years before.

Then, as if sensing in his audience a brooding nostalgia for Norway, he said, "How I wish there followed with me the fragrance of the forest of home—the roar of its waterfalls, the rushing of its rivers—that just for a moment you could look up and glimpse the melancholy mountains in the distance, see the glimmering light of those proud blue peaks, snow-covered even in summer.

"I have come to tell you about us [at home] as we are, neither worse nor better. I come bearing old and proud memories; I come with the story of our old sins and shortcomings. I come with confessions, for it is only through frank confessions that we can make improvements. I come with laughter and sorrow, with inspiration and bitterness. . . . I hope that something good will result from our meeting. I want to breathe something fresh into your languishing, half-forgotten memories, to strengthen the bond between you and the distant, yet ever near, motherland. I hope, too, that I shall carry back with me a message of a vigorous life, new ideas and strong wills."

As Janson began his greeting to America, he again altered the tempo:

"But before I roll up the curtain on my scenes, I must bow my head before this land whose earth I now have the honor to tread—Lincoln's land—Edison's land—Stanley's land—the land that has accepted the poor and downtrodden. . . . When in my dreams I envisioned my own country's future, I saw you as a lighted way in the distance. . . . I greet you, America, land of the republic, strong arm of democracy, home of the red-cheeked child, where labor is enthroned and freedom stands watch by the door.

13

"Here is a land not overshadowed by kingly power, where neither prejudice nor special privilege blocks the path, where every man makes his way with his own hands, his thoughts, and his will, where people live under laws they themselves have made, where birth does not endow the indolent and stupid with titles but where industry is the only mark of nobility—a land where a rail splitter may become president. . . . Your ship shall dominate the seas, your voice the assembly. With the authority that freedom gives, you will cut the bonds of thralldom which still bind Europe."

The applause that followed this introduction, *Norden* reported, "in truth must be called thunderous." Janson began his main address by telling Bjørnson's charming parable, "Hvorledes fjeldet skal blive klædt" (How the Mountain Was Clothed) from *Arne*. One can imagine a ripple going through the audience, for Janson did not tell the story as Bjørnson had written it—but in *landsmaal*. Many a person in the audience (still confused as to exactly what *landsmaal* might be) must have drawn in his breath sharply as he realized he could understand it perfectly. Expertly Janson told how the juniper, fir, oak, birch, and heather, dissatisfied with the lonely place where they grew, set out to scale the naked mountain wall on the far side of a deep chasm. Through centuries they inched along to the very brink of the abyss, reaching the path of a swollen mountain stream, which savagely uprooted them and flung them across the chasm to the mountain opposite. Recovering, they slowly climbed upward, through sleet and ice, rain and snow, until one by one they reached the summit, each uttering, as it came to the top, an exclamation of delight. Before them lay a full-grown forest. "This," said the juniper, "is what happens if one only tries." Janson then proceeded to relate the story to conditions in Norway. *Norden* reported the address as follows:

"The lecture on 'How the Mountain Was Clothed' was heard with great interest, the speaker being interrupted occasionally by vigorous applause. With Bjørnson's well-known story . . . as his text, Mr. Janson gave a political talk in which he presented Mother Norway's problems from his point of view, and the remedies. We shall not attempt a review of the address because Mr. Janson naturally expects to repeat it at other places. We shall restrict ourselves to a brief summary of its central thought:

"The Norwegian constitution of 1814 came into being because of the political conditions of the time, rather than because of a deeply felt need for freedom on the part of the people. The Norwegian people do not yet understand how to develop and utilize the freedom already assured them on paper. People still feel a great reverence for a monarchical form of government. They look up to the king and officials as solely responsible for the land's welfare, and expect them to take the lead in all matters. This blindness and dependency are entrenched by long habituation to monarchy. In democratic countries this is considered unsound; royal power is transmitted through inheritance and carries with it the conception that certain people have prior rights, which in turn leads to the granting of prerogatives and the making of class distinctions. The idea in a democracy, however, is equality. Monarchical rule will always hinder the development of the people's freedom. The struggle now going on in Norway between the people and the king will continue so long as the monarchy exists. The speaker hoped that the time would come when the Norwegian people would be courageous enough to form a republic. The spirit of republicanism was not, as some political groups at home believed, one of disorder, mobocracy, impiety, and ungodliness, but quite the opposite—one of loyalty, peace, order, morality, and industry.

"There was much that was true and significant in the address, but from our point of view it was a little one-sided. Mother Norway's faults were painted in strong colors and the monarchy received too much blame for these faults. Many of these, as well as various others, can be found in the hundred-year-old American republic as well as in other republics. But the faults of republics were not allocated a single word in the lecture.

"Norwegian Americans who know from experience what conditions are in a republic as well as under such a monarchy as that in Norway will hardly be persuaded to change their opinion on these matters because of Mr. Janson's address.

"Yet, although one could not agree with Mr. Janson in everything he said, it was nevertheless a great pleasure to hear him. The address contained, as we have said, much that was true and significant, and it was presented with a force, freshness, inspiration, and individuality, so far as form and delivery are concerned, that we have rarely seen equaled.

"Before the lecture we heard people here and there express fear that they would not understand Janson when he spoke in *landsmaal,* but his presentation of his text (Bjørnson's story) was one of the things that won the greatest applause, and the same persons assured us later that Janson's kind of *landsmaal* could be understood by any Scandinavian."[23]

F. A. Husher, the editor of *Fædrelandet og Emigranten,* also felt that

15

Janson had taken too pessimistic a view of conditions in Norway, saying that while many applauded, "not a few were disappointed that he had not a single good word to say about Norway." Other newspapers, however, were disposed to regard this as a relatively minor matter. *Verdens Gang* (Chicago) urged its readers under no circumstances to miss hearing Janson when he came to their communities, remarking on how pleasing his appearance and manner were, and adding that he did not flatter his audience, as American lecturers were wont to do, but spoke in such a forthright and intimate way that those who agreed with him were inspired and those who did not felt no ill will. *Skandinaven* did not summarize the lecture, on the grounds that it lived up to expectations in every way and would spoil in the retelling. The Swedish papers were also highly complimentary, *Svenska-Amerikaner* saying that Janson deserved to be included among the great scalds of the North.[24]

Janson, making Chicago his headquarters, spent some four weeks in the area, alternating local lectures with others in cities and settlements lying north along Lake Michigan. From his account in *Amerikanske forholde,* his curiosity about life in America was insatiable and his industry prodigious.

He gave a full account of Field and Leiter's mammoth store (the predecessor of the present Marshall Field), along with a description of the company's ingenious merchandising methods. He visited men's clothing factories, shoe factories, and the stockyards, marveling at what Americans could produce with steam-driven machinery. In rural communities he seems to have been equally busy. Willingly he tramped across fields to learn how corn was grown, inspected elevators and planing mills, attended church services, visited country stores, studied maps in land offices, inquired into every facet of local government, and listened with absorbed attention to what immigrants had to tell him of their past experiences.[25]

As *Norden* had predicted, Janson's lectures on Norse folklore were highly successful. In Lee, Illinois, where he gave "Fylgjesveinen" (The Companion), "Every ear pricked up and every eye sparkled." From a report of his appearance in Leland, Illinois, where he spoke in a church, we get a description of his method of presenting folklore. First he told the story, and then for a few moments paced back and forth as if to give his listeners time to absorb it before he began his interpretation. On his first visit to Racine, Wisconsin, which had a sizable Danish population, he spoke on "Grundtvig and His Times," so delighting his audience that he was offered Dania Hall, free of charge, whenever he wished to return.[26]

One Sunday, returning to Chicago after a week of speaking in country churches, Janson attended the Reverend Mr. David Swing's Central Church (which held its services in McVicker's Theater), amused at the paradox of his own lecturing in churches and Swing's preaching in a theater. Swing, who was a Presbyterian clergyman, had been tried for heresy some years before and acquitted. He had been called to Central Church by an insurgent group from his old congregation who felt that a minister should be given greater freedom than was allowed by the presbytery. Every Sunday, Swing attracted great crowds. The services were conducted in an informal fashion, with people laughing at the minister's sallies and now and then applauding him. Janson liked all this, remarking that ancient peoples had worshiped in an easy, natural manner. He was deeply impressed by another preacher, Dr. H. W. Thomas, a Methodist who prayed for sects other than his own. In 1879 Dr. Thomas was already under surveillance because of his liberalism, and in 1880 he faced heresy charges in a trial notorious for its bitterness and acrimony. At times during the tour Janson visited other American churches (the times and places cannot be pinpointed); he thought the sermons so recondite that they could not have been intended for working people.[27]

Although Janson lectured twice in Milwaukee, his addresses were not reviewed in the Norwegian papers in Chicago. His three subsequent lectures in Chicago were as well attended as his first. In two he dealt with Norse fairy tales, and *Norden* remarked that few in the audience had realized how much of life's wisdom was to be found in the simple stories. In Janson's final lecture he retold the saga, "Kongen og bonden" (The King and the Peasant), as well as two of Bjørnson's stories, "Faderen" (The Father) and "Ei farlig friing"—his *landsmaal* version of Bjørnson's popular tale about a "dangerous" courtship.[28]

4

By November 15 Janson was moving away from Lake Michigan. He had sent an enthusiastic letter dated November 2 to a friend in Norway; it appeared in *Bergens Tidende* and was later reprinted in *Budstikken*. His lectures were going well, he said, and everywhere people were hospitable and helpful. Yet he had hardly seen the typical America, for he traveled everywhere among Norwegians and spoke only Norwegian. At the time of his writing he was headed toward Neenah and Eau Claire in Wisconsin, and Minnesota. "I have a thousand-mile ticket on the train," he wrote. "I expect to go west to see the Mormons and then way out to California."[29]

On November 17 he spoke in Neenah, and moved on to Winchester, Waupaca, and Scandinavia, in Wisconsin. He was struck by Scandinavia's close resemblance to a Norwegian community. On the streets, in stores, one heard only Norwegian. The church was a replica of those at home; the minister wore the vestments of the state church; the hymnbooks were the same as those used in Norway. While Janson did not disparage all this, he apparently saw no particular merit in it either. He was much more interested in the immigrants who were taking full advantage of the opportunities in America. It was the custom in Norway, Janson remarked, for the "better classes" to regard the peasant as sluggish, wholly lacking in ambition and enterprise—but here one saw how absurd such a notion was.[30]

What one saw in the old Illinois and Wisconsin communities, Janson declared, was absolutely amazing. There lived men who had been *husmænd* in Norway—tenant farmers or cotters, belonging to the lowest stratum of the peasantry. In America the former *husmand* now lived not in a hut but in a two-story frame house, painted white with green shutters on the windows. In back were a spacious barn and a granary, and costly machinery stood in the farmyard. Entering the house, one came into a carpeted parlor, attractively furnished with an organ, a sofa, comfortable armchairs, and decorative lamps. At dinner a lavish meal was served, American style, with a soup course, a meat course, cakes and pastries, and crackers and cheese as an extra dessert. Coffee or tea was served with the meal, and ice water and lemonade were offered, should the guest fancy them. After dinner, in one instance, the daughter of the house played the organ and sang—English songs. She had worked as a domestic in American households and had brought home customs she found there. Her father owned, in addition to his farm, an elevator and a planing mill. Janson gave other examples of similar prosperity, and although he was quick to add that not all immigrants had fared so well, he saw everywhere a tendency among the Norwegians to be more fastidious in the preparation of food than they were at home and to make a conscientious effort to raise their standard of living.[31]

Yet, in Janson's eyes the important thing was the personality change in the immigrant, not his prosperity. In Norway, when addressed by one of his "betters," he had stood abjectly humble, eyes downcast, cap in hand, and mumbled a reply. In America he had a straight back

18

and a direct gaze; he was poised and hospitable. The transformation filled Janson with gratification: "When one considers," he wrote, "that these men—prosperous farmers owning their own farms—once slaved year after year without in any way improving their lot, one must be grateful to America for giving our countrymen opportunities to develop." Their lives had dignity because they had become responsible citizens who chose their officials from among themselves. And once knowing this independence, Janson declared, men found it the *sine qua non* of existence: "These people, through their freedom, have felt the soundness of their own enlightened might, and they love America. A few, clinging to memories of the mountains and fjords of home, sometimes give in to their longing and return. But they are back not more than a few months before they feel they must return to America. They cannot stand the class distinctions at home. I heard that time and time again."[32]

Janson came to realize, early in the second month of his tour, how divisive church strife could be. He lectured November 18 in Winchester, a small town in northern Wisconsin. Side by side on a hill stood churches of the Norwegian Synod and of the Conference for the Norwegian-Danish Evangelical Lutheran Church, and the two congregations regarded each other with bitter enmity. On one occasion, Janson was told, hysteria had risen to the point where a body was exhumed from the Synod churchyard and the coffin hoisted over the fence to the Conference cemetery. This act was prompted, Janson said, by a concern lest the righteous be embarrassed on Judgment Day by the presence of the unrighteous; he documented his account with a statement taken from a book by Professor A. Weenaas.[33]

Rasmus B. Anderson had planned to sell a translation of Bjørnson's play, *Leonarda* (1879), to *Scribner's Monthly* for $1,000. The project fell through because the work had already appeared in a German version; the *Atlantic* also refused it. When Janson was in the woodland of central Wisconsin, he learned that his mother had died; shortly afterward he had the onerous task, assigned him by Anderson, of writing Bjørnson that *Leonarda* had not been accepted. In the letter, Janson spoke of having heard from Drude, his wife, that Bjørnson was deeply depressed and was even thinking of selling Aulestad, his home. He urged Bjørnson to take heart, adding that he spoke only from faith; his own spirits were low, and he was saddened by the news of his mother's death and by the prospect of having to give up his own home in Norway.[34]

In the Wisconsin forests Janson saw what grueling labor the immigrants undertook in clearing land. He visited two brothers, former *husmandsgutter* from Toten, each of whom had a beautiful farm. Both maintained that people in Norway did not know what work was and that they themselves would not repeat their experience for any price. Janson readily believed them, for he could still see the marks left by the gargantuan tree roots. Often immigrants did not take time to grub roots, but let them rot in the ground. Merrilan, Wisconsin, Janson said, had a comic appearance; there were tree stumps in the middle of the street. He himself had penetrated a wilderness of rotting stumps, broken-down branches, and fallen logs before reaching a hut where a bleak face peered out—that of an immigrant who was just beginning to prove his claim.[35]

By November 25 Janson was in Eau Claire, where he went through the sawmills and visited a wagon factory; he was impressed by the use of machinery in America. Early in December he was lecturing on both sides of the Mississippi; visits to Rochester, Valley Grove, Rushford, and Zumbrota marked his penetration into Minnesota. In some towns his portrait went on sale in anticipation of his arrival. A month and a half before he gave his first lecture in La Crosse, *Fædrelandet og Emigranten* advertised photographs at fifteen cents for visiting-card style and thirty cents for cabinet size. Below the picture was a verse from one of Janson's poems, beginning, "Forth to freedom, to all that is good."[36]

On January 2, 1880, Janson gave his first lecture in La Crosse, where attendance was less than might have been expected in a town with so many Norwegians. His talk was a development of two fairy tales, "De tre mostre" and "Lurvebetler" (The Three Aunts and The Shabby Beggar). F. A. Husher, editor of *Fædrelandet og Emigranten,* gave a reserved report of the address, saying that many of Janson's judgments were distorted and false; he granted, however, that from the applause the speaker's views were shared by others. A member of the audience sent a report of the lecture to *Budstikken,* which printed it and Husher's account on January 13, 1880. This listener did not share Husher's opinion: he said it was a great delight to hear Janson, who deserved big audiences wherever he went.

Janson was somewhat disappointed with the people in Wisconsin. As he said later, he liked the Minnesotans better, just as he came to prefer rural folk to those in the city. An experience he had in Wisconsin apparently rankled for a long time, for he mentioned it in his autobiography as well as in *Amerikanske forholde.* Hardly had he finished lecturing when a troop of young people stormed into the room. Boisterously proclaiming, "Now *we* will have a meeting!" they proceeded to clear the floor for a dance. It was not their boycotting his lecture that distressed him, Janson said, but their complete lack of intellectual interest. They were neither fish nor fowl and were without concern for the land of their forefathers and indifferent to the opportunities lying before them in America. When he mentioned this to their parents, they blamed it on the fact that the community was torn by church strife, but Janson could not concur with this. The parents, he maintained, had worked hard and wanted life to be easier for their children, but they made the mistake of indulging them to the extent that the young people felt that nothing was expected of them.[37]

In the same community in Wisconsin, people wrangled with the ticket seller to have the admission price reduced to fifteen cents from the twenty-five charged elsewhere. Failing in this, they stood outside and listened, something the thin board walls of the building permitted.[38]

5

As Minneapolis awaited Janson's coming, Luth Jaeger, editor of *Budstikken,* reminded his readers that in Chicago five hundred people had greeted the speaker and urged that Minneapolis do as well. His hope was doomed, for throughout Janson's stay there his audiences were relatively small, an understandable disappointment to Jaeger. No one had done more, all through the tour, to keep Janson in the public eye. Besides reprinting reviews of the lectures from other papers, Jaeger carried a lengthy article by Egil Elda entitled "Kristofer Janson and the Nationalist Movement in Norway."[39]

Janson's first lecture in Minneapolis was scheduled for January 16, the title being "Enevælde og frihed: Historiske billede fra forrige aarhundrede" (Tyranny and Freedom: Historic Scenes from the Last Century). Although it was now winter, the weather was comparatively mild, with daily temperatures ranging from four to thirty degrees Fahrenheit. When Janson arrived in Minneapolis, which he announced would be his headquarters in Minnesota, he was the guest of Gudmund Johnson, one of the publishers of *Budstikken.* His lecture drew only three hundred and thirty people, mostly men, a situation that prompted Jaeger to remark that presumably the women were busy with their housework, indeed a regrettable circumstance. Jaeger was also disappointed to find so few ministers in the audience. Professor Georg Sverdrup of Augsburg Seminary could not attend because of a cold, but students from Augsburg were present in considerable numbers.

21

After the lecture Janson was serenaded at his host's residence on Nicollet Avenue. Exactly who did the serenading was not specified, but the implication was that it was the college students. Jaeger's review follows:

"Since Mr. Janson expects to give the lecture again, we will not, at his request, give a full report of its content. We shall merely remark that the existence of the monarchy was at first a historical necessity for protection against the encroachments of barons and other petty lords. However, the situation tended to encourage the development of the monarchical power until it reached the absolutism found during the reign of Louis XIV in France. Of that ruler's personal talents, Janson gave a striking, indeed almost a photographic account, describing the spirit of the age as it was embodied both in the magnificent palace at Versailles and in the ever-increasing assumption of power. The dark side of the picture, the misery of the people under Louis XIV, was also portrayed with analytical clarity. He told about the outstanding writers of the period and how their influence brought on the French Revolution. It was not the speaker's purpose to teach history, but to present a historical period, so that his listeners would have an insight into the forces that brought on the revolution and gave it the precise form it took, the terrible upheaval that occurred in consequence of violating eternal law. For monarchy had reached its summit; it could go no higher. The people had sunk so low that they could not endure more and survive.

"In the French Revolution the monarchy received its death blow, and a new day dawned. That was the central theme of the address, and it was developed with wonderful clarity and sharpness. In that respect the speech was the richest in learning and enlightenment that has ever been given before a Norwegian audience in this city, and no one went home without feeling his own understanding greatly enlarged and his soul enriched with a wealth of thoughts and impressions that he had not had before. So much for the content.

"The effectiveness of any lecture depends upon the manner in which it is delivered. Here Kristofer Janson demonstrated his mastery. To say there is no Norwegian in America who can be compared with him is perhaps not great praise, but we must add that among American lecturers it would be hard to find his equal—a full sonorous voice, now vibrating in righteous anger, now calm and mild, and then soaring in inspiration as he relates something beautiful and good, always the bearer of glowingly poetical, eloquent words. In that respect, we must single out the introduction as the best part of the lecture. From

22

the attention of his audience it is clear people realized what a rare cultural delight they were privileged to experience."[40]

In the week's interval between Janson's first and second lectures in Minneapolis, he had a light schedule, speaking once in St. Paul on January 19 and once in Red Wing the next day. In *Amerikanske forholde* he devoted relatively little space to Minneapolis, although he seemed to have been impressed by the efficiency of the mills, mentioning that a train brought the grain to one end of the building and another carried the flour away at the other. As was mentioned earlier, he liked rural people better than those of the city. He spoke of being irked by immigrant women living in cities (although he did not specifically mention those of Minneapolis). Many of them were accustomed to an aristocratic environment and liked to dwell on how agreeable life had been in Norway and how unsatisfactory it was in America. Janson mentioned, too, the "servant-girl flock" (again without definite reference to Minneapolis), saying that their duties were generally lighter than those of domestics in Norway—especially if they worked for Americans.[41]

On January 23 Janson gave his second lecture in Minneapolis, entitled "Hvorledes Norges frihed blev født" (How Norway's Freedom Was Born). During the last week in January, he was the dinner guest of Professor Sven R. Gunnersen and later attended a meeting at Augsburg Seminary, where students provided a program of music and declamations and held a debate on whether civilization was causing mankind to advance or regress. Janson, for his part, related some incidents from Bjørnson's *Arne* and told his own story, "Gale Arne" (Crazy Arne).[42] In the same week Janson spoke twice at St. Peter, and at Waseca and Madelia. From Madelia, only a few miles from where Janson was to establish his Nora Free Christian Church in Hanska less than two years later, a correspondent sent in a glowing account to *Budstikken*. The lecture was held in Flanders Hall, where Tosten Hovde, dressed in the costume of his native Romsdal, introduced Janson to an audience of about three hundred. Janson spoke on "Political Conditions in Norway," the new title given to "Hvorledes fjeldet skal blive klædt," presumably in response to criticism that the more flowery name did not indicate the content of the lecture. He was interrupted frequently by cheers and applause. "Here and there," said the account, "one saw tears rolling down bearded cheeks when the audience was reminded what humble people had had to endure in Norway." Almost everyone was well satisfied with the lecture, the reviewer continued; the few who made critical comments were not

23

competent judges. After the speech, the audience gave three rounds of cheers for Kristofer Janson and Bjørnstjerne Bjørnson. The account ended with the statement that no one would regret the money spent for admission.[43]

Two days later Janson gave his third Minneapolis lecture, "Fylgjesveinen" (The Companion). In the fatherland, Janson explained, the city man not only ignored folklore but was so influenced by foreigners that he imitated them. Thus, he said, Norwegian literature, both of the past and of the nineteenth century, had been dominated by an alien culture. Now that the Norwegians had become a free people, Janson declared, they must go to the peasant who had serenely clung to the native songs, epics, and fairy tales, if they were to reclaim this silver heritage.

Following his usual custom, Janson proceeded to tell a story, an account of a young man who interrupted his quest for a princess while he gave Christian burial to the body of an unscrupulous wine dealer—a corpse that had long been encased in a block of ice, spat upon by everyone passing by. Janson then explained the deep meaning to be found beneath the surface of the story. In reviewing this part of the lecture, *Budstikken's* editor commented:

"Kristofer Janson's interpretation was indeed a great revelation to the majority of his listeners. That the tale could contain so many truths, teach much that was beautiful, had escaped most of us, but it is certain that in the future every thoughtful person will look upon such tales with greater understanding and appreciation than before. We cannot give the poet's full treatment, but merely remark that it concerned the necessity of living for an ideal, and showed how the ideal might triumph. The boy was always true to his vision. What was most significant for our Norse-American circumstances was the boy's treatment of the wine dealer's corpse. The young man had come into the land of the righteous, where, in accordance with the law, the wine dealer had been executed and his body frozen in ice. The boy, however, was merciful and loving, and when he buried the wine dealer, the man's soul was released and ascended to God. Love is stronger even than righteousness; it does not condemn, but forgives, stretching out its arms to the sinner." Jaeger was again disappointed at the attendance; he said that two hundred and fifty people were not many, and urged that more turn out for the final address on February 13.[44]

Meanwhile, Janson himself was looking forward to hearing another lecturer. When he arrived in Minneapolis he had noticed placards that read, "Mrs. Livermore Is Coming!" followed by others that read,

"Mrs. Livermore Is Here!" If he read the *Minneapolis Tribune* for February 3 (and probably he did), he saw, prominently displayed on the front page, "Mrs. Livermore Tonight!" In *Amerikanske forholde* Janson mentioned the placards as another instance of American ingenuity in advertising, saying that his own curiosity was aroused. The lady was a prominent lecturer whose two addresses in Minneapolis bore the titles "Beyond the Sea" and "Concerning Husbands." Since Janson had a free evening on February 3, he attended the first talk.[45]

Mrs. Livermore's speech was based on observations she had made during a trip to Europe. She was seriously concerned with the status of women, and spoke feelingly of the contempt with which they were treated abroad, even in England. If consideration of women was an index of a nation's level of civilization, Mrs. Livermore declared, "Our land is 'way ahead of the rest of the world." She spoke of the achievements of American women and went on to say that they were also the best-looking in the world. Even the actress Lily Langtry, so celebrated in England for her beauty, would hardly cause a head to turn in America. Janson apparently was in complete accord with all this. In no other country, he said in *Amerikanske forholde,* were women treated with such chivalry as in America. He spoke of the laws that had been enacted for their protection. "I have never seen a finer, more beautiful, or nobler group," he added. "They are ordinarily smarter than European women, with intelligence lighting up their lively, alert faces—with charm and assurance revealed in their every movement. On the streets of New York, Philadelphia, Baltimore, and Chicago, every third woman one sees is a beauty."[46]

Janson spoke in Willmar February 4 and in Benson the following day. Then, during a four-day interval, he made a flying trip to Chicago. In a note to R. B. Anderson dated February 9, he spoke of going to the Griggs Publishing Company and receiving nine copies of *The Spellbound Fiddler.* He also announced that he would take a week off, beginning the following Sunday, February 15, to visit Boyesen in Ithaca, New York. Apparently that trip did not materialize, for the *Budstikken* review of Janson's last lecture, published February 17, indicated that he was going on to Fargo, where he was to speak February 20. He was not returning to Minneapolis after that but would go directly south. Until the end of March he was to be lecturing, concluding the tour in Chicago. From there he would go to the East, where he expected to spend a couple of months. His previous plan of visiting California had been abandoned. Instead, he expected to

25

sail for Europe early in June, stopping off in England before he returned to Norway.[47]

Attendance at Janson's final lecture in Minneapolis dropped to two hundred and twenty, and Jaeger interpreted this as evidence of a deplorable lack of cultural interest among the people. The talk, a repetition of the first given in America (now called "Political Conditions in Norway"), prompted Jaeger to say that Janson, though obviously a warm and sincere republican, was hardly a practical one, for he said nothing about how a Norwegian republic might be implemented. This, however, Jaeger added generously, was actually outside the speaker's purpose, and indeed Janson did say that the republican idea was being spread by the letters of immigrants to relatives back home. Janson also mentioned specific problems that demanded immediate attention, among them the extension of the franchise, the position of women, the flag controversy, and the state church. To Jaeger, the value of the lecture lay not only in what Janson said. "Back of the speeches stood a man. One recognized that fact instantly, and without doubt it played a part in the warm reception he won everywhere. . . . There was always a faithful and by no means small circle of people who listened to him with interest and enthusiasm, really appreciating the value of what he said. In their name and in the name of the Norwegians here generally, we feel justified in wishing for Janson's return and in promising him a warm welcome should that wish be realized in the future."[48]

Comments like the above drew a mild protest from Erik L. Petersen, an Episcopal minister in Faribault, himself an accomplished lecturer. Writing Professor Anderson on February 19, Petersen said: "Janson is doing well here in Minnesota, but I think the reviews in *Budstikken* are too one-sided, almost fanatically so, and it becomes tedious in the long run."[49]

6

In the middle of February, Kristofer Janson was traveling across the frozen Minnesota prairies en route to Fargo. From the first, the prairie had fascinated him—months before, when he had seen the Illinois plains, and more recently in Brown and Kandiyohi counties in Minnesota. The vast stretches of land filled one with loneliness, he said; it was like being at sea. Danger was always imminent, for storms and blizzards could erupt without warning. Yet there he found people who seemed to be nature's own children, as spirited and adventuresome, he said, as if the piercing wind that was always blowing had found its way into their blood streams.[50]

Visiting a sod house, he saw how primitive the life of an immigrant could be. He also mentioned how this rude shelter came to be supplanted, in time, by a log cabin and eventually by a frame house, the latter two phases indicating great strides in prosperity, for the logs and lumber had to be hauled immense distances. He saw the privations endured by pioneer pastors—often greater than those of their parishioners, for they were frequently housed in makeshift dwellings where the snow sifted in on their beds at night.[51]

On one occasion Janson spoke in a primitive community in which an unheated warehouse had been cleared to make space for the audience. Some of the more agile of his listeners climbed up to the rafters, where they perched so precariously that Janson, in his preliminary remarks, implored them to hold on firmly, lest they hurtle down on the audience or on him. Huddled before him on the cold plank benches, half buried in robes, were people who punctuated his address at intervals by stamping their feet to revive circulation. In overcoat and cap, bundled up in scarves, Janson held forth. The title of his address gave an ironic note to the whole proceeding. It was "Iceland."[52]

In *Amerikanske forholde* Janson gave considerable space to describing the rigors of life on the prairie. He spoke of the arduous work of plowing up the coarse prairie grass, an operation slow to bring results, for the earth had to lie fallow for a time before it could take the seed. He spoke of the problem, created by the alkaline soil, of getting good drinking water, of the threat of Indian violence (largely past by 1880, as he acknowledged), of the danger of prairie fires; and he climaxed all this by saying that the immigrants' worst troubles were those they had brought with them: drunkenness and immoral customs, in particular one he designated as "night courtship." Such things, Janson wrote, gave his countrymen a bad reputation among Americans, whom he found to be an unusually courteous and morally upright people.

These serious faults (and Janson added another by maintaining that all Norwegians, in both Norway and America, were sorely lacking in graciousness) resulted from ignorance. As has been mentioned, Janson remarked several times in *Amerikanske forholde* that most immigrants were from the working classes and had virtually no education beyond the ability to read and write. Often he was distressed to find an audience amused by the antics of a drunken man. On other occasions—apparently more than once—intoxicated men actually vomited

27

in the lecture hall. Since many people drove for miles through the bitter winter cold to get to the lecture, Janson understood that they might need a warming drop or two, but, as he said, the custom of standing treat prevented moderation in drinking. The Norwegians needed to be taught how degrading it was for a man to lose possession of himself.

"Night courtship" Janson traced to customs immigrants had brought with them from rural communities in Norway. He maintained that Americans looked upon this with great repugnance, and consequently regarded Norwegians as a morally loose people. As Janson saw it, the practice could best be discouraged through improved community life, one in which young people were given more opportunities to meet openly.[53]

7

From Fargo, Janson returned to La Crosse. There, on February 26, he wrote Rasmus B. Anderson. He was showing signs of weariness. He told Anderson to accept no more engagements, that he had decided to forgo Michigan altogether. He was still concerned over Bjørnson and the *Leonarda* matter, and urged Anderson to write and relieve Bjørnson's anxiety.[54] A few days later he was on his way again, revisiting Rushford, Lanesboro, and Spring Grove in southeastern Minnesota. On March 2 he arrived in Decorah, Iowa, where his stay was to culminate in what was virtually a community celebration.

Accepting an invitation received shortly after his arrival in America, "should Decorah be on your itinerary," Janson became the guest of the Reverend Laur. Larsen, president of Luther College. On March 3 he gave a lecture based on "The Three Aunts" and "The Shabby Beggar." According to *Decorah-Posten,* an audience of three hundred and fifty people awaited eagerly. Promptly at eight o'clock Janson appeared on the platform. The reporter described his surprise:

"So you are Kristofer Janson. I had not expected *den djærve maalstræver,* who so early broke with tradition and endured hate and abuse because he dared to speak to Norsemen in their own tongue, to look like this. I had anticipated someone who seemed harder. But there stood a tall form with a mild, friendly face and the eyes of a dove, which lighted up as a torrent of thoughts flowed from his lips in eloquent words. It must be that his life in poesy and legend has preserved in him the vigor of youth and protected him against the attacks which his inordinate labors for his ideals have brought upon him."

28

The writer went on to say that Janson's interpretation of the first tale showed what might result from human effort that is not guided by the light of the spirit. In the second, the poet explained how industry and beauty, when properly blended, might be utilized in the education of women. Often, he said, they are regarded as delicately nurtured plants, or as dolls in a dollhouse. The account concluded with the statement: "A member of the audience said at the close of the lecture, 'I have seldom heard so many truths expressed at one time.' He was not alone in his opinion."[55]

Janson's schedule was a tight one. The evening after his first appearance in Decorah, he spoke at Ridgeway, Iowa. The hall was decorated with flags and greenery, and there was a good audience. The next night Janson was back in Decorah, delivering his address on "How Norway's Freedom Was Born." The subject matter was familiar to his hearers, but Janson seems to have held people enthralled. So vividly did he depict the political and religious awakening of the time, interweaving the account with intimate biographical sketches of such figures as Kristian Lofthus, Hans Nielsen Hauge, and Kristian Fredrik, that the audience felt that the whole era had come to life.

Students from Luther College attended Janson's lectures in great numbers. On Saturday morning, he spent half a day in the college convocation hall reading his *landsmaal* version of a fairy tale, "Austanfyre sol og vestanfyre maane" (East of the Sun and West of the Moon). Meanwhile the citizens were preparing a banquet; for, as *Decorah-Posten* explained, "They had received so much that was good and beautiful from Janson that they wanted to show their appreciation with something more than applause."

That evening, between two and three hundred people, most of whom had brought food, were present at the dinner. Following selections given by a mixed chorus (which won the praise of the guest of honor), Professor O. J. Breda spoke. Professor Thrond Bothne told a charming fairy tale in which a boy (Kristofer Janson) freed a bewitched princess (the Norwegian people in America). It is interesting that the correspondent in *Decorah-Posten,* in describing Janson's effect on the community, used figurative language similar to his. Janson was "the sower," who "took with him a friendly memory of his countrymen in our little city. We, for our part, have loved him. We hope that the winged, shining seed which he has sown among us will grow quickly and bear good fruit."[56]

Before leaving Iowa, Janson spoke in St. Ansgar and in Northwood; then, crossing into Minnesota, he visited Albert Lea and Fountain

29

before returning to La Crosse. A report of the March 13 address given in Albert Lea that appeared in *Budstikken* indicated that people had been somewhat surprised by Janson's remark that the Norwegians were inclined to be suspicious of the word "free," often confusing freemindedness or liberalism with freethinking. The writer predicted that Janson was likely to meet opposition from those "who stood in fear of authority," but apparently there were no other reverberations from the talk. By mid-March Janson was in Madison, where he remained for about two weeks. Then, on his way to Chicago, he stopped off at Beloit. *Norden* spoke of the tour as a "triumphant journey."[57]

8

Janson lectured in Chicago on April 1, and appeared in Racine the following night. On April 7 he attended a memorial service held for William Ellery Channing at the Central Music Hall in Chicago. There, before a huge audience, tribute was paid Channing's great contribution to American culture by Episcopal, Baptist, Presbyterian, and Jewish clergymen, as well as by other prominent men with no designated religious affiliation. Janson, profoundly affected by what he heard, described the occasion in *Amerikanske forholde,* and recalled it some thirty years later in his autobiography: "I sat amazed. Were such things possible? Could such tolerance and cooperation between sects actually exist? I thought of the Lutheran congregations that devoured one another in hate with accusations of heresy. I thought of conditions at home, where the heretic was branded, condemned, and hunted down."

Curiously, in the autobiography Janson described his reaction to the services much more graphically than he did his own final address, "Den saa-kaldte rene lære" (The So-Called "Pure Teachings"), which he delivered the following night. He did not mention this lecture in *Amerikanske forholde* and spoke of it only briefly in his autobiography: "Before I left, I held a lecture in Chicago in which I strongly criticized the church's fundamentalism and intolerance. The speech aroused both acclaim and great bitterness and was the event that led to my later return to America as a minister."[58]

On April 8 the scene was again Aurora Hall. Janson began, mildly enough, by remarking that the church strife was indeed regrettable. During his tour, he said, whenever the minister of one synod entertained him, the pastors of the others warned their parishioners to stay away from him. He related the incident of the corpse being removed

30

from the Norwegian Synod graveyard. Once, he went on, a minister invited him to read a manuscript entitled "To What Congregation Should I Belong?" Janson expected the paper to state that one must choose the church that he feels teaches the truth—"for a man must never be a hypocrite before God." Instead, the writer insisted that the choice must be the Norwegian Synod, the only one that possessed God's teachings pure and undefiled. All other synods, Janson commented sardonically, were thus consigned to "a certain warm place."

How unfortunate, Janson continued, that a realm in which love should prevail had been pre-empted by a fanatical zeal to protect "the pure teachings." All groups claimed the Bible as their authority, and cudgeled one another with Biblical citations. Yet the Norwegian Synod was the apostle of ignorance: It opposed the public schools, warned its parishioners not to read American periodicals, and held the threat of church discipline and excommunication over its people. Thus Norwegian Lutherans were hermetically sealed off from American society. For the most part, the theological debate was over the heads of the laymen. A few persons with the ability to make fine logical distinctions entered the controversy and became procurators, but the majority slept through it. Being so isolated, the Norwegian immigrants did not even know the names of the leading American writers. Janson declared he had never encountered a policy more likely to create freethinkers or to cause people to become bored with Christianity than the one the Norwegian Synod had adopted to protect its doctrines. Later generations, he predicted, would go over to other denominations— if they did not go in an opposite direction and become followers of Robert Ingersoll.

Janson was not, he said, attacking ministers personally. He had had many opportunities during his tour to talk freely with pastors of both the Norwegian Synod and the Conference. He was impressed with their dedicated stand, their patience, their selflessness in enduring all kinds of privation. These men, Janson declared, were better than the organizations they served. At home they were lively and full of jest; it was only in their official capacity that they became harsh and narrowly parochial.

Throughout history, Janson continued, certain groups had declared themselves to be sole possessors of the pure teachings. In Jesus' time it was the Pharisees who put their faith in outer forms—in a literal interpretation of the sacred writings. Jesus himself had no creed or dogma but advocated love, and his apostles had done the same. Paul had said that there was one God, and only one medium between

31

God and man—Jesus, who offered himself as a sacrifice. The division into sects and the persecutions followed later. The early church fathers formulated the Athanasian Creed, which turned the emphasis from Christianity to dogma.

At the beginning of the sixteenth century, Janson continued, the Catholic Church proclaimed itself the guardian of pure teachings. Luther and Calvin became the leaders of the opposition. Later, in ignorance, they, as well as the Catholics, burned dissenters without really knowing what the dissenters believed. In America, Janson said, he had heard unwarranted attacks on freethinkers. If you are to oppose a man, he insisted, you must do it on the ground of what he says, not what he did not say or did not intend.

Luther did not consider himself infallible, Janson went on. He had the prejudices and superstitions of his milieu: He believed in witches; he had personal encounters with the devil. If one holds such beliefs, the devil becomes the central figure, stronger than God and Jesus together. For his own part, Janson declared, he could accept all Christians as brothers, be they Catholics or members of the Reformed sects. The Augsburg Confession was not intended to be binding for all time. Fear of critics and freethinkers should not cause one to crawl under dogma for protection from the lightning. Since the Reformation, man had only two options: to be a Catholic and accept the Roman Church as the sole authority, or to be a Protestant and believe in the freedom of individual conscience. One thing on which all Christians are agreed is that God is our father and Jesus is our saviour. Rely on a pope and you bind the individual conscience. Unfortunately, Protestants made the mistake of by-passing essential Christian principles. Janson concluded with a plea that love be given its place, quoting I John 4:7—"Beloved, let us love one another: for love is of God."

Throughout the Middle West the Norwegian-American community was stunned. Neither *Fædrelandet og Emigranten* nor *Decorah-Posten* reviewed the lecture, and Hande's first reaction was that he would ignore it in *Norden*. After reflecting, however, that the speech would be widely discussed and that those likely to be offended could not help hearing about it, he decided otherwise. "It is Janson's final word, his judgment of us," Hande wrote. "He has talked of coming back in a few years, and now people will know what to expect. The tone and the spirit of the speech were un-Lutheran, to say the least. But there is truth in it. The quarreling over religion has been conducted in an uncharitable, brawling, and cruel manner, but that is not the

32

fault of the teaching. Even with Janson's doctrine that God is our father and Jesus our saviour, there would be differences as soon as people sought to determine in what sense God was our father and Jesus our saviour."[59]

In Minneapolis Luth Jaeger, staunch defender of Janson though he was, reported the comments of the various papers scrupulously. As the debate gathered momentum, editors accused one another of misinterpretation and even duplicity, and the discussion enlivened the Norwegian press in this country until Janson returned to Norway. Thus *Budstikken* reported how *Verdens Gang* had taken *Den Nye Tid* to task for calling Janson a hypocrite. *Verdens Gang,* which in its own way now looked on Janson with a jaundiced eye, stated that he had faithfully expressed what lay before his inner vision "when he entertained the public with a new act of his 'American Fantasies' at Aurora Hall." Jaeger also quoted the editor of *Red River Posten,* who stated that it was unfortunate the speech had ever been given, and hoped that Janson's ideas would make no inroads among Norwegians. Jaeger then published a satirical piece from *Verdens Gang* (and later reprimanded the paper for its scurrilous gibes at *Norden*):

"Our readers now know the principal content of Janson's farewell address. It is superfluous to remark that there is nothing new in it that has not been said many times before, both verbally and in print. What gives his words a significance on this occasion is that Janson has now returned from what *Norden* has called his 'triumphant journey' in the Northwest, and the ministers and congregations which Janson now criticizes in the sharpest terms are the very ones who have been singing of his triumphs. The situation is almost laughable. When Janson was in Decorah, the Synod's professors, ministers, and students gave a reception in his honor at which time one of the professors told a fairy tale (in *landsmaal,* naturally!) called 'The Bewitched,' that dealt with a prince who freed a princess under a spell, the allusion being that Janson was the prince who had come to America to dispel the intellectual darkness which envelops our people here. When the Synod professor reads this week's papers, he will realize that he had the wrong fairy tale. He should have chosen an Arabic one called 'The Princess Who Got a Long Nose.' This Oriental tale has now been performed on American soil; the prince, Kristofer Janson, after spending many pleasant days, and carrying a well-filled purse, has forsaken the disappointed princess, the Norwegian ministry, which now has a long nose in return for its efforts to tempt Janson with endearing overtures and flattery.

33

"Norden expresses—exactly as one would expect that sycophantic, hypocritical paper to do—its great distress, yes, even shock, over Janson's lecture!"[60]

Jaeger, himself long a critic of church controversies, regarded the criticism Janson made in his last address to be fully justified: "It was a torch cast into the fields of the Philistines, and we hope it will burn, for enough inflammable stuff is there. As *Verdens Gang* says, there is really nothing new in it, but never has the issue been represented so basically and comprehensively.... It is Janson's judgment of us, and we can't flatter ourselves that another would have interpreted the situation otherwise.... His judgment is an enlightened stranger's view of conditions. Coming from a man of his gifts, with his reputation, the criticism will carry greater weight than it would otherwise. It will not give us too flattering a reputation abroad. Perhaps it will open our eyes."[61]

9

Meanwhile, Janson was already in the East. Apparently he stayed in Chicago at least until noon of Sunday, April 18, for that morning he attended services in a spiritualist church there, drawn to it through his omnivorous reading of American newspapers. Through the medium, Mrs. Cora Richmond, "the late Dr. Thompson" delivered a sermon, which Janson found satisfactory, although he questioned the identity of the author. After the service he bought a copy of a sermon William Ellery Channing had presented earlier in the same manner. In *Amerikanske forholde* he related the whole experience with droll humor, remarking on how onerous it must be for the dead to be on call for such duties.[62]

Two days after this incident, Janson reported in a postcard sent to Professor Anderson from New York City that he was having a good time. That evening, he said, he expected to see Edwin Booth as Iago in *Othello*, and the following evening he would see him in *Macbeth*. Then he was going to Philadelphia to attend the Lincoln memorial services conducted annually by Walt Whitman. In Philadelphia he also visited historic shrines, industrial sites, and department stores. He thought Wanamaker's a notable achievement, particularly because Wanamaker was a self-made man. (The great number of Americans of lowly origin who had risen to prominent positions impressed Janson throughout his visit in the East.) He called at the luxurious home of Henry C. Lea, the historian, and was awed by Lea's comprehensive knowledge of the eddas and Icelandic saga lore. He went to Camden, New Jersey, to call on Walt Whitman but unfortunately did not find him at home. He did, however, gather considerable information on the poet's simple mode of life, all of which increased Janson's admiration. As he continued to question Americans, he found, more often than not, that he himself knew Whitman's works far better than they did.[63]

Early in May, Janson was in Washington, D.C. Meanwhile, the excitement engendered by "The So-Called 'Pure Teachings' " was still at a high pitch in the Middle West. On April 27 the Reverend Erik L. Petersen wrote Professor Anderson his opinion of the lecture: " 'The Pure Teachings' is brilliant, but it will hurt him very much—especially for any kind of a future in this country. I have often said the same and *worse* from the pulpit—but in Janson's place, I don't believe I would have spoken so frankly. It was brilliant—but it will hurt him."[64]

By this time the Norwegian Synod had replied to Janson's lecture in its own publication, *Evangelisk Luthersk Kirketidende*. Someone must have sent Janson a copy, for he seems to have read the article before it was reprinted in the weekly papers. It began with the observation that Janson had, in the course of his tour, delivered many fine lectures drawn from Norwegian history, presenting them in excellent form. Therefore, the account continued, it was all the more distressing that his farewell address should have been "The So-Called 'Pure Teachings.' " And what, the writer asked rhetorically, was the summation of this talk? That the greatest and most beautiful accomplishment of our people in this country, building our church and preserving the faith of our fathers, had been put into the same class as the activities of the Pharisees and the atrocities of the Inquisition—a fate that the Synod must share with the ancient church for protecting the pure teachings of the Bible.

True enough, the article continued, Janson admitted that the pastors were honorable men. But in dealing with differences between churches, he mentioned slander.[65] He had also said that the author of "To Which Congregation Should I Belong?" had relegated members of all other church groups to "a certain warm place." Since the Synod's reply to Janson appeared in its church calendar, some four to five thousand copies of which had been distributed, the falsity of his charge could be readily ascertained. Again, Janson had remarked that his own belief was broad, that he was willing to accept Catholics and members of the Reformed sects. By the same token he might also, it seemed, include Jews and Mohammedans. Finally, Janson attacked the Athanasian Creed, formulated at the Council of Nicaea, and spoke of the doctrine of the Trinity as the work of men. "When he attacks Christianity on fundamentals—in its essential tenets which, in the clearest manner possible, are in agreement with Scripture—something accepted by all church groups—then we will have to tell him that regardless of how much church strife there may be among us, the members of the various churches who regard themselves as serious Christians will have nothing to do with him should he ever again come to our country as a guest."[66]

From Washington, on May 4, Janson answered the criticism in a communication to *Budstikken*. He had known, he said, that the lecture would cost him friends, but because he expected to air the same views on his return to Norway, he had felt it only honest to state his opinions candidly before leaving America. As he was now on his way home, he did not wish to become involved in any long discussion of the Trinity. He admitted that his own religious belief was broad—to love those of other sects whom he considered to be as Christian as he. Nevertheless, he insisted, it must be remembered that he was a Christian—not a Jew or Mohammedan. He was criticizing not the building of the church but its reliance on outer form. "When I look at the fruit, I cannot admire the result." Janson went on to say that he understood why the Norwegian Synod might warn people to stay away from his lectures when they dealt with religion, but he could not see why such a prohibition should be placed against those about fairy tales and saga lore. Nor was he to be forced out of the Christian fold. He still believed in the articles of faith in which he had been baptized, and he felt he had as much claim to salvation as the author of the *Kirketidende* article.

Jaeger, in publishing this reply in *Budstikken*, added his own defense of Janson. Janson, the editor declared, had not compared the building up of the church to the activities of the Pharisees or the atrocities of the Inquisition, but had attacked the uncharitableness, intolerance, and prejudice that had accompanied the task. Janson's criticism, Jaeger stoutly maintained, was wholly justified, for in the church history of the Norwegians in America so much emphasis had been put on doctrine that everything else had been thrust aside.[67]

Meanwhile, Janson was going about in the nation's capital where he was struck by the paradoxes evidenced in American life. On one occasion, when he was a dinner guest at the home of a Northern Civil War general, he was surprised to hear the host speak of Negroes with great disdain. As Janson was quick to discern, the position of the Negro, even for one of proven ability, was far from enviable. Sympathetically he followed the newspaper accounts of a young Negro cadet then at West Point. He had been found bound to his bed, his body marked with superficial wounds; investigation revealed that he had arranged the predicament himself with some help from a classmate. Visiting Congress, Janson found himself drawn to Senator Blanche K. Bruce, then its only Negro member, a man so light-skinned that he might have been taken for an Italian or a Spaniard. Janson was disappointed that he missed seeing him act as temporary presiding officer in the Senate, for he had heard reports of how bitterly Southern senators resented Bruce's gavel. On the other hand, he was amazed at the lack of ostentation he found at the White House. When he called on Rutherford B. Hayes he was quietly ushered into the chief executive's office where the President, dressed as any other businessman, cordially shook hands with him and invited him to sit down.[68]

He took a trip down the Potomac to Mount Vernon, where he saw tablets indicating that Washington's lineage could be traced to the English and Scottish petty nobility. Janson disparaged this, believing that the President had reflected honor on the nobility, rather than the reverse. The traveler was pleased to see bills of lading displayed that showed how Washington had sold his produce like any other farmer. On May 11, Janson sent a card to Professor Anderson saying that he had had a fine trip through Philadelphia, Baltimore, and Washington and was going to Boston, where he intended to stay for a week.[69]

By May 20 he was in Cambridge, where he called on Longfellow. Again he brought up the subject of Walt Whitman. Longfellow "in his usual mild manner described Whitman as a wild, untamed spirit whose poems were nevertheless (he apparently had not read many of them) full of warm, forceful thoughts."[70] Janson also ventured to ask Longfellow about Mrs. Victoria Woodhull, only to have the poet shake his head resignedly. Some time later Janson attended a meeting of Mrs. Woodhull's Free Love League in Boston. He was disappointed to find that the lady was lecturing in England, but he listened to the speeches of her colleagues, both Negro and white, finding the ideas presented somewhat visionary but in no way shameful or indecent. The league's reform program was based on the assumption that man is inherently good and should be released from the restrictions placed on him by government and orthodox religion—particularly the latter. It roundly berated Christianity and its concept of original sin, tracing most of society's evils to that source. Janson, reporting all this in *Amerikanske forholde,* was prompted to make a spirited defense of Christianity, finding in the league's attack additional evidence of how people con-

37

fused dogma with what he regarded to be essential Christian principles.[71]

Janson, searching as he was for ways in which America differed from Europe, found little in American art or literature that interested him. Pictorial art, when it was not humorous, tended to be tediously sentimental, causing him to remark that the American artist could not depict a young girl looking up at the sky without having the heavens open and angels descend. He considered the architecture more promising. The imposing mansions in the East and the buildings erected in Chicago after the fire displayed an ingenious use of red sandstone, white marble, glass, and iron. Poets and writers—with the notable exception of Walt Whitman—followed traditional styles and frequently drew their material from faraway places and remote times. Such writers as Mark Twain and Bret Harte, who did deal with the American scene, were, in Janson's judgment, faithful reporters but hardly men of great creative talent.[72]

On May 23, shortly before he sailed for home, Janson heard Henry Ward Beecher preach in Brooklyn and was agreeably impressed by his informality, much as he had been by that of the Reverend David Swing in Chicago months before. He arrived in Kristiania on June 3; he had abandoned his earlier plan to spend some time in England.

In the Middle West the controversy over "The So-Called 'Pure Teachings' " was still being threshed out in the newspapers. *Norden,* piqued at Jaeger's stout defense of Janson, had remarked that the editor of *Budstikken* was apparently unaware that Janson, long before he had any personal experience with conditions in the New World, had given essentially the same speech in Lillehammer, Norway, later tailoring it to fit his audience in America. Jaeger admitted that he had not known this before, but insisted that the news in no way altered the central issue: "When a man with Janson's gifts criticizes how we conduct our spiritual life, it is what every intelligent stranger with Janson's opportunity to see and hear must think, even if he does not say it to us."[73]

More than a month later, *Budstikken* reprinted a second article on Janson from the June 4 issue of *Evangelisk Luthersk Kirketidende.* In acknowledging Janson's response to the previous *Kirketidende* article, the commentator called attention to the poet's statement that he did not want to become involved in a long theological discussion. All of this bypassed a vital point, he said. The question was not whether Janson was "Synoden" or a Lutheran, but whether he was a Christian. He had spread slander. In spite of his having heard the account of the cemetery incident from a pastor, he should have known, by reference to the eighth commandment, that Christians are in duty bound not to carry such tales. Furthermore, Janson claimed to believe in the articles of faith in which he had been baptized. If so, he had taken out the kernel and kept merely the shell, for the articles were nothing more than an acceptance of the triune God.

How, the writer asked, could Janson consider Christ his saviour if he did not consider him to be divine? He could not be a Christian unless—as another paper had suggested—he was a Unitarian. If he was not a Christian, he was not a Lutheran. "No serious Christian will have anything to do with him, should he ever visit our land again. His words will be regarded as poisonous. He came as a guest, was honored as a writer and a son of the fatherland. He will not be so treated by Christians again. Had he been sufficiently honorable to give his talk at the beginning of his series rather than at the end, he would have seen that we are right."[74]

Curiously, Rasmus B. Anderson failed to mention "The So-Called 'Pure Teachings' " in his summary of the lecture tour. The omission was serious, making Anderson's account a distortion: "Kristofer Janson was at the time, though somewhat tainted with Grundtvigianism, thought to be fairly orthodox in his theology. In his addresses he abstained rigidly from touching upon religious topics. Accordingly, he was hospitably received at all Norwegian Lutheran parsonages, and he was permitted to speak in a large number of Norwegian Lutheran churches. He was received and entertained as one of Norway's distinguished sons and his visit did much to promote an interest in Noregiandom on this side of the Atlantic."[75]

In *Amerikanske forholde,* Janson gave a more comprehensive and far more devastating description of church conditions in America than that in "The So-Called 'Pure Teachings.' " He spoke of five rival synods, naming the Norwegian Synod and the Conference as the largest and most acutely inimical. He elaborated at some length on the Norwegian Synod's claim to the sole possession of the "pure teachings," of its adamant stand on a literal interpretation of the Bible, and of its complete rejection of latter-day Biblical scholarship. He described the Norwegian Synod's close affiliation with the German Missouri Synod; this was the only other Lutheran body with which it was in accord, for it found the Lutheran Church in the Scandinavian countries and Germany to be lacking in vigilance against the encroachment of liberal elements.

The Norwegian Synod, Janson went on to say, characteristically took a narrowly partisan stand on public issues, viciously denounced those who differed with it in theological matters, and exercised a tyrannical control over its own members. He spoke of the Synod's opposition to the public schools and its earlier defense of slavery. He cited instances of attacks on pastors of other synods, documenting his statements. He spoke of the multiple prohibitions placed on its parishioners, listing secret engagements and marriages, lotteries, life insurance, membership in secret societies, lending out money at interest, and a widower marrying his deceased wife's sister as forbidden activities. Transgressors, Janson maintained, were subjected to such severe disciplinary measures as public examination and excommunication.

In the conduct of family affairs, Janson saw the Synod exercising a pernicious influence. He reported that it gave parents absolute authority over their children, and the husband complete dominion over his wife. To illustrate the latter point, Janson cited two cases. The first (which he later used as the nucleus for his story, "Wives, Submit Yourselves unto Your Husbands," in *Præriens saga*) concerned a woman who fled from a brutal husband and was forcibly returned to her home on the advice of a minister. This account, Janson declared, he heard from the woman's brothers. The other case was the Bernt Julius Muus story, which Janson described at some length, drawing details of the pastor's alleged callous treatment of his wife from testimony reported in the newspapers during Janson's stay in America.[76]

To what extent Janson looked upon his lecture tour as a tryout for a career in America is not clear, but there are indications that the prospect was in his mind. In a note to Bjørnson written at the time of his departure from Norway, he hal spoken of "what the tour might mean for the future"—although the phrase is broad enough to suggest various possibilities.[77] During his trip he must have spoken often of coming again, for the newspapers discussed it in reviews of "The So-Called 'Pure Teachings.'" Erik L. Petersen apparently saw the trip as a sort of trial balloon, for he mentioned to Anderson the harmful effect Janson's final lecture was likely to have on his future in this country.[78]

His judgment proved to be correct. Although it is unlikely that the memory of "The So-Called 'Pure Teachings'" would fade quickly in any event, in this instance it was shortly to be revived. In the winter of 1881, the indomitable Bjørnstjerne Bjørnson visited the Middle West. Unlike Janson, he made no bones about his *vantro* or heresy, and at once raised the hackles of the orthodox in all the synods. On his return to the East, Bjørnson gave his impressions of the immigrants in an interview that was later reprinted in the *Freeborn* (Minnesota) *County Standard*: "They [the Norwegian Americans] are unfortunately still a priest-ridden people. The Norwegian church synod in the West, composed of 175 pastors, controls the conscience of almost all our emigrants, and, for fear the latter may lose faith in their rigid Calvinistic creed, they are forbidden even to attend American public schools. They grow up in ignorance of the great social questions of the day and are good only for manual labor."[79]

Small wonder that—after Bjørnson had gone—they found Rasmus B. Anderson's announcement in *Skandinaven* insufferable: "I have the honor and pleasure to inform the public that I received a cable from Kristofer Janson today in which he says he will be in Madison by November. In the course of the fall and winter, he expects to hold a series of lectures, and he has authorized me to arrange the preliminaries. Any further recommendation from me is superfluous, for his name is so well known and many had the pleasure of hearing him two years ago. Those organizations or committees in the West that wish to secure a visit from the famous poet and lecturer should write to me so that I can arrange his route as soon as possible. I will then send information on costs, etc. Let us give our renowned countryman a worthy reception."[80]

Several protests appeared in the Norwegian press, but one will suffice here. On October 12, 1881, a notice appeared in *Norden*, signed only "J":

To the Norwegian Church People in America

The Norwegian press tells us Kristofer Janson is coming again. Last time he was given a warm welcome and entertained by our pastors. At first he hid his beliefs and then lashed out at our churches. Now when the freethinker and poet comes again, what? I call upon Norwegians of any Lutheran Church body to oppose this man who is trying to lead us away from our childhood faith. Regardless of his gifts, which are considerable, do not listen to his lectures even though they do not deal with religion. Norwegian Lutherans, what choice will you make?

2

A Beginning
Ministry

LATE IN the fall of 1880, some five months after Kristofer
Janson had returned to Norway from his lecture tour in America, he
and his wife, Drude, went to Italy on a vacation. The trip was the
fulfillment of a promise he had made the year before, should the
American venture be profitable—as indeed it was. Their seven children
were left in the care of a farm woman who had long been attached
to the family. Some of their relatives, particularly Dina Krog, Drude's
sister, disapproved of this arrangement. She felt the Jansons were
somewhat negligent parents not to leave an "educated" person in
charge.[1]

In Rome, the Jansons' final destination, they found lodgings on
Via Purificatione. Two Norwegian artists, Eilif Petersen and Kristian
Ross, and their families joined them as neighbors. All became part
of the sophisticated Scandinavian colony then in Rome, of which
Ibsen was clearly the Olympian figure, but which also included such
persons as Magdalena Thorsen and Camilla Collett—the latter, according to Janson, an ardent feminist virtually to the point of fanaticism.[2]

Attractive, still young, the Jansons seem to have been an engaging
couple, alike in their zest for the new but otherwise highly individual
in tastes—Drude, paradoxically, being somewhat the more radical and
certainly the more practical of the two. Family legend has it that
Drude was much admired in Rome, and this is not hard to believe,
for so urbane a man as the Danish scholar and critic, Georg Brandes,
who had met her a few months before in Kristiania, told how attracted
he had been to her, finding her highly original and very charming.[3]

42

For the Christmas festivities held by the Scandinavian group in Rome, Kristofer wrote a poem which won praise from Ibsen. Janson, in his autobiography, has told of taking long walks around Rome, of reading his short play, *Et kvindesjæbne* (A Woman's Fate) before an admiring audience. He was then working on his novel, *Vore besteforældre* (Our Grandparents), which gives an old man's account of events in Norwegian history from 1790 to 1815. On one occasion the Jansons borrowed costumes of the period of the story from Kristian Ross and invited their friends to a party. Drude's dress is not decribed, but Janson wore knee breeches, shoes with silver buckles, and a three-cornered hat, and, thus attired, read from his manuscript. During this period Ross painted Drude's portrait, a large canvas showing the three-quarter length figure of a poised young matron whose slender form and unlined face belied the fact that she had borne seven children in some nine years. When the newspaper *Dagbladet* arrived from Kristiania carrying Bjørnson's accounts of his stay in America, Janson discussed them with Ibsen, who had caustic things to say about Bjørnson, then his foremost rival as a Norwegian litterateur. At some time during this Italian holiday—the date cannot be pinpointed—Janson himself received a letter from Bjørnson, saying that a plan was afloat to bring Janson to America as a minister, and this prospect, as he revealed later, filled him with great excitement.[4]

Abruptly the Jansons' luck turned. Drude became ill, and, before she had recovered, word came from Norway that their son Sigmund was not expected to live. Kristofer rushed homeward, arriving in Lillehammer the day after the child had died. From such details as we have of the event, it was a lonely time for him. The older children, shocked by their first experience with bereavement, longed for their mother, and a younger one, Arne, was unable to realize what had happened. Janson had to face, besides his grief, the recriminations of Dina Krog, who made it clear that she hoped the event had taught the parents a lesson. The late Dr. Eilev Janson has reported that Janson conducted the child's funeral himself.[5]

Early in May, 1881, Drude returned home. By that time Janson had received a proposal from Professor Rasmus B. Anderson of the University of Wisconsin that he return to America to organize a liberal religious movement among the Scandinavians. Janson was at first inclined to refuse, dreading the prospect of another long separation from his family, and Drude advised him at least to sleep on the matter.[6]

Anderson's letter has not survived, but in his autobiography he gave this account: He wrote Janson immediately after meeting two prominent Unitarian clergymen, Jenkin Lloyd Jones and Henry Martyn Simmons, in Madison. He had promised Bjørnson that he would do something to establish Janson in America but had no idea how to proceed. This chance encounter with the ministers, whom he knew well, gave him an opening. If the Unitarians were interested in missionary work among the Norwegians in this country, he had the ideal man for them, and he described Janson's career as a writer and speaker and his theological training at the university in Kristiania. Jones and Simmons were at once interested; they were going to Boston for a church conference, where they would present the matter before the American Unitarian Association. Anderson then suggested that Janson be guaranteed an annual salary of $1,000 for the first three years. They agreed, promising to write Anderson from Boston. Encouraged by all this, Anderson at once wrote Janson, saying that if the matter turned out as he expected, he would send a one-word cable, "Come!" Sometime afterward Anderson received confirmation of his proposal, whereupon—to quote the professor—"I cabled the word 'come' to him and he immediately packed his grip and came."[7]

No one can doubt that Anderson was responsible for bringing Janson to America as a minister, but he has gilded his story a bit. Things did not move so fast. If (as Janson said) he received the professor's proposal early in May, he must have mulled the matter over through a great many nights, for he did not reply until the middle of July. Then he did not mention the Unitarians, apparently considering the ministers' show of interest a flimsy prospect on which to risk his future. Much of Janson's letter was given to an analysis of his own situation. He was forty years old and had six children to support. His wife was not robust and needed household help. Janson, knowing full well the privations some Lutheran ministers and their wives had to endure in America, could not tolerate Drude's giving up a comfortable life in Norway for one of hardship in America. Unless he were assured an income of at least $1,500, he would not consider the matter.

Yet, as he ruefully explained, his prospects in Norway did not seem good. He felt isolated, for those who shared his religious views differed from him politically, and vice versa. Nor did he foresee much of a future as a writer. Public interest in tales of rural life had waned in favor of the social novel and drama, a field Janson felt had been pre-empted by Ibsen, Bjørnson, and Alexander Kjelland. Furthermore, the *landsmaal* issue had been resolved, for that language was even taught in the schools: Janson was no longer needed as its champion.

But more than anything else he wanted to go into religious work; were he able to get congregations, he would give all his energy to the development of their spiritual life. Anderson had suggested that he establish churches in several localities, dividing his time among them. Janson agreed to this but vetoed Anderson's recommendation to include Chicago. He was set on living in Minneapolis, and traveling between the two cities would be too wearying. Besides—and here he asked Anderson to respect his confidence—Janson had not much liked the Scandinavians in Chicago, and though he might lecture there from time to time, he did not relish closer contact with them.

Janson then instructed Anderson how to go about organizing congregations. He drew up a proposed program, sending three copies, which he called circulars. Each was to go to an energetic but discreet man in one of three cities: Minneapolis, Fort Dodge, Iowa, and a third that Anderson might pick—possibly Madison. In each town, the man selected was to call a meeting at which Janson's program would be discussed, and those willing to support a congregation based on the principles given were to sign their names and pledge an annual sum, to be continued for at least three years. All of this, Janson cautioned, must be kept out of the newspapers, for if orthodox ministers got wind of it, they might frighten away people who would otherwise support the movement. After the circulars had made their rounds, Anderson was to forward them to Janson with whatever explanation was necessary. Toward the end of the letter Janson asked if it was legal in America for a man who had not been ordained to function as a minister, reminding Anderson that he had not been; nor could he go through the rite in Norway, for ordination there required taking an oath to uphold the Augsburg Confession.[8]

Had Anderson tried to put this plan into operation, he might well have been thrown back on his heels, for it is hard to publicize a man's activities and be quiet about them at the same time. But he faced no such dilemma. By the time he received Janson's letter, he seems to have been sufficiently confident of his own plans to disregard the circulars. Instead of a single-word cable, he wrote Janson, and while this letter too is lost, its contents can be surmised from the response it drew. Anderson seems to have made it clear that the time for ambivalence was over. Prospects for support from the American Unitarians were good, but they were not going to commit themselves until they had met Janson. He must come to America in the fall, accepting the risks, or the matter would be dropped. While negotiations were going on, he could be lecturing, with Anderson again acting as his manager. A friend of Anderson's in Madison, John A. Johnson, had offered to keep Janson at his home until he was permanently located, and to donate a sum of money to him, a suggestion that was apparently tantamount to saying he would support Janson for a time if the worst came to the worst.[9]

On September 8 Janson cabled that he would come. In a letter of the same date, Professor Anderson wrote *Skandinaven* in Chicago, announcing that Janson would return to America in the fall for another lecture tour.[10]

In Norway, Janson agonized over the sudden turn of events. On September 9, the day after he had sent his cable, he wrote the professor, revealing his anxiety over the future and his humiliation at coming under such circumstances. "Your letter gave me a great shock! All my plans have been ruined. Had you realized what you were doing, taking me away from my home, my wife and children, giving me a long voyage across the ocean, forcing me to come—uncalled—to struggle with an uncertain future, you would have thought twice about it. However, now I have cast my lot, and I must try. I have set my life's hope on a future there with you. If I fail, woe is me!"[11]

Janson went on to say that he expected to arrive before the middle of October. He gratefully accepted Johnson's offer of hospitality but not the money, which he would accept only in extremity and then strictly as a loan. He was, nevertheless, concerned about finances; he had to earn enough to support his family in Norway and to lay aside money to bring them over and establish a home. For a lecture he needed a minimum guarantee of twenty-five dollars, and fifty dollars in the larger cities. He hoped to stay out of controversy, adding resignedly that he supposed that was unlikely, at least so far as the Norwegian Synod was concerned. He added in a postscript that Bjørnson disapproved of his decision to go and could not understand why Anderson had done nothing with the circulars. "I would stay in Norway until a congregation was knocking at my door," he quoted Bjørnson as saying.[12]

Anderson apparently felt no qualms. Shortly after his ultimatum went to Janson, he wrote Bjørnson that he was working on the Janson matter and had good prospects for getting him a yearly salary of $2,000. Just what encouragement he had received thus far is not known, but it is clear that the American Unitarians were talking about Janson and were indeed eager to see him. On September 27, Aubertine Woodward, who had translated Janson's *Den bergtekne* (The Spellbound Fiddler) two years before, wrote Anderson from Boston that the Reverend James de Normandie, editor of the *Unitarian Review and Religious Magazine,* wanted to get all particulars from her on Janson, about whose coming he had heard from the wife of a Unitarian clergyman. On October 11, in the postscript of another letter to Anderson, she wrote: "I have seen Mr. De Normandie. He is delighted about Kristofer Janson, and says he must by all means come to Boston where he will himself introduce him to the Unitarian Board and he has not the slightest doubt of getting a salary appointed for him. He also says that the columns of the Unitarian Review are open whenever we want to use them. . . . Mr. De Normandie is very influential, and passes much time in Boston."[13]

Meanwhile many readers of *Skandinaven,* unaware of any prospective ministry for Janson, read Anderson's announcement of another lecture tour glumly. Even the Reverend Erik L. Petersen, who a year and a half before had applauded Janson's outspoken final lecture, "The So-Called 'Pure Teachings,' " now thought that enough was enough. "Let as many cablegrams come as will," he advised readers of *Skandinaven.* "Twice you have been taken in; don't let it happen a third time," he said, citing the proverb that a fool and his gold are soon parted. "Neither Kristofer Janson nor Rasmus B. Anderson is a poor man," he continued, "and you would be foolish if you filled Janson's purse with thousands to use in enjoying himself later in Paris or Rome while you slave in the summer heat and winter cold. If you love God, you won't put out a cent for those who scorn God and His Holy Word, and whose living is made by driving Christianity out of the believer's heart."[14]

Janson apparently arrived in New York rather early in October. His initial activities are not known; possibly he stopped there to visit Hjalmar Hjorth Boyesen, something he had speculated on in his letter to Anderson of September 9. He may, under a directive from Anderson, have gone to Boston to meet directors of the American Unitarian Association. It seems likely, not only because the way had been cleared for such a meeting but also because missionaries were paid by the association from Boston, even though those working in the Middle West were directed by the Western Unitarian Conference. By October 24, 1881, Janson was in Madison, still awaiting definite word from the Unitarians. On that day he wrote a twenty-page letter to Jenkin Lloyd Jones, secretary of the Western Conference. Probably he had not yet met Jones, for he was, in effect, introducing himself. Quite likely the first letter Janson ever wrote in English, it reveals his early difficulties with idiom and syntax but also indicates that the shift in language did not hamper him from presenting himself in an appealing way: "You must excuse me, that I dare to trouble you with a so very long letter, as this seems to be; but when you have read it through, you will find reason in it, I hope. To you perhaps have been told, my friend in Madison, Prof. Anderson, had written to me a while ago a letter, asking me to emigrate to America for the purpose of working for a more liberal spirit among my countrymen here, especially concerning their religious views, and make them good American citizens. I felt a desire to do it, because it seems me a necessary and blessed work too—but I had a large family, I was well off in my home, and I did not dare to do it without any assistance. Then Mr. Anderson told me about his meeting with you and your readiness to accept his proposals. I was quite surprised, for such a thing could not happen in any other country than America, I suppose, where public confidence has become an educating power. Relying upon this magnanimous and noble offer, I have left my home and am willing to try the hard task. I hope that you, dear Sir, may be able to get Mr. Andersons proposals realized, and that your confidence in me will not be misplaced. I hope, that the spiritual capital, which my countrymen, when once awakened, will bring to their new fatherland, will reward the generosity of your society toward me and the Scandinavians. I promise you as an honest man to put in all my vigour and energy in this work."

Janson went on to a description of the dissension among the Norwegian Lutherans in America—the five rival synods, and the Norwegian Synod's affiliation with the German Missouri Synod, the schism then threatening it over the predestination issue, and its actions in the past: its defense of slavery, its opposition to the common school, its rigid fundamentalism, and (the allegation Janson had made before) its policy of keeping its parishioners cut off from American society. With some stylistic changes, this discussion was later printed in *Unity,* the publication of the Western Unitarian Conference, and then was widely disseminated when an excerpt from it appeared in the *Independent*, an interdenominational magazine devoted to news of the various Protestant churches.

Janson next assessed his chances of success as a missionary: "I thought it my duty, dear Sir, to tell you the very truth about the distressing condition of my fatherlands church here in America. You may see that my task will not be easy, and that I may not hope to organize free societies in a hurry. I am sure, that all the Lutheran congregations will agree in my persecution. I have already got a little

48

taste of it by several mean articles in the Norwegian newspapers here. In one of them they recite the words of St. Paul as a salutation to me: 'if any man preacheth unto you any gospel other than that which ye received (from the Norwegian synod?) *let him be anathema.'*

"But I will also find my defenders.

"Besides the members of the mentioned congregations you will find many thousands of Norwegian people outside the church, floating and drifting for all winds, spread over all the country. Among them I will probably find the first stones for my church. But I am not sure, how far I will succeed among them. A large part of them have thrown the christianity over board and do not care for any Christian membership; another part are business men, who are afraid to loose [*sic*] their customers if they declare themselves to be members of a free church. For it is not so among the Norsemen as among the Americains [*sic*], that nobody in affairs asks, whether a man is Methodist or Episcopalian or not—no—they make business with their own fellows and look at the others with a shy look as something strange and horrible.

"Without your assistance I will be compelled to lay my religious work a side and earn my living by lecturing about esthetical, historical, and social subjects. With your assistance I will put my other lectures in the background and employ all my power in a labor for a free church, and shall be able to stay here for a number of years at least. In that case I intend to go back to the old country next May, arrange my affairs there and take my family over with me. The summer months spent at home I will use for collecting a hymn book, which will be necessary, because the largest number of the common hymns in the Norwegian church are so inwoven with old creeds and singular Lutheran dogmas, that these will be of no use to me.

"Finally, I may beg your pardon, dear Sir, that I have engaged your attention for so long time. You may also excuse my bad language, but I am a beginner and must still compose my letters by means of the dictionary. In a year or two I hope I will improve so much in English, that I may be able to preach my sermon in that language. That will be necessary, if I shall think upon conquering the growing up people. If any of this information should have interest for your society, I will leave them entirely at yours disposal."[15]

This prospect of support made it mandatory for Janson to become known to the American public. Apparently Anderson has this in mind. He had recently published a translation of Bjørnson's *Arne*, and arranged to have Janson review it. The article, composed in English by the reviewer himself, appeared in the November, 1881, *Dial*, and

49

was entitled, "A Norse Prose Idyl"; the fact that Janson spoke well of the translator's work does not seem strange under the circumstances. As soon as the magazine came out, Janson sent a copy to Jones.

In the last week in October, Janson received favorable word from the American Unitarians, and the news that his ordination would take place in Chicago during the following month. On November 1 Janson wrote Jones, asking if Sunday, the thirteenth, would be convenient—not, it appears, because he had a preference for that date but because he was considering giving a free lecture in Chicago while he was there and needed to make preliminary arrangements. Four days later he gave an address, "Vore forfædre" (Our Ancestors) in the assembly hall of the University of Wisconsin. It was of course delivered in Norwegian, but received a lengthy and very favorable review in the *Wisconsin State Journal* (Madison) which, in translation, appeared in *Skandinaven*.[16]

On November 21, 1881, the directors of the American Unitarian Association formally accepted Janson's application into its ministry and voted him $1,000 for the first six months of his work. On Friday evening, November 25, he was ordained in the Third Unitarian Church in Chicago. Besides Jones, three other Unitarian clergymen, Brooke Herford, E. L. Garvin, and George C. Miln, took part in the ceremony. After the ordination, Janson, apologizing for his English, spoke of the event as one of the highlights of his life, likening it to the day he became a university student, the day his first book came out, the date of his marriage, and that of the birth of his first child.[17]

The event had extensive coverage in Unitarian journals. In the *Christian Register,* the official organ of the American Unitarian Association, the article was entitled "A New Prophet in Israel." In *Unity,* Jenkin Lloyd Jones quoted Bjørnson that no better protest against the dogmas of the orthodox church could be found than in Kristofer Janson's liberal religion, "sustained by the purest personal character and most charming intellect." Jones, extending the good wishes of the Western Conference to its new missionary, made use of Norse mythology: "May his be Thor's hammer to smite wrong, and Balder's smile to woo the right."[18]

Meanwhile Aubertine Woodward had been waiting until after the ordination to write about Janson. In the *Unitarian Review and Religious Magazine,* under her pseudonym, Auber Forestier, she described the ordination, gave a biographical account of Janson, and spoke of Professor Anderson as the man who had paved the way for Janson by his truthfulness about the Norwegian Synod and his "brave, single-handed fight on the common school question." The work of the two men would harmonize, she declared, concluding her article with a eulogy of Janson:

"And now this man, so rich in endowments, in experience, in honors, a true liberal in religion and politics, his poetic nature and loving heart overflowing with a Christ-like yearning to aid and lift up his people, leaves his home with a self-sacrifice that we can perhaps scarcely estimate, and comes among us on a noble and exalted mission. His genial presence, his deep earnestness, his strong personal influence, cannot fail to help his cause and attract many about him. May his endeavors be crowned with the grandest success!"[19]

On the Sunday following the ordination, Janson gave his free lecture, "The Norwegian Synod," in Chicago. *Skandinaven,* in an objective account, reported that every seat was taken, on both the main floor and in the balcony, and crowds took standing room in the back of the hall. Otherwise, the Norwegian press of the city took a dour view of this as well as the proceedings of the Friday evening before. "He chose a rich theme for one who claims to be the apostle of brotherly love. Janson is a hypocrite," *Den Nye Tid* lashed out angrily. *Norden* concluded its remarks with the statement, "We hope Janson's mission will have no future among our countrymen." *Verdens Gang* was more temperate. Janson's significance, as both poet and theologian, had been greatly exaggerated by his admirers, the editor maintained. Nevertheless, his coming meant a struggle which should stimulate the spiritual life of the Norwegians, something they greatly needed. A man had a right to ally himself wherever he chose, the editor continued, even if it meant breaking with the old. In Norway many in the higher classes were certainly not Lutheran, were actually closer to Unitarianism, and it was better for church and society that they be openly so. The editor felt, however, that Janson's Sunday lecture did not leave a good impression, because of its bitterness and the circumstances under which the material had been gathered—the latter a reference to Janson's lecture tour of 1879–80.[20]

In La Crosse, Wisconsin, *Fædrelandet og Emigranten* prefaced its account of the ordination by saying that Unitarians accepted only one God and denied the divinity of Christ and the verbal inspiration of the Bible. In England, the editor continued, they were considered freethinkers. In America they tried to gloss themselves over as Christians, but were really freethinkers, nothing else. The same issue of the paper carried another column-long article entitled "Unitariernes sekt," a history of Unitarianism beginning with Servetus and concluding with the statement that in America there were no more than 17,960 members.[21]

On December 2, Anderson wrote exultantly to Bjørnson:

"I must report the news on Janson. He received the salary from the Unitarian Association that I predicted at the outset. Beginning yesterday (December 1) he has $2,000 as a missionary to the Norwegians in the Northwest. . . . Slightly over a week ago he was ordained in Chicago, and soon afterward he gave a fine address in the old Turner Hall before a *packed* house. Theme: the Norwegian Synod, and it took! Yesterday he went to Minneapolis. There will be a life-and-death battle, but Janson, with the backing of the Unitarian Association, can laugh at the neck-breaking exertions of the opposition. He will bring life and the Norwegians will develop into independent thinkers. I hope Janson himself will become a more independent man, for he still holds on to a great many dogmas. However, by this he builds a bridge for many others. I shall keep you informed; you can depend on that."[22]

2

At this time Minneapolis was entering a decade of great expansion; its population was to increase fourfold, from 36,887 to 164,738. The great influx of Norwegian immigrants had already begun; their number was to grow with every passing year, increasing from 2,500 in 1880 to 12,624 in 1890.[23] Nor do these figures tell the full story: for one thing, the census of the time did not include the native-born children of immigrants, and for another, there were, every year, newcomers streaming into the city who used it as a stopping place before moving on to find homes elsewhere.

Minneapolis covered some thirty-three square miles, extending seven and a half miles from north to south and slightly over six miles from east to west. As one might expect, immigrant life was humble, although it in no way approached the squalor found in the tenements of New York and Chicago. Even so, most newcomers got along on the narrowest financial margins, and accounts of suicide in Norwegian weeklies of the time point the trail of those who could not make it. Immigrant life was to become increasingly hard with the years. The nation as a whole had known a labor shortage in 1870, but this situation was to be reversed in the period 1881–1900, when immigration, technological changes, and other factors were to swell the number of unemployed to a million.[24]

Although it may be assumed that there were Norwegians living

52

in all sections of the city when Janson arrived, places of their heaviest concentration may be identified. The largest colony—and the area where Janson first directed his efforts—lay along both sides of Washington Avenue, roughly bounded on the north by Eleventh Avenue South, moving toward Cedar Avenue and the Riverside area. Washington Avenue from Eleventh to Fifteenth was lined on both sides with establishments kept by Scandinavians—grocery, dry goods, shoe repair, furniture, and hardware shops—and saloons. Some buildings towered to three stories, but most seem to have been single-story, gable-fronted stores. To the west of Washington Avenue, on the corner of Second Street and Twelfth Avenue, was Beard's Block, a three-story building commonly known as Noah's Ark, which contained some sixty apartments renting from eight to thirteen dollars a month. In windows throughout the area were such signs as "Scandinavian Boarding Day or Week" and "Scandinavian Midwife." A few blocks off Riverside Avenue was Augsburg Seminary, the theological school of the Norwegian-Danish Conference, the second largest of the five Norwegian Lutheran synods. This academy had been in the city since 1872, and the church established by the Conference—Trinity—also in this area, was the oldest Norwegian congregation in Minneapolis. There were four other Norwegian churches: Two were Lutheran, Our Saviour's and St. Paul's—of the Norwegian and Hauge synods, respectively—while the other two were Methodist and Baptist.[25]

A second colony, in north Minneapolis, extended north from Plymouth Avenue to what is now West Broadway, and from Second Street North westward toward Emerson. This group, drawn largely from the Trondhjem province in Norway, seems to have been generally interspersed with other nationalities, for the area as a whole was not dominated by Scandinavians. Years before, these Norwegians had made some efforts to form organizations: In the early seventies a number of families banded together to set up a primary school but abandoned it after a few years. In 1874 the Conference established St. Olaf congregation, but this too had petered out by 1877, and in 1881 the Norwegians in north Minneapolis had no church. In northeast Minneapolis was another colony about which little is known except that it was sufficiently large to maintain a church, Immanuel, established by the Norwegian Synod in 1874.[26]

3

Such, in brief, was the city and such its concentrations of Norwegians when Janson arrived on December 3, 1881, to try his luck.

While all the Norwegians certainly were not pleased at the prospect, the event caused virtually no surprise. Months before, in the spring of 1881, a rumor had circulated that Janson was to organize a liberal congregation in the city. The report reached Norway, where it was laid to rest by Janson himself in *Dagbladet*—a denial which was printed some time after he had opened his correspondence with Anderson. Although the statement was reprinted in *Budstikken* in Minneapolis (which traced the rumor to the efforts of a Pastor R. Egeland to organize a "free" congregation), many people who had heard the report seem not to have read the denial, for after Janson's ordination, correspondents to the paper frequently spoke of it as something they had been hearing about for a long time.[27]

In announcing Janson's arrival, Luth Jaeger, editor of *Budstikken,* said he was sure the majority of his readers would join in wishing Janson a hearty welcome. Janson had come, not to destroy the Synod, but to work for religious toleration and spiritual freedom. Now prospects were better than ever for the Norwegian people to be emancipated from blind dogmatism, Jaeger said, adding, "All free-minded Norsemen who, like us, long for this, will wish Janson the best of luck."[28]

In many ways Janson was fortunate in his choice of Minneapolis. He had prominent friends there, among them Dr. Karl Bendeke, Andreas Ueland, and Dr. Jacob Schumann. Besides Luth Jaeger, the publishers of *Budstikken,* Gudmund Johnson and John Gjedde, were friendly to him and from the beginning the columns of the paper were open to him. He was welcomed by the minister of Unity Church in St. Paul, the Reverend W. C. Gannett, a man with impressive Unitarian credentials, for he was the son of the famed Boston preacher, Ezra Stiles Gannett, and the namesake of the great William Channing, who had, indeed, christened him. Then Janson was to have the guidance of a Unitarian colleague near at hand—the Reverend Henry Martyn Simmons, who, the month before—in November, 1881— began what was to be a long ministry in Minneapolis when the already organized Liberal League became the First Unitarian Society. The two men liked each other from their first meeting.[29]

The time when Janson arrived—even though it was wholly adventitious—was also in his favor. The two major Norwegian Lutheran organizations—the Norwegian Evangelical Lutheran Church, popularly known as the Norwegian Synod, and the Conference of the Norwegian-Danish Evangelical Lutheran Church in America, generally referred to as the Conference—paid little attention to him, absorbed as they were in internal problems. In the Norwegian Synod a controversy had erupted (as Janson had mentioned in his letter to Jones) over the issue of predestination, led by a group that came to be known as the Anti-Missourians. In the Conference, efforts to raise an endowment fund of $50,000 for Augsburg Seminary had been received coolly by some congregations and was sparking some newspaper debate. It has been said by those who knew Janson, among them his protégé and successor, Dr. Amandus Norman, that Janson was denounced from pulpits; if this was the case, these attacks were not reported in the papers. What Janson had to endure was harassment from laymen—some of it so crude that it aroused public sympathy for him.

Six days after Janson arrived, on Friday, December 9, he lectured about the Norwegian Synod before an audience of 249 people, a fraction of the number who had heard the same address in Chicago; but those in Minneapolis paid twenty-five cents admission. Shortly afterward he was invited to give the speech in St. Paul. Thus far, however, he was only warming up. What he regarded as the opening salvo of his mission was a mass meeting he called for the following Sunday. For this he hired the largest auditorium in Minneapolis, Harrison Hall, on Washington and Nicollet avenues. According to Simmons, who attended as an observer, the crowd was so huge that people thronged the aisles. Janson has told, with sardonic humor, incidents that immediately followed the meeting. At the end of the address he announced that he would remain for a time in a small adjoining room, available to anyone who wished to talk with him. First to take advantage of this offer was an old woman carrying a copy of the Lutheran catechism. Brandishing the book, she demanded whether he was going to uphold its teachings. On hearing that he would not, she warned him that she would call down a curse on his work. Another person was an elderly man, his eyes glistening with tears, who clasped Janson's hand warmly. But then—as Janson has described it—the man suddenly came to his senses, and, realizing that the devil had been tempting him, hurried away.[30]

These instances, however, were mere bagatelles and did not depress Janson in the slightest. That night he wrote Professor Anderson—in English—his salutation revealing his exultant mood:
"My dear, sweet, young old boy Rasmus!

"I have just delivered my program—a splendid meeting, the large hall crowded. I think 1500 persons were there! When I protested the tyranny of the ministers and abolished the eternal hell there was perfect joy and applause: only two whistles were heard, but I do not know if they whistled in *American* or on [*sic*] *Norwegian*. I suppose the latter. It seems as if my program has made a deep impression. My friends told me that many people, walking out, declared they would join my congregation. Next Sunday I will commence my regular services, in the beginning at the same hall 3 o'clock in the afternoon. My first theme will be: 'God is Love!' After my lecture several persons walked in to me—and clasped my hands with sparkling eyes; the largest number of them *Swedes*. In Sweden, you see, those thoughts are not quite unknown, there has Nils Ignell and V. Rydberg worked and I think I here in Amerika will gather the fruits of their work in Sweden."

He mentioned two prominent persons as likely members of his church: Miss Nanny Mattson, Luth Jaeger's fiancée and the daughter of Colonel Hans Mattson, and Alfred Söderström, editor of *Svenska Folkets Tidning* (Minneapolis). He had other reasons for being encouraged. Even before his mass meeting he had been approached by N. T. Sjøberg and a group of the latter's friends about forming a congregation. These men, Janson explained to Anderson, had withdrawn or been expelled from Lutheran churches because they had joined fraternal organizations with life-insurance programs. They showed Janson the constitution they had drawn up. He was momentarily dismayed: "It was just the same as every Lutheran church— the name ought to be a Norwegian *Lutheran* congregation and they would oblige the minister on symbolium, Nicanum, Athanasianum." Janson told them he could not accept it and, after explaining his reasons, asked if he had frightened them away. They answered that he had not, and after that they had sold tickets for him and performed other services. He also received a letter from a group in rural Brown County and in return sent them what he called a "friendly and prudent letter," saying he would soon deliver a lecture in nearby Madelia, and when he was in the area he would preach for them and hold a conference to discuss their offer. He had been busy with other things too: working out a constitution which he planned to present to Sjøberg and the group in Minneapolis and later take with him to Brown County, preparing the announcement of his program for publication in *Budstikken* and *Skandinaven,* compiling a small hymn collection to be used at his services, and sending out a list of the titles of lectures he was prepared to give, for advertisements to be run in *Budstikken, Skandinaven,* and *Fædrelandet og Emigranten.* "I answer letters, make acquaintances, write sermons—so you will see I have my hands full," he wrote Anderson, adding cheerfully, "But I

56

have good hopes of success, old fellow, and I see it will only depend on my personal influence, so I have to be as amiable and vigorous as possible. I have suffered from backache these last days, and that is not very pleasant, but I must be thankful that my head is clear and that I can work."[31]

The following day he sent off a lengthy report to Jenkin Lloyd Jones, of much the same content as the one to Anderson. This letter, although more restrained in tone, was also buoyantly optimistic. Balder's smile, he remarked, referring to the secretary's comment in *Unity,* was likely to be more useful than Thor's thunderbolts. Still feeling the need to interpret the Norwegians to Jones, he added a few comments on a letter from the people in Brown County:

"The man [Johannes Mo] who writes it, writes in the name of a lot of Norwegian peasants [farmers] who have separated themselves from the Synod because they were always quarreling there. They ask me to come and be their minister, and they send me their constitution— the same as the former 'Nicanus Athanasium, the confession of Augsburg, etc.['] They do not know any other thing, poor fellows, and they will try to do it as well as possible. I returned a very friendly letter, thanked them for their confidence in me but told them I preferred to be a Christian for [rather than] a Lutheran." Janson had asked them if it was not time for the different Christian churches to unite rather than separate.[32]

4

"Kristofer Janson's Program," which was published in *Budstikken* on Wednesday, December 13, informed those who had not attended his mass meeting how Janson interpreted his role as a clergyman. It had long been his wish, he said, to engage in religious work, but his convictions were such that he could not serve within the state church in Norway. As for otherwise serving the liberal cause there, Norway was already well supplied with active leaders; his efforts could be put to better use among the Norwegians in America. Since most of them came from the working class and had little education, it was hard for them to develop a leader from their own ranks. Janson wanted to become their spokesman, helping them in their adjustment to American life. Lutheran pastors, he said, were tyrants rather than helpers. They had changed the Bible into a procurator's lawbook and embalmed Christianity into a mummy with their literally interpreted scriptural passages. This tyranny, Janson declared, he would oppose with full vigor.

Outside of that he wanted no controversy. He had no intention of going into congregations seeking converts, for he respected all faiths; he was instead making an appeal to Scandinavians who could not accept the dogmas of the orthodox church but were unwilling to renounce Christianity. The liberal church he planned to organize would be founded on "love to God the Father, and to our Saviour, Jesus Christ." Listing his major principles, Janson said he followed St. Paul in regarding Jesus as "the one mediator between God and man." He did not accept the divinity of Jesus, saying the crucifixion of a god amounted to an absurdity. Nor did he consider the Bible to be verbally inspired: The Old Testament he regarded as the history of the Jewish people and the New Testament as the earliest account of the lives of Jesus and the apostles, but both were the work of men who bore the prejudices of their own milieu. He did not accept the doctrine of the Trinity; he did not believe in an everlasting hell—although he was convinced that all wrongdoing was punished by mental and physical suffering, in accordance with natural law.

For his church services, Janson would use some of the practices of the church in Norway. Unless parents wanted it otherwise, he would baptize in the name of the Father, Son, and Holy Ghost. In celebrating the Lord's Supper, he would follow some of the conventional usages of the church at home.

Some parts of this statement seemed paradoxical; and Janson was shortly to be called to account. Yet, in terms of his rationale, it was entirely consistent. There was one God; Jesus was indeed the son of God, but not because of any mystical circumstances attendant on his birth, rather in the sense that all human beings are the children of God. Nor was he the Saviour for having served as a sacrificial lamb who redeemed mankind, but because he had, by his teaching and example, shown the way to God. Christians were to be identified by their way of life, not by a mere profession of faith. To Janson, what one believed was an intimate, personal matter, governed by inner conviction. An earnest Christian, looking to Jesus for guidance, never presumed that his particular belief of the moment constituted a monopoly on truth; instead he strove for new insights so that his religion, never a static body of doctrine, was always growing and developing.

Since belief was a matter of the individual conscience, no one who joined Janson's movement was under any compulsion to agree with him on what he had outlined as the major tenets of his faith. He was to meet shortly with those who could not, and this fact he accepted with equanimity. He also recognized that people were emotionally attached to many Norwegian church customs, associated as they were with memories of home. He saw no reason for dispensing with these when they could be reinterpreted by deleting the mystical elements. Thus Janson accepted the use of baptism, the Eucharist, confirmation, and other established practices.

All in all—as an outsider might view it—the orthodoxy Janson rejected and the "free" Christianity he espoused differed most fundamentally in that the latter lacked the punitive features of the former (a Jehovah punishing the sins of the fathers upon their children unto the third and fourth generation, a hell awaiting those who would not accept prescribed articles of faith) and in the breadth it gave religion; according to Janson's definition, one could find Christians in all places and ages—even among the ancients who had lived before the time of Christ—and Janson frequently did find them. Yet even his denial of the divinity of Christ becomes academic, for one is hard put to find greater reverence for Jesus than that in Janson's sermons and poems.[33]

In the week following the appearance of Janson's program in *Budstikken,* it was reviewed in *Folkebladet,* a weekly also published in Minneapolis. The paper was owned and edited by Sven Oftedal and Georg Sverdrup, professors at Augsburg Seminary, the theological school of the Conference, which had its headquarters in Minneapolis. Although the professors used *Folkebladet* to expound their views on issues related to the seminary and the Conference, it was essentially a secular paper, written in a highly readable style. Of the two editors, Oftedal was to emerge as Janson's most implacable critic, and until 1887 he was to be nipping at Janson's heels much of the time. The differences between him and Janson—so Oftedal declared—were not to be interpreted as *en lærestrid* (a theological debate), for the professor could not be drawn into any such discussion with a person who denied the divinity of Jesus.

He was not one to shrink from controversy and, once involved, he used little restraint in verbally pummeling an opponent. Long before Janson appeared on the scene, Oftedal had become well known for his broadsides. In 1874—shortly after he arrived in America—he had published a scathing attack on the Norwegian Synod that, even in those days of bitter exchanges, made something of a high-water mark.[34] Later, angered by the prospect of Bjørnson's lecture tour, he belittled the poet as a "clown," an epithet critics then and later found singularly inept.

Kristofer Janson in America

After Janson's ordination, *Folkebladet* contained allusions to Janson that seemed to be in Oftedal's idiom. Janson was mentioned as "a petite edition of Bjørnson" and as "one of Bjørnson's living proof sheets"; in the latter case, there was an added comment that all such persons might better be removed to Alaska, where the wilderness would appreciate their new form of civilization. Yet, all this was missing from the treatment of Janson in the December 22, 1881, issue of *Folkebladet*. For one thing, a dispatch written by a correspondent in Madison for a paper in Norway, highly complimentary to Janson, was reprinted without comment .Then—without any recourse to name calling—Janson's program was reviewed. As none of the articles was signed, the author cannot be identified with certainty. But the piece suggests a hand other than Oftedal's—that of Georg Sverdrup, an introspective man, somewhat austere in bearing, who today has the reputation of having been an unusually able dialectician. The review was not an exercise in dialectics, however, but more of a satire in which the writer generously conceded Janson's talents and then thrust the dagger where he was vulnerable.

The writer in *Folkebladet* reported Janson's statement about coming to serve as a leader for the Scandinavian people in America, adding with quiet irony "since they have none other than Lutheran ministers." Citing Janson's five major points as well as his resolve to retain practices from the church of Norway, the reviewer noted that although Janson denied the Trinity, he would baptize in the name of the Father, Son, and Holy Ghost; and while he did not accept the divinity of Christ, he would celebrate the Eucharist using the words, "This is my body" and "This is my blood." Janson would be both pastor and teacher; he would preach and deliver lectures. "Such is the program," said the writer, adding resignedly, "and so it must be, coming from a Unitarian." He assessed these principles as outworn rationalism, something long since discarded by Europeans but propounded in America by the Unitarians. This teaching could only be regarded as freethinking. Serious as the threat was, one could take comfort by recalling events in Norwegian history: It was just such rationalism that had precipitated the great religious awakening led by the lay preacher, Hans Nielsen Hauge.[35] One must remember this precedent while grieving over Janson's defection:

"It is disheartening to see a Norwegian poet become a minister in order to propound such a teaching, one regarded in the Lutheran countries of Europe as stable fodder and a crop of potatoes. It is discouraging to see a man who has fought for freedom now work for the teachings once preached in Norway by men who put Hauge in prison and sought to quell the workings of the spirit by physical force. It is disappointing to see a talented man from the Norwegian church openly declare views which the Christian church has never acknowledged.

"There is no reason, however, for Norwegians in America, who have worked to establish free congregations to safeguard the teachings of their childhood, to nourish anxious or bitter thoughts over Pastor Janson and his mission. The same thing has often happened in the history of the church, that heretical and rationalistic views have been preached and people have had to protect themselves by regarding them critically. That is especially true in this country, which has so many sects. Congregations must choose between the new teachings and the proven truth."[36]

Janson seems to have been somewhat puzzled about how to answer. He had no wish to quarrel with the Conference. The Norwegian Synod had been his prime target, and on several occasions he had praised the Conference, both for its confederation of independent congregations as against a centrally administered synod and for its use of lay preachers.

In his reply, Janson began by thanking the editor of *Folkebladet* for the generally courteous tone of the article, saying, "In these days of bitter strife, that is something one rarely encounters in an opponent, especially here in America." If the writer chose to adopt an attitude of levity and superiority toward his program, Janson must accept that interpretation. The same might be said about the comments on his similarity to the clergymen who had persecuted Hauge, although Janson added parenthetically that he was well versed on these men and on Hauge too, having recently dealt with them in a still unfinished book—a reference to *Vore besteforældre*. He could not acknowledge these ministers as his kindred, nor did he feel, especially at Christmas, any inclination to preach on potatoes. "All such imprecations," he said, "strike me as making use of old, but, unfortunately, not outworn tactics, designed to create mistrust in people's eyes. And I must admit I am surprised that you express yourself thus, for recently in my lecture on the Norwegian Synod I spoke of my admiration of the Conference's use of lay preachers. Do you call that persecuting Hauge?"

Janson complained that his program had been reported in terms of contradictions, and that such practices as the use of the Eucharist were not part of original Christianity but had been introduced by the early church fathers in the year 381. He conceded, however, that it was natural that he and the Conference should look upon such matters differently; each must choose according to his taste. He thanked the editor for reprinting the favorable dispatch by the correspondent from Madison. And he agreed that future debate between him and the Conference was unnecessary, adding, "I should value it very much if you would accept me as a neighbor with whom you could be on personally friendly terms, and that both our congregations might work side by side without either casting aspersions on the other."

This overture was rebuffed. Janson's letter was printed in the January 5, 1882, issue of *Folkebladet* and followed by editorial comment couched in coldly civil terms:

"Folkebladet has printed the above communication from Pastor Janson because it clearly reveals his rationalism as much as anything we could have written. Christianity is not, for us, something one chooses according to his taste, and it cannot be for any Christian. There can be no talk of working side by side with a man or an organization that denies the divinity of Jesus, which Christians have acknowledged through the ages, not just since 381, but from the days of the apostles. If Janson is familiar with the events of Hauge's time, he knows that the ministers who opposed him had a spiritual lack, intricately bound up with their heretical views and their denial of the divinity of Christ. Mankind, therefore, is prepared to fear the fruits that come from the same root in church work."[37]

5

The exchange took several weeks. In the meantime, Janson proceeded with his original plan to hold services every Sunday. Thus, one week after his mass meeting, he preached in Harrison Hall in Minneapolis at three in the afternoon before an audience of twelve hundred. In the interval between the two events, he heard from Jenkin Lloyd Jones. We do not have Jones's letter, but Janson's reply indicates that the secretary had some misgivings about Janson's hiring the largest hall in the city to attract great crowds, most of whom attended out of curiosity. He seems to have felt, too, that any further pillorying of the Norwegian Synod was unproductive, that Janson could be better employed emphasizing the constructive aspects of his mission.

"Thank you for your kind advice," Janson began in his reply of Monday, December 19. "I will try to get so sagacious as possible and behave as a 'business man' in all regards. Though I do not like serpents at all, I will nevertheless be 'as wise as the serpent and harmless as a dove.' " Yet, though he was willing to be counseled, he wanted

Jones to know that he had been prudent in his management and by no means neglectful of the real purpose of his mission. As long as people continued to come, he had to have a place large enough to accommodate them. Daytime rental of Harrison Hall was ten dollars, but there had been no difficulty meeting expenses. Rent for the mass meeting had been paid from proceeds of his lecture on the Norwegian Synod; for the two following Sundays, friends had offered to assume the burden; and thereafter he planned to take up a collection to cover costs. He went on to say that at least Norwegians knew he was in the city. "I have been reported, that the Norwegians do not speak about other things now, whether they meet one another on the street, in the shops or in the saloons. The worst thing is I have abolished the eternal hell; they cannot dispense with their pet child. I have been very careful in my utterances, trying not to frighten them away." Then, as if to reassure Jones, he summarized his sermon of the day before:

"Yesterday I spoke of 'God is love.' I took my starting point from the beautiful story of Elias when he stares for the Lord in the sturm [*sic*] and the earthquake and the consuming fire—but the Lord was not there. And then came a mild breeze, and the prophet covered his head for the Lord was near him. With short pencil strokes I painted to them the development of the Jewish opinions of their Jehova[h], first as a Sun-God, then as a War-God and the God of their nationality til [*sic*] the idea reached its highest top in Jesus Christ who taught 'the father in heaven.' That was one of the reasons, I said, why there is such a confusion in my countrymen's reading in the Bible and in their religious opinions, that they do not make any difference between the Jewish God and the Christian God. I showed them, how that is to disgrace God to tell that he sends famine and pestilence and war, etc. as special punishments upon us, how such an opinion is reminiscent from olden times, when they stared for God in the sturm, in the earthquake, and in the consuming fire. I showed them, how all suffering here on earth are brought by the humanity over the humanity, but the blessings, which sprout from the sufferings are his, our father's, and advised them to trust upon him as the boundless mercy and charity."

Several staunch Synod men had been in the audience, yet Janson was told that on their way out they had remarked that they could see nothing harmful in what he had said. "May I not then have been sagacious, Brother Jones?" he asked, a bit slyly. He said he expected to hold his next service on Christmas Day, and on the following day preach in Fort Dodge, Iowa. Enclosing four photographs of himself, he asked that Jones keep one and distribute the others to the rest of the clergymen who had taken part in his ordination.[38]

On the same day that Janson wrote this letter, Anderson sent one off to Bjørnson. Still relishing the fact that he had been "right all along," he reported that Janson was assured of a salary of $2,000 a year from the American Unitarian Association. On this point, however, Anderson was overstating the case. True enough, the salary was to become a reality and the professor's statement may only reflect his confidence in Janson's ultimate success. Janson had no such assurance: he was going through a trial period of six months, for which he was to be paid $1,000, and although, as it turned out, subsequent support was to be forthcoming, the understanding was that the American Unitarian Association would continue this only until Janson's congregations became large enough to bear their own burdens. Yet Anderson was in no mood for qualification. Janson was doing wonderfully, he reported, better than all expectations. He would get congregations in Minneapolis, Madelia, and Fort Dodge. "The struggle with the synod will be a life-and-death one, but he is on top. Attacks on him have already started in a thousand ways, and there is the same irresponsibility and bitterness in the attacks as those on you last year."[39]

6

A newspaper article that Anderson seems to have found especially "irresponsible" had appeared in *Fædrelandet og Emigranten* on December 6, characterizing the Unitarians as a small sect of about 17,960 people. Anderson, in a letter to *Budstikken* published December 20, 1881, declared the estimate to be patently false. Acknowledging that he had not the exact figures, he said he would judge the number to be nearer 300,000, and, more than that, they included the most gifted and distinguished citizens of the United States. To illustrate, he listed an impressive array of presidents, poets and novelists, historians, clergymen, teachers, and philanthropists, concluding with a suggestion that he found men of distinction and Unitarians to be virtually identical:

"To the Norwegian people in America I have only this to say: Watch out for the talented, worthy, popular, great poet and speaker, Kristofer Janson. If you allow yourselves to be led astray by him, you may find yourselves, on the other side of the grave, with the men and women I have named in this article, and among them you will also find Milton, Locke, Macaulay, and James Martineau from England. A dangerous society, is it not?"[40]

64

At Christmas Janson received gifts from the Andersons and Miss Woodward; he was the dinner guest of Dr. and Mrs. Karl Bendeke. At his service on Christmas Day (which in 1881 fell on a Sunday) an incident occurred that incensed his friends. As *Budstikken* described it, three persons attended who obviously did not belong there. One was a Swede, the other two, Norwegians—one of the latter so staunch a Synod man that he did not send his children to the public school. During the sermon he and his Swedish friend kept up a lively conversation in spite of repeated remonstrances from Janson. At one point they walked out but returned shortly, continuing to make comments. Finally when another person went out as if to summon the police, the men became frightened and left. Such conduct was inexcusable, Jaeger declared, warning that if such an incident was repeated, he would publish the names of the offenders.[41]

On January 2, 1882, a month after Janson had arrived in the city, he organized the Free Christian Church in Minneapolis. (Four years later, after it had erected its own building, it became known as Nazareth Church.) As congregation records are not available, the exact number of charter members is not known, but in February Janson wrote Anderson that he had thirty-four, some of them men with families.[42] The immediate result was that on the following Sunday, January 8, the time of the services was shifted from afternoon to the conventional morning hour. Attendance dropped from the great numbers he had been drawing at afternoon meetings, but it was still much larger than the actual membership count would indicate, ranging throughout the winter and early spring from two to four hundred people—the fluctuation, according to Janson, depending on the weather.[43]

Certainly some who attended Janson's church services, not only in the early days of his ministry but later, too, were there to see the man. This is mentioned not only in memoirs but also in the immigrant fiction of the period; one of the first things a Norwegian newcomer did on arriving in the city was go to hear Janson. Yet the sermons were memorable in themselves—rich in imagery, with illustrations drawn from all places and all times. Sometimes they had evocative titles ("When Will the Day Come?" "How Wonderful to Be a Human Being!"). Luth Jaeger found one, "Our Leading Stars," magnificent and published it in *Budstikken*.[44]

The theme of the sermon is how one finds the Christ child. Each of us, Janson says, carries the spirit of God within him, but one is also a free agent. From the myriad of stars that beckon him, he must

65

choose the right one. Others have done so to the benefit of mankind, the speaker declares, reading a passage from a Hindu writer who lived long before Jesus. The words are noble and elevating, remarkably similar, as Janson notes, to the Sermon on the Mount. Despite the period in which he lived, the writer was a Christian rather than the Norwegian of a latter day who gets drunk at Christmas while he noisily professes himself a "true believer." Then, as if to assure his hearers that this judgment is not merely his own notion, Janson cites the early church father Tertullian as saying that the noble ancients living before Jesus were "Christians by nature."

All this does not mean that faith plays no part, only that the profession of it may be superfluous, for if one lives as a Christian, men will know. Janson speaks of the importance given to good works in the epistle of St. James and that placed on faith by St. Paul. Briefly he discusses the Catholic emphasis on good works and that of the Lutherans on faith, concluding that such differences may be dismissed as theological abracadabra. Both are necessary. One must believe that the teachings of Christ present one with the best option, and that if he earnestly tries, he can live up to them. Faith is the root and one's actions the fruit of the tree.

Early in January, 1882, Janson was the victim of a trick which aroused considerable resentment in the Norwegian community. One morning a man invited him to take part in a program given by a young people's literary society. The group, according to the caller, had been organized by the Norwegian Synod pastor, the Reverend Ole P. Vangsness, but it was open to anyone who cared to join. As Janson explained later, he was pleased to hear of the organization; he thought it fine to have a society in which Norwegian young people, regardless of church affiliation, could meet. Ordinarily, on the evening in question, Janson attended a literary group organized by Henry M. Simmons, but he said he would gladly forego that. The caller asked what subject Janson would choose to speak on, saying that programs were to be printed. When Janson said he needed time to make a choice, the two agreed that "Reading by Kristofer Janson" would serve. On leaving, the visitor said he would give this information immediately to Dr. Prydz, chairman of the program committee.

When Janson entered the hall on the evening of the meeting, one of the first persons he met was Pastor Vangsness, who greeted him courteously, but, as Janson later recalled, seemed somewhat surprised to see him. No printed programs were in evidence; instead Dr. Prydz announced each number. As the evening wore on, and one selection followed another, Janson began to feel apprehensive. Finding an opportunity to speak to the chairman, he asked when he could expect to be called upon. Jocosely Dr. Prydz answered him, "Your turn will come next Sunday!" Stung, Janson found his way back to his seat; someone helped him with his coat, and he left the hall. Recounting all this in *Budstikken,* Janson concluded the tale of his humiliation somewhat bitterly, "I hope none of the righteous men and women who remained contracted a disease as a result of having so dangerous a person in their presence for a few hours."[45]

Exactly who was responsible for the trick seems never to have been ascertained. Dr. Prydz later stated that he did not know that Janson had been invited, adding that he considered his refusal to allow him to speak justified "on Christian grounds." The matter enlivened the columns of *Budstikken* for several weeks. One correspondent, signing himself "En Bondegut" (A Farm Lad) found Dr. Prydz's excuse a lame one. It was impossible, he declared, for the committee to be unaware that Janson had been invited. Yet even had that been the case, Dr. Prydz knew that Janson had been in the hall for several hours before he made his inquiry, and then, the writer declared angrily, the doctor's rude retort had been made on "synod grounds" rather than "Christian." Somewhat later, Peter J. Hilden wrote from Montevideo, commending "En Bondegut" for his letter and implying that it was high time for the Norwegian farmers to forget their subservience to the "better classes" and act independently. "Better conditions are in store for Norwegian Americans," he prophesied. "We have Kristofer Janson, who has studied us well. . . . I give you this advice: Don't be afraid to hear Janson or others." To this he added a bristling statement: "I am the son of a *husmand.* Some may think I have no right to express an opinion, but I certainly have."[46]

The greatest impact of the incident was felt by the literary society itself. A strong faction insisted that an apology be sent Janson. When, after several meetings given over to stormy debate, one was not forthcoming, the group withdrew to form a rival society which they called "Fram" (Forward). An active organization from the first, it frequently invited Janson to take part in its programs.[47]

7

Humiliating as Janson had found the incident, he was soon to have a gratifying experience of a different sort. On January 10, 1882, negotiations came to a head with the already organized congregation in rural Brown County. Janson became the minister of what was thereafter to be known as the Nora Free Christian Church. What perhaps makes the history of this congregation unique is that up to the moment when the parishioners met the man who was to be their preacher, their sole intent was to continue as Lutherans.[48]

This group had been part of the Lake Hanska Lutheran Church. In the summer of 1881, months before Janson arrived in this country, they broke away, saying that they could no longer tolerate the bitter dissension that characterized congregational meetings. Presumably several issues were at stake, but one of them centered about who should be permitted burial in the church cemetery. In August the seceding members met in a local schoolhouse and organized an independent congregation. Shortly afterward they drew up a constitution and elected officers, with Johannes Mo as president. From time to time in the months that followed, they invited a Lutheran minister from another synod to preach (the Lake Hanska Church had belonged to the Norwegian Synod) but were always refused. At one time they considered writing the university in Kristiania for a theological candidate but gave that up for financial reasons. In December they read of Janson's ordination. Many of them had heard Janson lecture in nearby Madelia less than two years before, when he gave an address on peasant reform in Norway that so captivated the audience that at the end they gave three rounds of cheers for Kristofer Janson and Bjørnson. In December, 1881, the Brown County group, somewhat uncertain what to make of Janson's Unitarianism, had instructed Mo to write him, sending their constitution.[49] In return, Janson sent them a cordial but guardedly worded letter.

When Janson faced the congregation on that January day, the time for reticence was over. "I told them openly and honorably where I stood, making it clear I was opposed to the kind of preaching to which they had been accustomed." Watching his auditors as he spoke, Janson noticed from time to time that men would nudge and eye one another, nod and smile. When he had finished, some of them declared that on many issues they had long felt much as he did but had never dared say so openly. They found it easy to relinquish dogmas of the Trinity, the verbal inspiration of the Bible, and the existence of hell, but some found it impossible to give up their faith in the divinity of Christ. These Janson comforted by saying that they not only should but *must* continue to believe it if it seemed to them to be the truth. Before the meeting ended Janson was asked to revise the written constitution; this and other practical matters were completed shortly. In February

Janson wrote Anderson that he had forty voting members and twenty-five children under eighteen. The "peasants," however, as he still called those living in farming areas, were poor and could not pay their minister much. Several non-members in the neighborhood pledged support, but even then he could expect no more than $140 to $150 a year.[50]

In the months that followed, the congregation was bitterly assailed but stood its ground, with Johannes Mo acting as chief spokesman. Much of the opposition apparently came from the immediate neighborhood of the church. Thus, shortly after Nora Church was organized, when *Budstikken* announced that Janson had preached and lectured in Madelia and Waseca and started a congregation in the former, M. Olson wrote to reprove the editor, denying that such a church had been established. Unitarianism, he said, was a bloody pillow under the sleeping head. Then, wrathfully mixing his metaphors, he added, "I hope this dangerous teaching will not throw dust in the eyes of our countrymen. *Budstikken* would do well not to champion a movement aimed at destroying Christianity." Luth Jaeger, unrepentant, admitted that he had erred about the location of the congregation: "It was one in the vicinity of Madelia which had the honor of calling Janson as its minister."[51]

In January, 1882, *Evangelisk Luthersk Kirketidende,* official organ of the Norwegian Synod, reprinted a section of an article by Janson, his account of the shortcomings of the Synod that had originally appeared in *Unity.* Accompanying the excerpt was an editorial statement that no comment was necessary, the implication being that the charges were preposterous. Yet at the same time similar criticism of the Synod was being aired in the *Critic,* when Hjalmar Hjorth Boyesen published an article on Janson. After sketching his career as a writer, a pioneer in the *landsmaal* movement, and a teacher in the Norwegian folk school, Boyesen said that Janson was merely transferring his work to a new field—the Middle West—where the Norwegians needed enlightenment:

"They are sorely in need of the liberalizing influence of just such a man as Mr. Janson, having been too long shut off from intellectual contact with the Nineteenth Century by their 'evangelical' Norse Lutheran Synod. It speaks very poorly in fact for the culture and intellectual status of the Norwegians that they have allowed themselves to be ruled so long by a corporation which would find its proper place in a museum of antiquarian remains. It is the soul-paralyzing tyranny of this body of clergymen that Janson is endeavoring to break, apparently with encouraging success."[52]

Janson was succeeding far beyond his expectations. He had lectured in St. Paul and Lake Park in Minnesota and La Crosse, Wisconsin. Subscription lists for the support of his work were circulating in Eau Claire and La Crosse, besides several in Minneapolis, and he had recently received $112 from Dodge City, Iowa. All of this he mentioned in a letter to Anderson. If his letters to the professor frequently mentioned money, it must be remembered that at the time he was wholly self-supporting, having as yet received no payment from the American Unitarian Association. Through Anderson, lists also circulated in Madison.[53]

8

Grateful though Janson was for the professor's help, he came to realize that at times Anderson's patronage was a mixed blessing. Long before Janson arrived in the United States, Anderson had become involved in a bitter feud with Halle Steensland, a businessman in Madison, over the latter's candidacy for secretary of state in Wisconsin. After a series of acrimonious exchanges in the newspapers, Steensland sued Anderson for libel. Anderson had called upon his friends for support. John A. Johnson in Madison and Bjørnson in Norway both wrote articles, and Janson, after his arrival in America, wrote an account for a newspaper in Norway. Since Steensland was known to be a strong supporter of the Norwegian Synod, Anderson represented himself as the liberal champion engaged in a desperate struggle against orthodox tyranny, publicly appealing to those who sympathized with him to send ten-cent contributions for his defense. While many did so, cooler heads among the liberals (Luth Jaeger, for instance) disapproved of Anderson for having started the feud in the first place. Steensland, for his part, bitterly resented the interference of Bjørnson and Janson; shortly after the latter's ordination, he reproved him sharply in *Norden,* concluding bluntly, "Mind your own business, Reverend Sir, and let those who have not bothered you live in peace."[54]

After the turn of the year, the dispute having become increasingly bitter, Steensland turned more of his attention to Janson. On February 9, Janson wrote plaintively to Anderson:

"And what to say about that story with Halle Steensland! I very seldom felt myself so like a wet rooster as on that occasion. I had myself drawn my formidable sword defending you and now *quil bruit pour une omelette.* That was the little mouse the mountain brought forth after all woes and throes in the newspapers and the ten-cent subscription and the boasting of your lawyers. The result of all is that he now threatens me with libel suit too! He has written several letters to me and promised that my expressions in the article to 'Verdens Gang' shall cause me trouble."[55]

Fortunately, by the time Janson wrote this letter the matter had already been settled out of court when Anderson made a public apology in *Skandinaven* on February 24, 1882. And Janson, worried though he might have been, had not let the matter interfere with his work. Shortly after the organization of his Minneapolis congregation, he announced that he would give a series of weekly readings from literature. Because of difficulties in finding an evening when Harrison Hall was available, these did not begin until January 23, when Janson read the first part of his *Fante Anne* (Gipsy Anne) before an audience said to be as large as the hall would hold.[56]

Throughout February Janson's work went on with encouraging success. *Unity,* commenting on the growth of the two new Unitarian churches in Minneapolis, observed that St. Paul had better watch lest Minneapolis eclipse it and become the cathedral city of Unitarian Minnesota. Professor Anderson, beguiled because Janson was not getting more opposition from the orthodox, wrote exultantly to Bjørnson:

"What's so amusing is that the Synod is in the midst of a great struggle within its own ranks on the predestination issue, a fight that is driving people out of the Synod and will eventually divide them a thousand ways. They are so absorbed in this internal quarrel that they have wholly forgotten Janson, who takes one province after the other from them. In the Conference things are not better. They are fighting over something they call the issue of professors' salaries and go at one another like mad dogs."[57]

Yet, if Janson was escaping attack from official quarters, Nora congregation was feeling the wrath of laymen and clergy alike. Late in March, Johannes Mo wrote to *Budstikken,* recounting the history of the church and pleading that Norwegians in America live and let live. From the time the group had left Lake Hanska Church, they had been barraged with slander and abuse on every side, even from pulpits. They had been called mockers of God, a rotten congregation, freethinkers. Attacks had appeared in *Nordvesten* in St. Paul, in *Norden* and *Skandinaven* in Chicago. A letter in the last-named paper, bearing the signature of a neighbor in Brown County, had berated Mo and

71

Ole Serumgaard for being leaders of a congregation served by Janson, who was undermining Christianity. No one, Mo went on, need speak for Janson, who was fully able to defend himself. Instead of destroying, however, he devoted himself to raising the downtrodden and righting what was wrong and false. In his last sermon, Janson, knowing the calumny people had endured, had urged them to be patient, not to repay evil with evil. Mo, for his part, was not ashamed of his function in the congregation but was proud of the confidence others had placed in him.

The writer of the letter to *Skandinaven* had said that the group left the Lake Hanska Church because of a dispute over the graveyard. Mo, insisting that this was only one issue, explained that Nora Church was going to have its own burial ground, and in it anyone, regardless of creed, might bury his dead. Even Norwegian Synod ministers who had denied that privilege to those who had left their congregations might find a final resting place there. Expressing doubt that the neighbor was actually the author of the *Skandinaven* letter but had allowed his signature to be affixed to one composed by another, Mo spoke of his regret that an old friendship should be severed in such a manner, and ended by appealing for better relations: "You better-thinking men of Lake Hanska, Linden, Madelia, and Butternut Valley congregations —Norwegians, near and far—leave fanaticism and hate and live together in peace and charity."[58]

9

In March Janson was making plans to wind up his affairs in Minneapolis temporarily so that he could go back to Norway and get his family. Early in the month he received a letter from Jenkin Lloyd Jones asking him to take part in the Western Conference convention, to be held in Cleveland early in May. Somewhat bewildered by American practices, Janson replied:

"What do you mean by 'devotional exercises'? Do you mean only a short prayer, or a prayer and a short sermon? or what? What I wish to do at the meeting is *to read a paper about the Scandinavians and the Scandinavian movement.* Will that be permitted instead of any platform speech? You must think upon, that I am a foreigner and can not move in the English language like a fish in water. Please answer these questions, and I shall then decide what to do at the meeting. I should like rather to be a listener than a speaker on that occasion."[59]

Jones's reply did not wholly satisfy him. When Janson wrote again on March 20, he was still concerned with what kind of topics might be of interest to the convention and asked Jones's opinion on "Do We Christians Always Treat Our Adversaries Fairly?" as a subject. He had questions about how long it took to get to Cleveland from Chicago and where the other ministers were staying, saying he would very much like to have company. Yet, more than that, he was wondering when he was going to be paid, being badly pressed for money. He had sent off his report to the American Unitarian Association sometime before, channeling it through Jones, whom he knew to be a busy man. As he visualized Jones's desk, need took precedence over delicacy:

"And what shall I think of the Unit. Assoc. in Boston? I have not received a single cent yet, and now we have the 20th of March. What makes me impatient is, that I have not been able to send a cent for the support of my family in Norway, and my wife has been obliged to borrow money. Now she will start for the western part of the country with the children in the last part of April for the purpose of taking farewell with her old father, and she needs money for that journey. And it takes three weeks before a letter reaches her from here. You are sure you have forwarded the report, brother Jones, so that it has not been hidden among your many papers? Excuse my question."[60]

Some time before his departure from Minneapolis in the spring, Janson received what came to be known as the "salt pork letter." The anonymous sender had mailed it from Lanesboro, Minnesota, addressing it to "Rev. Kristofer Janson," and enclosing a piece of meat. Punning on the abbreviation for "reverend" (in Norwegian *rev* is the word for fox), the writer said that Janson had acquired his rightful title. He was sending the morsel in the hope that it would satisfy the fox who had come to devour the cock on the church steeple, and failing in that, was trying to undermine the church with its claws.

Janson forwarded the letter to friends in Lanesboro. On April 18 a statement appeared in *Budstikken* saying that the friends had only contempt for the sender and hoped that Janson would not think such boorishness characteristic of the Norwegians in that locality. They promised to try to find the culprit, but it was not until the middle of May, when Janson was on his way to Norway, that they openly accused someone. Using ruses, they had written to several persons they regarded as suspect, and compared the handwriting of the replies with that of the anonymous letter. The man they charged was a teacher and a choir member of a Lutheran congegation in the vicinity. Luth

73

Jaeger also examined the letters and found the writing similar, but, characteristically, he offered the accused an opportunity to defend himself in *Budstikken,* and shortly afterward he did. The man denied any knowledge of the "salt pork letter," but much of his communication was given over to a denunciation of the investigators, saying that they had brought no honor upon themselves by using such a "Jesuitical trick." He was forced to face trial, and although *Budstikken* did not give the final outcome of the case, Janson has stated that the man was forced to leave the community.[61]

Before Janson left, he was assured that his report had, indeed, reached Boston. The *Christian Register,* reporting the monthly meeting of the American Unitarian Association, spoke of the full and striking account received from "a new laborer in a new field, Rev. Kristofer Janson, our missionary to the Scandinavians in the States of the Northwest," who had already gathered five or six little congregations. Since there were only two formally organized churches, the others may have been places where Janson's subscription lists circulated and where he hoped to establish permanent organizations.[62]

En route to Cleveland, Janson had stopped off in Madison, where he preached in the Unitarian church, something Anderson regarded as noteworthy, as it indicated Janson's increased confidence in his use of English. He picked up an American flag to be presented as Professor Anderson's gift to Bjørnson when the latter commemorated the twenty-fifth anniversary of the publication of his *Synnøve Solbakken* the following summer.[63]

Whatever fears Janson may have had about appearing before the convention seem to have been groundless. The *Christian Register,* reporting how he conducted the devotional service, said his opening prelude had been "like a bit of Norse poetry, made especially winning by the foreign accent and gentle speech." Janson had told a legend about a contest among birds to choose as their king the one that could fly the highest. The eagle was expected to win, but just before it took wing, the smallest bird perched on its back and was borne up higher than the eagle, to become king. God's love was like the flight of the eagle, Janson said, adding that he would like to be like the little bird, looking down upon the world in the light of God's love. *Unity* reported that Janson had delivered two papers, one on tolerance (presumably a development of his idea on treating adversaries fairly), and another on the Scandinavians in America. Both, the editor said, were worthy of the author of *The Spellbound Fiddler,* and remarked that Janson's accented speech added to the attractiveness of his address. "Under any circumstances we should have admired the fine thought and nice diction but with the speaker's gracious smile and quaint pronunciation added thereto they become altogether fascinating." Even the handwritten minutes of what seems to have been a business meeting mention Janson. The secretaries recorded that when the Reverend Grindall Reynolds, secretary of the American Unitarian Association, spoke, he emphasized the work being done among the Scandinavians by Kristofer Janson.[64]

10

Clearly, Janson had stimulated considerable interest in his work. His paper, "The Scandinavians in America," was published in the *Christian Register* in three installments, beginning June 22, 1882. The first two, written in a lucid, interesting style, were largely background material for the third, which discussed Janson's activities since his arrival in Minneapolis the preceding December. Thus the first part dealt with the poverty that induced most emigrants to leave their homeland, the localities where they had mainly congregated, and their efforts to improve their standard of living. The Scandinavians in America had two enemies, Janson declared, the bottle and the priest. Often the hardships of their life in Norway (those of fishermen, for example) had led them to alcohol. In America the practice of standing treat in saloons encouraged drunkenness. The priests gave their people no outside interests but held the fear of hell over them. They were not cruel men, but they felt they must put aside human considerations when acting in an official capacity. The immigrants came to this country with great reverence for the Bible and a deep respect for the clergyman's learning. "It will be years before the yoke is broken," Janson prophesied. "The opposition already has its martyrs and I my predecessors." In other words, it was dangerous to contend with the Norwegian Synod.

The second installment of the paper dealt with the division of the Norwegian Lutherans into five synods, the church strife, and the restrictions imposed on parishioners by the Norwegian Synod—matters Janson had discussed in *Unity* in December, 1881. Underlying the third part, Janson's activities, lies a philosophy which today is often spoken of as the Protestant ethic: the assumption that hard work and a careful husbandry of one's resources inevitably bring success. In colorful, specific detail Janson recounted his experiences, beginning with his first lecture and going on to tell how he used the proceeds to hire the largest hall in Minneapolis for his mass meeting. With wry humor he described both the old woman who brandished the catechism and the old man who belatedly realized that the devil was tempting him, and then told of those who had welcomed him and had formed the nucleus of his congregation. He mentioned the number of listeners he had preached to every Sunday, adding that he attracted more men than women. Yet he was confident that he would win the women too, for in his congregations they had the same rights as men. He spoke of his evening readings from literature, where, although no admission was charged, a collection was taken. From this and from the contributions at his Sunday services, he had covered his expenses.

He gave a poignant account of his Brown County congregation. Because the farmers were saddled with heavy mortgages and their crops had been ravaged by grasshoppers, they could pay their minister only seventy dollars a year, but friends of the church had pledged an equal amount. The parishioners had difficulty finding a suitable meeting place. When they met in a small schoolhouse, the crowd overflowed and windows had to be kept open so those standing outside could hear. Sometimes they met in a grove, but that would not be pleasant in winter. They had bought an acre of ground on which they hoped to build a chapel. "But where to get the money?" They would need $1,500 to $2,000.

Janson spoke of his great attachment to this congregation; he had found many highly intelligent people among them. They knew nothing of Unitarianism, but wanted a gospel of love, comfort, and peace. Like the Minneapolis congregation, that of Brown County was known as a "free Christian church." Admitting frankly that he avoided the name "Unitarian," Janson said he did so partly because he did not like sect names, and partly out of discretion, adding, "I must be wise like the serpent." He closed with a direct appeal:

"I see a great and blessed work before me. I cannot fully enough thank the Unitarian Association for its valuable assistance, without which I had been unable to do what I have done. I feel assured the society will not withdraw its assistance until my young congregations can stand on their own feet."

3

The Work
Expands

WHEN Janson returned to Norway in the late spring of 1882 to conduct his family to their new home in America, he found them at Fana Prestegaard in Flekkefjord, the girlhood home of his wife Drude, where they were enjoying an extended farewell visit. There her father, Hans Jensen Krog, a pastor in the Lutheran state church, administered his parish, one of the finest in Norway. His residence, then some two hundred years old, was a rambling L-shaped building set in a stone-paved courtyard with a garden lying in the crook of the house. His household was ordered and gracious, with his two unmarried daughters, Kitty and Dina, in charge.

To accommodate the Jansons, the Krogs had rented a peasant's house (*bondegaards hus*) not directly located on the grounds of the parsonage but half an hour's walk away. In addition to her own brood of six, ranging in age from thirteen to three, Drude had also brought Anne, the maid who had agreed to go with them to America. Early in the morning, the Jansons managed their own breakfast of rye porridge, but at eight o'clock coffee and open-faced sandwiches were served at the pastor's residence, where the visitors had all their other meals.[1]

To the end of his days, Janson was to speak of the pastor with affection. Hans Jensen Krog was a kindly man who, before he was through, was to have his full share of heartaches over the troubles of his children. While it is unlikely that he looked upon his son-in-law's Unitarian ministry with favor, he and indeed all the Krogs had more or less given up trying to advise Kristofer and Drude.

77

Some time during the summer, the children were taken to Bergen to pay their respects at Damsgaard, a stately house which had belonged to the Janson family since 1795 and which is today reckoned as Bergen's most beautiful mansion (*herskapshus*) of the rococo period. At that time it was the residence of Helmich Janson, Kristofer's younger brother. For the visit, the children had been primed on how the structure was linked with Norwegian history from the days of the Eidsvold convention in 1814. Much of this information may have been lost on the younger children, but the two older boys were deeply impressed with the old mansion, especially with the tapestried walls of the Blue Room and the second-floor portrait gallery, as Dr. Eilev Janson recalled more than seventy years later.[2]

Early in August, Kristofer and Drude made a brief visit to Aulestad, Bjørnson's home in Gausdal, where the poet celebrated the twenty-fifth anniversary of the publication of his novel, *Synnøve Solbakken*. As 110 congratulatory telegrams streamed in, Bjørnson heard himself eulogized by distinguished guests from all over Scandinavia. Janson also took part, reading a poem he had written for the occasion and presenting gifts to Bjørnson—a purse from the women of Bergen and an American flag from Professor Rasmus B. Anderson of the University of Wisconsin. Before the festivities came to a close, the poet delivered a trenchant speech, spelling out his grievances against Christianity.[3]

Because of their imminent sailing, the Jansons could not linger for any private talks with Bjørnson. By mid-August the family and Anne were on board the "Kong Sverre," a ship of the Thingvalla Line, which was also engaged in the immigrant traffic. When Janson found that the infirmary was not in use, he quartered his family there, for it was located in the section least affected by the roll of the ship.

As chance would have it, Janson was to have as traveling companions two rival Lutheran pastors from Minneapolis, Hans Gerhard Stub of the Synod and Sven Oftedal of the Conference. For the duration of the crossing, Stub found that he could have nominally pleasant relations with Janson, and the two of them took part in the ship's programs. Oftedal held himself aloof. In his autobiography, Janson was to say he thought Oftedal's conduct was prompted more by hatred of his fellow Lutheran than by dislike of the heretical Janson. On this point his memory must have failed him, for we have ample evidence that, whatever feelings Oftedal might have had about Stub, he certainly had no tolerance for Kristofer Janson.

During the crossing, Janson wrote to Bjørnson. He had not liked

Bjørnson's speech at the *Synnøve Solbakken* anniversary, and he warned
his friend that he would antagonize many if he continued in that vein.
Bjørnson, Janson wrote, made the same mistake as the American Robert
Ingersoll by blaming Christianity for what was really the fault of the
dogmatists. Having said that, he dwelt on his gratitude for the poet's
friendship and his own hopes for the future. At long last, he had found
his true vocation, adding—as if to imply things could hardly be more
promising—that his relationship with Drude had never been better.[4]

2

The Jansons' marriage was hardly a conventional one for the time.
From the first, they had determined it was to be a partnership, regardless of what St. Paul had said about the husband being the head of the
household. Both were earnest advocates of the emancipation of women.
They had agreed to be completely honest with one another, scorning
all hypocrisy and intrigue.

Drude Janson was a talented and indeed a charming and spirited
young woman. Even as a girl, she had been so greatly admired—as
legend has it—that all Flekkefjord had turned out for her confirmation. Some months before her twenty-second birthday, she had married
Janson and a year later had enthusiastically gone with him to be
part of the folk-school community which Christopher Bruun had
organized. It had been a good testing ground for youthful idealism,
for the teachers lived in cottages with thatched roofs and shared the
humble fare of peasants, strong on fish and potatoes. (In later years,
members of the Janson family liked to recall a comment of the young
couple's firstborn, Ivar: "This has been a good week," the child said
solemnly. "We have had meat twice.") Drude had fitted into that
community very well, having been unusually successful in winning the
confidence of the young adult students. In the summer, when the
school was not in session and Janson was on lecture tours, she had
occupied herself with translating into Danish the stories her husband
had originally written in the peasant vernacular (*landsmaal*). As a
result, they became so popular throughout Scandinavia that some were
translated into German and even into Italian. She could also sew expertly and was a gifted pianist.[5]

Much as Janson theoretically upheld a wife's right to have opinions
and beliefs different from his, he was sometimes wounded by Drude's
independence. After the folk school was moved to Gausdal, Janson
was deeply troubled when she—like the rest of the community—was

completely captivated by the eloquence of Christopher Bruun, whom Janson found too rigidly puritanical. It was at a time when Janson felt that his contribution to the school was being completely overlooked, a situation doubly galling when he was not getting the support he craved from his wife. And Drude did not have the religious commitment of her husband; long before Janson had given up his orthodox faith, she had abandoned hers, and, although she was ready to explore every new movement that came to her attention, her approach seems to have been intellectual rather than emotional as was the case with him.[6]

At Gausdal they had built a house on a hill overlooking Bjørnson's, calling it "Solbakken" in honor of the famous novel. They spent many hours with the dramatist and poet who, in the course of time, was to use both of them as models for characters in his plays. In Janson, Bjørnson was to say, he had found the "noblest Christian he had ever known." He considered Drude alert and inventive, attractively feminine with an appetite for whatever seemed new and interesting. Bjørnson often teased her by predicting she would one day run off with a "Spanish skipper."[7]

At the time Drude arrived in America, she was about a month short of being thirty-six, a brown-haired, tall, slender woman with quick movements and an erect bearing. In New York Janson put up his family in a hotel where they quickly discovered that the ship's infirmary had not been such a good place after all, for they had picked up lice. After that unhappy situation had been corrected, Kristofer and Drude set out for the Winter Garden to attend a concert. On the way, a pickpocket relieved Janson of his wallet. Luckily the tickets to Minneapolis had been paid for, and Drude had enough money to settle the hotel bill and to keep them fed until they reached their destination.

3

Arriving in Minneapolis on Thursday, September 14, 1882, the family moved into a flat on Franklin and Thirteenth, an area heavily populated with Scandinavian immigrants. Church work began immediately. The evening after their arrival, Drude was introduced to the congregation at a meeting held in the home of N. T. Sjøberg, a few doors away on Franklin Avenue. Two weeks later a gala reception for the Janson family was given at Harrison Hall to which all those who had contributed to the church fund were invited.[8] The following Sunday, October 1, Janson began regular services for the season in Harrison Hall, delivering a sermon with the evocative title "Under

What Banner Shall We Christians Assemble?" It was one that Janson was to repeat in many places throughout the Middle West, and it was finally included in his compilation of sermons, *Light and Freedom,* published in 1892. Far from the gloom and doom preached in orthodox churches, it pictured religion as dynamic, always developing and changing.

All Christians, including every sect, Janson said, make up a mighty army, flying aloft the banner of Jesus Christ and fighting for the triumph of the good and beautiful over all that is base and ugly. True enough, Janson conceded, the orthodox did not look at it that way: they wanted to exclude liberals or at least force them to remain in the background. But Janson, for one, was not willing to submit to such treatment. He wanted to be in the forefront where every bend in the road might expose some new danger. He implied that this was a national characteristic: "There is something in the Norseman's nature that loves danger and welcomes a challenge!"

Being in the vanguard was not easy, for one must prove his worth by *living* a Christlike life, as it was taught in the three synoptic gospels. (The fourth, that of John, differs so radically from the others that it can not be regarded as historically reliable.) In Matthew, Mark, and Luke, one finds the great principle of Jesus. It may be summarized in a single sentence: God is our Father. In Jesus' day this was new and startling, for the Jews had looked upon God as a stern taskmaster who had selected their race as His chosen people. Jesus had taught that He loved all men and was an eternal spirit present everywhere—on land and sea, in the hall where Janson was speaking, in the brain of each one of his auditors.

Jesus had said, "Be ye perfect even as your Father which is in heaven is perfect." It was nothing more or less than that: man should strive to be like God. Jesus himself had supplied the model by His blameless life. It was in that sense—as the pathfinder, not as a sacrificial lamb—that He was the Saviour. Every human being must work out his own salvation, as St. Paul has said, by giving himself up to God and being filled with His spirit.

Janson was sure, he told his audience, that many who heard him might not agree with him at the moment, but they would later. By that time, however, he himself might in one respect or another have changed, for religion must not be static. This was the reason the Unitarian Church did not bind its members with a restrictive creed but stated its purpose in a single sentence: "In the love of truth and the spirit of Jesus Christ we unite to worship God and serve man."

81

Janson concluded it would be his purpose to bring Christianity back to its original simplicity by following the teachings of its great leader.[9]

4

As a Unitarian, Janson was already demonstrating that he belonged to the conservative branch of the Western Conference. The definition of Unitarianism he had given was one coined by the Reverend C. G. Ames, which some of his colleagues found too limited. It excluded a small but growing number of clergymen who had become humanists. The liberals favored a phrase of Jenkin Lloyd Jones: "Freedom, fellowship, character, and intelligence in religion." The matter had been debated for some time and was to bring about a division in the Western Conference by 1886. Neither side, however, even remotely approached the vehemence displayed by the Norwegian synods in their disputes. Actually the difference was juridical rather than theological. The conservatives—those supporting the Ames statement—were fully in accord with the liberals that each clergyman must have the freedom to preach the truth as he saw it. The conservatives felt that the Jones slogan made the Unitarian Church indistinguishable from the Free Religious Association or Felix Adler's Ethical Culture Society, while the Ames definition emphasized its historic moorings in Christianity. Ironically, neither of the two leaders among the liberals, Jenkin Lloyd Jones and William Channing Gannett, was personally a humanist; rather, each was a Christian theist.[10]

A conservative Western Conference Unitarian, yes, but otherwise Janson in his sermon reveals that he fitted very well into liberal American Protestantism. One sees that he accepted the immanence of God, a doctrine which came to be widely proclaimed in the 1880's. It was an interpretation which the distinguished Washington Gladden was later to declare broke down the old distinction between the sacred and the profane; if God is inherent in all of His universe, He is on the street, in the factory, and in the chamber of commerce as well as in the church. It was a doctrine that led to an organic theory of society and to the acceptance of the human race as constituting a brotherhood. Then, as Janson said, increasingly in the late nineteenth century, liberal Protestant ministers were interpreting Jesus and salvation in ethical terms. The individual is revitalized by following the teachings of Christ, and as a consequence he brings about a regenerated society or the presence of the kingdom of heaven on earth. Janson's disavowal of the harsh God of the Old Testament in favor of the all-loving

Father finds a parallel in a later statement by President Charles William Eliot of Harvard to the effect that the earlier concept of God as an angry, vengeful deity had given way to one which looked upon Him as "one of supreme power and love, filling the universe, working through all human institutions, and through all men."[11]

Conducting the "Scandinavian mission"—as it was usually called in Unitarian periodicals—meant more than having a sermon ready every Sunday. On Monday evenings, Janson gave his literary readings. A ladies' aid (*kvindeforening*) had been organized, in which Drude must stand ready to help. Every day she spent four hours working with Janson as his secretary, and she also kept all the accounts. On Friday evenings, she and Janson entertained at musicales in their apartment at first for members of the congregation, but, as their acquaintances grew, also for others—among them Americans. Janson had organized a religious school for children which met on Saturday morning rather than on Sunday. In addition to teaching the primary class, Drude taught sewing to the girls.[12]

5

The older Janson boys had been placed in the public school, a new experience for them, for in Norway they had shared a tutor with the Bjørnson children. Knowing no English, they were put into an elementary grade with very small children. That was humiliating enough, but their presence there (they were thirteen and twelve) attracted the attention of older pupils. When school was out, they delighted in chanting after the Janson boys:

> Swedish, Swedish,
> Stock and straw!
> Can't say nothing
> But ya, ya, ya!

Dr. Eilev Janson could still repeat the doggerel when he was eighty-eight years old, but he chuckled over it for the persecution had been short-lived and growing up in Minneapolis had been very pleasant. But, when some of these early experiences had been reported at home, Janson was concerned, and later in a sermon, "Our Boys" (Vore gutter), he spoke of it.[13]

During the fall, Kristofer and Drude visited the Nora Congregation in Brown County. From the first, Drude was delighted with the prairie. She never seems to have more than tolerated Minneapolis, and as the years went by her distaste for the city grew. But Brown County was always a refuge to her. On her first visit to the original Hage farmhouse in the fall of 1882—as the late Emil Hage recalled—she found the prairie awe-inspiring with its stretches of flat land and great expanse of sky. While she was there, an electric storm came up which drew her to the screen door, where she stood watching the lightning cut into the vast expanse of sky, marveling at the magnificence of the scene.

The church situation in Brown County was, of course, fundamentally different from that of Janson's congregation in Minneapolis. He had organized the city church himself and had to keep priming it with readings, concerts, clubs, and the like to bolster membership, but the Nora congregation, in existence before Janson came, had "called" him and had been fortunate to have him accept. By the fall of 1882, the people at Lake Hanska had bought land for a burial ground and church, the latter to include living quarters for the minister and his family, and they expected to have the building ready by the following summer. The dispatch with which this recently transformed Unitarian congregation managed its affairs rankled with some of the neighbors. Just at the time the Jansons arrived in Minnesota, H. Ahlnes had published an article in *Nordvesten*, a paper printed in St. Paul. The writer said that Janson would consider any offer of payment a personal affront, thereby implying that any congregation could get ahead if it could avoid such an expense. Quite naturally the people of Nora congregation were nettled, and in the October 3 issue of *Budstikken*, Johannes Mo set the record straight. "As president of the congregation," he wrote, "it is my duty to Pastor Janson and the reading public to correct falsehoods." Nora would meet the same obligations as any other church. Janson was paid $150 a year; this total meant that each family would contribute $7.50, actually more than families gave who belonged to the Lake Linden and Lake Hanska Lutheran churches. Furthermore, neither he nor the other members of the congregation could see how paying a minister for his work could in any way be interpreted as an affront.[14]

It is a fair guess that, at the time Mo's denial appeared, Janson was already at work on an article dealing with American life for *Nyt Tidsskrift,* a prestigious journal of opinion published in Kristiania. In it he described American politics, religious life, and societies for the improvement of this and that, as well as giving a candid picture of what the city of Minneapolis was like in 1882. It is probably as graphic as any account of the period now in existence. Yet, even though Janson could spell out the crudities of new-world life in great detail, he regarded them as passing features bound to disappear as people became better educated. To Drude they were galling, not correctable during her lifetime—and more and more she came to resent having to spend her youth in Minneapolis.

In the lectures Janson had given after his tour of 1879–80, he had praised religious tolerance in America. Now he was forced to admit that even in the United States such religious tolerance was still in its infancy. Better than Europe, yes, but still inflexible. The Young Men's Christian Association was organized to be interdenominational, but it was open only to orthodox Trinitarians and excluded Unitarians and members of other liberal sects. American Protestantism was narrowly pietistic, so fanatical in its insistence on a puritanical observance of Sunday that clergymen had been known to expel milkmen from church membership for delivering milk on the Sabbath. All candidates for public office, if they were to have any chance of winning, must represent themselves as "blue noses," eternally vigilant lest Sunday be desecrated. Janson was to cite many instances of such absurd zeal, one of them concerning Dr. A. A. Ames, the mayor of Minneapolis, who was later to come up for his full share of notoriety in Lincoln Steffens' *The Shame of the Cities*. Ames, according to Janson, was a convivial man and well known for the laxness of his administration, but he was ambitious to go to Congress. He had therefore threatened the editor of the *Minneapolis Tribune* with arrest for permitting his staff to work on the Sunday edition after midnight on Saturday. Ames withdrew his charge only when the newspaper publishers openly defied him, promising their own disclosures.

Any critic of orthodoxy in America was publicly vilified. At this time, Robert Ingersoll was the most prominent one. He gave lectures across the country, always drawing huge crowds who cheered and applauded him. Yet the next day, according to Janson, the same people who had laughed at the speaker's sallies at the expense of orthodox Christianity would shake their heads, denouncing Ingersoll as morally depraved. Janson had attended a lecture at the University of Minnesota, where another well-known orator was supposed to have spoken on Voltaire. Instead, he spent most of his time denouncing Ingersoll, and, when he did get to Voltaire, discussed him wholly apart from the milieu in which he had lived.

85

The Unitarians were the only ones who did not have this facade of piety. Shortly after the Jansons had arrived in Minnesota, Kristofer and Drude had been guests of honor at a reception given by Unity Church in St. Paul. Then ten years old, the congregation had just moved into its new building which Janson reported had a German medieval style, agreeably adorned with porticos and projecting windows. Within, besides the main auditorium, it had a lower lecture hall and several carpeted and attractively furnished rooms to be used by the many organizations of the church. The building also had a kitchen and rest rooms and thus had the warmth of a home. It was in use every day of the week, Janson reported, adding that it certainly contrasted with the churches in Norway, which stood empty six days of the week and held a bored audience on the seventh.

Janson went on to say that the First Unitarian Society in Minneapolis had not progressed so far as the St. Paul church, being much newer, but it had already organized a Biographic Club and a Unity Club. The first, meeting every Tuesday in private homes, studied the lives of famous persons. Each member in turn had to prepare a talk intended to lead to a general discussion. After Janson joined, the club had dealt with Victor Hugo, Garibaldi, Napoleon III, and Bjørnstjerne Bjørnson, the last-named being Janson's contribution. Often members asked naive questions, revealing deplorable ignorance—all of which Janson thought showed the need for just such an organization. Unity Club met directly after services on Sunday morning—the only time when the men were free—and dealt with such political and esthetic topics as the separation of church and state and the new French school of naturalism.

He also discussed the campaign for the general election which had just been completed. As he was writing his article, bands stomped down the streets by day and torchlight parades marched by night. Banners that screamed "Vote for Ames" or "Vote for Washburn" decorated horses, buggies, and sometimes even people. Political meetings were held nightly, and newspapers vied with one another in sanctifying the candidates they were endorsing and vilifying the opposition. At the time, the most heated contest had been between the Norwegian immigrant, Knute Nelson, and a wealthy American, Albert Kindred, for a seat in the House of Representatives. The latter was said to have spent $150,000 on the campaign and was charged with buying up newspapers, bribing voters, and the like. Janson was pleased that Nelson won, remarking that at long last the Norwegians in America had found something they could agree on.

Yet even when a political campaign was not going on, American life moved at a hectic pace. Unlike Norway, according to Janson, people did not wait for officials to initiate reforms but took it upon themselves to champion all causes; moreover, the women were as active as the men. One could not blame them, for, when one realized what criminal, ignorant, and impoverished elements had made their way to America and had been granted equal rights with the native-born, he realized what an effort it was going to take to create a stable citizenry out of this raw mass. On the other hand, the constant, nervous activity robbed American home life of the tranquillity it should have. The restlessness was actually contagious; Janson himself had the feeling there was so much to be done that he felt guilty if he so much as sat down a few minutes to read a newspaper. It characterized even the children. He said he had never known youngsters who screamed and fought as those in America did, adding that docile immigrant children were not in this country very long before they behaved in the same way.

Drunkenness was widespread, the writer went on, and the temperance zeal of reforming Americans was fanatically pietistic. They regarded alcohol as an evil in itself, denouncing even the moderate use of it as sinful. They formed societies pledging themselves to total abstinence and sought to get laws passed prohibiting the sale of alcoholic beverages within the state. All of this Janson abhorred, saying he could see no reason why liquor should be withheld from those who might like an occasional glass of wine or a dram of whisky. People must be taught that it was a matter of individual responsibility. Prohibition would only encourage illegal traffic. He felt that the problem could best be dealt with by placing the sale of liquor under state control and introducing in the schools an educational program on alcohol.[15]

7

As the year advanced, Janson shifted his services from Harrison Hall to Peterson's Hall at Washington and Thirteenth avenues south. There, two days after Christmas, his religious school gave a program before an audience that taxed the capacity of the hall. During the holidays, the Jansons were deluged with cards from well-wishers in the East. A women's organization in Providence, Rhode Island, sent substantial gifts: 250 books for the church library in Minneapolis and $250 for the building fund of the Brown County congregation. *Unity* remarked how reassuring Janson's quarterly report had been and how worthy of support the Scandinavian mission was: "There are Unitarians in this country whose lives would be happier if out of their well-filled purses, they would send forth to this brave voice in the Scandinavian wilderness of the Northwest money enough to build in Minneapolis the substantial chapel that is needed there.... We shall be glad to lend a hand to the one or many."[16]

The church in Minneapolis had bought a small organ, and the women in the congregation had undertaken to pay for it by giving a series of suppers during the winter and into the spring. People paid an entrance fee and were both fed and entertained with a program, the latter always including an anecdote or reading by Janson. For his Monday night readings, Janson had chosen accounts of the heroes from the Icelandic sagas—Olav Trygvasson, Kjartan Olafsson, Stein Skifleson, Erling Skjalgson, and finally St. Olaf. Virtually every issue of *Budstikken* contained a poem or sermon by Janson. Gudmund Johnson, the publisher of the paper, was a trustee of the church. After a sermon had appeared in the paper, he allowed the minister to use the type forms, and Janson was thus able to put out the sermon in a pamphlet, getting 5,000 copies at a cost of no more than $30 or $40.[17]

He did not receive such good treatment everywhere. In mid-January, 1883, he was scheduled to give a lecture at Norden Hall in La Crosse, Wisconsin. On arriving in the community he set about to have handbills printed. Of the two Norwegian papers in town, *Norden* had always turned down his business, but *Fædrelandet og Emigranten,* though editorially critical, had never refused to do job printing for him. But when the editor saw that the subject was to be "Is the Bible the Inspired Word of God?", he would have nothing to do with the handbills. Janson went to a German printshop which had the same type as the Norwegians used. He had a good audience for his lecture, and the incident supplied him with good copy for an article in *Unity* on what he sometimes met with in the "Scandinavian wilderness." *Budstikken* was also to capitalize on it: "Not only did *Fædrelandet og Emigranten* refuse to allow its sacred columns to be besmirched with a review of the lecture but, with a fatherly concern for the spiritual welfare of its presses, refused to print the handbills. Because the only other Norwegian paper in town had turned Janson down before, he had to go to a German shop where, with a boldness truly amazing, they printed the bills."[18]

8

Although the La Crosse incident does not seem to have disturbed the Jansons unduly, Drude found her first winter in America difficult. Yet now and then a printed sermon would find its way to a Norwegian living some distance away, who would write to ask where he or she might get other copies. One such letter came from a widow in Texas who had written that she had been a Unitarian for a long time without realizing it. This message seems to have impressed both Kristofer and Drude and kindled the idea that Janson should put out a periodical of his own. Apparently he wrote to Rasmus B. Anderson asking for his support in presenting the matter to Jenkin Lloyd Jones of the Western Conference. When the professor responded coolly, Drude took things in hand and—without Kristofer's knowledge—wrote to Anderson.

His letter had been a great disappointment, Drude began. "If you had been here and talked with Kristofer, if you could have seen how hard he works, how old, drawn, and nervous he has become this winter, you certainly would have realized that if he is to have any success, he must have all the help and encouragement you can give him." The mission to which Anderson had called Janson was not an easy one, Drude continued; she had enough knowledge of the world to know there was not another man living who would take such an obligation upon himself and give himself to it so wholeheartedly. She added: "There is not another man with his talents who has such a childlike, naive faith in people and such an unbelievably strong faith in the triumph of the truth. You perhaps think it strange that I, who am so close to him, should praise him so highly. I do so because I am the one who knows him best, and because I—as he himself acknowledges—am his severest critic. His weakest trait—and the one which may ruin him in spite of all his other wonderful qualities—is that he can tolerate so little coldness and misunderstanding. Therefore he suffers more than others would when he meets it where he expected affection and trust. I am sometimes afraid he will never regain his old sunniness and confidence, though there is still some youth in him." Support him in the way he wants to work, Drude urged, even if it should not be exactly the way Anderson might go about it. He gets letters all the time from people who want more reading material, and it grieves him when he cannot satisfy them. Telling them to subscribe to *Budstikken* or *Skandinaven* on the chance that they might find articles by Janson would be impractical, she said, and besides a paper of his own was needed for his parishioners in

Minneapolis. "Every Sunday he has audiences ranging from 400 to 500 who would be better off if they could do a little studying on their own."

Drude did not mince matters. If the Unitarians were going to conduct a mission, she wrote, they must realize it was going to cost something. Apparently Anderson had suggested that Janson get an assistant; Drude wondered how he would be paid. Janson's salary had not increased since he began, and the income from his churches during the past year had been $400 at the most. She also felt that the American Unitarian Association would be likely to favor the idea of Janson's putting out a periodical. In fact, the secretary of the American Unitarian Association, the Reverend Grindall Reynolds, had repeatedly urged Kristofer to make known his needs. Janson was not an ordinary man, Drude insisted. He could much more easily make a living by lecturing than by being a minister, but he loved his people and wanted to free them from the tyranny of the orthodox ministers. Every Sunday he delivered excellent sermons, attacking one fanatical belief or prejudice after the other. She brought her letter adroitly to a close by speaking of the confidence she had in Anderson: "I hope you won't be angry with me because of this, and I am sure you will not, if you are the man I believe you to be. . . . About the lecture you spoke of, Kristofer will write later. He has been so busy he has not had time to think about it. . . . We have so much wanted to see you and talk with you."[19]

Anderson does not seem to have been offended. Three weeks later, in reporting Janson's progress to Bjørnson, he was to quote Drude's figures on the Sunday audiences, saying it was a good thing Janson had been brought to America. Interest in him seemed to be growing among Americans, too, for the *Christian Register* in Boston had carried an article about him, the editor remarking that no more profitable mission was to be found than that of the poet-preacher from Norway. Actually, Janson did not get around to prepare the prospectus for his proposed paper or periodical until April. By that time, it was clear that Drude's letter to Anderson had not harmed her husband's chances and may indeed have helped them. In sending what he had proposed, Janson almost jauntily suggested that the professor talk it over with John A. Johnson of Madison and then send the material to Jenkin Lloyd Jones in Chicago with their approval or disapproval. The request was granted, and Janson would have put out the first copy of *Saamanden* the following September had not a tornado in July upset the normal progression of the Scandinavian mission.

The winter of 1883 was anything but a happy period for Drude. She found it hard to adjust to the climate. Dissension broke out in the congregation, and, while news of it never reached the papers, it brought both Kristofer and Drude many an uneasy moment. In his autobiography, years later, Janson was to say that many who would follow him when he was attacking orthodoxy became indifferent when he turned to the constructive work of his mission. On April 18—after the crisis was over—Janson was to deliver a sermon entitled "True and False Liberals" (Sande og falske liberale), a title he had borrowed from a sermon by the Reverend J. T. Sunderland, which had appeared in the *Christian Register*.[20] The most poignant expression of what Drude had gone through came when she poured out her heart to Bjørnson in a letter dated April 9, 1883: "We have gone through a winter none of us would willingly relive: *pettiness, crudity,* and *slander*, such as we have never known in our lives. There were times when I worried that Kristofer's happy nature would leave him forever, and then for the first time I realized he was the sunshine of our home—and I felt I could weep blood. . . . Now things are going well, and I believe Kristofer has come out of it, as he is a bit wiser about the world and people. And it was all necessary: now both sides understand each other, and there is more seriousness on the whole. The dissatisfied have gone out (eight persons) and those who remain will follow him and not want only enjoyment, which they certainly should have known all along if they had only thought. When things had developed to that point, we were on top of them, but up to that time it was awful."

Kristofer was giving excellent sermons, carefully developed and rich in content, Drude said, and as a result more and more people were coming to join him. All this compensated her for her past grief and when she felt well, she was happy. The experience of the last winter had made her nervous, and at times she had been irritable. But she felt she had become a much better wife, assuring Bjørnson he need not fear she would run off with a Spanish sailor, adding: "However, if my husband were not the man he is, I should have taken off a thousand times." Janson was soon to publish a hymnbook, she reported. Although she was not in agreement on all the selections, she thought it was a good piece of work on the whole. In the fall, his paper would come out, and she was going to help with it. "I am happy we can work together as much as we can and be united in spite of our differing points of view on certain matters, and I rejoice with all my heart in his work." They had a small group of friends in Minneapolis whom they enjoyed and saw frequently: the Bendekes, Luth Jaeger and his fiancée, Andreas Ueland, and Dr. Schumann.[21]

9

Drude seems to have had reason to be worried about Janson, for he was showing a cantankerousness that was unlike him. It was perhaps not strange when he snapped at T. Paulson in the columns of *Budstikken,* in replying for the umpteenth time to the charge that he was not a Christian. "I will work for God's kingdom on this earth," he wrote, "to get people to be true Christians, to love God and their neighbors, and to follow Jesus as their leader." That was more profitable than memorizing a catechism, he said, going on to suggest that Paulson would do well to turn a critical eye on his own Christianity. "I don't think you serve either God or your neighbor by spreading falsehoods against me and another sect. One day the Norwegian people will have their eyes opened and see how their ministers have misled them, and revenge will come of itself."[22]

However, when Janson lashed out at Jenkin Lloyd Jones, one might suspect that his nerves were frayed. The time was approaching for the annual convention of the Western Conference which was to be held in Chicago. As he had the year before, Jones had requested that Janson take part in the program and apparently had asked for a detailed report on all of the minister's activities. He even suggested that Janson organize a Unity club in his church. In reply Janson fumed: "Do you think I remember how many lectures I have delivered and on what subjects? Shall I dig up among all my papers to find out every little bit of speech I have made, and waste my precious time with that useless work? No Sir. Unity Club! Do you think my house-mover and my tailor and my carpenter or men coming home late, worn out and hungry, are fit for studing [*sic*] Longfellow and Bryant? As you know I have tried to educate them by delivering lectures on the Scandinavian history and litterature [*sic*] every Monday night, and invited them to come to my house every Friday evening, and spread heretic seeds among them every Sunday. You must not ask my congregation for studies and clubs. They are hand-workers not spirit-workers."

In response to the secretary's question concerning whether he had had any particular needs, Janson wrote: "Well, we have just bought a lot $2,000 and wish to pay it as soon as possible—that is our special need for the present moment." The outburst seems to have done Janson good, for he could then be more conciliatory. He would deliver a fifteen-minute report on the Scandinavian mission and then give another ten-minute address. He would be pleased to attend the Channing Club social, and while he was in Chicago he intended to deliver a lecture to the Scandinavians in the city. But Jones was not to trouble him any further with demands for "red scraps of paper." After his signature, Janson affixed a doggerel:

> "When we meet from papers free,
> how jolly dogs we'll be."[23]

Drude was to accompany her husband to Chicago. After the convention, he was sending her on to Madison, while he remained in Chicago to lecture. When he joined her in Madison, he would fulfill a promise he had made to give a lecture in English for the benefit of a building fund for the Unitarian Church there. All this he outlined in a letter to Professor Anderson, saying that the advertisement should be headed " 'Between the Battles,' a drama in one act by Bjørnstjerne Bjørnson with an introduction by Kristofer Janson." Along with this, he enclosed statements to John A. Johnson, Aubertine Woodward, and others who had pledged yearly support for the Scandinavian mission, adding apologetically that it looked as if he would have to count on their help for some time to come.[24]

Things seem to have gone smoothly in Chicago. According to the minutes of the Conference meetings, Janson had given an interesting talk about his work, good humoredly telling about some of his difficulties, and then speaking of his satisfaction with the hymnbook he had compiled and the great hopes he had for the paper he would publish in the fall. By request, he had sung a Norwegian hymn of his own composition. On May 15, as the meetings drew to a close, Miss Woodward sent off an account to Professor Anderson: "Kristofer and his dear wife are delightful, and it would do you good to see the enthusiasm they create. Dozens of people asked me after Kristofer's missionary report and little song if I was not proud of my countryman, and Mrs. Janson says it helps her to feel at home to know people take me for her countryman. She says she would not go back to Norway. She is proud of the success of her husband in his work, proud of the confidence the society places in him, and like myself she is moved by the bond of fellowship, in which thought is free, that unites the members of the Unitarian association in their efforts to uplift humanity. She says no one can know what this conference has been to her, and I share the same thought. Several people, men and women from the East, have been with us, among them good Mr. Reynolds, our Eastern Secretary, who fully appreciates Mr. Janson. 'His enthusiasm does me good,' Mr. Reynolds said to me in a long talk I had with him. . . . Tomorrow I go with Mr. and Mrs. Janson to a 17th of May celebration at Aurora Hall. Kristofer speaks. It will be charming. . . . On Friday Mrs. Janson and I start for Madison."[25]

10

At the time, Janson was involved in newspaper controversies in both *Skandinaven* and the *Albert Lea* (Minnesota) *Posten*. The latter argument was with Th. Ylvisaker, a Norwegian Synod pastor. It was unusual—at the beginning—in that the clergyman was not at all vituperative. Early in April, Janson had given his lecture "Jesus and the Jews" in Albert Lea, and Ylivsaker had been in the audience. Although he had been somewhat surprised to find out that Lutherans had been among those who had invited Janson to Albert Lea, he said there was much to enjoy in the lecture—poetic diction and fine delivery, which allowed one to hear every word distinctly. Furthermore, in picturing Jesus as a Jew among Jews, Janson had portrayed a very noble character, but a limited one (as might be expected from a Unitarian) and certainly not one to satisfy Christians who wanted the whole Christ or none at all.

In his reply, written shortly before he had gone to Chicago, Janson thanked the minister for the courteous tone of his article, saying it was logical that he and a Lutheran should differ theologically. He did think it strange that the pastor should find a historical interpretation of Jesus and his times as "an argument against Christianity." He asked "How long are you ministers going to tell your congregations (They are ignorant enough already!) that Unitarians are not Christians? Stop such accusations. They are not worthy of you." If he had dwelt on the historical Jesus, Janson went on, that is what he found in the New Testament; although he knew texts were often cited concerning Jesus' godliness, these were either open falsifications of the Greek original or poor translations. And why, Janson wondered, should Ylvisaker be disturbed that Lutherans had been among those who had invited him to Albert Lea. As far as he was concerned, he would gladly hear a Catholic priest, the evangelist Dwight L. Moody, or Henry Ward Beecher. It was absurd to isolate Lutherans from all outside influence.

On his return from Chicago, Janson was to find that Ylvisaker had answered him in *Albert Lea Posten*. From then on, the exchanges continued, growing increasingly bitter, until the middle of June, when the editor refused to accept any more contributions. The Lutheran pastor was to characterize himself as a "watchman on the walls of Zion" who must warn parishioners against a Moody or a Catholic because they distorted Scripture. Such a watchman must—in the case of a man like Janson—"extract the Unitarian horns." Janson later accused the pastor of citing an apocryphal Bible passage, arguing that Luther himself had condemned it as such, and taunted Ylvisaker that God had not appointed him as His grand inquisitor. Yet there was one time when Janson felt the Lutheran pastor's thrust—a charge that stung him later when it was repeated by others. In the wrangling on who was or was not a Christian, the pastor had said Janson's followers did not belong to Christendom but to Kristoferdom. As he always responded when he felt a direct attack, Janson retorted that he was shocked to find he had not been dealing with a gentleman.[26]

During this time, *Folkebladet* in Minneapolis was no longer badgering him. The owners of the paper, Professors Oftedal and Sverdrup, had for some time been severely criticized by their colleague Professor Gunnersen and by ministers within the Conference, all of whom felt that the welfare of Augsburg Seminary was being jeopardized because of the time the two were devoting to the paper. In an effort toward reconciliation, the two men had withdrawn from the staff of *Folkebladet* and hired an outsider, Johannes J. Skørdalsvold, as editor. Although he did not join Janson's church until some eight years later, he was friendly toward the Unitarian minister, and the columns of the paper began to reflect the editor's attitude. This favorable relationship lasted for only a short period. In the summer of 1883, the Conference was to vindicate Oftedal and Sverdrup and to let Gunnersen leave, all of which seemed to signal a go-ahead to Oftedal, for in January, 1884, he again took over the editing of the paper. Janson's time of grace was over, but in late June, 1883, with Skørdalsvold at the helm, *Folkebladet* had reported that Janson's congregation would close its season with a picnic at Lake Harriet on July 1. Instructions were given about where one could buy trolley line tickets to get to the picnic grounds, what refreshments would be on sale there, and the nature of the program which would include a talk by Janson entitled "What a Leaf in the Forest Teaches Us."[27]

11

On July 4 Janson gave an address in Northwood, Iowa, where he told his audience that American independence was largely the work of such religious liberals as Benjamin Franklin, Thomas Jefferson, and Thomas Paine. Back in Minneapolis, the family were getting ready to leave the Franklin Avenue apartment for good. Their departure for Brown County had been somewhat delayed until their living quarters were completed to the point that they could move in. In September, when they returned to the city, they would occupy a fine new house that was being built at 2419 Nicollet Avenue, a site then somewhat on the outskirts of the city but conveniently reached by the motor line that ran out to Lake Harriet. It was a location chosen by Drude, far enough away from the Scandinavian district of the city to give her a sense of refuge. Distraught now with problems of building and moving, she wrote to Mrs. Rasmus B. Anderson to ask for some clarification on contributions received from Madison. "I am not almost sick; I am sick," she wrote unhappily, adding that she would have to put up with it all in the hope that one day things would settle down.[28]

Early in July, 1883, Professor Anderson wrote Bjørnson that Janson was becoming more firmly established every day and was drawing larger audiences than any other Norwegian minister in America.[29] Certainly he was getting good attendance at his services in Minneapolis, and, when the family arrived in Brown County in time to hold services on July 8, Janson must have felt a surge of pride in what he had accomplished, for there was the newly constructed church awaiting him. It had been designed in the shape of a cross, the two arms providing living quarters for the Janson family. These rooms were ready for occupancy, and, although the main sanctuary still had no windows or pews, it could be used on Sundays by making benches out of planks of lumber supported on stacks of shingles. This was the arrangement for July 8 and 15; by July 22 the carpenters expected to have the pews in place and the windows installed. On Saturday, July 21, the building was leveled by a tornado. Miraculously, the Janson family and the carpenters, who were in the building at the time—sixteen people in all—escaped unhurt.

For about a week before, the weather had been unsettled, with electrical storms building up, usually at night. When the sky again clouded on this Saturday morning at ten o'clock, the family felt relieved, believing that the outburst would at least come by day and not disturb their sleep. Eilev Janson, then thirteen, was in the arm of the building containing the kitchen, where he had been set to work washing dishes. As it grew darker, lightning flashed and a strong wind arose. Frightened, the boy left his work, and, walking through the church where the carpenters were hastily boarding up windows, he joined the other members of the family in the living room located in the other arm of the building. By that time it had grown so dark that a lamp had been lighted. The carpenters left their work and joined the family. Suddenly the wind died down and an unnatural stillness followed. Going out on a little porch, they could see a dark green cloud on the horizon moving very fast and whirling houses and haystacks before it. All returned inside. Drude sat in a deck chair, with two little girls in her lap; the rest of the family gathered around her. The carpenters braced themselves against the wall facing the storm; as the first gust struck, it shook the living quarters, caving the wall inward. A second blast, stronger than the first, followed, and with the third, the walls and the roof detached themselves and went flying down the hill. Only the floor remained, but soon it too was lifted up, sending the sixteen people on it through the air and then dropping them onto the wreckage. Except for bruises, all were alive and uninjured, but two of the children and a carpenter had become separated from the others. A heavy hailstorm followed and then a bolt of lightning struck the church proper. It, too, came flying through the air but fortunately in a different direction from where the people were huddled. They were able to crawl to a wooded area and to thread their way to a neighboring farm. Some time afterward, the missing carpenter came with the children. Later, when the Jansons measured the distance they had been carried through the air, they found it to be approximately a hundred feet.[30]

The family lost everything except the clothes they were wearing at the moment. Although no one else in the neighborhood had quite so terrifying an experience, many had buildings destroyed and fields ravaged. The Jansons rented a three-room cottage in nearby Madelia, where they remained for the rest of the summer. Four days after the storm, Janson sent off an account of their misfortune to both *Unity* and the *Christian Register*. By that time, he could report that the carpenters had cleared away the rubble from the site of the church and had found that they could salvage about a third of the building material. Sitting amid the ruins—so Janson described the scene—the men determined to rebuild the church.

From articles Janson had published earlier in Unitarian papers, the Nora Free Christian Church was already an appealing group to Eastern Unitarians. Now he gave a vivid account of the storm and followed that with a detailed account of how the congregation stood financially. They would have only $250 after meeting all their earlier

97

obligations, and they would need $700 to rebuild. Hardly had the account been printed before donations began to stream in—clothing for the Janson children and others, a suit of clothes for Janson, bedspreads and tablecloths for Mrs. Janson. In addition, before the year was over, money gifts aggregated over $2,000. In his autobiography, Janson has said all this largesse came without any prompting on his part. This, however, was not an exact statement. Janson had made a direct appeal, but there was nothing abject and sniveling about it. Instead, it was a gallant bit of evidence that his misfortunes had not caused him to lose his sense of balance and dedication.

He had written: "Alone we cannot do it, we need aid. Will you not still lend a hand, Unitarian brethren and sisters? It is of great importance to get the church up as soon as possible, because that will break up the powerful efforts which now will be made by our opponents to destroy my work. The two months I intended to spend here they have all announced meetings forenoon and afternoons on Sundays, to prevent their people to listen to me. At first the Lutheran people here did not at all believe that we should be able to raise a church, and they made fun of us; when they saw the church rise, they said that we had changed God's pure word into a wooden house. One of their ministers prophesied that the church would not stay long, and it has been uttered privately that Lutheran Christians here wished that church burned to the ground and the false prophet Kristofer Janson drowned in the lake. I urged the farmers to get it insured as fast as possible, I did not know how far 'Christian' zeal could go. . . . We must have the chapel raised again to show the people that liberal Christianity does not fall to the ground on account of a cyclone, but is backed up pretty well by friends in all states."[31]

Janson's detractors in the neighborhood were ready to argue that the destruction of the church was an act of divine vengeance. In a letter dated July 23, a correspondent, who signed himself "A Lutheran," aroused deep resentment among the members of Nora Church when his communication appeared in *Nordvesten*. Ole Jorgensen, who answered it in *Budstikken,* characterized the letter as "evil beyond words." No copy of the original is now in existence, but Janson did send *Unity* what he said was a literal translation of it, although it is clear he allowed himself a few interpolations:

God Will Not Be Mocked At

On Sunday, the 15 of July, Mr. Kristofer Janson announced in his church in Linden, Minnesota, that on Sunday coming he would preach a sermon in said church in which he should prove, that there is only one person in the Deity. Mr. Janson still persists, you see, in his terrible blasphemy, denying that Jesus Christ and the Holy Ghost is true God, like God the Father in all things. Mr. Janson appeals to the Bible and calls himself a Christian still he is impudent enough to deny the deity of Christ, and in that way spit God straight in the face. A nice Christian, an excellent pastor! As before said, Mr. Janson intended last Sunday to prove Christ is not true God. But he failed to get the opportunity to do that, because "God is not to be mocked at." What happens? On Sunday [*that is a convenient lie for it was on Saturday*] a furious hurricane arose which throws the church of the blasphemer from its foundation. The storm takes again the fated house and tears it completely to pieces. Sixteen men, among them Mr. Janson and his family, were all inside the church walls. Not one of them was hurt. What a miracle as the church was quite destroyed! A striking proof of God's long suffering. Dear reader, a word to you: take heed of the false prophets who come to you dressed as sheep but inwardly are ravening wolves. Keep on the old paths, cling to God's pure and unfalsified words, to the old and tried Lutheran doctrine which is a true reflection of the Bible. Remember: God is not to be mocked at.

Madelia, July 23   A Lutheran[32]

Obviously the letter did not disturb Janson, for he was receiving so many others expressing sympathy. Just about every day brought pleasant surprises—notes from donors, many of them well known across the nation, such as James Freeman Clarke, Samuel Longfellow, and Ramabai, a Hindu then visiting the United States. People wrote to ask for the titles of the books he had lost, saying they would like to replenish his library. Others—for example, a Mrs. Tinkham—sent money for Janson's personal use. As he was to write to his benefactress, this gift was indeed welcome, for he had learned that the new house in Minneapolis was going to cost more than he had anticipated. But fortunately not all that had been blown away by the storm was lost: farmers came in with five- and ten-dollar bills they had found in trees and in their fields (Janson had had $100 with which he intended to pay the carpenters lying on a table when the storm broke). Others brought manuscripts which, when they were dried and brushed, sometimes turned out to be legible. When the Jansons finally came to write home to Norway about their experience, their report was on the whole cheerful, reputedly causing Dina Krog to shake her head and say, "When Drude and Kristofer cannot manage in any other way, they fly through the air!"[33]

12

It was some time after the storm that Janson first saw Knut Hamsun, who was working in a lumberyard in Madelia. The only account of their first meeting is that given by Janson in his autobiography. It was a chance occurrence on a Sunday, when Janson noticed a tall young man with an aristocratic bearing and an intelligent face. He invited young Hamsun to go for a ride with him, and before that was over, he had offered his new friend a job as his secretary, and the latter had accepted. It is from a newspaper account that Hamsun wrote a year and a half later that we get a brief account of the Jansons that summer after the storm. The cottage in Madelia was small and poorly constructed. During the day, Janson wrote at a table in the living room, surrounded by children and their toys and frequently interrupted when a brisk prairie wind blew open the door, rumpling the rug on the floor and flapping his papers. Hamsun attended services of the Nora Free Christian Church, which, weather permitting, were held at the site of the ruined church. The young man was anything but a sentimentalist, but he was to say that he found the religious meetings very touching. Whole families were there—mothers with small infants, children, aged grandmothers, and farmers, their faces tanned and wind-burned from work in the fields. Hamsun said he had never known an audience to give a speaker such rapt attention. They had complete trust in Janson, and (Hamsun was to report this when he no longer worked for Janson) he was equally devoted to them, ready to concern himself with all their problems, even those of the most practical nature.[34]

Services in Minneapolis began on September 9. In the latter part of the same week, Janson moved his family into their new home at 2419 Nicollet Avenue, with Hamsun still as his aide. Although the house was not finished, it was in such condition that it could accommodate them on a makeshift basis. A red-brick structure with white stone trimming, it had two and a half stories with a tower on the south side. The open-air tower room soon came to be a refuge for all members of the household; from it one could view a sizable part of the city, at least its most desirable residential district. Hamsun was to report that one could see the mansions of Washburn, Blaisdell, and other rich men. Janson came to use it as a place to do his writing whenever the weather was fair, for he, like Drude, had the romantic's appreciation of nature. He had to be able to see the sky and hear the twittering of the birds to be fully at ease. The second story of the house was given over to bedrooms, with the first floor containing the minister's study, a living room or drawing room, a dining room, kitchen, and an additional bedroom. Beneath the house ran a full basement which, from time to time in later years, would temporarily house a destitute family until Janson could rally enough help to locate them in permanent quarters. Of all material possessions, what Janson valued most was "a pleasant and comfortable home"; the phrase runs like a litany through his letters, but he was also incapable of looking on the misery of others without trying to do something about it. This was a quality that Janson's son, Dr. Eilev Janson, and Drude's niece, Mrs. Kolderup, spoke of many times. She said that Drude accepted the situation, even though it often caused her inconvenience and forced her to stringent economies. "She was a genius at mending," said Mrs. Kolderup, "and she needed to be with such an improvident husband!"[35]

In the fall of 1883, however, only the Jansons and Knut Hamsun occupied the house on Nicollet Avenue. Plans for putting out a magazine had been postponed, but Janson had been allocated $500 for help with publications by the American Unitarian Association. It seems that out of this fund Hamsun was to be paid, receiving in addition his room and board. Donations from private persons in the East had provided funds for rebuilding the church in Brown County, clothing for families there who had been hard hit by the storm, and enough money for Janson personally to allow him to meet his current obligations. He had acknowledged these gifts with letters to the donors, but in early autumn he sent a note of thanks to the *Christian Register*. It appeared in a September issue.

"American friends, men and women: In these hard times of trial, you have treated me as if I were your brother. . . . America is no longer a foreign country. I have now living proof of what the society is, educating to fellowship and common responsibility. I think the American people the finest in the world to answer promptly and generously every real need in such a way that it hurts neither the pride nor the modesty of the receiver."[36]

13

The Jansons had been in America a year. On October 4, with carpenters and painters still at work in the house, he wrote a twelve-page letter to Bjørnson, who had just sent the Jansons a copy of his new play, *A Glove* (En hanske) and thanked them for the congratulatory telegram they had sent for the Bjørnsons' twenty-fifth wedding anniversary. The telegram had been a stupid thing, Janson wrote, not at all what he and Drude had originally planned. He had written a bit of sprightly verse. He and Drude had then been in Madelia, but they had sent it to friends in Minneapolis to be cabled to Norway, only to find that it would cost more than $50 (double because it was in a foreign language). They had to conclude that no verse was worth that much, especially when they realized it would probably be garbled when it got to Bjørnson.

He need not tell of the storm nor of their "paradise in Madelia"; Drude had written about all that. Yet when all was said and done, in a way Dina Krog had been right—much had been accomplished by flying through the air. None of them would care to repeat the experience. Janson admitted that he became squeamish when the sky darkened, and the children were frightened—especially Arne, who became hysterical whenever a wind arose. This was something to worry about; they could only hope the child would grow out of it. The ordeal had left Drude weaker physically, but Janson was thankful that she had remained in good spirits. There was no denying that the donations had helped with their most pressing money problems. Unfortunately, the new house was going to cost $2,000 more than he had expected; that was going to mean additional lectures to meet the payments, but having a pleasant, comfortable home was worth it.

His Brown County church was secure—and not only financially. Orthodox ministers still thundered against him, but he had many intelligent men in the congregation who had read Thomas Paine and Robert Ingersoll, and these writers had served as a plow, preparing the ground for him.

Janson had great hopes for his hymnbook. There had never been one like it, containing verse from Walt Whitman, not to speak of seventeen selections from the humanist, Bjørnstjerne Bjørnson. Here and there, he had been obliged to make slight alterations in the text, but he hoped Bjørnson would find the changes to be in good taste. He was grateful for *En hanske* and had already announced that he would use the play for his reading the following Sunday evening and would also read it for a small group he and Drude were entertaining in a few days. The play was critical of society's tolerance of a double moral standard for men and women, a point of view Janson heartily agreed with. He congratulated Bjørnson on having come round to that way of thinking and reminded the dramatist that some years before in private conversations, Bjørnson had argued that young men who could not afford to marry were justified in going to prostitutes.

Janson had also written a play, or, to be more exact, a "dramatized sermon" entitled *The Children of Hell* (Helvedes børn). It would be sure to attract considerable attention. He was sending Bjørnson a copy, knowing that it would please him, for it dealt with holding the fear of hell over people. Janson also had plans for a series of short stories dealing with life on the prairie, although these were thus far only in his head and had not made their way to paper.

All in all, things were going well. The Americans were indeed an unusual people. They could sometimes be irritating in small ways, but on important matters they were nothing less than wonderful, and the Scandinavians had something to learn from them. He had received $20 or $30 from the Scandinavians, but nothing from the wealthy individuals among them. Contributions were still coming in from the Americans; that very day he had received $55. "Between us," he confided to Bjørnson, "I am the favorite child of the Unitarians at the moment. My mission interests them very much. It is their first attempt to introduce their ideas among the foreign-born."[37]

4

Difficulties
Beset Unitarians

WHEN Rasmus B. Anderson resigned his professorship in the fall of 1883, President John Bascom of the University of Wisconsin offered the position to Janson. In his autobiography, Janson has said that the offer was tempting—a good salary, long summer vacations, and the prospect of living in Madison, which he had always found a delightful little city. He pondered the matter overnight and then refused. The minister, he was to write, had triumphed over the professor.[1]

The academic position would have given him greater security—and perhaps that was its only advantage. Anderson had been paid $1,800 a year while Janson was receiving $2,000 from the American Unitarian Association, although on a provisional basis until such a time as his congregations would be able to support him. Of course, Anderson had augmented his income by lecturing, and Janson would have been able to do the same. Money, however, does not seem to have been the deciding factor. Nothing succeeds like success. After having gone through a difficult trial period, Janson knew he had awakened an interest in the rank and file of the American Unitarians, and was, as he had said, "their favorite child." No one would want to quit at such a time. Possibly his ministry opened up a wider field for him than a professorship. He was getting an increasing number of invitations to speak before American audiences. As long as he remained in America, he never ceased to deprecate his English, really without reason, for his American audiences understood him readily, and when allusion was made to his accent, it was only to say that it gave his speech a piquant charm.[2]

He seems to have had an unusual sensitivity to what an audience needed or expected from him. To the end of his life, he regretted that he had not had more opportunity to speak to cultivated audiences. Yet people never seem to have felt he was talking down to them. No one can explain how a talented person performs the way he does, but Janson has hinted that his folk-school experience may have had something to do with it. In his autobiography, he has told that in his early years as a folk-school teacher he used methods that had been employed by his teachers in the Latin school—with dismal results. Then he "caught on" to the Grundtvigian philosophy and everything changed.[3]

In his *Bjørnstjerne Bjørnson og folkehøyskolen,* Olav S. Midttun has an illuminating chapter on the basic philosophy of the folk school entitled "Folkehøyskolens idegrunnlag." Grundtvig did not look upon man as totally depraved, but as having a God-given spark within him which could be ignited under the right circumstances. That was not done by cramming facts down a student but by kindling an enthusiasm within him, getting him to love what he was being taught. Consequently, the atmosphere of such a school was friendly and benign, with no examinations or punitive measures. Instruction was by word of mouth, for print was cold, and a young person could be reached by a teacher who loves what he is teaching. The student was to be taught the legendary lore of his own country, along with its history, music, and poetry. He would find himself in its stream, bridging the gap between the past and the future. He would love his country and develop a new awareness of the blessing of having come into conscious life. That was all-important, for Grundtvig held that the Christian concept of eternal life was meaningless unless one loved life itself. Loving his neighbor, the student would stretch out beyond national boundaries to all men. According to Midttun, behind the Grundtvigian philosophy was the basic concept, "Respect for life itself, which is something greater than man, a godly gift, which in the last analysis is common to all."[4]

2

By the fall of 1883, Janson had Knut Hamsun as his secretary. In his autobiography, Janson said that he wanted Hamsun to translate articles for his monthly, *Saamanden,* but found that his young friend's English was not up to the task. This is puzzling, for *Saamanden* did not come out until September, 1887, long after the young Hamsun's employment with Janson had ended. It is true that Janson had originally planned to issue *Saamanden* in September, 1883; his reason for postponing it may have been that he did not have adequate help. As he had written Bjørnson, Drude was not in robust health and could not give him the assistance she had in the past.

In October, Janson set about lining up extra work to pay for his new house. He announced in *Budstikken* that he would be available for lectures through October, November, and December, asking a guarantee of $25 for each appearance. He offered a choice of esthetic, historical, or religious subjects, his lists including such new titles as "Scenes from Life in Italy," "Ibsen's *Brand*," and his own newly completed *The Children of Hell* (Helvedes børn). The same issue of *Budstikken* contained advertisements of pamphlets he had for sale as well as his hymnbook, available at a cost of seventy-five cents in flexible cloth and a dollar in hard cover with gold lettering.[5]

Apparently he was gone from the city much of the fall, for the newspapers carry no announcements of his sermons, and Knut Hamsun, in the article mentioned earlier, speaks of Janson's getting invitations from such far-flung places that he could not possibly accept. Even so, he traveled about quite widely, and the marvel was that he accomplished as much as he did. He could not have done this, Hamsun went on, if he had not had an unusually capable man as president of the congregation, Christian Haug, formerly of Kristiania, who could take over with great competence when Janson was absent.[6]

Perhaps in those busy days Janson felt some disappointment at the reception of his hymnbook. He had taken his motto for the book from Henrik Wergeland's great epic, *Man* (*Menneske*):

> Greet the pastor: freedom of thought
> Is a human need
> Vibrating to heaven from earth
> Through the grave of Jesus.[7]

This choice of a motto, Janson had confided to Bjørnson, was flinging the gauntlet in the face of orthodoxy, going on to say that the more he studied Wergeland, the more he felt the latter was the forerunner of Unitarianism in Norway. Wergeland (1808–45) is a towering figure in Norwegian literature.[8] Georg Brandes has said that, with the exception of Shelley, Wergeland was the greatest lyric poet Europe had produced. The man's brief life also had an epic sweep. The target of bitter criticism, he espoused a grass-roots Norwegian culture, established libraries, championed the cause of the peasants, the Jews, and indeed all the oppressed. Like other Romantic poets, he felt a mystical bond with nature; as he roamed about the countryside, he carried seeds in his pocket, scattering them wherever he found a fertile spot. It was to him—when he lay on his deathbed— that the Danish poet, Meyer Goldschmidt, wrote, "When I think of you, Wergeland, I am proud to be a human being." Many have felt so since, and more than one Norwegian writer has aspired to the mantle of Wergeland. In identifying his cause with that of the great poet, Janson perhaps saw more than one parallel. Wergeland had been trained in theology in the established church and had for years applied for an appointment as a clergyman, always to be refused. Yet his religious views were so unconventional that, as some critics have said, the wonder was that he should have applied at all.[9] For himself, Janson was to adopt the image of the sower, and more than once in later years, when he found the going rough, he was to remark (perhaps taking comfort that Wergeland had known the same trials) that ridicule and contumely were "the fate of the sower."

Janson's hymnbook received attention only in places where he was sure of a favorable verdict. It was a small book, about six inches long and four wide, containing 330 selections, a few of them in English, and a section of responsive readings translated from Gannet, Blake, and Hosmer's *Unity Hymns and Chorals*. The words *Jansons salmebog* were on the cover, but the title on the first page read *Salmer og sange for kirke og hjem* (Hymns and Songs for Church and Home). In its mid-November issue, the *Christian Register* found the book to come up to all expectations, reminding readers that some of the hymns by Janson had already appeared in translation there and in *Unity*. It quoted Bjørnson: "I think some of the hymns written by him are the best in our language since the days of Grundtvig."[10]

Budstikken judged it to be like no other hymnbook, containing as it did so many selections of high literary value. Some of them, the reviewer said, were not hymns in the ordinary sense, as for example, those by Wergeland and Bjørnson, but they presented an exalted view of life. Traditional hymns from Landstad, Luther, Kingo, and Ingeman were included as well as many by Grundtvig, and those by Janson were permeated with his mild and charitable Christianity. The reviewer noted that some alterations had been made in Bjørnson's texts, and he questioned Janson's right to take such liberties.[11]

By December, it seems that Janson had either completed his tour or was speaking in places close enough to the city for him to get back for the weekend and preach on Sunday morning. Whenever he did get home, an avalanche of mail awaited him. Hamsun has said he received so much every day that the carrier, described as a "young, quick Yankee" had said of Janson, "He was the damndest fellow to get letters you ever saw." The bulk was from Norway—all correspondents wanting help in finding work in America. Some were pathetic requests that Janson find a place for "my son Ola" or "Sigrid, my god-daughter." Other writers appealed in their own behalf, and among these, according to Hamsun, were laborers, skilled workers, schoolteachers, telegraph operators, and store clerks. Janson answered them, joking that the Norwegian government should rightfully give him a stipend for the service.[12]

Yet the fall of 1883, although a busy one for Janson, seems to have been peaceful. He could meet the payments on his house, and on December 10 he enjoyed an oyster supper given by the ladies' aid of his church. *Budstikken* again carried advertisements of his Sunday sermons: on December 9, "The First Christian Congregation of James, the Brother of the Lord," and on December 16, "Jewish Christians and *Heathen* Christians—the First Theological Warfare" (Jødekristne og hedningekristne—den første kirkestrid).[13] Attendance always shot up when it was known that Janson was to be in the pulpit, and Hamsun reported, "He certainly never lacks an audience for his sermons. Members of the Norwegian Synod as well as of the Conference attend."[14] Somehow during the autumn and early winter, Janson had found time to write the first of his stories of the prairie, "Wives, Submit Yourselves unto Your Husbands" (Kvinden skal være manden underdannig). In December he scheduled three lectures in Chicago for the following January, using the new story for one, his play *The Children of Hell* (which he called a "dramatized sermon") for the second, and rounding out the series with Bjørnson's drama, *A Glove*.

As it turned out, the period of tranquillity was soon over. From January, 1884, until well into 1886, Janson was involved in one brouhaha after the other, with only brief interludes of comparative quiet. Clergy and laymen alike took part, some of the latter lining up with Janson and others against him. Synod ministers and zealous church members came forward with arguments; prominent among them was Sven Oftedal of the Conference (again in command of *Folkebladet*). The issues were often so absurd as to seem highly ludicrous today, but they spawned claims of duplicity, unseemly conduct, money-grubbing—the latter charge to be leveled at Oftedal. This was the period between tornadoes for Janson, for in the spring of 1886 his second church was to be destroyed. It was the aftermath of this catastrophe that brought the quarrels to a crescendo, drawing in Americans, making headlines in the Minneapolis and St. Paul newspapers, even becoming enough of a *cause célèbre* to draw comment from the *Herald* in Boston. Then, by late 1886, the fury subsided—much as if Janson's detractors had exhausted themselves, for even Sven Oftedal, who had seemed indefatigable, was nearly through. Now and then he would make some attack on Janson, but he refused to take part in any prolonged exchange. The public also had become bored, their interest having centered in a battle in another part of the field. Since 1880, trouble had been brewing between the Missourians and the Anti-Missourians in the Norwegian Synod, and this quarrel broke out in white heat in 1886, when the Anti-Missourians severed their connections with the Synod, virtually decimating that once powerful church body.

3

The story of the bitter disputes among the various Norwegian Lutheran synods in this country is well known; these quarrels date back to the 1850s. Later they became so virulent that present-day Lutheran church historians, in describing them, have used such chapter headings as "Theological Warfare in the 70s" and "Theological Warfare in the 80s." While no one can question that the Norwegians were able to hold up their end when it came to religious feuding, it would be a mistake to assume they were the only ones to be so occupied, or that they necessarily surpassed other sects in fanatical zeal. According to Arthur M. Schlesinger—a pioneer in the study of American religious activity—in no period of American history has Christianity known so much unrest as in the last quarter of the nineteenth century. Everywhere Protestant orthodoxy was on the defensive, as traditionally minded clergymen girded themselves against the onslaught of Darwinism and other developments in the natural sciences, studies in Biblical criticism, and research on world religions. The Bible as the inspired word of God was laid open to questions by scholars in European universities, who produced evidence that it had been assembled over a long period of time and was a compilation of history, folklore, poetry, biography, and discourses. Anthropologists were finding parallels between Christianity and other ancient religions.

By 1880—according to Schlesinger—some clergymen had found that they could come to terms with Darwinism by arguing that religion and science belonged in different spheres. By this reasoning, the Bible was a guide to faith and conduct but not a textbook in science. They could argue that the account of creation in Genesis, allegorically interpreted, could be found to support Darwin's thesis. The general public became more susceptible to a wider religious view. In 1871 James Freeman Clarke (who was one of Janson's benefactors in the Brown County disaster) had published *Ten Great Religions,* a book which went through twenty-one editions in fifteen years. The agnostic Robert G. Ingersoll toured the country during the 1880s, charging orthodox Christianity with being overridden with superstition.

Throughout the 1870s and 1880s, the Methodists and Presbyterians held heresy trials. Professors in various colleges and theological seminaries were dismissed because of their liberalism. Orthodoxy was defended by such men as Professor W. H. Green of Princeton Seminary and the Reverend De Witt Talmadge. Dwight L. Moody, though not an ordained minister, conducted evangelistic crusades, preaching a fundamentalist Christianity to thousands, and answering those who charged that the Bible had inconsistences by saying, "The Bible was not made to be understood."

New sects were drawing converts. In 1875, theosophy, which one historian has described as a blend of spiritualism and both Brahmanic and Vedic lore, was introduced to Americans by Madame Helena P. Blavatsky. The same year, Mary Baker Eddy published *Science and Health,* the textbook of the Christian Scientists. From England, the Salvation Army was brought to this country. In 1876 Felix Adler organized the Ethical Culture Society, which attracted so many that it largely came to supplant the Free Religious Association founded in 1867. In addition, interest in spiritualism was revived.[15]

While Norwegian immigrants in the mass do not seem to have been very much affected by all of this, their clergy were knowledgeable men, and they were touched by it, more than peripherally it seems. The defensive slogans of both the Synod and the Conference, while they might serve in intra-Lutheran debate over a disputed passage, were clearly intended against the multiple American sects. The Synod, in its quest for a theological seminary where it could send men to be trained for the ministry, had visited many American Lutheran institutions, only to find them tainted with liberalism. Finally, its leaders had decided that the German Missouri Synod alone was worthy of their confidence, for in this group they found a literal interpretation of Scripture as firm as their own. As a "watchman on the walls of Zion," the

Synod pastor, Th. Ylvisaker, would not go to hear Dwight L. Moody, Henry Ward Beecher, nor a Catholic priest because he felt none of them had "God's word unfalsified." Professor Sven Oftedal was to lament that the Baptists, Episcopalians, and Universalists all had missionaries to the Scandinavians, and, while they had drawn off very few, the situation called for vigilance among those who would "remain true to their childhood teachings"—a phrase often used by the Conference.

These clergymen—Synod and Conference alike—read the *Independent*, the most widely circulated periodical on church activity in the country, and a paper which contained word of new programs, of the movement of ministers from one congregation to another, and occasionally of a clergyman's shift from one denomination to another. Apprehensive of all non-Lutherans, they were most fearful of Janson, for he was bringing ultramodern ideas of the Bible's authority up to their very doors and drawing too many auditors.

The series of disputes which were to engage Janson in one way or another for the next several years was set off by his Christmas sermon in 1883, although at the time it aroused no unusual attention. It was entitled "The Glad Tidings of the Orthodox and the Liberals" (De ortodokses og de liberales glæde evangelium). If they examined their doctrine, Janson held, the orthodox had no reason to be glad. If man was by nature depraved and could in no way change this situation through his own effort, he was in the power of the devil, not God. The idea of atonement—that an innocent man should suffer and die for the sins of others—was immoral, a concept no reasoning person would ever apply to everyday life. And if every word in the Bible was literally true, one could not escape the conclusion that God himself was a shabby actor, inciting people to deceive and steal. Concerning this, Janson cited several examples from the Old Testament. The liberals, on the other hand, believed that man was a free agent who could develop his character and thus make for a better world. He held that evil was traceable to human error; each man was responsible for his acts. He knew that all wrongdoing would sooner or later be punished in accordance with the natural law of a just and loving God.

Late in the spring of 1884, *Budstikken* published this sermon. Shortly afterward, a man in Faribault wrote a letter to *Nordvesten*, calling for greater vigilance against heresy. Janson did not reply, but he translated the communication for *Unity*, as an example of the kind of opposition he sometimes ran into:

111

Kristofer Janson in America

To the Norwegian Lutheran Ministers

In *Budstikken* there is a printed Christmas sermon by Kristofer Janson. Such an abominable, blasphemous product I hardly ever saw except in *The New Time,* a Socialist paper. Should it not be the duty of some of you to write to the Norwegian papers against such a blasphemy? Cry aloud and spare not, because the salvation of many dear-bought souls is at stake.

Ministers of the gospel! Read the Christmas sermon and see if it be a lie that I tell you. Judge for yourselves, if that can be called a Christmas sermon. That is a production of hell which is worse than any free thinker paper, for everybody can see what that is, but not so with Mr. Janson's products, because he uses God's word as a false pretext. Therefore, priests, awaken! stand up against such a doctrine. Speak, write, do all you can, for the time is short, and there are many souls who are on the way to be deceived for their salvation under Mr. Janson's guidance.[16]

Budstikken was to reprint the original from *Nordvesten* and to follow it with the comment that the "abominable" sermon was available in pamphlet form for five cents.

4

All this was in the future as Janson prepared to lecture in Chicago early in 1884. He had advertised well in advance, and five Synod ministers responded by publishing "A Warning to Lutheran Church Members" (Advarsel til det lutherske kirkefolk). Dated January 16, 1884, this admonition lacked the generalized fury of the letter from the man in Faribault.[17] For a long time, they charged, Janson had been working to undermine Christianity, denying the Holy Ghost and the divinity of Jesus. Didn't he know that St. Paul had said a man should love and honor his wife, showing her consideration, and that the apostle had also said that the wife should be subservient to the husband? Yet Janson held these teachings up to ridicule, acting as if they were the invention of Synod ministers. If it were only that he displayed amusement and malice toward the doctrines of the Lutheran church—that is, the content of the Scriptures—the pastors would be disposed to hold their peace. But their concern went beyond this to what was deeply disturbing to all committed Christians: whether thousands of their fellow Norwegians would be alienated from their Christian faith, whether many, already touched by doubt, would inadvertently, with Pastor Janson's help, be led into heresy. To all of those who did not want to find themselves doomed at the hour of death, the pastors would issue a warning: let them remind themselves as well that whoever denies Christ, him will Christ deny before His heavenly Father, and that everyone is guilty of denying Christ who does not believe He is the true God and the eternal life.

Yet, before the final paragraph of warning, the pastors revealed a new outrage. Janson had announced that one of his offerings would be a "sermon in drama form." They wrote: "Were we to be silent, we would be blind watchmen whom the prophet Isaiah calls dumb dogs that cannot bark. Pastor Janson also uses the drama to serve his purpose, namely to get faith in Christ as God eradicated and to substitute something else in its place. That is so unworthy a way to preach religion that the Unitarians, however free they might otherwise be, hardly find it serves the purpose. Even among them there are regulations that if a minister feels drawn to offering scenes or dramatic presentations, so must he first resign his pastorate, for a man cannot be both a minister and an actor. We refer here to the Reverend [George C.] Miln of Chicago. But for simpleminded Norwegians such a thing seems to be good enough."[18] The central characters in "The Children of Hell" are a Synod pastor and his wife. The minister has been called to the deathbed of a young man who has refused to admit his innate depravity and therefore cannot be given communion. The young man declares his own faith, "God is good," and dies, leaving the pastor without any means of comforting the youth's mother. But the pastor's wife, who has long had some doctrinal doubts, finds this insupportable. She cannot live "in falsehood" and leaves her husband and children. All of this forces the pastor to examine himself, and, as the play progresses, he seems almost at the point of giving way, when he is visited by colleagues who tell him that this trial has been sent to test his faith. As the play ends, the differences between husband and wife seem irreconcilable.[19]

In his autobiography, Janson has said that the Synod pastors' protest over his "Children of Hell" only served to increase his audience. Shortly after he had delivered the dramatized sermon, he read his story, "Wives, Submit Yourselves unto Your Husbands," which was also polemical, and had the Norwegian Synod again as its target. Ola and Emma had met in a folk school in Norway. Emma belonged to a "better" family than Ola, who was a cotter's son. Because of the rigid class distinctions in Norway, they could not marry. They immigrate to America, where they are married and then go out to the Middle West to homestead land. By hard work, they progress from

113

a sod hut to a log cabin and then to a frame house set within acres of prosperous farmland. But Ola, who had been a handsome, light-hearted young man, now lives only to increase his holdings. He cannot understand his wife's longing for books and the like, taunting her before their children that she has these uppity tastes because she came from "better people" in Norway. Except for brief respites when she bears a child, Emma lives like a slave, working in the fields and caring for cattle in addition to cooking and ministering to children. She is beaten and kicked, a brutality Ola justified by saying the Bible teaches that the wife must be subservient to her husband. During a storm, an American woman takes refuge in their home. Appalled by Emma's wretched existence, she leaves Emma ten dollars, suggesting she use it to escape to her brother's home in Minneapolis. When, shortly afterward, Emma suffers further indignities, she steals away to her brother's home, taking her infant child. She is well received, and for some weeks lives a contented life. When Ola finds out her where-abouts, he sends the Synod minister to bring her back. By quoting Scripture, the minister persuades the brother that the wife must be brought back to her husband's house. She is taken forcibly, and a day or two after her return she drowns herself and the baby.

This synopsis does not do justice to the story, which is skillfully built up and is related in such gripping detail that one accepts both Emma and Ola as living characters. Janson's third presentation offering, Bjørnson's *A Glove,* consisted of a reading of the play followed by his interpretation. Since Janson had given all three lectures before, they were presented in a highly polished form.[20]

On February 2, Dr. J. Julson of Chicago wrote his opinion of the series in a long article inappropriately entitled "A Little on Pastor K. Janson's Latest Appearance Here in Chicago." This was printed in *Skandinaven* in March, 1884, in a supplement to the regular edition.[21] Little is known about Dr. Julson except that he had attacked Janson several times before, arguing that the minister's objections to the Synod stemmed from his inability to live up to the high level of discipline it demanded.

Both Bjørnson and Janson, Julson thought, could make better use of their talents by inspiring the working man, giving him the courage and will to make a mighty thrust against the tyranny of capi-talism. Why had they not come forward championing the cause of the oppressed and working for social improvement, instead—as they had done in the past—of clamoring for political freedom? (Norway was then restive under the union with Sweden; both Bjørnson and

Janson wanted Norway to become a republic.) In writing *A Glove,*
Bjørnson had his head in the clouds, fancying he could abolish immorality and like evils by choosing controversial themes for his plays.
Janson should have known better than to read such a play publicly,
for calling attention to its contents only led to increased immorality.

It was clear, Julson felt, that Janson was determined to destroy the
Norwegian Synod. Not being a Christian himself, he had no right
to attack the clergy in "The Children of Hell." Furthermore, the portrait
of the pastor was a lie; no man such as Janson depicted was to be
found in real life. The characterization of Ola in "Wives, Submit
Yourselves unto Your Husbands" was also a libel, and Dr. Julson
had only contempt for the character Emma. Obviously she had not
married Ola for love, but for sensuality. She had been attracted to
the embrace of a raw, primitive man. And she was not a "cultivated"
person, but quite the reverse, a woman with a blown-up imagination
that had been nourished by bad reading. Dr. Julson added that he
and Synod pastors would be willing to meet Janson in debate about
these matters.

The article was not answered by Janson but by his secretary, Knut
Hamsun.[22] Whether he was asked to do it or had volunteered, we do
not know, but it is a safe guess that he was willing and even glad to
take care of the matter. In answering, Hamsun made short work of
Dr. Julson. His article was printed in *Skandinaven* in April, 1884.[23]
Dr. Julson's whole trouble, Hamsun said, was that he was stupid;
he had not comprehended the lectures—or perhaps he lacked the will
to understand them. Hamsun's tone is one of exasperation. To Dr.
Julson, his elder, he wrote brashly, "It doesn't look good when old
people begin to imagine things—be assured it seems absolutely ludicrous."

Until the doctor had done more reading, Hamsun recommended
that he keep away from writing. Four and a half columns! One began
with Dr. Julson and ended with a chatterbox. When a man is going
to oppose someone, he should make some preparation, especially when
he is going to criticize such persons as Bjørnson and Janson, among
the most intelligent men of the time—men who raise the great contemporary questions that no one can ignore, for they concern all men. At
this point Hamsun added parenthetically, "who are not idiots."

The doctor lacked even an elementary knowledge of human nature,
Hamsun continued. When he had listened to "The Children of Hell"
and couldn't fathom the psychological development, instead of being
offended, he should have asked for an explanation. "That's what

people do when they want to find out something; they don't jump up and prattle nonsense—'in the name of truth.'" Dr. Julson's four and a half columns contained many errors. Janson had not reproached the Synod pastor because he refused a freethinker the sacrament. The pastor is portrayed as a good, honorable person, one-sided, naturally, but genuinely concerned about the dying man. The book would soon be out in print, Hamsun assured the doctor, and then he would be able to study it. "But you should have someone to explain it to you."

Hamsun spent little time on Bjørnson's *A Glove,* except for saying that Julson might read the criticism written by Professor E. J. Lockmann in *Nyt Tidsskrift.* So far as "Wives" was concerned, Ola was anything but a caricature; he was so faithful a copy that there were many men who had recognized themselves in him, and many wives had thanked Janson for raising his voice in their behalf.

Hamsun found Dr. Julson's suggestion of a debate worthless. No discussion was meaningful unless the participants recognized some common ground. Julson and the Synod ministers would stress the righteousness of the orthodox view, he said, adding parenthetically, "now and then using apocryphal Biblical passages."[24] And they would have none of what Janson would present: history and Biblical research. But if Dr. Julson, in the meantime, should "really wish to know what Janson teaches and what he teaches with, there is a rich Unitarian literature which is open to everyone. In particular, I refer you to Victor Rydberg."

The article brought no reply. Its appearance in *Skandinaven* would seem to imply Janson's tacit approval, but what he thought of it otherwise is not known. Meanwhile he had many irons in the fire. During the winter, he had given "The Legend of St. Christopher" at Chicago's Universalist church and was invited back two weeks later to present "Our Ancestors." This lecture was printed in June in *Scandinavia,* a magazine published in Chicago, following another English translation by Janson, "Bishop Grundtvig and the Peasant High School," which had appeared in the spring. He was still delivering "The Children of Hell" and "Wives," but the latter had become the favorite of audiences, so he was at work on an English version of it.[25]

5

The building fund for the Minneapolis church was not growing fast enough. Appealing through Unitarian periodicals was a bit awkward, because Janson was still receiving contributions for the church in Brown County. (He acknowledged a total of $794 on March 27 in the *Christian Register*.) In his autobiography, Janson has said that this constant begging was the most mortifying of his experiences in America. If so, he must have felt humiliated much of the time, and often his dispatches showed it. People are likely to be coy when asking for donations or favors; Janson's appeals were whimsical, playfully self-deprecatory. There was an old proverb, he wrote in *Unity* in mid-January, "If a certain man has got the finger, he will take the hand also." His country church was completed, and by spring the little parsonage would be ready as well. Ladies' organizations in Boston and Providence had contributed a great deal toward his first church in Brown County. When that was destroyed, the orthodox had said God's vengeance was at work, but they had failed to make clear whether God was displeased with Janson or with the good ladies of Boston and Providence. Now everything was secure in Brown County, but his Minneapolis congregation was still homeless, having shifted from place to place. Harrison Hall, the largest, was used for a dime museum during the week, and on Sunday garish posters still hung on the walls. The Minneapolis congregation had already bought a lot, and they must get a building on it. If there were women's organizations which had not chosen their winter project, they might keep his Minneapolis congregation in mind.[26]

"Wives, Submit Yourselves unto Your Husbands" was first read in Minneapolis in March, as a benefit for the building fund. The fame of the story seems to have justified raising the price of admission—twenty-five cents instead of the usual ten. Janson mailed subscription lists to Rasmus B. Anderson in Madison, saying, "Send them back with good names and good money so we can get the church up by winter."[27] Contributions were solicited in *Budstikken*. The Minneapolis church now had a choir, directed by Samuel Garborg, a brother of Arne Garborg, the Norwegian writer who already had two novels to his credit. (Samuel Garborg, for a time a member of the Janson household, seems to have been a versatile man and was eventually to become a Unitarian minister. In the summer of 1884, he opened a Scandinavian-English evening school in Minneapolis.) By April, the choir had progressed to the point that it could appear, together with a quartette from it, on a prestigious program given at Market Hall. Henry M. Simmons, the witty minister of the First Unitarian Society, gave an address in English and Nicolai Grevstad one in Norwegian. Gustavus Johnson, one of the best-known musicians in the city, presented piano solos.[28] (He was also the organist for Janson's church, apparently

117

not discouraged by the small organ the congregation had bought. If he brought along his small dog on Sunday morning, to sit quietly beside him as he played, no one thought things were any the worse for it.)[29] The program included selections by Jacob Seeman, described by *Budstikken* as unquestionably the best violinist in the Northwest—all in the service of the building fund.

While Janson was gone from the city, Knut Hamsun took his place in Harrison Hall, speaking on "The Ancient Egyptians' Religion."[30] *Budstikken* did not bother to report on it—as was usually the case when Janson had substitutes—but two days later, when the Norwegian Women's Society (Norske Damers Forening) announced a five-day bazaar with a different program for every evening, Hamsun was the featured speaker for Saturday evening, the others being Andreas Ueland, Rasmus B. Anderson, Janson, and Nicolai Grevstad.[31] (On Sunday, when Janson appeared, Jacob Seeman's accompanist had been Mrs. Oline Muus, whose divorce action against Pastor Bernt Julius Muus of the Norwegian Synod, some four years earlier, had revealed the pastor to be a household tyrant. The disclosures in court had shocked the entire Norwegian community. In 1884 she was making a living as a piano teacher in Minneapolis.) On another level, Mrs. Kristofer Janson had helped the bazaar by donating an embroidered boudoir pillow, surely a salable item in an age that admired ornamental needlework on doilies, antimacassars, pillows, and the like. Such work always taxed Drude's patience; her niece, Mrs. Kolderup, has said that Drude thought embroidering such folderol a waste of time.

When May came, Janson returned to Chicago to attend the annual meeting of the Western Unitarian Conference. As in the previous year, he also spoke at a Seventeenth of May celebration, sharing the platform with Mayor Carter Harrison, and giving what *Scandinavia* declared to be "a brilliant oration."[32] But the Western Conference meeting— Janson's third—was unsettling, and he could sense that the "Issue of the West" was by no means resolved. As mentioned before, American Protestantism everywhere was apprehensive of the liberals they found in their midst. Janson had observed at his first meeting in the spring of 1882 that the ministers present were of such mixed opinions as to be unable to agree on a definition of Unitarianism. But Janson had known then and there that he was on the side of the conservatives, and he had incorporated the Ames statement—"In the love of truth and in the spirit of Jesus Christ we join for the worship of God and the service of man"—into his sermon, "Under Which Banner Shall We Christians Assemble?" This had been his opening sermon after he returned to the United States with Drude and his family. The Ames declaration was to be the doctrinal cornerstone of every one of his churches.

For the conservatives, Jones's "Freedom, Fellowship, and Character in Religion" was wholly inadequate. The Reverend Jabez T. Sunderland, who was to emerge as the leader of the conservative faction, pointed out that "Freedom and Fellowship" had been the motto of the Free Religious Association. He felt Jones's phrase ignored "an historic connection with a great past—with what is highest, sweetest, most vital in Christianity." In the East, Unitarians were wondering exactly what was going on in the West, and officers of the American Unitarian Association, as well as the general secretary, the Reverend Grindall Reynolds, were concerned.

The air was rife with charges that Jones's permissive policy had led to secular teachings, lecturing instead of preaching, and that there were Unitarian ministers in the West who had declared God and immortality to be fictions. Some of the conservatives—like Janson—had originally belonged to orthodox church bodies: Sunderland had been a Baptist; M. J. Savage, S. M. Crothers, and Reed Stewart had been Congregationalists. Others, like W. G. Eliot of St. Louis, Missouri, a severe critic of the Western Conference, were birthright Unitarians.

One of the most agitated of the conservatives was the Reverend Jasper L. Douthit of Shelbyville, Illinois, who had resigned from the Western Conference in 1880 in disapproval. After watching developments, he had—by 1884, as he wrote Secretary Reynolds of the American Unitarian Association—"become so sick and tired of this sort of business that I cannot in good faith keep silent any longer." In April of that year, he had mailed an extra edition of his paper, *Our Best Words,* to every Unitarian minister in the country asking for plain answers to the following questions:

1. Does Unitarianism mean the Christian religion in its simplicity and purity or does it mean something else?

2. Are we Unitarians an organized body of Christian believers with the Holy Son of God as our Captain or are we only a nebulous, tenuous mass of humanity, believing anything and everything in general and nothing in particular?

3. Are Unitarians unequivocally and aggressively Christian in character or are we merely a heterogeneous multitude clamoring for Freedom, Fellowship, and Character in Religion with a com-

119

placent indifference as to whether the divine religion of Jesus is voted up or down?[33]

Yet if we are to trust what Janson says of these meetings in his autobiography, the forthright Douthit was a rarity among the Unitarians. They operated as a mutual admiration society, he said, adding that he (Janson) became known as "the frank Norwegian" because he always spoke directly to the point.[34] Surely, if they responded to one another as Jones did to Douthit, debates must have been circuitous. Jones's reply appeared in *Unity* on May 16. He was not disturbed about belonging to "a nebulous, tenuous mass of humanity," for he liked humanity. More than that, he liked Douthit, and it seems that nothing the man might say would cause him to change his mind. Jones wrote: "Douthit's religion is larger than his theology. If of our work he can say 'my soul abhors it,' in his work we can heartily say our souls delight. He may deny the Western Unitarian Conference; I am sure the Western Conference will still delight in him. He may turn us out of his church but he cannot keep himself out of ours. If Freedom, Fellowship, and Character are marginal things to him, they are central to us; consequently we must count him in though his freedom in Christ counts us out."[35]

At the meeting, Janson took a verbal shot at one of the extremists present. His remarks were printed later in the *Christian Register*, possibly to comfort Easterners that, if the Western Conference did contain every kind of a radical, at least the National Association was not importing any. The paper did not identify the man Janson took issue with, except to say that he "laid special emphasis on the scientific method of moral training and of appealing to facts as an ultimate source of knowledge." (One suspects he might have been a logical positivist.) "But Rev. Kristofer Janson rose in reply and his musical words ran as follows: 'I but wish I could express myself in a foreign language, for then I should have something to say to the gentleman who spoke of scientific facts. There is one thing we must not forget, and that is that there are unseen facts as well as seen facts. There are unseen realities. The unseen realities are not all scientific. We cannot prove God mathematically or scientifically. We can prove his laws; we can show a child his laws, and those laws point to a lawgiver; but we cannot prove God himself. Still I think a child is to be placed face to face with the Eternal Being he cannot see and understand. I think fathers and mothers should speak of him as the Eternal Blessed Spirit that carries all life in his arms. A child cannot understand it wholly but he can understand enough. Eternity, immortality—we cannot prove that or show it to any child as a scientific fact. It is beyond our reach. We can prove the probability of it, because it is a cry of our own souls. It is a craving of all our faculties that there should be such a thing, and I think that it is our duty to place the child face to face with that unseen reality.' "[36]

In the end, the conservatives won out, for the Reverend J. T. Sunderland was elected Western Conference secretary to replace Jones. Jones remained as editor of *Unity* and turned to the problem of erecting a new building for his expanding All Souls congregation. In his acceptance speech, Sunderland thanked Jones for his long, invaluable service, praising him for his "zeal, self-sacrifice, devotion and large prophetic vision." Douthit openly rejoiced that at last the Western Conference had a secretary "with Christian principles" (Jones was personally a Christian theist like Janson), but Douthit thought Sunderland had not pushed his victory hard enough, for in his acceptance speech he had not made "one loyal or loving reference to Jesus Christ." Wearily, the delegates returned home, some of them having found the division tasteless and absurd—for Unitarians whose basic tenet was freedom of conscience, for laymen and clergy alike. Among them was Henry M. Simmons, Janson's colleague in Minneapolis. Others seem to have been influenced by practical considerations: Unitarianism must not lose its identity as a church. The year before, the Ethical Culture Society had organized a unit in Chicago, and societies were being formed in Philadelphia and St. Louis.[37]

For the rest of May and into June, Janson traveled about lecturing, moving as far south as Kansas City, getting to Sioux Falls, South Dakota, and stopping off at Humboldt, Iowa, where the Iowa Unitarian Conference heard "The Legend of St. Christopher." In his absence, Knut Hamsun took over on Sunday, June 8, in Harrison Hall, speaking on "Unitarismens levnetsløb," which appears to have been a historical sketch on Unitarianism.[38] Shortly afterward, another Norwegian entered the Unitarian ministry: Hans Tambs Lyche of Kristiania, Norway, who had been trained as an engineer there, and who had graduated from the theological school at Meadville, Pennsylvania, where he delivered an address, "Law, the Nature of the Eternal."[39]

6

In July, when the Janson family should have gone to Brown County for the blessed summer vacation, the four youngest children came down with whooping cough. It was disappointing, as the new church there was to be dedicated and the little red parsonage was ready. Janson went to the rural parish, taking Eilev along to be his housekeeper. Hamsun seems to have been left behind, how occupied we do not know, but there was a week-long bazaar coming up in the fall for the building fund, and getting ready for that was enough to keep several secretaries going. In Brown County, the dedication took place on July 13. Janson described it in *Unity*: "At ten o'clock the teams commenced to come from north, south, east, and west, the wagons loaded with farmers, their wives and children. I think there were about a hundred teams. The crowd present was about 400 and the church was not able to take them all as the gallery was not yet fixed. They stood packed in the aisle, in the door, and outside the windows. The church was decorated with white muslin bar put up with wild vine picked fresh from the forest. Wreathes and garlands of wild flowers round the walls and on the pulpit. The back wall was covered with a large Norwegian flag, which bound a dark blue cross in white and red ground; we had applied in vain in Madelia for two American flags as curtains for the entrance; people down there must not be very patriotic. Over the head stood N M (Nora Menighed, that is, Nora Congregation) wound up in wild flowers. There were many members of the Lutheran churches present, who were surprised to find Unitarians prayed to God; they had been told they were all free-thinkers and that is in the Scandinavian opinion the same as an Atheist. At the close of the service they wondered we were not worse; they found there was sense in what I preached.

"After the service all present were invited to a feast in open air on lemonade, crackers, and cake, while a band played. The Scandinavians are suspected to be terrible drinkers and it proved true, as they emptied two big barrels with lemonade before they left. In the afternoon I read to the same crowded audience as before my novel: 'Wives, submit yourselves unto your Husbands' in the Norwegian language.' "

The following Sunday, Janson went on, he had held confirmation.[40] This, he explained to his Unitarian readers, was a custom from the old country, greatly cherished by the settlers. Janson had thought it to be a good way to instruct the young people in the Unitarian faith. Although he did not conduct the ceremony exactly as the Lutherans did, in general he followed the old form. At one point—instead of exacting vows—he held the hand of each confirmand, spoke to the child personally and then gave him or her a written copy of the talk, much as orthodox ministers would present a certificate of confirmation. Following this, he administered the Lord's Supper.[41]

Later in the summer, he was back in Minneapolis. On Sunday, July 27, he had scheduled service in Harrison Hall, where Jenkin Lloyd Jones would be present to speak. (Jones's leaving the secretaryship seems in no way to have altered their relationship, and the dispute, although it continued to grow in the Western Conference, never seems to have emerged in the Minnesota Conference, organized somewhat later.) Shortly after, he wrote to Bjørnson. The four children were still down with whooping cough, suffering their worst spasms at night, a great drain on Drude. That day she also was in bed with a gastric upset, running a fever. "Such are the comforts of home!" His real reason for writing was his concern over Solbakken, his house in Norway. It seems to have been standing empty since 1882, a "dead treasure," for Janson had to keep it insured but derived no revenue from it. One man had wanted to buy it, but he discovered that Janson did not have a clear title to the ground on which it stood because of a prior mortgage that had been taken on the Aulestad estate. This buyer had urged Janson to get a release from Bjørnson, saying that this would be a minor matter for the poet but one of great importance to Janson, for his property would be in jeopardy if the Aulestad estate were to be sold. Would Bjørnson try to clear up the matter?

Then to other things: the newly built parsonage was all he could want. Eilev was a fine housekeeper and a good provider, going out hunting every day and coming back with wild ducks and prairie chickens. Janson had had plenty of milk and could gorge himself on cream morning, noon, and night. He could sit and write close to nature, had finished "A Buggy Minister," and hoped to put out a volume of tales of prairie life soon. The stories he had thus far completed would serve for his Sunday evening readings in the fall. On the exact anniversary of the tornado in 1883, another storm had come. He and Eilev had shivered through it in the cellar of the parsonage, but thankfully no buildings had whirled through the air, and no one in the neighborhood had been hurt. Drude would write when she was able; both the Jansons had enjoyed Bjørnson's letter more than he would ever know. But life had been hard for her; the family had also had some scarlet fever in the house before Christmas.[42]

7

In the fall, services were again shifted to Peterson Hall. There, during the first week in October, the congregation gave its bazaar.

The tastefully decorated room, *Budstikken* declared, was filled to overflowing every night; a great variety of fine things were on sale; the excellent programs put everyone in a good mood, especially the tableaux, which drew rapt attention. Even Hamsun was impressed. "To raise money for their new church which will seat eight to ten hundred people," he wrote a few months later, "the little Unitarian congregation gave a grand bazaar, the most elaborate ever given by Scandinavians in Minneapolis, and they made over one thousand dollars."[43]

But for a time it looked as though the bazaar had been Hamsun's undoing. At one point he served as auctioneer, straining his voice in order to be heard. Suddenly he felt something give in his chest and he spat up blood. He went to a doctor—a Norwegian—for immigrants did not trust American physicians, and Norwegian doctors, dentists, and midwives all advertised they were *"Norsk examinert."* The physician told him that he had galloping consumption, brought on by the harsh Minnesota climate, and advised him to return to Norway at once. Janson and others collected funds for his passage, and Hamsun was sent off. Sick though he was, Hamsun had his own ideas on how to cure consumption. On the way to New York, he sat in the locomotive, allowing a stream of steam to pass through his lungs. Arriving in New York three days later, he felt much better, and was entirely well by the time he reached Norway.[44]

Before he left, Hamsun seems to have been a disruptive element in the Janson household. The chief evidence of this fact is contained in a letter written by Peder Ydstie, a good friend of Janson, to Torkel Oftelie, who had known Kristofer and Drude Janson from his days in Norway. Ydstie's letter is not dated, but it is clear that it was written after Janson had returned to Norway and had made his decision not to come back to America. In his letter, Ydstie discusses the divorce of Kristofer and Drude, saying that Kristofer had assumed the full responsibility for the dissolution of the marriage, even though in fact that was not the case. He related that once earlier the marriage had gone through a crisis, when Drude told Janson she had fallen in love with Knut Hamsun and wanted to be free.

It was Hamsun who balked at that arrangement, according to Ydstie. For a time, Hamsun had basked in Drude's admiration and was not averse to harmless coquetry, but that he should ally himself with a woman who was a dozen years older, the mother of many children, was unthinkable. According to Ydstie, Drude was disappointed at this turn, but she recovered to beg Janson's forgiveness, which she received, and the two were reconciled.[45]

Rasmus B. Anderson has said that Drude was "delighted if not infatuated" with Hamsun, adding that she had told Anderson she found it invigorating, mentally and physically, to be in the same room with the young man. Hamsun himself has written of events that took place in the Janson home. In America, he had lived a sexually abstinent life, finding the strain grueling. This he later described in a letter, dated December 26, 1888, to the Danish writer, Erik Skram. He wrote that he had frankly told Fru Janson what bothered him and seems to have been surprised when she answered that she could understand that. Later he sold his watch and in all secrecy hired a carriage to take him to a brothel. He was sick at the time and felt that the experience would kill him, but he was nevertheless intent on it. Yet Fru Janson could not have understood after all, he wrote, for she dismissed the carriage.

A short time later, Hamsun continued, he had the opportunity to "sin" in the very house where he lived; it was *offered* to him in so many words. (Hamsun italicized the word.) He was to have a key, told of a red bow in the curtain, given a designated time, and requested to give one knock on the door. He had not accepted, he wrote, saying that perhaps he might have done so if he had been the aggressor rather than the one solicited.

8

Some time after the bazaar, the Norwegian Synod held its district meeting in Madelia, a few miles from Janson's Nora Free Christian Church. Here Pastor W. M. H. Petersen spoke on "The Gross Errors of the Unitarians in Respect to Sin and Grace." When the address was published in *Evangelisk Luthersk Kirketidende,* a footnote explained that it was delivered with special reference to Kristofer Janson. The pastor never mentioned Janson by name, but early in the speech he said he hoped that God would help him to make clear his message since the most shameful (*skjændigste*) of all false teachings, under the guise of Christianity, was making inroads among the Norwegians. Janson never answered it and possibly never saw it. But the speech illustrates how closely the Synod pastor had studied his subject and that he knew of the turmoil in the Western Conference and of Janson's position in it. He did not bother with Jones's broad tolerance of "Freedom, Fellowship, and Character in Religion," nor with any logical positivist, but marshaled his examples from the stalwart conservatives: James Freeman Clarke, the Unitarians' most prestigious theologian, W. G. Eliot of St. Louis, Samuel J. May, and Jasper L. Douthit.[46]

As he had done the year before, Janson scheduled a lecture tour for 1885, although a relatively short one. In his absence, should anyone want ministerial aid, he was to leave his name with Christian Haug at the Goodfellow and Eastman store on Nicollet Avenue. In the meantime, Drude's life had brightened. Her sister, Mrs. Wilhelmine Behr (it had been Beer in Norway and was changed for an obvious reason) had moved from Chicago to Minneapolis together with her two young daughters, Agnes and Dina. She was the wife of Johan Beer, whose financial machinations had brought the family to ruin in Norway. For a time, Mrs. Behr had operated a *pensionat* in Kristiania, but soon her husband's creditors swarmed about her, bringing that venture to nothing. She had taken her children to Chicago, where she conducted a boardinghouse and was a cateress, activities that she took up in Minneapolis.

From the first, the Behr girls and the Jansons were good friends. Mrs. Behr lived in the Scandinavian community in south Minneapolis, but her daughters soon learned how to take the motor line out to the Janson house. Agnes was already showing talent as a pianist, and she eventually became a music teacher. Both the girls would frequently stay overnight, and they soon found Tante Drude a much stricter disciplinarian than their mother. No sweets for children; in the morning, milk and a bowl of oatmeal with very little sugar and no nonsense—as Mrs. Dina Kolderup later recalled. She has said that Drude was very frugal with meat, too. The roast would go around the table once with everyone getting a piece, and then Tante Drude would carry it into the kitchen, "with a gleam of triumph in her eyes," Mrs. Kolderup said, thinking of the times she had wished there might be seconds. The Janson girls were always glad when they could visit their cousins, for Mrs. Behr would indulge them with cake, cookies, and even candy. The Behr children were promptly enrolled in Janson's Saturday school, and they later came to take part in tableaux for various programs, as did the Janson youngsters. Beginning in 1885, they always accompanied the Janson family to spend July and August in Brown County.

During the 1880s, Minneapolis had two ministerial societies: the Orthodox Ministers' Association and the Liberal Ministers' Association. It is not known whether the Norwegian Synod pastors were members of the former, but some of the Conference leaders were prom-

126

inent in it. Both societies convened on Monday mornings, and their meetings were usually reported in the city newspapers. The liberals were made up of Unitarians, Universalists, and Jewish rabbis. One of the latter was the Reverend Henry Iliowizi, known to be a learned rabbinical scholar and admired as an effective speaker and a man of ready wit. (He was to be called upon for the principal address at the dedication of the First Unitarian Society in 1886.) He and other rabbis and Janson were to exchange platforms occasionally, as when Janson, in the early fall of 1884 had read "King Hodding's Journey into Unknown Lands" to an audience in a synagogue. There he followed his usual practice of first relating the story and then interpreting it to show its wealth of folk wisdom.

At best, relations between the two ministerial societies were strained. As Janson had said in his *Nyt Tidsskrift* article in 1883, Unitarianism was the *enfant terrible* of American Protestantism. Unitarians were not eligible for membership in the Y.M.C.A. (nor, for that matter, was anyone else who was not an orthodox Trinitarian). In the Twin City area, according to Janson, Unitarians could contribute to any good cause espoused by the orthodox, but they were never named to steering committees. If the Norwegians—in both the Synod and the Conference—were bitter about Janson's activities in the city, so also were some of the American orthodox, who were more resentful of him, it seems, than of his American colleague, Henry M. Simmons.

It was December, 1884. Janson's attention had been called to an article that had appeared in the *Independent* shortly before, saying that the attempt to draw Scandinavians into Unitarianism had been a failure, and that Janson was giving up. On the sixth of December, he wrote to set the record straight, as usual adopting a light satirical tone. Such news, he knew, would gladden many, but there was not a word of truth in it. "I am, alas, in full health and vigor as before, my mission is prospering, we have built one church in Brown County and intend to build another one in Minneapolis pretty soon. My hall is well filled, and I have not the slightest thought of giving up. I keep my regular services every Sunday."[47]

The weather was bitter: the winds were strident, the streets smoked with cold, and even indoors, with all the stoves going; it was drafty around windows and the floors were chill. Ivar, the Janson's oldest son, in mid-December caught a cold which worsened, and he was soon down in bed. It was just at that time that Janson found comments of Sven Oftedal in *Folkebladet* rankling; soon they were to be battling on two fronts.

127

For about two years, Oftedal had been silent about Janson. The Norwegian Conference, like the Synod and the Western Unitarian Conference, had its own internal strife, centered in Augsburg Seminary. As mentioned before, Professor Sven Gunnersen objected to Oftedal's and Sverdrup's ownership and editing of *Folkebladet*. Like the Synod pastors who believed the ministry could not be combined with acting, Gunnersen had felt that editing a paper and the teaching of theology could only mean neglect of the latter. He had come to have some following among Conference pastors, and, to appease these dissidents, Oftedal had turned the editorship over to Johannes Skørdalsvold. This had not satisfied Gunnersen, and in the spring he resigned, to the great surprise of his colleagues. Uneasy about being the center of the controversy, Professor Sverdrup also resigned, and Oftedal did so shortly afterward. When the Conference held its annual meeting in the summer of 1883, they had no faculty for the upcoming fall term at Augsburg Seminary. After some discussion, the convention turned to choosing professors. All three were nominated, but only Sverdrup and Oftedal received enough votes to be elected. Both accepted, and, in a session charged with emotion, they asked forgiveness for the worry and sorrow they had caused. Oftedal announced that *Folkebladet* would be placed in the hands of a corporation, saying that steps had already been taken in that direction. But by December, 1884—a year and a half later—Oftedal seems to have sensed that the objections to his being associated with *Folkebladet* were no longer an issue.

Later, Janson may have regretted that he had challenged Oftedal on so minor a matter. In December, Oftedal reported that the Reverend Martin R. Schermerhorn had left the Unitarian church to go into the Episcopalian ministry. It was not surprising, Oftedal felt, that Schermerhorn had had enough of so retrogressive a faith. (That Unitarianism was retrogressive had been the view taken by *Folkebladet* in 1881 when Janson began his ministry. The writer at that time—presumably Sverdrup—had said that Norwegians would recognize Unitarianism as the same worn-out rationalism that had prevailed in Norway in the early nineteenth century, until it was dispelled by the evangelism of the peasant lay preacher, Hans Nielsen Hauge.) Oftedal went on to say that Schermerhorn's move illustrated the plight of Unitarians, who were neither fish nor fowl, not Christians and not freethinkers—a situation which was untenable.

It was the word *retrogressive* that rankled with Janson. That, he maintained, was an unworthy thing to say. His reply was printed in *Folkebladet* the week after Oftedal had written of Schermerhorn's defection. Perhaps, Janson said, in his next move Schermerhorn might join the Conference. Orthodox preachers frequently went over to Unitarianism. Why was that not reported in *Folkebladet*? For that matter, Janson was sure there were many members of the Conference who agreed with the Unitarian view but were afraid to say so.[48]

Beneath this letter was printed Oftedal's "Brief Reply." Janson's comments, Oftedal said, were typical of freethinkers and Unitarians as well as of Catholics and Missourians, all of whom had such partisan narrowmindedness that they had only belittling things to say about those who had other views. Furthermore, Janson might look to his own Unitarian congregations; if he were to examine them, he would lose more members than the Conference would. Members of the Conference held to their faith through personal conviction, and indeed they knew how to evaluate Yankee funds for missionary work among the Norwegians at its true worth.

Janson turned to *Budstikken* the next week. He had additional information on Schermerhorn. (Neither Janson nor Oftedal knew the man.) Shortly after Oftedal's report, Janson had had a visit from the Reverend Grindall Reynolds, secretary of the American Unitarian Association. When told that Schermerhorn had accepted the Trinity after serious study, Reynolds had smiled, saying that four days before going over to the Episcopalians, Schermerhorn had asked for a Unitarian church. According to Reynolds, he was a restless, unsteady man who had wanted to serve in well-established churches and did not want to go where development was needed.

Janson wrote of the orthodox ministers who had become Unitarians. (He could name fifty-four but felt there were undoubtedly more.) He spoke of the growth of Unitarianism in the United States and Europe, citing increases in England, Ireland, Scotland, Germany, and even Sweden. Norway had not advanced that far as yet.[49]

Folkebladet would not acknowledge Unitarians to be Christians; they were neither fish nor fowl. But they did not feel ambivalent and were content to be "simply truthful and sound people."

9

On December 23 Oftedal introduced in *Folkebladet* a matter that, for the moment, far overshadowed the Schermerhorn affair. Janson had libeled the Norwegian people *before Americans*. He had read one of his stories in which a brutal husband had driven his wife to suicide, implying that such treatment was the direct result of the teachings of the Lutheran church. This was a falsification for the sake of American applause. "To call the whole thing insane would be merciful."[50]

Oftedal was referring to "Wives, Submit Yourselves unto Your Husbands," which Janson by this time had translated into English. Early in December, he had read the story to an audience which included a reporter, a woman from the *Minneapolis Evening Journal*. She had been deeply impressed, and on December 10 her account, "A Pathetic Story," appeared in the paper. Mr. Janson, she said, was a celebrated author in his native Norway, standing next to Bjørnstjerne Bjørnson. He had been in this country only two years, but he had a summer home in a farming region in Minnesota and had had the opportunity to observe the home life of immigrants first hand. "This life, barren as it might seem to an outsider, he finds full of pathetic interest. In many a humble Norwegian home is being enacted a tragedy that enacted on the stage would melt the hardest heart. Especially has the position of the wives of Scandinavian farmers moved him—lives of drudgery and mental degradation."

Giving a résumé of the plot, she explained, "There are five sects of Lutherans, holding a wide range of belief from extreme bigotry to advanced liberalism." The husband of Emma [the wife in Janson's story] belonged to the strictest sect, one which did not send children to the public schools, allowed no American books in the house, and limited reading to the Bible and the Catechism in the mother tongue. The husband looks upon a woman as his inferior, and, taking his cue from the priest, "dings constantly in her ear his favorite text, 'Wives, obey your husbands.' "

After hearing the story, the reporter wrote, one realized that the novelist need not go abroad for themes but could find them at his very door: "In listening to this true and tragic recital, one ceases to wonder that the majority of suicides in the Northwest are farmers' wives. It is to be hoped that this story of Mr. Janson which is soon to appear in print will awaken public interest and sympathy in behalf of a class of our own Minnesota citizens whose position is as truly deplorable as that of the plantation slaves in the old days before the war." Oftedal had many objections to the story, but that it should give outsiders the impression that all Norwegian farm women lived under conditions comparable to the slaves in the South was insupportable. If Janson had not left the Lutheran church so early, he would have remembered that the Catechism explicitly states that a husband should love his wife as Christ loved the church. (Janson had graduated *cum laude* in theology from the same university as Oftedal.) But Oftedal

130

could only plead with Janson, as a matter of honor, to cite an instance— just one—in which a Norwegian farm woman had killed herself because of the particular circumstances given in the story.

This was the way things stood between the two men at Christmas. Shortly before the holiday, Drude wrote to Aubertine Woodward in Madison, showing herself to be so unhappy and discouraged that Mrs. Rasmus B. Anderson became alarmed. Both she and Miss Woodward immediately sent cards and letters to Drude so that they would reach her on Christmas Eve. On New Year's Day, Drude wrote to thank them, sending her letter to Mrs. Anderson. With illness in the house, life had been especially hectic; she had not had a second to herself. Her mood had improved somewhat; she was not as depressed as she had been when she had written to Miss Woodward. For one thing, Christmas had been better than anything she had anticipated. Ivar had been well enough to be downstairs on Christmas Eve for the family festivities. Then her sister and niece had been with them, and she had found it pleasant to have some of her own relatives around once again. It was still bitterly cold; Minneapolis certainly did not have a climate fit to live in. She supposed it affected her so deeply because she was not very strong in the first place. It was horrible when one lost courage and happiness in living, but she had been depressed all fall. She hoped better things were in store—not so much sickness. "I am so egotistical," she apologized, "for I write only about us and what we have gone through—but it is still so close to me."

Kristofer was slaving away and fighting, Drude continued, in a bitter feud with Professor Oftedal, who had attacked him hysterically. Oftedal was supposed to have said that he had to do it to keep his position—to prove his devotion to the pure teachings—but Drude felt he enjoyed it. "I don't know another person for whom I have such contempt."[51]

131

5

Janson
Versus Oftedal

THE DANES, Kristofer Janson wrote in the *Christian Register* of June 11, 1885, were light-minded and amiable, but they were the least religious of the Scandinavians. The Swedes had strong feelings but were inclined to sentimentality, and the Norwegians were critical and tenacious and thus most fit for a rationalistic view of religion. Not in his wildest dreams could Janson have hoped to bring Sven Oftedal to look with a sympathetic eye on rationalistic religion, but the man certainly met the criteria. As he and Janson had ended the old year, so they began the new. But Oftedal was by no means the only one incensed over the *Journal's* review of "Wives." Early in 1885, a Minneapolis paper printed the following letter:

"Editor Journal: Journalistic ignorance of the characteristics of a nation may be excusable but a wilful misrepresentation of the people is a dishonor; therefore as an American citizen and a Norwegian by birth, I protest Rev. Kristofer Jansen's misrepresentation of the Scandinavian farmers and their wives as exhibited in the *Evening Journal* of December 10, 1884.

"I do not blame Rev. Jansen because he does not stand next to Bjørnson as an author, neither do I blame him because he is a Unitarian missionary; but when he upbraids the Norwegians because they are Lutherans and wilfully misrepresents the moral and intellectual conditions of his own countrymen, then self-respect ceases to be a virtue.

"Can our American friends really believe that the Scandinavian farmers as a class are sordid, bigoted, and brutal; that their wives live a life of hopeless drudgery and mental degradation; that the farming community of the Northwest is a neighborhood of suicides; that secret marriages and divorces is the true characteristic of the Norwegians; that they are destitute of American books and forbid their children to attend the common schools of the land? If so, I pity your credulity. Minneapolis may be an elysium for runaway wives, but that is no reason why a class of intelligent men and women should be insulted and abused.

"Mr. Editor, it is but simple justice to publish this protest and thereby correct an erroneous impression made by Rev. Jansen's 'Wives, Obey Your Husbands.' In behalf of justice and equal rights, O. J. Rollevson, School Supt. of Chippewa Co., Minn."[1]

Shortly thereafter, Oftedal again took up the Schermerhorn issue in *Folkebladet*. During the Christmas interval, he had written to Schermerhorn, and thus he had the latter's own word that he would gladly have remained in the Unitarian church had he been permitted to preach "three persons in one God." The Reverend Grindall Reynolds had certainly known this, Oftedal wrote, adding that Unitarians could not have much of a foundation when they had to resort to such repressive devices. "Possibly Pastor Janson's missionary work will make them better," he said. Janson would find this news a bitter pill to swallow.[2]

Janson still had not answered Oftedal's objections to "Wives," and now he must also respond to the latest news about Schermerhorn. Fortunately, Rollevson had asked only for justice and equal rights, demands easily satisfied by the printing of his letter. Janson sent his response concerning Schermerhorn to *Folkebladet,* and that on "Wives" to *Budstikken*. Both appeared on the same day.

In *Folkebladet,* Janson said he was aggrieved that the secretary of the American Unitarian Association had been accused of lying and that he himself was considered a dupe. He was, however, glad that they now had Schermerhorn's own word he had wanted to preach the trinity as a Unitarian, but it did strike one as strange that a man should want to stay in a sect and preach against its basic tenet. One thing more: the *Christian Register* had reported that George C. Cressy of the Presbyterian Andover Seminary had entered the Unitarian ministry. Was Oftedal interested in going into that?[3]

In *Budstikken,* Janson systematically took up Oftedal's charges, from the point that "Wives" was a re-hash of the Muus case[4] to his willfully defaming Norwegians before Americans. "Wives" had nothing to do with the Muus case; it was based upon events related to Janson by the brother of Emma, the suicide in the tale. Oftedal would have

133

realized that, if he had known the story instead of relying on the *Evening Journal*. Janson had read the piece to audiences in Chicago and Minneapolis; no one had been insulted, but many had told him that the circumstances depicted were true. (He had evidently forgotten Dr. Julson, or possibly had been persuaded by Hamsun that the physician was too stupid to be considered.) So far as belittling his own people was concerned, this was precisely the kind of criticism that had been leveled at Ibsen, Bjørnson, Lie, and Kielland when their work had been translated into French, German, and English. And Oftedal need not be disturbed that the *Evening Journal's* reporter had spoken of Janson as being second only to Bjørnson. All that indicated was the newspaper writer was not acquainted with Norwegian literature—or that some people put a higher value on Janson's writing than did Sven Oftedal.[5]

This exchange was to draw in others. Women addressed letters to *Folkebladet,* assuring Oftedal that he was right in objecting to the willful misrepresentation of Norwegian farm women. Writers to *Budstikken,* a liberal paper, generally hid behind pseudonyms. Silo Sagen wondered why Oftedal had not also written to Secretary Reynolds. "Keep on missing, Professor," he wrote. "When you lay in a new supply of cannons, get round ones, for the pointed may bounce off the church wall." Sixtus Decimus aired his resentment against Oftedal, sarcastically referring to him as "King Svein" and "Prelate Svein." It was pitiful, he said, to observe Oftedal's regard for the spiritual welfare of his people, but, if he kept on as he had been doing, he was not likely to get many converts, and he might as well give up on Janson. The professor worked hard for temperance. (Oftedal was an earnest crusader in that field and apparently an effective one, for his work was later—in more peaceful times—to draw a tribute from Janson.) He also collected money for his church, Sixtus Decimus continued. After one of his speeches, people had come forward to make donations. But Oftedal had urged larger contributions, asking people to give notes, which they did. These, the writer charged, the professor had sold to a bank which charged the donors ten per cent interest. "Whichever is the greater humbug," Sixtus Decimus asked, "to sell whisky or collect church funds in this manner? I will let others judge."[6]

2

While this was going on, Janson had been eyeing north Minneapolis as the site of another mission. By and large the immigrants there were

134

spread over a wider area than those in south Minneapolis. The Conference had not succeeded in establishing a stable congregation in that area until the late 1870s, and it was 1884 before the Synod had a congregation of ten families, even though the settlement of the vicinity by Norwegians went back to the mid-1860s.[7] They had not been drawn into the many clubs and organizations in south Minneapolis. Many of them were from Selbu, a province in Norway near the city of Trondhjem. Norwegians in south Minneapolis didn't know quite what to make of them. More than seventy years later, old men and women who had lived on the south side spoke of the Selbygs as if they were still puzzled by them. "Nothing wrong with them at all! Finest kind of people, honest and hard-working—but a little odd." (Ironically, it was these north-side Norwegians who were to organize the Sons of Norway ten years after Janson first attempted his mission. When it became known that they had decided to call themselves the Sons of Norway, Norwegians on the south side took it as something of an affront, commenting dryly that the "Sons of Selbu" would have been more appropriate.)

Janson, who began holding services every Monday evening in Hunt's Hall on Plymouth Avenue in mid-January, 1885, never spoke of this activity with the enthusiasm that characterized his other new ventures. Certainly he had more reason to be hopeful about a discussion club he organized about the same time, which met every Saturday night in a hall on Third and Nicollet, for the purpose of dealing with social and political issues—not religion.[8]

Throughout these days, he continued to cudgel his brain for new ways of raising money for the church building. The American Unitarian Association had offered the Minneapolis congregation an interest-free loan of $5,000 on condition that the group raise an equal sum. This Janson explained in an article in *Unity* in mid-April, saying that they already had $2,000, were busily soliciting in Minneapolis, and had mailed letters to every Unitarian church in the United States, asking each for a five-dollar contribution. Hopeful of a flow of funds, he had organized a committee of prominent American businessmen to oversee and audit all contributions. The committee, headed by Robert Hall, secretary of the Board of Trade, included S. C. Gale and Dr. A. Barnard.[9] By April, *Scandinavia* had concluded its serialization of the English version of "Wives," and the editor commented that opposition to the story could be interpreted as a sign of national weakness among the Norwegians, who were unwilling to look on the darker side of the lives of their own people.[10]

135

In June, Janson attended the National Unitarian anniversary meetings in Boston. After these, Janson remained in the East to lecture in Massachusetts, New York, and Rhode Island—for the benefit of the building fund. By that time, Easterners had read of the disputes over Schermerhorn and "Wives" which Janson had reported in the *Christian Register*. He had also revealed that ground had been broken for the church and that the congregation would again hold a week-long bazaar in the fall. He had been forced to add, however, that he doubted the bazaar would bring in enough money and so additional appeals to American Unitarians would be necessary.[11]

When he returned to Minneapolis, he had over $300 from his lectures and from additional contributions. The basement walls of the church, at Twelfth Avenue South and Ninth Street, were up, and there was an outside chance that the basement might be ready for use in the fall. In his absence, the women's society had given a strawberry festival, clearing $112; with the $160 already in their treasury, they would be able to pay for benches and chairs. This heartening news Janson relayed in another *Christian Register* article beginning, "It will be a relief to many to know I have now left the Eastern States for a while, so the churches need not any longer to pray, 'God free us from the furious Norseman.' " He listed the names of individuals and organizations which had helped, going on to say that the contract for the basement was for $6,025. This sum was to be paid in three installments. The first two they could raise, but the third—the $1,525 due on the first of September—they could not as yet pay. The letter-writing experiment had not been entirely successful, many of the letters "having gone to that sad place called the wastebasket, I presume."[12]

Years later, in his autobiography, Janson was to speak gratefully of the generosity of the Americans, which no one could doubt. Very much the same appeal was sent to *Unity,* where Jones commented that two churches—the First Unitarian Society and the Scandinavian mission—were erecting buildings in Minneapolis at the same time. If the Americans ever grumbled at Janson's incessant pleas, such rumblings never reached the surface. Jones was to remind readers that the Norwegian poet-preacher was both a home and a foreign missionary, working alone in a large field. "Creed-bound evangicals are our heathen," Jones declared, "and none are more creed-bound than the Scandinavian Lutherans."[13]

While Janson was in the East, Drude, her daughters, and the Behr girls sewed every Saturday afternoon, in preparation for July and August in Brown County. They did not make their own clothing, but they worked on costumes for tableaux and plays. They sat in the tower room, which first had to be cleaned because of Eilev's pigeons which roosted in the tower. Bats also hung there; the girls did not seem to mind them, but it was quite a task, Dina Behr Kolderup later recalled, climbing up the steep stairway which led from the girls' bedroom, burdened with soap and water, to wash up after "those awfully dirty pigeons." Eilev, then fifteen, had interested his brother Ivar in his varied collection: tumblers, blowers, blue-blacks, fantails, carriers. (As an old man, he spoke of the birds with pride, remembering that when he later quit high school to try his luck out West, he gave them to a boy named Lars Smeby, the son of a policeman.) In those days, Eilev could hardly wait to be through with school to get back to his pigeons, always carrying wheat in his pockets so that the birds swooped down as he approached the house, perching on his shoulders while he filled each hand with grain to feed them.

Late in June, the Jansons set out for Brown County—a party of eight. "Old Anne" (Gamle Anne), the maid who had accompanied them from Norway, was no longer one of the household; she had married a farmer and lived near Mankato. Dina Behr Kolderup has described the trip, and—while she did not specify 1885 precisely—the pattern was unvaried. They took the train to Madelia, where a lumber wagon drawn by two sturdy brown horses awaited them. Drude and Kristofer, with Borghild, the youngest child, sat up beside Hansa Nils, the driver. Ivar and Eilev rode on the horses, and the rest of the children, along with the luggage, found places in the bed of the wagon. They bumped along for fifteen miles over pitted roads and under a broiling sun. Finally, as they rounded the woods, they could see the parsonage and church on the hill, and the children shrieked with delight. Soon bags, boxes, and suitcases must be unloaded, each person taking care of his own. "And then began the most wonderful country life ever a child could have. Tante held us to regulations: the girls must help the maid—Signe and I one week, Borghild and Agnes the next, with Ingeborg, gentle and sweet, helping all the time. She was an angel; I thought she surely would become a minister."

On weekdays the girls wore only one garment—dark blue seersucker bloomers, with an overblouse of the same material. No girls anywhere wore anything like it, Mrs. Kolderup recalled. Drude had designed it as practical; the dark blue did not show dirt and the seersucker did not have to be ironed. When washday came, Kristofer and the girls managed with water from the Ourens' well. Every morning after breakfast, each person made a sandwich to tide him over the noon hour and to insure Kristofer and Drude an unbroken day for writing or study. After morning chores were over, the young people kept out of the way of their elders, who sat working on the screened porch, moving as the sun advanced. The girls often visited neighboring farms, where they were permitted to "help" in one way or another, and the boys usually went hunting or fishing. Late in the afternoon the whole family went for a swim, *au naturel,* for they had the lake to themselves. On Saturday nights, the boys usually attended square dances in the neighborhood. The girls sat on the screened porch while Janson read from the manuscript he was working on, asking Drude for criticism. As darkness came on, Dina was allowed the privileged place in Kristofer's lap, where she made braids with strands of his beard. They all sang "Fred dveler over land og by" (Peace Dwells over Land and Town) and other favorites. As Mrs. Kolderup later wrote, "We watched the thousands of fireflies playing in the bushes and listened to the crickets chirping their accompaniment. We were as close to heaven and God and Jesus Christ as anyone ever could be on this earth."[14]

The church and parsonage were located (and still are) on a hill said to be the highest point in Brown County. According to legend, Jesuit missionaries, making their way through the wilderness, named it Mount Pisquah after a range in ancient Palestine. Janson liked the name and frequently used it, but popularly it was called "the Hill" (*haugen*). Sunday was festive with the congregation arriving about ten in the morning and staying until sundown, when the farmers had to return home for evening chores. The day began with Janson in city ministerial dress, which included a stiff white shirt and a long Prince Albert coat. Accompanied by the girls—sometimes wearing Norwegian national costumes but always in their best—he raised the flag. From this eminence, they watched the teams arrive, waving and calling to the children of the various families who responded in turn. All brought food to supply the minister and his family for the coming week: eggs, butter, milk, sweet and sour cream, vegetables, chickens, meat, baked goods, which must be placed in the pantry or cooler. This bounty was part of the idyll, with only now and then an irregularity—as when an old woman brought butter packed in a chamber pot![15]

The services began with Drude at the parlor-size organ, pumping with her feet as she played and lowering her head to peer at the notes, for she was nearsighted and would sometimes dispense with her pince-nez glasses in the stifling midsummer heat. Janson, using the sermons he had given in Minneapolis, stood before the congregation, manuscript in hand, now and then laying it down on the lectern as he mopped his brow or waited until a mother could carry out a wailing infant.

After church, everyone gathered on the lawn for a picnic, the adults getting coffee dispensed from the parsonage porch. Later, visiting and small talk followed as a band played what Mrs. Kolderup recalled as "patriotic tunes." As the afternoon wore on, the adults gathered together—still out of doors—and Janson read to them one of his own stories or a selection he had used for his Sunday evenings in Minneapolis the winter before. Then, after the singing of a hymn and prayer, parents rounded up their children, wagons were loaded, and team after team made the descent down the gradual slope from the hill.[16]

During those weekdays on the screened porch, Janson wrote a novelette, *Vildrose* (The Wild Rose). His spirited heroine, Gunhild, had grown up in the Minnesota forest region, where she had made friends with the Indians and won the devotion of an Indian boy who comes to be known as Clever Hjort (Flink Hjort). Curious about what city life might be like, she runs away to St. Paul but finally returns to her forest home, where she dies a heroic death. Sentimental and melodramatic as the story is, it does contain an engrossing account of the Indian troubles in Minnesota in 1862.[17]

4

When the Jansons returned to Minneapolis in September, the church basement was still not ready and services had to be held in Peterson's Hall. How the congregation met the payment of $1,525 due on September first we do not know. For some reason, plans for another bazaar were given up—possibly because the one of the year before had set so high a standard that the congregation shrank from the work involved to beat their own record. Instead, they gave a program and dance on Sunday evening. Had Janson reckoned with how critical and tenacious Professor Sven Oftedal could be, he might possibly have decided that the bazaar was the better option after all. And, later, Oftedal might have had second thoughts about the whole thing, too, for he found himself using the pointed cannon Silo Sagen had spoken of—if that somewhat cryptic remark has been rightfully interpreted.

On the fateful Sunday of October 4, Janson delivered a sermon entitled "The Many Evils of Intemperance" in Peterson's Hall. As he had said in his *Nyt Tidsskrift* article two years before, the evil did not lie in alcohol but in human weakness. He could see nothing wrong in an adult's indulging in an occasional dram, so long as he had enough self-respect not to degrade himself. But if one knew that such moderate drinking was impossible for him, he should abstain completely. Unfortunately, there were many Norwegians who drank to excess, and Janson went on to say that much of the poverty of immigrant families was traceable to drunkenness. The sermon was reported the next day in the *Minneapolis Tribune.*[18]

In the evening, the program and dance were given, the affair lasting until one o'clock, with Janson present until the end. At one point, a group of Irishmen entered, going on the dance floor while wearing their hats and smoking cigars. When told such conduct would not be tolerated, they affably put out the cigars and removed their hats. The dance had been well attended and was marred by no other incidents.

The following week "A Temperance Talk and a Congregational Ball" appeared in *Folkebladet.* Janson's advice, summarized as "Drink, but do not get drunk," was bad enough, but he had gone on to say that the drunkenness of the Scandinavians was a disgrace to the city. He had also asserted that many immigrants lived in misery because of drunkenness. Such words were not likely to raise people's standards. And Janson had not only said this, but had had his remarks printed in the *Tribune,* again maligning his own nationality before Americans. While some Scandinavians did drink, Editor Oftedal admitted, both moderately and immoderately, they were not worse than any other people, and it was heartless of Janson to condemn them in such a manner. "If, for a moment, Pastor Janson will desert his Yankee easy chair and go among the poor, he will find many who are so because they are without work, and, scarlet with shame, he will go back to his Yankee mission realizing the need among our people that is not caused by drunkenness."

This was only the half of it. In the evening, Janson's congregation had given an entertainment—first a program, and then the floor had been cleared and people had danced until late at night—on a Sunday and under the auspices of a Unitarian minister. "Oh, if only a warning voice had been sounded to the young people."[19]

Janson had not said that the Scandinavians were a disgrace to the city; the *Tribune* had misquoted him—or so he replied to Oftedal two weeks later in *Folkebladet.* However, he had maintained that much of the poverty among the Scandinavians was due to drunkenness, and this he still believed to be true. He was surprised that *Folkebladet* should object to his telling people to leave liquor alone if they could not drink in moderation, and puzzled why the Sunday evening entertainment should be criticized, for it had proved people could get together and enjoy themselves without drinking. Coffee, lemonade, and ice cream had been served, and the affair had been orderly in every respect. If *Folkebladet* objected to dancing, that was its privilege; Janson regarded it as a pleasant type of recreation. Sunday had been chosen because that was the day most people were free, and furthermore the Scandinavian Lutherans did not, traditionally, hold to the Jewish conception of the Sabbath. If Janson enjoyed slandering his own people, he surely would not spend his time working among them. And he could not see why he should be criticized for accepting a salary from the American Unitarian Association while his congregation was still young and struggling.[20]

So the exchanges began. Janson did not get to strike a telling blow until early in November, when the discussion centered on who had been present at the dance. He admitted the Irishmen had given him a few moments' concern, but they had at once mended their ways and conducted themselves so well that no one could object to their presence, especially since this had been a public dance and open to anyone who paid admission. And there had been only a few Irishmen. Most of the outsiders present had been Conference people. *Folkebladet* had stated that respectable young people would not attend such an affair, but Janson said that hardly seemed to be the case. They had been very well behaved, he declared, adding that he had always found Conference people to be so, as long as they kept out of *Folkebladet*.[21]

Oftedal could use mockery too—and better the example. "Pastor Janson Is Hopping!" (Pastor Janson hopper!) was the headline of an article in *Folkebladet*. Janson was described as jumping about in complete confusion—first on one foot and then on the other, gyrating from head to foot because three things bothered him "as a hot floor affects cold feet": that the public dance had been given under the auspices of his church, that he was in the pay of the Yankees, and that he had slandered his own people.

Janson had made no attempt to deny that the dance had been free for all, Oftedal continued, and that he had been present until one o'clock in the morning. The Irishmen, wearing hats and smoking cigars, had invaded the dance floor, but on being reproved had behaved themselves, and the affair had been orderly and respectable. But on

141

that point Pastor Janson was wrong; not even the best people could make such a gathering respectable. Furthermore, by saying that many Conference people had been present, Janson had slandered young people. Who were they? Until he named names, *Folkebladet* must assume the statement to be false.

Janson, Oftedal charged, became nervous when his salary from the Yankees was as much as mentioned, saying that the Conference would rather have him starve. Nothing could be further from the truth, but they did not want him to take money from strangers for unworthy work. If he had written his defamatory statements about his own people in Dano-Norwegian, people would have known how to judge them. Instead, they were written in English, to shame the Norwegians before the Americans. Certainly the Yankees were not entitled to everything for one thousand a year.[22]

Janson answered briefly in *Budstikken*: "*Folkebladet* has honored me with an attack of such a nature that I cannot descend to answer it. I believed, in the last analysis, I was dealing with a gentleman. That belief I am forced to relinquish, and it grieves me."[23] This was merely an evasion, *Folkebladet* countered. Until Janson named the Conference people present at the dance, his statement would be regarded as a falsehood. "We wait patiently for the evidence."[24] Janson remained silent, but on Christmas Eve *Budstikken* published a letter from Willmar containing shocking news, signed with the initials "L. A." On December 12, the Conference church in that town had sponsored a dance. In the morning posters, placed in prominent places, had announced:

To-night! To-night!
Coffee and Cake
Sociable
In Tvedson Bros' Hall
After refreshments the floor will be cleared
and a social Dance will follow
Proceeds for the Conference Church Christmas tree

The word *dance,* L. A. declared, had been printed in letters three inches high. He was not, he wrote, a member of either the Conference or of Janson's congregation, but he hoped this news would help people judge the petty attacks *Folkebladet* had launched against "a noble opponent."[25]

L. A., *Folkebladet* was to inform readers later in December, was Ludvig Arctander. (He was a teacher in Willmar who had just passed

142

his bar examination; in future years, he was to have a long career as an attorney in Minneapolis.) Under the caption, "Another Christmas Greeting in Support of Pastor Janson," *Folkebladet* reprinted Arctander's letter from *Budstikken*. Before going into how audaciously the man had misrepresented things in Willmar, Oftedal reminded his readers that Janson still had not come up with the names of the Conference people at the dance. The goings-on in Willmar had been the result of a series of errors. A person—not a member of the Conference church—was to get the placards printed. When he asked whether or not there was to be dancing, he was erroneously told dancing would follow refreshments. As soon as Conference members saw the posters, they systematically removed them and had others printed. The social was held. After the ice cream and cake had been served, private persons present hired a musician for $2.00 and dancing followed. As soon as the music began, the Conference people left, and their church did not accept a cent from the proceeds. This explanation had been given by G. Berger Quale of Willmar, who wanted it printed so "the truth be known." His account was verified by Thos. Osmundson, president of the board of trustees of the Conference church in Willmar.[26]

There were other exchanges—repetitions of what had passed before—between Janson and Oftedal. When "H.P.P." in a letter to *Budstikken* complained he was sick and tired of the whole thing, he probably expressed the feeling of many others. Nevertheless, he tried his hand at arbitration: he did not think holding a dance was an appropriate way for a church to raise money, but he couldn't see why Janson should be criticized for accepting a salary from the Unitarians when he had been ordained by them, nor why there was so much ado about the Unitarians having a missionary to the Scandinavians, when the same practice was followed by the Baptists and Methodists.[27]

5

All of this had not kept the Jansons—nor Oftedal either, for that matter—from going about the work of the day. By January, Janson seems to have recovered from his disappointment at not finding Oftedal a gentleman and could treat the whole thing jauntily again—no doubt bolstered by Arctander's news from Willmar. When he described the children's Christmas program at his church, he mentioned that the youngsters had joined hands and circled the Christmas tree, explicitly instructed to keep time to the music. "We intend to make a clean breast of such things hereafter."[28] Yet, while important events had taken place in the Jansons' lives in the fall of 1885—the dedication of the basement, the official naming of the church, and the convention of the Women's Suffrage Association—throughout it all, the newspaper feud cast some shadow.

The dedication had taken place Sunday morning, November 15. "This was the happiest day of our lives since we came to Minneapolis," Drude wrote to Mrs. Rasmus B. Anderson. She and Mrs. Gudmund Johnson had not only been in charge of decorating the church, but they, accompanied by Christian Haug, had also made the rounds of various business establishments in the city, asking for contributions for the furnishing of the rooms. They had come back with many beautiful things. The women's society had also been able to collect attractive articles. The basement had a large lecture room, a parlor, a library, and a kitchen. "The idea was to make the place look as much like a home as possible," Drude wrote to Mrs. Anderson. By the time they had finished, the parlor was delightfully furnished; light-colored curtains hung at all the windows and drapes at the archways between the rooms. Janson was later to say that the monotony of the white walls had been broken by a broad border of brown and blue and by photographs of the Sistine Chapel, and that other masterpieces of Christian art decorated the walls of the lecture hall. The library and parlor were ornamented with scenes illustrating events in Scandinavian history, photographs of the work of Scandinavian painters. All of this drew exclamations from everyone entering. Americans told Drude that the Norwegian church was much more attractive than theirs, even though their new Unitarian building had cost two to three times as much.[29]

An estimated 450 people had been present at the dedication; the next day the *Minneapolis Morning Tribune* devoted more than a column to it. Janson had preached on "Why Have We Built This House?"—explaining that the Unitarians looked upon Jesus Christ as their great leader. They believed in the spirit of God even though they rejected the Trinity and the person of the Holy Ghost, and regarded the religious life as growth and development rather than as blind acceptance of dogma. Following this sermon, he had spoken in English for the benefit of the many Americans present, regretting the language barrier that prevented closer cooperation between the two Unitarian societies, but adding that both could stretch out their arms and love one another. At intervals during the service, the choir of the First Unitarian Society sang, and later Janson introduced the Reverend Henry M. Simmons. who gave what the *Morning Tribune* described as "a very vigorous and lively address." Following that, all sang the doxology, "Praise God from Whom All Blessings Flow," and the service closed with a benediction. In the evening, Janson read Ibsen's *Brand* before a full house. Drude wrote to Mrs. Anderson that the basement showed up to great advantage when the lamps were lighted at night.[30]

Now that the basement was completed, the Scandinavian mission was beginning to approximate what Janson had envisioned from the first: the encouragement of intellectual as well as spiritual growth. So he wrote to Bjørnson early in December, 1885. The church basement was open all Sunday afternoon. People were encouraged to make use of the library, which was stocked with books, newspapers, and magazines. Late in the afternoon they could buy coffee and light refreshments and thus have no need to leave until after Janson had given his Sunday evening reading, at the time one of a series on *Peer Gynt*. On another evening, the discussion club met in the church. Every Monday morning, Janson's sermon of the day before appeared in the *Minneapolis Morning Tribune,* Janson himself doing the translating. He sent along a copy of one of them to Bjørnson, saying that the translating meant additional work but brought his mission to the attention of the Americans and gave him prestige with the Scandinavians as well. Then he spoke briefly of the newspaper feud: "Oftedal and his cohorts are at present attacking me violently, but, God be praised, with such extreme rudeness they hurt their own cause."[31]

Up to this time, Janson's congregation in Minneapolis had been sometimes called the Free Christian Church and was usually listed in city directories as the Second Unitarian Society. On December 13, 1885, it was formally named Nazareth Church (Nasaret Kirke). At the same time, the congregation adopted the Ames statement as its motto: "In the love of truth and the spirit of Jesus Christ, we join for the worship of God and the service of man." This was inscribed on a plaque and placed on the outside of the church. Janson's sermon had as its text the words of Nathanael in John 1:46: "Can any good thing come out of Nazareth?" He was to draw a parallel between the despised Nazarenes of Galilee and his own flock then being pilloried in the newspapers. Elaborating on the newly adopted motto, Janson hoped the congregation would emulate the Nazarenes—a gentle, serious people more intermingled with other races than the rigidly pietistic Jews of Judea. Unitarians would demand no confession of faith from members, only the promise to lead an upright life; they would regard all men as brethren, welcoming to their pulpit preachers of all persuasions, including Jewish rabbis and Mohammedan teachers—all who

145

worshipped the one God and practiced brotherly love. Of the two accounts of Jesus Christ given in the gospels—the one of the child born under miraculous circumstances in Bethlehem and the other of the man from Nazareth, the son of Joseph—they would follow the latter, the one verified by history. Thus committed, they would hope "something good might come out of Nazareth."[32]

Pleased as Drude was over the dedication and all that the beautifully furnished church basement promised, she had had another experience that had given her fresh vitality. Only Bjørnson would ever understand what this had meant to her. After a long silence, she wrote him shortly after the dedication. All spring she had been very depressed—with good reason—for her brother Morten had fallen into difficulties that had culminated in his arrest, and Drude had been worried over the welfare of his family and had grieved over the sorrow this had given her aged father. During that time, she could not write to Bjørnson; he would see through any facade. After a long period of groping and unrest, she had emerged from her depression, resolved to become as fine a person as possible. The event which had triggered the change in her was the convention of the Women's Suffrage Association held in Minneapolis in the middle of October, 1885. She had attended all sessions; it was one of the greatest experiences she had ever had. "You can't believe what it meant to me to see those women, most of whom have become gray in the service of ideas to which they had dedicated their lives—and yet remained so youthfully fresh and warm, so keen and intelligent that anyone not a beast or a mean-spirited person (and there are plenty of those among both the Americans and Scandinavians) had to love them."

The pearl among them, Drude continued, had been Lucy Stone, the president of the Association. An elderly woman with a round, childish face, pink cheeks, a charming smile, she had a voice the like of which Drude had never known. "One dared not move while she talked for fear of missing a single sound; her fine humor, the depth of her commitment, the deep seriousness with which she presented the cause she loved were all so captivating that she reached even the stupidest person." The last night, when she had delivered her farewell address, she had held her audience enthralled even though it was so vast it filled the huge Universalist church to the entrance. None of the others, Drude continued, was the equal of Lucy Stone, but every one was a true, serious woman. A Mrs. Duniway of Oregon was extremely unattractive in appearance but so gifted one forgot everything else once she began to speak. She had gone to Oregon Territory as a young woman, had made her living by sewing until she had been able to buy a printing press, and then she had begun publishing *The New Northwest*, the second paper devoted to women's rights in America.

Drude also described the dedication, enclosing a copy of Kristofer's address. She wished Bjørnson might have heard the talk given by the Reverend Henry M. Simmons—so humorous yet so full of fundamental goodness—a combination Drude found appealing and rather characteristic of American ministers, especially the Unitarian. Her sons, Ivar and Eilev, were becoming tall young men, very much absorbed in their pigeons. Arne, the third son and the child most affected by the Brown County tornado, had been placed in a private school where they hoped he would develop. The girls were thriving.[33]

Drude's good mood continued—shadowed only by "the horrible attacks on Kristofer carried in *Folkebladet*." Concerning these, she wrote to Mrs. Rasmus B. Anderson in January, 1886. They no longer saw the Gjertsens (not the pastor but the Gerhard Gjertsens, the younger brother of the minister, a man prominent in political activities). Drude supposed that they had allied themselves with Oftedal— all of which seems to show that the feud was acrimonious enough to affect social relations. But the Jansons had been delightfully surprised at Christmas by a coffee and tea serving set sent them by ladies in Boston. As usual, she found herself lacking energy in the winter, but she was grateful there had been no illness in the family. She was still an ardent feminist, signing herself "Drude Krog Janson" and explaining in a postscript, "You can see I have resumed my maiden name, something I have long thought of doing, feeling I should not drop it simply because I married."[34]

The same day, she sent off a cheerful message to Bjørnson, thanking him for copies of *Geography and Love* and *The King*. The latter she had not got round to reading, but *Geography and Love* she had found highly amusing, insisting that the leading character, the professor, was none other than Bjørnson himself. If she recognized the heroine, modesty may have kept her from acknowledging it, for—as Bjørnson has revealed elsewhere—she had served as the model.[35]

7

Early in 1886, the Scandinavians of the Twin Cities—those successful in business and the professions—were ambitious to form their own high society with a season of elaborate dinners and balls. In January, the residents of St. Paul invited the Scandinavians of Minneapolis to a banquet in the Ryan Hotel. The guests drove over to St. Paul in sleighs, somewhat in the Currier and Ives style, it seems. Minneapolitans were unable to respond until two months later, when they gave a dinner and dance in the new West Hotel, a million-dollar building widely advertised as the most elegant hostelry between Chicago and San Francisco. Committees for the invitations, programs, decorations, and floor arrangements set to work; the invitations were sent to the Danish and Swedish-Norwegian ministers to the United States, to Congressman Knute Nelson, Professor Hjalmar Hjorth Boyesen, and to prominent Scandinavians throughout the Northwest. The dining room, magnificent with marble floor and mahogany wainscoting, was adorned with a large painting showing three maidens—Svea, Dania, and Nora—embracing one another, as an elevated Goddess of Liberty poured down the flowers and fruits of her cornucopia upon them. After a seven-course dinner, each accompanied by an appropriate wine, telegrams from distinguished guests who had been unable to attend were read. Mayor A. A. Ames gave greetings from the city; Alden J. Blethen, publisher of the *Minneapolis Tribune,* told how fortunate the Midwest had been in having an influx of Scandinavians. Before the orchestra struck up the first waltz, a series of toasts was given to "Our Guests," "Our Hosts," "The United States," "Sweden," "Norway," "Denmark," and the like, culminating in Kristofer Janson's to "Minneapolis." He urged Scandinavians to interest themselves in political and social problems, to encourage art, literature, and science, and to improve life in their city of bizarre contrasts with its million-dollar buildings and deplorably muddy streets.[36]

The event closed the social season, and no other occasion of such magnitude ever followed. Perhaps others, like Andreas Ueland, found the self-praise cloying. The following week, he wrote of his irritation to Rasmus B. Anderson, then United States minister to Denmark, exempting only Kristofer Janson:

"Last week there was a Scandinavian banquet at the West hotel attended by the so called prominent Scandinavians from all parts of the Northwest, eleven of whom answering toasts, but not a single one, except Kristofer Janson, gave expression to a progressive idea. . . . Prof. Olson's speech was much applauded. We had a right to this country, for we discovered it and we were the best people in the world, but too modest. Now we should stick together and show the Americans what we amounted to, etc., etc. This is then the sentiment which is to lead the Scandinavians here! This shall make them prominent and useful in shaping the affairs of the country so as to secure lasting prosperity and greatness."[37]

8

Shortly before, Ueland had written to Anderson when the latter had inquired how Janson was getting along. Although the actual number of Janson's church members was small, Ueland thought, he was attracting large audiences at sermons and lectures, displaying such energy and enthusiasm that Ueland believed he would make a considerable impression on the Norwegian-American mind. That was at a time when the feud with Oftedal had worn thin.[38] Janson had published his *Saga of the Prairie* (Præriens saga), a collection of five long stories of immigrant life in rural communities. Although none of these created as great a sensation as "Wives, Submit Yourselves unto Your Husbands," they all made engaging reading. Most critics have preferred "En buggy-prest" concerning a minister who traveled about the country in a horse-drawn buggy. None of the stories was translated into English. Janson was what was commonly termed in the 1880s a "tendency writer"—one who used his fiction to propagandize.

In the story of the buggy minister, a certain freethinker (who had been a theological student in Kristiania and was knowledgeable about all that such theologians as Johnsen and Caspari had to teach) persuades the minister's young wife to his point of view. While this is the essence of the plot, much of the story deals with the hardships of the young clergyman who had accepted his call in Norway, having been falsely led to believe he was going into a prosperous, well-established new-world community. Instead, he finds a primitive settlement with a store, a post office, and several saloons. His parish covers a wide area; to visit members of his congregation he must go across the roadless prairie and penetrate swamps, under a merciless sun in the summer and always with the possibility that he might be caught in a blizzard in the winter. Indeed, it is the latter which brings him to his death. He and his wife are lodged in a storehouse set up on posts, and, while some additions are made to the structure, it is never more than a makeshift.

His parishioners, still resentful of the class distinctions in Norway, tell him that in America a pastor has no more prestige than anyone else, and he is able to discipline them only after he had learned the ways of the Synod. His wife, formerly a carefree young girl in Kristiania, who had been fond of joining the promenade on Karl Johan's

Avenue and of sipping chocolate at Günther's, was too frail to accompany him on his calls. Consumed with loneliness, she finds the freethinker's logic engaging, especially since he turns out to have been a former suitor of her mother. He also remembers Karl Johan's and Günther's. In the story, one recognizes the hardships Janson had spoken of as being the lot of pioneer ministers at the time of his lecture tour in 1879–80; he has also satirized the textual debates which had taken place at Synod meetings, At the time of his death, the pastor in Janson's story was on his way to a district meeting where ministers would discuss the Old Testament incident in which Elijah's mantle falls on Elisha, determining whether that garment had been made of camel's hair or of goat's hair. The young minister felt that he had conclusive evidence it had been camel's hair.

Two other stories, "The Enemies of the People" (Folkets fiender) and "The Czar of the Settlement" (En bygdekonge), have what critics of that day often described as "a strong tendency." In the first, the saloon and the Synod minister are the people's enemies. In the second, Lars Larsen, the settlement czar, is a shrewd manipulator who finds it to his advantage to get a Conference church organized in a community where there is already one belonging to the Synod, knowing that the two will be immediately embattled and thus draw away attention from his tricky dealings. The other story, "Love on the Cowcatcher" (Kjærlighed paa kofangeren), is comic, having nothing to do with ministers; instead, it reveals Janson's penchant for the Irish. In the fiction which he wrote in America, Janson sometimes used Germans, Swedes, and Danes as background figures; but immigrant heroes and heroines, when they were not Norwegian, were Irish, always sympathetically portrayed as in this case with lazy, luckless, good-natured Jim.[39]

Prœriens saga was published in 1885. Early in the following year, *Budstikken's* reviewer found it a courageous book, one making it clear that Norwegian immigrants would have no political or social influence so long as their pastors kept them away from participating in American society.[40] This criticism appeared just at the time when Janson's feud with Oftedal over the congregational ball was petering out; in the month that followed, Janson could see that others held him in higher esteem than they did Sven Oftedal. He appeared on a program given by the Scandia Lodge, Knights of Pythias, winning that fraternity's gratitude for the support he gave their movement, long ostracized by the orthodox. Svein Mo, president of the socialist organization, New Time, was to thank Janson publicly for his sermon, "Dynamite Persons," which, though it deprecated violence, was a warning that such acts were traceable to the wrongs suffered by working men and could be stopped only by correcting their causes.[41]

9

Janson's article in the *Christian Register* in February, 1886, contained mainly good news. His weekly meetings in north Minneapolis had a regular attendance of a hundred as against the eighty previously reported. He had lectured in Fergus Falls, Minnesota, and had been invited to Grand Forks, North Dakota, and to Montevideo, Appleton, Dawson, and Madison in Minnesota. In Minneapolis, he had been asked to take part in a program for the Norwegian Benevolent Association, and, in accepting, he had suggested that the meeting take place in his newly dedicated church basement. When some committee members had grumbled, saying Conference and Synod people would then likely not attend, Janson had answered that if his basement was not good enough for them, he was not either. "They dare not show prejudice against innocent walls," he wrote. His church library was growing, thanks to donations from ladies in New Hampshire and Massachusetts; he added what he had come to repeat like a litany, "If anyone feels a desire to assist, it will be received gratefully."[42]

As the spring advanced, the main structure of the church took shape: the red brick walls were up, the roof on, the steeple in place—and work had begun on the interior. On Sunday evening, April 11, when Rabbi Henry Iliowizi gave a talk on Judaism for the benefit of the building fund, he remarked on how long it was taking to get the church finished, saying he would have thought there were enough Scandinavians in the city to erect two or three such churches. However, he understood the circumstances, for he was to say he was glad to offer his bit for those who struggled against heavy odds, be they the victims of an irresponsible capitalism or of the tyranny of the majority. *Budstikken* reported that he had a large and attentive audience.[43]

Three days later, the blow came. On the night of April 14, a tornado moving in a northwesterly direction passed over Minneapolis to descend upon St. Cloud, devastating a wide area, killing many persons—so great a catastrophe that it was judged the worst storm within human memory. In its passage over the city, it had caught the steeple of Nazareth Church, the great force lifting the top structure of the building and strewing the streets with sections of walls and roof, twisted iron and timbers, and the decapitated steeple. Only the basement remained, and in the hail and rain that followed, its ceiling was

151

damaged, the carpets and furnishings within ruined. Nazareth Church was the only building in Minneapolis to be struck.[44]

In his autobiography, Janson has said that when he saw the destruction he wept.[45] In letters to Mrs. Anderson and Bjørnson at the time, Drude described the incident more graphically. Crowds had been standing around, people pointing out Janson, some of them jeering and openly taunting him. They were so ignorant, she was to lament, that they could easily be led to believe the destruction was an act of divine vengeance. But surely one should expect something different from educated men, she wrote Mrs. Anderson. Reverend Gjertsen had laughed when he had spoken of it, saying how pleased he was; Drude had that directly from Dr. Karl Bendeke.[46] To Bjørnson she wrote that she wanted to sob whenever she thought of Kristofer. They were thankful no one had been in the building at the time, realizing that they were fortunate compared with people at St. Cloud and especially Sauk Rapids, which had a heavy death toll. Nevertheless, it had been hard to hold services the next Sunday. They had begun as usual, singing Bjørnson's verses, "Forward! Forward!"—for, as Drude put it, there must be no thought of giving up. Kristofer had stood at his usual place and was about to give his sermon when the impact of the disaster gripped him afresh, and he could not speak. She had sat holding her breath—and many another, too, for the room was deathly still— but in a moment he had mastered himself and his voice was strong and firm. He felt it would be years before he could regain what had been lost, she wrote, but she was more hopeful. The Americans were very interested in his mission, and every setback he had experienced seemed to make them more eager to help him.[47]

Janson wrote an account of the storm for the *Christian Register* under the title, "A Twice-Told Tale." Estimating the damages at $3,000, he prophesied, as Drude had, that the orthodox would interpret the destruction as an act of divine vengeance, but he went on to say that that claim would be difficult to establish for the tornado had killed a Lutheran minister and his wife in St. Cloud. Yet he was to conclude with rather shabby histrionics: "And what am I to do? My congregation is poor and has made strenuous efforts which now prove to have been in vain. I am sitting like Jeremiah weeping on the ruins of his dear Jerusalem. I am tired of sounding again and again the never-ceasing cry about 'aid and help.' And people must at last lose their patience and get tired of me too. So—let me sit, then on my broken hope and mourn, surrounded by a gaping crowd, which sneers and points and asks, 'To what denomination did this church

152

belong? To the Unitarian? Well, that people must be awful wicked. The only church in Minneapolis gone—there you see!' "[48]

Drude had been right. In its next issue the *Christian Register* reported that contributions were already coming into its office.[49] And Janson had friends in Minneapolis, members of the Liberal Ministers' Association. They undertook a public drive for funds, and, among other things, wrote the Orthodox Ministers' Association, asking that it permit a letter of solicitation to be circulated through its congregations. The antagonism this group felt toward the liberal ministers may be sensed by the reaction. When the chairman read the request, the ministers listened in stunned silence. He then asked for a volunteer committee to recommend a course of action, but when no one responded, the request was tabled for discussion at the next meeting. As usual, a reporter was present, and, when the word spread of what had happened, both Minneapolis and St. Paul papers covered the next meeting.

All this public notice was to draw wider attention to Janson than if the orthodox ministers had quietly agreed to the request. In fact, one of them testily remarked at the May 3 meeting, "As usual the press will be on the side of that paper [the letter of solicitation] and against this body." The newspapers did give the proceedings of the evangelical pastors' meeting derisive treatment, the headlines of the *Minneapolis Evening Journal* being characteristic:

"We Are Orthodox"
So Say the Members of the
City Pastors' Association
Refuse to Aid Unitarians
A Hot Time at the Ministers' Meeting
Rev. Jansen Denounced

Yet at least one man was disposed to be generous, for, as the meeting opened, the Reverend Mr. Pitner moved that the Association concur in the appeal. "That started the whirlwind," in the words of the *Evening Journal*. Pitner immediately found his own credentials suspect. A colleague replied vehemently: "I hold that the man who would recommend the rebuilding of that church stultifies himself as a Christian minister. We preach the Lord Jesus Christ. They reach up and tear off his royal crown and trample it under their feet. Let us, if we will, express our sympathy with them, but as for building up error, that we cannot do." Others were just as hostile, and the reporters followed

153

the practice of quoting them verbatim: "There are types of Unitarianism that I believe to be doing good. The type of Unitarianism represented by Christopher Jansen is doing a great deal of mischief."—"The Roman Catholics might as consistently come in with a request of this kind."—"You may depend on it this appeal comes to us not in good faith. My motto is: Millions for the gospel of Jesus Christ, but not one cent for the upbuilding of ruinous error."[50]

The *St. Paul Pioneer Press*—as well as the *Minneapolis Morning Tribune* with slightly different wording—quoted Pastor M. Falk Gjertsen: "As this man, Janson, is getting used to having his churches blown down (the first one he built was destroyed by a storm) we are rather inclined to sympathize with him. But there is another question. Can we, as ministers of the gospel, consistently indorse any such society? If we should recommend others to aid, we ourselves should be willing to give for the same kind of thing. Now this church teaches sheer infidelity. That is what it is—out-and-out infidelity. We can't aid that. Moreover, that church is not built at great sacrifice by the Scandinavian society, as they represent, but by Unitarians of Boston. Janson is paid by them. We Scandinavians regard that church as a standing insult to our people and church. Shall this society participate in the insult? Rich Americans built that church, and can rebuild it. To ask Christians to aid a church that denies Christ is absurd."

As a result of the discussion, the Association passed two resolutions:

While we deeply sympathize with those who have suffered in the recent cyclone, which has lately visited a portion of our state, and while we are ever ready to respond to the appeal of human suffering, without respect to religious doctrine, or national belief, yet we decline to comply with this request for the following reasons:

First—That it does not come properly within the jurisdiction of this association.

Second—Because we believe the teachings of the congregation in question are on the whole harmful rather than helpful.

In the wake of these resolutions, the *Christian Register* devoted a page to the ministers' deliberations in Minneapolis, printing its article around a large drawing of the destroyed church and closing with editorial comment from the Boston *Herald*: "We presume that the evangelical clergymen acted conscientiously; but their action curiously illustrates the bigotry of creed. We should find it hard to reconcile ourselves to any theological system which held that Trinity Church and Old South are beneficent institutions, while the Church of the Disciples and the New South are only workers of evil to mankind. But we are so heterodox that we believe in the good work of any church which teaches man to worship the highest they are capable of conceiving."[51]

The same issue of the *Christian Register* contained an article by Secretary Grindall Reynolds urging that $5,000 be raised for the Scandinavian mission rather than the $3,000 Janson had mentioned. Another account, entitled "The Scandinavian Jeremiah," told the story of how the Old Testament prophet had been rescued from a dungeon. Following it came the suggestion that "if about thirty men would come to the rescue of Mr. Janson, each one bringing as a cushion a good bunch of bankbills, it would not take long to draw him from the depths of gloom into which this new blow of adversity has cast him."[52]

A week after the storm, *Folkebladet* had printed a short piece called "Superstition and Heresy" (Overtro og vantro). Human understanding is so limited one cannot really know why God operates as he does through nature, the article read. Assuming such knowledge leads to superstition; on the other hand, if God concerns himself with large things, he must also deal with the small.[53] Janson translated part of it for the *Christian Register*: "Many see in it God's punishment of Janson's blasphemous activity. Others go so far as to show malicious joy. . . . Janson is right in complaining of that sort of people. . . . It happens now for the second time that the storm demolished a church for Pastor Janson; and even if such a misfortune might serve to secure an extra collection of money, it would not be too much if this event might bring Pastor Janson to some reflections. There are, at all events, many, both Scandinavians and Americans, who do not rejoice at this disaster, but who for the second time have commenced to meditate on what foundation Pastor Janson and the Unitarians really build."[54]

To refute this reasoning, the Reverend Henry Simmons of the First Unitarian Society was to preach on "What Tornadoes Teach," again calling attention to the storm's having taken the lives of many Lutherans, among them a minister.[55] Chris. Anderson, writing in *Budstikken,* charged that *Folkbladet* made no mention of the same storm having destroyed a Baptist church because the Baptists were too strong to be attacked.[56]

155

The first volume of Janson's *Is Orthodoxy Right?* had come out shortly after the storm; for a time this publication was to be somewhat obscured by the tornado and its aftermath. Dealing with the verbal inspiration of the Bible, in appearance the tract was an oversized pamphlet, nine inches long by five in width and running to sixty-six pages. Subscribers paid a dollar for the first volume, after which the others would be sent to them as they came out. Future issues were to discuss the Trinity, the divinity of Jesus, the atonement, miracles, the history of the devil, and life after death. In Norway, Bjørnson gave the booklet an extensive review, and two state-church clergymen responded to its contents. In America, Janson's work went largely unnoticed.

For "Is the Bible an Inspired Book or Not?"—the first volume of *Is Orthodoxy Right?*—Janson drew on secondary sources, chiefly John Chadwick's *The Bible of Today.* Janson's tract is divided into two parts: the Old Testament and the New Testament. In the first, he explains and illustrates how many ancient people believed their sacred books to be of divine origin. In discussing authorship, he says that Moses could not have been the writer of the Pentateuch because Deuteronomy gives an account of his death; more important, the language of the Pentateuch is so similar to that of later books that it was impossible a thousand years could have intervened between them. He discusses documents in which God is referred to as "Jahveh," some in which he is called "Elohim," and still others in which both names are used. Janson delineates the cruelties described in the Old Testament—the murder of the innocent, including women and children, the selling of persons into slavery, and the persecution of those suspected of being witches. Such acts, he maintains, could not have been at the bidding of God. For three and a half pages, he reproduces citations from the Old Testament which contradict one another.

In the second part, Janson discusses early disputes about which books should be included, citing the Revelation of St. John as the most questionable; it was rejected by many, from the early church fathers to Luther. He mentions discrepancies in the Acts of the Apostles, going on to the authorship of the epistles and gospels, concluding that the writers did not consider themselves to be divinely inspired and therefore infallible. Many of the books, he says, are compilations drawn from several sources; some were not included until four hundred years after the church was first instituted. Many contain inaccuracies and contradictions. Furthermore, the idiosyncrasies of the various scribes stand out so clearly that their writings cannot be other than the result of their own thinking.

Because of the repairs going on in the church basement, Janson cancelled weekly discussion meetings for the rest of the season. He made the same decision about his sessions in north Minneapolis, but actually he had given up hope of ever establishing a congregation there.

Throughout the spring, he held regular Sunday services and gave his Sunday evening readings, using Max Nordau's *Capital and Labor* for the latter. He exchanged pulpits with the Reverend L. E. G. Powers of the Second Universalist Church, appeared at a Scandinavian temperance meeting along with Professor John F. Downey of the university, and spoke before Rabbi Iliowizi's congregation. He also lectured in Black River Falls, Eau Claire, and Chippewa Falls, all in western Wisconsin.[57]

11

In the middle of May, the Western Unitarian Conference was scheduled to hold its annual convention in Cincinnati. Although the destruction of Janson's church was to receive some consideration, the major thrust of the meetings was more or less foreordained by a pamphlet, *The Issue of the West,* written by J. T. Sunderland and mailed to ministers as well as to prominent church members a week in advance of the convention.[58] Something of a conservative action might have been anticipated, for the January before Sunderland and the Reverend Brooke Herford had begun a new monthly, the *Unitarian,* announcing that, while it would hold to the old freedom from dogmatic creeds, it would "stand clearly for belief in God and worship and the spirit of Christ." In his pamphlet, Sunderland explained that a determined group within the Conference, "men we all honor and love," wanted to cut Unitarianism off from its traditional allegiance to Christianity and change it to a free or ethical religion. However, those who believed Unitarianism to be Christian Theism could no longer remain silent. Sunderland would not have the denomination protect itself by persecution and heresy trials, but by insisting that everywhere it stand for "God and worship, the great immortal hope, the ideal of divine humanity that shines in Christ Jesus—what the A. U. A. stands for." He declared that such slogans as "Freedom, Fellowship, and Character in Religion" mistook revolution for evolution. A non-Christian attitude would remove the Unitarians from "the great band of Christian worshipers and workers, our Universalist brethren, the Broad churchmen of the Episcopal Church, the New Theology men in the Congregationalist body, such Christian independents as Professor Swing and Dr. Thomas." By substituting an ethical standard for the Christian and the theistic, Sunderland felt, the Unitarians would seal the fate of their denomination in the West.

W. C. Gannett, who led the opposition, declared that the Western Conference was not ready to give up its Christian character nor to exclude from membership those who were neither Christian nor Theist. After four sessions, Gannett succeeded in mustering votes to pass a resolution: "That the Western Unitarian Conference conditions its fellowship on no dogmatic tests but welcomes all who wish to join it to help establish Truth, Righteousness, and Love in the world."[59]

From Cincinnati, Janson appears to have gone to Madison, where a sectional Conference apparently was held. Just as he was about to leave for Minneapolis, he wrote to Rasmus B. Anderson, thanking the United States minister to Denmark for the hospitality the latter had shown him in absentia. Janson had spoken at the Unitarian church in Madison and at the university. At the latter place, he had had copies of *Is Orthodoxy Right?* for sale, and one of his new subscribers was none other than Pastor Severin Gunderson. For that matter, he had had delightful encounters with other conservative clergymen, having met Professor Hans Gerhard Stub on the steps of the Synod Theological Seminary where—according to Janson—the two had embraced one another warmly. That evening they were both dinner guests at the Anderson home, where the hostess, as well as the host, was missing. Nevertheless, the guests had been amply cared for by Miss Woodward and Anderson's daughter, Lotta. Julius Olson had been present, and another university professor had brought bottles of "the forbidden ale,"—all of which had made for a delightful evening. Janson's only regret was that Drude had not been with him; the Jansons did not have money enough to permit both of them to make the trip. In the light of later developments, this seems to have been a questionable decision because she, at home with the children so much of the time, languished for a change of scene and stimulating company.[60]

During this interval, other conservatives in the Western Unitarian Conference had gone home somewhat aggrieved. In an issue of his *Our Best Words*, the Reverend Jasper Douthit declared that the Conference now had an atheistic platform. The Truth, Righteousness, and Love resolution was essentially humbug, Douthit said, and suggested that the time had come to organize a Western Unitarian division which would cooperate with the American Unitarian Association.

Shortly afterward, Sunderland and the president of the Western Conference, Joseph Shippen, resigned their offices. On June 21, 1886, the Western Unitarian Association was formed, setting up its headquarters in Chicago. George W. McCrary, a prominent Kansas City lawyer, was elected president. In addition to Sunderland and Shippen, the directors included Jasper Douthit of Shelbyville, Illinois, Professor H. H. Barber of the Meadville Theological School, John Snyder of St. Louis, M. B. Hull of Chicago, and Kristofer Janson of Minneapolis.[61]

Janson makes no mention of this schism in his autobiography. So far as he was concerned, allying himself with the Western Association seems to have had only one benefit: it placed him squarely on record as a Christian Theist, clearing him from any subsequent attacks that he was in alliance with humanists, logical positivists, or the like. Even that seems to have been a negligible gain for after the denouement of the May 3 meeting of the Orthodox Ministers' Association, he was to remain viritually free from attack.

As Arthur M. Schlesinger has said, everywhere orthodoxy was on the defensive. To this Charles H. Lyttle, the historian of the Western Conference, has added that the schism brought on by the formation of the Western Association was the pattern that the struggle took among the Unitarians. While those who remained in the Conference, with *Unity* as their organ, found some supporters, at the time most of the weight of outside opinion seems to have been on the side of the conservatives. The faculty of Meadville Theological School supported the Association, as did Professor F. H. Hedge of Harvard and James Freeman Clarke, who were agreed that there could be no true religious progress outside Christianity. In religion, as in other fields, Clarke maintained, one must respect the authority of the expert, and in religion the expert was Jesus. Hedge felt that refraining from the worship of God could lead only to moral anarchy.[62]

Surely Janson had some intimation of the impending break in the Western Conference that night late in May when he enjoyed the company of Professor Stub. Urbane and polished, both men could forget their theological differences for the moment and possibly commiserate with one another. Janson had suffered the destruction of a church and was about to become (at least nominally) part of a splinter group. Professor Stub was, so to speak, the victim of Professor F. A. Schmidt and the Anti-Missourians, for in 1886 the Synod Seminary in Madison was reduced to seven students and two professors.[63] In another sense, the camaraderie of the evening was prophetic. The following year the Synod seminary was to be moved to Robbinsdale, a northern suburb of Minneapolis.

Valborg Hovind Stub, the professor's wife, was an accomplished singer who had been trained in a German conservatory; prior to her marriage, she had sung in the principal cities of the Continent. Like Drude, she was to find herself alienated from the society in which circumstances had placed her—in her case the wives of faculty members of the seminary. The two women were to become extremely close friends. As Drude later said, in describing her last agonizing year in Minneapolis, the only thing that kept her from madness was the comfort she derived from her sister and from her friend, Valborg Hovind Stub.

6

Champion of the
Social Gospel

IN THE summer of 1886, Drude Krog Janson began work on *En saloonkeepers datter,* her first novel. Her theme was the emancipation of women. As Kristofer had done in *Præriens saga,* she drew her material from the life about her, modeling her heroine after Mathilde Ilstrup, a beautiful and popular young lady who took part in amateur theatricals and was the daughter of a saloonkeeper. For the most part, the action of the novel takes place in Minneapolis, beginning about 1877 and extending into the mid-1880s. In the book, the heroine is a woman of extremely high sensibilities who longs for a life of beauty and refinement but finds it difficult to realize because of the meanness of her father's occupation. She is about to sell herself into a loveless marriage when she has an opportunity to discuss her troubles with Bjørnstjerne Bjørnson, who was in the city in January, 1881. Having so recently enjoyed the society of New England Unitarians, Bjørnson—after hearing her story—suggests that she go into the liberal ministry. Somewhat later, she is helped by the Reverend William Channing Gannett in getting a scholarship to Meadville Theological School. The novel closes with her ordination.[1]

Like Janson's fiction, Drude's novel is "tendency writing," slanted in favor of women—with a few notable exceptions. Pettersen, a minor character who seems to have been modeled after Christian Haug, is an exemplary individual.[2] Bjørnson and Gannett, perceptive in their recognition of a woman's need to develop as a *person,* are demonstrably men of vision. Otherwise the men in the book are a sorry lot: the heroine's calculating father, the wastrel son of a good family in Norway,

161

an idler who clumsily attempts petty larceny, a wealthy attorney who is also a libertine, working men whose burly proportions prove they take more than their share of the family food supply, and a miscellany of beer-drinking, tobacco-spitting roughnecks. Most of the women are sympathetically drawn: a physician gets along on a meager income because she does so much free work among immigrant families, the faithful old servant who had accompanied the heroine from Norway, and housemaids pathetically decked out in a cheap finery. These are also the wives of working men, always encumbered with children, their bodies worn down by hard work, their faces drawn from privation and constant worry. Only the wives of prosperous businessmen are censured. Elegantly dressed, they are spiteful or fawning, as suits their convenience. Either entertaining or being entertained, these shallow creatures have an appetite for scandal and salacious gossip.

Present-day critics have dismissed the book as overdrawn and sentimental. Judging it as a novel, few would dispute this. But as a document of the times, it has some value. During the 1880s, Norwegian immigrants were streaming into the city. In his *Nyt Tidsskrift* article, Janson had written of what a motley mass of humanity one found among the Norwegians, and immigrant newspapers verify this judgment to an extent.

In later years, Drude was to intimate that she had written the novel to assuage the loneliness she felt from lack of companionship, and one suspects that the heroine, except for exterior details, has in her makeup more of Drude than of Miss Ilstrup. Yet, for the late nineteenth century, the heroine's choice of a career was by no means far-fetched. The Unitarians had many women ministers; some of them had been among the speakers at the Women's Suffrage Association convention—an event that had inspired Drude. Later Janson was to praise them in his autobiography, singling out the Reverend Mary Safford as being extremely able and yet one of the most unassuming and feminine women he had ever met.[3]

In reference to women, both Janson and Drude were to use the expression "intellectual suicide." From their published works and letters, one finds that this condition occurs either when a woman has no access to books, lectures, concerts, and the like, or when she allows herself to become completely absorbed in motherhood and the minutiae of housekeeping.[4] Kristofer and Drude had long been alert to this problem; it seems that Drude, after the birth of her first child, had been encouraged to attend lectures at the folk school lest she become too engrossed in motherhood.[5]

162

In 1886, the Jansons had gone to Brown County the last week in June. Their family was smaller, for Ivar, then seventeen, had decided the previous winter that he had had enough of school and would try making his living in California. He wrote home frequently, saying that he had found work as a ranch hand and in no way regretted his move. Nevertheless, his mother was concerned, writing Mrs. Rasmus B. Anderson that she "hoped Ivar was doing the right thing." But the Jansons were to find teenage independence a hard thing to oppose. By the following winter, Eilev, the second son, had followed his brother's example, also heading for California; not wanting any special advantage, he deliberately chose a destination different from that of his brother.[6]

While Drude worked on her novel, Janson wrote *Femtende Wisconsin,* a fictionalized account of the Fifteenth Wisconsin Regiment of the Civil War, a unit made up of Scandinavians—largely Norwegians—and organized in Madison, Wisconsin, under the command of Colonel Hans Christian Heg. In this book, religion plays no part. It has vivid descriptions of battles at Chattanooga, Chickamauga, and Altanta, pictures conditions in Union hospitals and at the Confederate prison at Andersonville, and gives episodes of how the Norwegian Yankees provide asylum for runaway slaves and of how they are joined by a valiant drummer boy. In footnotes, Janson explained that some of these events were literally true, but he allowed himself to introduce highly improbable action into his fiction. The most unlikely concerned Ola and his Irish fiancée, Kate. When Ola joined the regiment, Kate refused to be separated from him. She married him, and, disguising herself as a man, joined the regiment where she was known as "Valdres Karl." She was successful in concealing both her sex and nationality (she had worked only for Norwegians since coming to America)—and she and Ola fought side by side until he was mortally wounded. Then her impassioned grief led to the uncovering of her identity. The book closes with accounts of reunions in Madison at the end of the war. The widowed Kate marries Siver, whose harrowing escape from a Confederate prison, Janson explained, was based on an actual happening—except that the actual hero had not been a Norwegian, but an Irishman.[7]

During the summer, Janson had received a letter from Amandus Norman, his youthful friend in Reynolds, North Dakota, revealing that Norman had finally decided to enter the Unitarian ministry.

Janson was always on the lookout for promising candidates, and by 1886 two Norwegians, Johannes J. Brauti and Herman Haugerud, were already enrolled at Meadville Theological School. His acquaintance with Norman had begun slightly more than a year before, when the young man had sent five dollars for books Janson had advertised. At the same time, he has asked for advice. He had finished high school and hoped to attend a university. He had read Ibsen, Kierkegaard, and John Stuart Mill, but Seneca remained his favorite author. Would Janson recommend additional books for him? That was a little hard, Janson answered, since the young man was doing so well on his own, but he did suggest a few titles and also asked if he were interested in entering the ministry. After a brief correspondence, Norman arranged for Janson to give a series of lectures in Reynolds. In the interim, he had become a partner in a store in that town and had independently begun the study of astronomy, having bought a large mounted telescope and other equipment. Janson had again written about the ministry, saying that this profession would allow more time for study than any other. He had even suggested that Norman enter Meadville in the fall of 1886. But when he received word of the latter's decision, he also learned that his friend could not possibly wind up his affairs in Reynolds in time for the beginning of the school term, and Janson felt that entering late would place a beginning student at a great disadvantage. He then suggested that Norman spend a year under his guidance, living in the Janson house, studying history, philosophy, literature, and art history, as well as developing his style in writing and getting practice in public speaking. Board and room would be furnished him as cheaply as possible, and if, at the end of the year, Norman had decided that the ministry was not for him, he would have lost nothing and actually would be much further along in his education.[8]

3

During those August days, when newspapers came in the mail, the Jansons followed the trial of eight men in Chicago on charges of committing murder, inciting to violence by speech and writing, and being accessory to these crimes in connection with the Haymarket Riot. On the evening of May 4, 1886, an open-air meeting had been called near Haymarket Square in Chicago to protest the brutal treatment striking working men had received at the hands of the police the day before. Early in the evening, Mayor Carter Harrison had been present as an onlooker, but, satisfied that the gathering was peaceful, he had left. Without the mayor's knowledge, a company of policemen had been dispatched to the meeting. As they arrived, a bomb had been thrown into their midst, killing one officer instantly and wounding others. In the mêlée that followed, the police fired and were fired upon. All in all, eight policemen lost their lives and an undetermined number of private citizens were killed or injured. The event gave rise to mass hysteria throughout the country. Serious trouble in connection with labor disputes had occurred before, but a frightened public felt the slaughter at Haymarket Square to be the ultimate, and the hue and cry was for law and order. The trial of the eight men accused began on June 21 and lasted until August 20. All, eventually identified as "anarchists," were convicted; one was sentenced to fifteen years in prison and the other seven were condemned to death.[9]

During the twenty years that followed the Civil War, increasing unrest in the country marked the change the United States was undergoing as it moved from a rural to an industrial society. Cities were booming. From 1880 to 1890, Chicago increased over a hundred per cent in population, to become the second largest city in the United States; the Twin Cities trebled in size, and other communities in the Midwest grew from 60 to 80 per cent.[10] With the increase of manufacturing and commerce, the wealth of the nation rose astronomically. In 1861 the United States had three millionaires; at the close of the century there were 3,800.[11] Great fortunes were made in railroads by Vanderbilt, Gould, and Huntington, in steel by Carnegie, in oil by Rockefeller, in finance by Morgan and Cooke, and in meatpacking by Armour. These men were looked upon as the personification of the American dream, admired as "captains of industry," "self-made men," and "rugged individualists"—estimates which time has downgraded; today they are more commonly called "tycoons," "moguls," and "robber barons." More than half of the nation's wealth was in the possession of about forty thousand families, or one third of one per cent of the population.

As great fortunes grew, the real wages of workers decreased, declining from $400 to $300 from 1870 to 1880, thus forcing women and children into the labor market. In 1869, the Noble Order of the Knights of Labor had been organized. Using aggressive tactics, including sabotage, the Knights won some victories during the late 1870s; the organization reached a membership of over a half million in 1886, after which it declined, to be supplanted by the American Federation of Labor. From 1881 to 1894, some fourteen thousand strikes and lockouts took place, confrontations that were virtually unknown up to the close of the Civil War.[12]

Modern Socialism had its beginning in this country in 1872, but it made little headway during the 1870s because of internal troubles. In 1882, the anarchist Johan Most came to the United States, and the following year the Socialists divided into two groups. The radical wing became known as the International Working People's Association. It advocated the abolition of class rule by any means possible, but it never gained much of a following. After the Haymarket Riot, this association was suspected of complicity in the affair, and, although the group denied playing any part, it was thereafter distrusted. The other, moderate, wing—the Socialist Labor Party—became the principal force in the national movement. Advocating such sweeping reforms as public control of the means of production and of transportation and exchange, it sought to bring these reforms about by means of the ballot and peaceful demonstration.[13]

The moneyed interests had ways of organizing to maintain their power. The rise of corporations on a national scale was followed by such combinations as trusts, pools, and monopolies. Secured from foreign competition by protective tariffs, big business resisted workers' efforts to organize for collective bargaining. It hired Pinkerton men to quell disturbances, kept spies in factories, and blacklisted employees who had taken part in protests.

Unrest was not confined to the cities. From 1870 to 1897, farm prices declined steadily. Farmers had grievances against the railroads for charging exorbitant shipping rates; they felt themselves victimized when they bought machines, clothing, fuel, and building materials. When they sold their produce, they considered that they were preyed upon by elevator combines, millers' rings, and packing trusts. Heavily mortgaged and paying high interest rates, most farmers in the West were bitterly resentful of money lenders. From 1887 onward, the National Farmers' Alliance, or the Northwestern Alliance, organized on a state basis, grew in strength in the Middle West, especially in Minnesota, the Dakotas, Nebraska, and Kansas. At first, they tried to get reforms through the Republican and Democratic parties, but, when these efforts were not successful, they organized the Populist Party in 1892.[14]

4

At the close of his lecture tour in 1880, Janson had still looked upon America as the land of opportunity. In admiring Walt Whitman's

Democratic Vistas, he had agreed that the nation had faults, but these he believed were bound to give way before "the enlightened might of a free people." Once he had marveled at America's generosity in taking the cast-offs of Europe and readily offering them citizenship. But after several years' residence in this country, he had revised his ideas considerably. He came to see immigrants not only as exploited people themselves, but as making up an endless stream of cheap labor used by rich employers to impoverish the working class in this country, native-born as well as foreign. This change in Janson's attitude came before 1886, as his sermon "Dynamite Persons" testifies, but generally up to that year he had been kept busy defending his religious views and building and rebuilding his churches. After the destruction of the Minneapolis church and the censure he had received from the orthodox ministers, he was, for the most part, to be free from attack. He joined a growing body of concerned Protestant clergymen whom Charles Howard Hopkins has called the "social gospelers," the forerunners of the Christian Socialists of the 1890s. It must be said in fairness, however, that throughout the 1880s Jewish and Catholic clergymen were denouncing the inequities of the age and pleading for reform.

The condemnation of the accused men in Chicago's Haymarket Riot was to arouse the conscience of many clergymen of all faiths, and some of them lost their pulpits as a consequence. The execution of the seven prisoners had been set for December 3, 1886, but as the year advanced, appeals to higher courts brought a stay of sentence. As Janson began his fall program in Minneapolis, he chose "Can Anything Justify Anarchism?" as the subject of the first discussion meeting, announcing that the gathering was open to the public without charge and urging as many as possible to attend.[15] This forum was followed by at least one on the Socialist platform and several on the Social Democrats. Since there were no organized Social Democrats in America at the time, this approach at first seems puzzling, but an event which took place in the fall of 1886 may throw some light on it.[16]

The American Socialist Labor Party—the moderate wing—had made appreciable gains in membership, allowing it to establish new party papers, organize new sections, and send out lecturers. Of the latter, the speakers who attracted most attention were Wilhelm Liebknecht, the veteran leader of the Social Democrats in Germany, Eleanor Marx Aveling, the daughter of Karl Marx, and her husband, Dr. Edward Aveling. In the autumn of 1886, they addressed some fifty meetings in the principal cities of the United States. Liebknecht spoke in German and the Avelings in English.[17]

We have no record of any conversation Janson may have had with Liebknecht when the trio visited Minneapolis. He may have talked with Liebknecht, however, or the latter may have been present when Janson called on the Avelings at their hotel in Minneapolis. The only record of this visit is a letter that Mrs. Aveling wrote almost two years later to her friend, Havelock Ellis, recalling her pleasure at seeing Janson. She was knowledgeable about the Norwegian literature of the time, having been one of the first to translate Ibsen's *A Doll's House* into English; Ellis also was aware of current trends, for, in speaking of Janson, Mrs. Aveling wrote, "Of course, you know his books, and that he, too, is one of the 'new school.' " Janson, she said, had spoken most sympathetically about their work, telling the visitors that Ibsen was also a Socialist. Describing Janson, she wrote, "He is a great big fellow, over six feet and broad in proportion, and he has the clearest, honestest blue eyes I have ever seen."

On this occasion, finding themselves in agreement on Socialism—according to Mrs. Aveling—the group had shifted their conversation to Ibsen. Janson, Mrs. Aveling wrote, seemed to worship Ibsen's genius and to love the man, but he had said, "When we are together, we quarrel all the time." Mrs. Aveling then related the story of an argument the two had had over *landsmaal,* Ibsen becoming so irritated that he seized a chair and threw it at Janson and stomped out of the room. After a quarter hour, Ibsen returned to present Janson with a little bag of chocolate creams as a peace offering. Mrs. Aveling concluded: "If only you could have seen this enormous man, the idea of bringing him a little bag of sweets would have struck you as it did us. It was impossible not to scream with laughter, though apparently the absurdity had not struck Janson who told it quite seriously. It seemed to me a very characteristic incident. It is quite the sort of thing Stockmann would do. Certainly I do not believe such a scene, so ended, could occur between two great writers, one a man of immense genius, of any other nation than the Norwegian. I thought such a detail as this might interest you. I know I have *loved* Ibsen the man ever since Janson told it to us."[18]

5

In 1886, for his sermons on Sunday mornings, Janson had begun with a series on resurrection: the beliefs of the pagans, the doctrines of the Jews and what Jesus taught, the interpretation given by the apostles, and the teachings of the early church. He concluded with the views of the Universalists, the Swedenborgians, and other liberal sects of the time. For his Sunday evening readings, he opened with Bjørnson's *Det nye system,* following it with Marius Janzen's play, *Helene Krag,* which deals with the Franco-Prussian War. His own *Femtende Wisconsin* was ready, but Drude does not seem to have finished *En saloonkeepers datter,* for Janson did not read it until the following spring. Nevertheless, she took the time to write a couple of articles for *Nylænde,* a journal in Norway devoted to the advancement of women. For these, she had used material from the *Woman's Journal* of the American Women's Suffrage Association. Published early in 1887, the first of Drude's articles dealt with how intelligently women used the ballot, once they had the chance to vote; all of her argument was based on conditions in Washington Territory, where women had full suffrage. The second was a biographical sketch of Mrs. Abbey Kelley Foster, whose death at seventy-seven had closed a long, useful career which included work for the abolition of slavery, the advancement of women, and other humanitarian causes.

In October, a five-day church bazaar was held, forcing the congregation to come up with new ideas for raising money. *Budstikken* spoke of the "artistic enjoyment" awaiting people, but that came to be overshadowed by the grand prize of a $950 piano which was to go to some lucky winner. A contest (at ten cents a ticket) was held to determine the most popular young lady, the winner to receive a diamond ring. (Mathilde Ilstrup won easily with over two thousand votes, some eight hundred above her closest competitor.) At ten cents a vote, one could choose political candidates—Ames versus McGill for governor, Swenson versus Brackett for sheriff, and Rand versus Von Schegel for municipal judge. In each instance, the first named won, although the results did not always tally with those of the election the following November.[19]

It was at about this time that Janson delivered what seems to have been his first sermon on Spiritualism, "Spiritism and Orthodoxy: The Objections of Reason."[20] In his autobiography, Janson says that he first began his investigation of the subject when members of his congregation told him of experiences they had had.[21] Later, Amandus Norman was to say that during the year he spent as Janson's student hardly a week went by when they did not attend a seance.[22] Yet, for the times, such an interest was by no means unusual. People were curious about the subject much as they are today. In May, 1885, the *Christian Register* had carried an article, "Spiritualism from the Standpoint of a Believer," by the Reverend Herman Snow. We have no direct evidence that Snow was a Unitarian minister, but, since the Unitarians were willing to explore any issue that presented itself, he

169

may well have been. The Reverend Minot J. Savage, a prominent Unitarian in the East, became convinced that communication with the dead was possible, and the philosopher William James felt the subject to be so much worth investigating that he was holding a series of seances with a Mrs. Piper, a well-known medium of the time.[23] In appealing to Scandinavian liberals, Janson had encountered many agnostics and atheists who challenged him saying that neither he nor anyone else knew anything about the immortality of the soul. In answering these charges, Janson, the advocate of rational religion, had been forced to rely on what he called "probabilities." His assumptions were that an all-loving God would not bring human beings to life to suffer the many trials of this existence merely to obliterate them completely, and that men of all faiths, pagan as well as Christian, had believed in eternal life since time immemorial. The main attraction of Spiritualism for Janson was that, if he could find communication with the dead to be possible, he would have "proof" of personal immortality, one of his most cherished beliefs.

When Janson wrote to Norman, some time after the bazaar, to inquire about when they could expect him, he said that the church was off to a splendid start.[24] He gave very much the same report the following December in the *Christian Register*. His Sunday evening readings, which he considered "a sort of Unitarian education," were well attended; and the Monday evening discussions were given over to the burning issues of the day. His theological work, *Har ortodoksien ret?* had met with greater success than he had anticipated, not only in the number of subscribers, but in the many encouraging letters he had received from readers. He added that the opposition had calmed except in Dakota, where a Lutheran minister had ordered a rural parishioner to burn some of Janson's books that the pastor had discovered in the farmer's house. When the parishioner had not obeyed, the clergyman, on his next visit, had walked away with the books, an act which prompted Janson to say that the minister should learn the seventh commandment. Such incidents, of course, were only amusing. "All in all, the outlook is brighter than ever before."[25]

6

In the late fall, the Liberal Ministers' Association, increased to fifteen members, embarked on an ambitious winter study program. Each member was to present a paper to be read at the weekly Monday morning meeting, beginning with that of the president, H. M. Simmons, whose offering was "The Relation of the Liberal Churches to the Modern Theories of Creation." Rabbi Iliowizi was to follow with "Is Modern Biblical Criticism Tenable?" Others were "The Organization of Labor and Its Bearing on Modern Civilization," "Scholasticism and Medieval Theology," and "Ministerial Responsibility in Reference to Truth," which was to be given by Rabbi S. Freuder of St. Paul. "How to Prevent Skepticism among the Young" was the topic of a newcomer, the Reverend Marion D. Shutter, who had recently left his orthodox church in Minneapolis to become a Universalist. Shutter had graduated from the Baptist Theological Seminary in 1881. He had become minister of the Olivet Baptist Church in Minneapolis, and during his tenure the congregation had erected a new building. Gradually he had been growing away from his old faith, but it came as a surprise to his congregation when, one Sunday morning, he quietly told them so. Without having formed any new connection, he resigned his pastorate and withdrew from the Baptist denomination. His action aroused considerable attention, and some time afterward Dr. J. T. Tuttle of the Universalist Church of the Redeemer invited Shutter to speak at his church. There he met with a sympathetic response, and in 1886 he was invited to be Tuttle's associate, a position he was to hold for five years until the latter retired, to become pastor emeritus. At that time, Shutter became his successor, serving a long pastorate at the Church of the Redeemer.[26]

Janson's time to appear in the series did not come until early in 1887, when he spoke on similarities found in the lore about Buddha and the mystical events described in the gospels surrounding the birth of Jesus. This was to draw fire from *Folkebladet*; while the brief article was not signed, Janson assumed the author to have been Oftedal. The writer charged: "What Voltaire had not been able to do, Janson had—namely, with the stroke of a pen—reduced to nothing what the twelve simple fishermen had 'fabricated.' Poor worm! The second psalm reads, 'He that sitteth in the heavens shall laugh!' And when the dust of Janson is hidden and forgotten, poor sinners will rejoice eternally because of their faith in the despised and mocked Nazarene."[27]

When Janson sent his remonstrance to *Folkebladet,* the manuscript was returned with the brief comment that *Folkebladet* could not enter into a discussion with him on Buddhism and Christianity. In this reaction, Oftedal was being consistent. He might criticize Janson's practices, but he had said years before that he would not enter into a theological discussion with one who denied the divinity of Christ. Janson then resorted to *Budstikken.* He had indeed called attention to the similarities found in the supernatural events connected with the life

171

of Jesus and those related some five hundred years earlier about Buddha, he wrote, but he could not see that this constituted an effort to destroy Christianity or to mock the Nazarene. "I cannot lie about or dictate history. If it's so, it's so—and Professor Oftedal is free to investigate. Whether or not he agrees with my conclusion is another matter, although I cannot see how it is open to more than one interpretation." If Christianity rested on such tales as the journey of the three wise men and the killing of infants, it was poorly founded, Janson continued. "How can one 'mock' what he admires and loves? I wonder if the Lutheran churches have a more fervent evangelist for Christ than the one in Nazareth Church."[28]

He drew no response. As things turned out, this was the last of the exchanges between the two men. The image of Jesus that Janson projected in his sermons was always that of the man. In his Christmas sermon of 1886, he had suggested that even at that season one might dispense with the account of the birth of the infant, appealing and poetic though it was. Choosing as his title "The Hero from Nazareth" (Helten fra Nasaret), he intended to call attention to the fact that, in many respects, Jesus was one of us—the common people. At the age of thirty, when he was baptized and began his vocation, his hands were calloused by hard toil, he had no special education, and he went about in the garb of a worker. This was the image that the advocates of the social gospel were to present—and, even more emphatically that of the Christian Socialists. Later Janson was to sharpen the portrait to deplore the shamelessness of the churches, professing Christianity but revealing indifference to the misery and suffering all about them.

In this Christmas sermon, Jesus is portrayed as our master and teacher because He achieved what he admonished the rest of us to do: "Be ye perfect even as your Father in heaven is perfect." He was without sin—a circumstance that at first appears mystical, as the rest of us seem so heavily endowed with it. But as one follows Janson's rationale one finds that the spirit of God is within each of us, and, as we are creatures of free will, we can rise to ever greater heights, if we have the determination. This interpretation was at the core of the Unitarian Christian theism of the last half of the nineteenth century. It is the central thought of Oliver Wendell Holmes' poem, "The Chambered Nautilus," which everyone brought up in America has read and whose last stanza millions have memorized:

> Build thee more stately mansions, O my soul
> As the swift seasons roll!

172

Leave thy low-vaulted past!
Let each new temple, nobler than the last,
Shut thee from heaven with a dome more vast,
Till thou at length art free,
Leaving thine outgrown shell by life's unresting sea!

No one can claim that this concept is an American one; it is the romantic idea of the perfectibility of man. In the struggle for perfection, one must not hesitate to speak out against the evils of the established order in the way that Jesus did; he cut through the hypocrisy of the time, ignored racial prejudice, refused to follow such fossilized customs as the rigid observance of the Jewish Sabbath, and did not recognize class distinctions. It is to be remembered that he associated with the most despised, including tax collectors and prostitutes.[29]

7

As social historians point out, most advocates of the social gospel in Janson's time concerned themselves with the industrial ills of the cities, but he was to champion the cause of the farmer as well. More and more he was penetrating into North Dakota, and what he did not learn from personal observation Norman was at hand to tell him. He was an avid reader of current books advocating this or that means of curing the nation's ills. Of these, the two most important in the 1880s were Henry George's *Progress and Poverty*, first published under that title in 1879, and Edward Bellamy's novel, *Looking Backward*, which came out in 1888. Although the latter seems to have influenced Janson more than the first, he greatly admired Henry George, and after George's weekly, the *Standard*, appeared in the spring of 1887, Janson was one of its faithful readers.

Both Henry George and Edward Bellamy were deeply religious men. George was a Philadelphian by birth. As a young man, he had gone to sea; later he learned the trade of typesetting, and in the late 1850s he settled in San Francisco. On a trip to New York City in 1869, he was appalled by the contrast between the squalor and filth of tenement living on the East Side and the palatial residences on the West Side. He has said that for a time this experience threatened his faith in a benevolent Creator. He came to feel that such circumstances were not the will of God but traceable to the gross errors of man—
"the monopolization of the opportunities which nature freely offers to

173

all." As civilization advances, poverty increases. "Where population is densest, wealth greatest, and the machinery of production and exchange most highly developed—we find the deepest poverty, the sharpest struggle for existence, and the most enforced idleness."

Two factors brought on this starvation in the midst of plenty. First, as an area became settled and the supply of labor grew plentiful, wages were forced down. Second, the best and most accessible land, well in advance of the coming of settlers, was bought up by monopolists—the railroads and speculators—and either sold to those who came later at extravagant prices or rented at exorbitant rates. Henry George argued that the enhanced value of land was an unearned increment, created by population and thus rightfully belonging to society at large. He advocated placing a tax on it, saying that the revenue would be so large that all other taxes could be abolished; thus his proposal came to be known as the "single tax." He was to win the enthusiastic support of Father Edward McGlynn and Rabbi Gustave Gottheil, and, to one degree or another, that of such prominent Protestant clergymen as H. Heber Newton, Lyman Abbott, and Henry Ward Beecher. In later years such well-known advocates of the social gospel as Walter Rauschenbusch and George D. Herron acknowledged that they owed their "awakening" to Henry George, as did William D. P. Bliss, the pioneer in the Christian Socialist movement. In 1887, shortly after he had founded the *Standard,* George organized the Anti-Poverty Society in New York City.[30]

Some measure of the influence of *Progress and Poverty* on the clergy can be gauged by the appearance in 1889 of a Christian version of Henry George's doctrine in *The Bible and Land* by the Reverend James B. Converse. The author demanded the adoption of the single tax because it was the only form of taxation "in accord with the Creator's plans." The book was to receive the official endorsement of the Swedenborgians.[31]

The Unitarians—whom Charles Howard Hopkins has characterized as "that gadfly of American religion"—were in the vanguard of the social gospel movement. Close behind them were the Universalists and Swedenborgians, but their numbers also included clergymen belonging to the liberal wings of the Congregationalists and Episcopalians. In answer to criticism that ministers should restrict themselves to spiritual or theological matters, they responded that anything of concern to human beings was clearly within the province of the pulpit. Speaking before students at Hartford Theological Seminary, the Reverend A. J. F. Behrends said that ministers should be knowledgeable about the problems of the day in order to be ready to apply the principles of the New Testament to their solution. Episcopal Bishop Frederic Don Huntington wrote in the *Church Review* that the duty of the various classes to one another was more fully treated in the Gospels than in the pulpits of the day.[32]

At the time, there was no organized science of sociology, although beginnings were to be made in that direction before the decade of the 1880s was over. The earnest advocates of the social gospel looked upon the New Testament as a textbook on the ordering of society. Like Janson, they accepted the doctrine of the immanence of God. This meant, as William D. P. Bliss was to explain some years later, that they looked upon every member of society—Mohammedan, Jew, agnostic—as the child of God. To be a Christian, said Bliss, who had moved from the Congregational to the Episcopal church, one must recognize the relationship of God as the Father and of all men as brothers. This kinship, he maintained, meant a radical change in the function of the church. It did not exist to make men children of God, for they were that already, but to impress this relationship upon them and to make them see that they must live as members of the same family. In his book, *Ruling Ideas of the Present Age,* published in 1896, Washington Gladden said that the doctrine emphasized the sanctity of all life, rendering the old distinction of the sacred and the profane "meaningless and almost blasphemous."[33]

On January 23, 1887, Janson first delivered his sermon, "Den gjøende hund," which came to be widely admired both for its content and for the poetic expression it gave his thought. Under its English title, "The Barking Dog," it was given before American audiences, winning accolades from laymen and clergy alike. This sermon marks the beginning of a new era for Janson, in which he could turn his attention to the injustices about him and show how completely he was in accord with the advocates of the social gospel.

The sermon begins with a Buddhist parable. Dismayed by the machinations of an unscrupulous king, Buddha descended from heaven transformed as a hunter, accompanied by Devi Matalee who had been changed into a dog. As soon as they were within the royal palace, the dog began to bark so loudly that the walls of the building shook. When the king asked why the animal was behaving so strangely, the hunter answered that it was hungry. The dog was immediately given food, which it devoured, but after every huge portion, the dog resumed its howling. When the creature appeared to be insatiable, the hunter said that only the flesh of its enemies would appease it. When the king inquired who these might be, the hunter answered that they were those who committed such evil acts as oppressing the poor, waging war, and being cruel to animals. The king trembled in fear, and at that point Buddha revealed himself.

The parable was timely, Janson continued, for perhaps at no previous time was the dog howling as it was at the present. The barking of the animal, Janson went on, was the awakened conscience of man. All through history, people had suffered oppression, but always at some point injustice awakened the humane feelings of man (the dog began to howl), and he fought and persisted until the evil was abolished. Janson went on to illustrate this power to bring about social justice by citing such examples as breaking the tyranny of the church, abolishing slavery, and crushing monarchy in the French Revolution. These historical allusions brought him to the climax: "The black clouds now hovering over us are formed by the labor issue. They are erupting in thunder and lightning over Europe. One can no longer gloss over the matter with mere talk or try to appease the howling dog with surrogates. What is needed is a complete change in the system. What is demanded is that the spirit of brotherhood govern the ordering of society, not license for the few to extend their greed and power. The howling over the tyranny of money now shakes the earth, even here in America where the capitalists are in control. Men are asking if it is human or just for a few to accumulate millions while others starve, for a few to crush competition and get control of the various industries so that others dare not enter or are destroyed if they make the attempt.

"Giving millions to charitable institutions is a mere surrogate; it will not silence the just demand for food and shelter, for a peaceful life here interspersed with the occasional pleasures that brighten existence. The dog will howl until it gets justice or until every man and woman wakes up and attempts to change things."

Before he closed the sermon, Janson gave a brief review of Zola's *Germinal,* dealing with the wretchedness of French miners. This book, published in 1886, was another example of the howling of the dog. If the rich did not heed its message, and if the church continued to ignore the precept that one should love his neighbor as himself, the unrest in the world might erupt into violence, for man's conscience would not be quiet until a righteous order had been established on earth.[34]

That winter and spring, Janson devoted his Sunday evening readings to modern Norwegian literature: Ibsen's *Rosmersholm* and *The League of Youth,* Kielland's *Snow,* and Garborg's *Peasant Students.*[35] Drude had finished *A Saloonkeeper's Daughter.* The manuscript had been sent to a publisher in Copenhagen, and Janson had scheduled it for reading in April and May. Years later, Laura Frisvold told how she vowed every Monday that she would be sensible and not go to the reading the following week. She worked long hours as a housemaid in the home of a wealthy family. On Monday morning she had to be up at four o'clock to heat water for washing clothes. Every garment and piece of linen had to be rubbed on a scrub board; she boiled the white clothes and cooked starch for a great number of shirts and petticoats. In the winter and spring as well as in the summer, she carried heavy baskets of laundry outside to hang on lines; later in the day, when she brought them in, during the winter and on raw spring days, they were icy and stiff. By evening, every bone in her body ached, but when Sunday rolled around again, she was never able to stay away from Janson's readings.[36]

Drude did not get to hear her novel read. As the season turned toward spring, the Jansons' eldest daughter, Ingeborg, developed an ear infection. Worried that she might lose her hearing, the Jansons decided she must be taken to specialists in Norway. In April, Drude and Ingeborg sailed on the "Hekla," and Mrs. Behr took over the management of the Janson household.[37] Shortly after Drude left, Janson began the reading of his wife's book. Later that year, it was published under the title *En ung pige* (A Young Girl), the publisher evidently feeling that *En saloonkeepers datter* would not be meaningful in Scandinavia. On December 4 of that year, Andreas Ueland wrote to Rasmus B. Anderson, curious about how the book was being received in Norway and Denmark. "It would be difficult for us to form an opinion of its artistic merits, if we *were* good judges (which we are not) knowing the originals of her characters so well."[38] Ueland did not have long to wait to get a report from Norway. Two days after he had written, *Budstikke*n printed a review from *Verdens Gang* of Kristiania, one which was, on the whole, favorable. Mrs. Janson had a message, the critic said: that no aspiration is too high for a woman if she has the courage to follow her own bent and develop her talents. While the book was one-sided, the reviewer did not feel that it was unrealistic, adding that one got a vivid impression of the coarse elements to be found among the Norwegians in American cities. Since it was quite common for women in America to take part in civic and intellectual activities, the critic did not find the heroine's choice of a vocation at all unlikely, and he predicted that many women in Norway would welcome Drude's novel as a fresh breeze from the West.[39] Apparently the book did not fare as well in Denmark, for, some time later, Janson wrote Bjørnson that *Politikken* had dealt harshly and unfairly with it. According to Janson, the reviewer revealed his contempt for women, as well as his appalling ignorance of the conditions in America which Drude had depicted with almost photographic fidelity.[40]

By the spring of 1887, Hamsun was back in Minneapolis, having spent the previous winter in Chicago. Meeting him one day on the street, Janson learned that the young man was trying to write but was finding this activity almost impossible because of his need to make a living. Janson immediately told Hamsun that he might stay at his house until the family went to Brown County late in June.[41] Hamsun accepted, and soon he and the scholarly young Amandus Norman found the tower room a good place for their discussions of the new school of "Bohemian writers" which was emerging in Kristiania. These authors, influenced by Zola and other French naturalists, were subjecting such hallowed institutions as marriage to scrutiny and expressing themselves so candidly on sexual matters that Norwegians in America were shocked, looking upon the movement as evidence of moral degradation. The subject had a good airing in Minneapolis. People had heard of Hans Jæger's *From the Bohemia of Kristiania* (*Fra Kristiania-Bohemen*), a book that was said to be scandalous. In the spring of 1887, C. Kallum toured the Middle West giving public readings of Christian Krohg's *Albertine*, a novel which had been published in Kristiania on December 20, 1886, only to have all available copies confiscated by the police the following day. Krohg, who was also a painter of distinction, had written a realistic story of a seamstress' descent into prostitution. Well in advance of Kallum's appearance in Minneapolis, *Budstikken* had carried an article sympathetic to Krohg, characterizing him as both an artist (in writing as well as painting) and a reformer. This drew fire from a reader, "Dixi," who somehow or other had obtained a copy and had found the book "tedious, long drawn out, and completely without foundation." After Kallum had read the book in the city, Hamsun came to its defense in *Budstikken,* starting a controversy that attracted "Dixi," "Incognito," and even Kallum, who launched such a personal attack on "Dixi" that the editor reproved him sharply. Janson took no part in this exchange. Although he seems to have admired Krohg's artistry in *Albertine,* both he and Drude had reservations about the Bohemian school of Norwegian writers.[42]

He, however, was involved in a dispute with the Reverend Otto C. Ottesen, a prominent Synod pastor. Janson was to take the initiative, first sending his protest to the editor of the *Minneapolis Evening Journal,* where it was printed under the title "Scandinavian Orthodoxy." His communication read: "Last Sunday a lady came to me after the service and asked me if I remembered that I had baptized her child. Some time ago she had been visiting her parents up in the country where the child died. She took it to the church to be buried and asked the Luthern [*sic*] minister to perform the last ceremony at the grave; but when the minister heard that I had baptized the child, he refused to do it, and the deacon, hearing that, refused to sing at the funeral. The poor mother felt very sorry about it and asked me what to do. I said: 'The child is safe in the care of God, and if the ministers want to make fools out of themselves, let them.' The woman did not belong to my society. The same minister has now moved to Minneapolis, so that we are now blessed with his presence. I know that in the short time he has been here, he has refused to receive as witnesses to his baptisms people who do not belong to my society, only because they sometimes go and listen to my services. I wonder if such ministers think to promote Christian ideas in that way, and I wonder how long the Scandinavian people will tolerate and sustain this priestly tyranny."[43]

Two days after the letter first appeared, it was printed in *Budstikken,* satirically headed "Orthodox Love for One's Neighbor." Some six weeks later, Ottesen replied in *Budstikken.* Janson, he said, should be more careful about his facts: the Synod pastor had been in the city almost four years and thus was not a newcomer. The parents had not been concerned over the child's salvation during its life. The only consolation the pastor had to offer was to present Christ as the son of God and the Bible as the inspired word of God, all of which Janson denied. Furthermore, the pastor had not refused sponsorship to those who might now and then go to hear Janson, but when people had told him they agreed with Janson on such matters as the divinity of Jesus and the inspiration of the Bible, he did deny them. He said he was baffled by the fact that such people would want to be godparents, knowing what it entailed.[44]

Janson was to pursue the matter further. The incident of the funeral was not the only occasion when Ottesen had behaved tyranically.

179

Laura Frisvold often attended services at Nazareth Church, but was not a member; she had been rejected by the pastor after she had been asked by friends belonging to the Synod to be the godmother of their child. This was followed by a statement from Miss Frisvold attesting that Janson had reported matters correctly. Ottesen did not deny that he had refused to accept the young woman but insisted that the particulars were not exactly as Janson had represented them. Thereafter he was to put Janson on the defensive, reviewing such matters as the portraits Janson had given of Synod ministers in *Præriens saga,* his Christmas sermon on the glad tidings of the orthodox and the liberals, the use he made of legends and myths, as well as his denial of the divinity of Jesus and of the verbal inspiration of the Bible. No one else entered the dispute, a fact which may have indicated that even the liberal readers of *Budstikken* felt that Pastor Ottesen had the right to decide who was or was not an acceptable sponsor at baptisms.[45]

9

While this was going on, *Præriens saga* had been brought to the attention of the American public when Hjalmar Hjorth Boyesen reviewed it in the *Critic,* reporting that Janson had depicted in striking colors "the obscurantism and the spiritual thraldom to which a majority of the Norse emigrants submit, and which often keeps them for a whole generation aliens in the land of their adoption."[46] By this time—a year after his Minneapolis church had been destroyed—Janson had raised enough funds for work to be resumed in rebuilding.[47] For several months, he had been conducting services every Sunday afternoon in Unity Church in St. Paul, finding these meetings more promising than his venture in north Minneapolis. The theological differences between him and M. Falk Gjertsen and Sven Oftedal had not kept the three of them from joining together to form a Norwegian Art Association for the purpose of importing paintings from Norway. The group also included Dr. Karl Bendeke, Dr. Tønnes A. Thams, A. C. Haugan, and Professor O. J. Breda of the University of Minnesota.[48]

On May 12, a working man's group in Minneapolis held an "Indignation Meeting" at Bridge Square, and Janson was asked to be a speaker. He was well acquainted with the labor situation in the city, he told his audience. Most of the members of his church and most of his countrymen were of the working class, and he thought it might well be that most of the labor supply in Minneapolis was Scandinavian.

He could give an example of something he was "indignant" about.

A well-educated man from Norway had met with bad luck at home and had migrated to America with his family. In Minneapolis, he had found work in the streetcar barns washing horses, for which he had been paid $1.45 a day. This was not the most suitable work for a man of his ability, but he felt that it would be endurable if he could have Sundays off. When he asked for this concession, he had been told that he might have every sixth Sunday off if he would pay for a substitute. This he refused to do but finally he learned that he might have half a day off every sixth Sunday without paying for someone to take his place. The man's employer was a millionaire, Janson went on. This business leader attended church every Sunday and was supposedly part of a Christian society. Workers in America had less leisure than those of Europe. In this country, competition for jobs was so keen that they always went to the lowest bidders, a practice that forced the working class into greater and greater poverty.

Janson hoped that the lowly and underprivileged would come into their rights and that workers would have better conditions. Amassing wealth that cannot be used up by the most luxurious living, while others lack the bare necessities, could not be tolerated. Change could be brought about without violence if a nation that pretended to be Christian actually became so and practiced the principle of brotherhood.[49] At the time, Janson was already at work on a novel about the labor situation in Minneapolis. At long last, he had also found the way clear for him to issue his own monthly magazine, a publication he had originally planned for the fall of 1883 but had been forced to postpone. Early in June, he announced that the first issue would come out in September, 1887.[50]

10

As usual, the Western Conference held its annual meeting in mid-May. Janson does not seem to have attended, probably because a Minnesota Conference was in the process of formation, in which the old quarrel was to be conveniently bypassed by giving each congregation complete autonomy. The Western Association, however, was well represented at the convention. Douthit came with an "extra" edition of his *Our Best Words* to advance the cause of Christian theism, and Sunderland brought copies of his "Address from the Western Unitarian Association to the Conference." The "Ethical Basis" advocates were under considerable pressure from the American Unitarian Association at least to agree that all missionary work undertaken be soundly Christian theistic in character or to transfer all such work to the A. U. A. All this the delegates found too prescriptive. Freedom of thought meant exactly that. Finally the Conference passed a statement prepared by W. C. Gannett, written in luminous prose strikingly like the idiom of Janson. It was entitled "Things Commonly Believed Among Us":

The Western Conference has neither the wish nor the right to bind a single member by declarations concerning fellowship or doctrine. Yet it thinks some practical good may be done by setting forth in simple words the things most commonly believed among us,—the Statement being always open to re-statement and to be regarded only as the thought of the majority.

All names that divide "religion" are to us of little consequence compared with religion itself. Whoever loves Truth and lives the Good is, in a broad sense, of our religious fellowship; whoever loves the one or lives the other better than ourselves is our teacher, whatever church or age he may belong to.

The general faith is hinted well in words which several of our churches have adopted for their covenant: "In the freedom of the truth and in the spirit of Jesus Christ, we unite for the worship of God and the service of man." It is hinted in such words as these: "Unitarianism is a religion of love to God and love to man." Because we have no "creed" which we impose as a condition of fellowship, specific statements of belief abound among us, always somewhat differing, always largely agreeing. One such we offer here:

"We believe that to love the Good and live the Good is the supreme thing in religion;

"We hold reason and conscience to be final authorities in matters of religious belief;

"We honor the Bible and all inspiring scripture, old and new;

"We revere Jesus, and all holy souls that have taught men truth and righteousness and love, as prophets of religion.

"We believe in the growing nobility of Man;

"We trust the unfolding Universe as beautiful, beneficent, unchanging Order; to know this order is truth; to obey it is right and liberty and stronger life;

"We believe that good and evil invariably carry their own recompense, no good thing being failure and no evil thing success; that heaven and hell are states of being; that no evil can befall the good man in either life or death; that all things work together for the victory of the Good.

"We believe that *we* ought to join hands and work to *make* the good things better and the worst good, counting nothing good for self that is not good for all;

"We believe that this self-forgetting, loyal life awakes in man the sense of union here and now with things eternal—the sense of deathlessness; and this sense is to us an earnest of life to come.

"We worship One-in-All—that life whence suns and stars derive their orbits and the soul of man its Ought,—that Light which lighteth every man that cometh into the world, giving us power to become the sons of God—that love with which our souls commune."[51]

The *Christian Register* hailed the statement as "a glorious presentation of Unitarian beliefs."[52] Later Janson was to translate it into Norwegian for his monthly.[53] But Sunderland had wanted a wording that gave stronger allegiance to "pure Christianity," and Douthit said bluntly, "The dog remains the same kind of dog; they have simply tied a statement on the end of its tail." The Conference continued to publish *Unity* and the Association, the *Unitarian*. Each put out books and pamphlets. But they had no theological quarrel; they did in fact form a "mutual admiration society" as Janson has said—for each side always wrote appreciative reviews about the productions of the other.

11

In June, the new building of the First Unitarian Society was dedicated, with Rabbi Iliowizi as the principal speaker and with Janson rounding out the program by telling a legend and giving its interpretation. His own church would be rebuilt by the fall, but the congregation was still short of funds for lathing and plastering the interior. Now and then contributions came in from women's organizations in the East, and on June 23 the congregation gave a St. John's Day or midsummer festival. On this occasion, in addition to violin and piano solos and Janson's own contribution, Knut Hamsun gave a sprightly talk and Mathilde Ilstrup a declamation.[54]

A few days later, the Jansons, Amandus Norman, Mrs. Behr, and her two daughters went to Brown County, and Hamsun took off for North Dakota, where he was to find work in the wheat fields. The Jansons had reassuring news from Norway about Ingeborg: she was under the care of a doctor in Bergen and improving. But Drude—to judge from letters she wrote Mrs. Rasmus B. Anderson and Bjørnson at the time—was finding Norway somewhat disappointing. In May, she wrote to Mrs. Anderson, who had been her traveling companion on the "Hekla" and was then in Copenhagen: "It was wonderful to come home to my old father. He has not aged much in appearance but in mental alertness and is more like a child, a lovable elderly child, and it affected me very deeply to see him so. Now I have only one wish for him—that he can live to get some good news of my unfortunate brother who is in America trying to make a humble living for himself and his family—and die. My sisters and all my dear ones here were happy to see us and have treated us wonderfully. They were all very taken with Ingeborg and thought she was so sweet and good. . . . From home I have had several letters, and everything is going well. My sister is looking after them wonderfully, and it is a comfort to know she is there. But Kristofer is longing for me, and I am longing for him. I will be happy beyond words to get back again, and I have the feeling I would never thrive here in the long run. I think for certain I'll go back on the 'Hekla' September 15. . . . I heard from someone who knows Amalie Skram that her oldest son has been completely ruined. He has been one of Hans Jaeger's most devoted followers and living in accordance with his theories. Now the mother has taken him in hand to try to save whatever can be saved by now, poor woman! I thought thankfully of my sons living a wholesome life as laborers in California."[55]

For one reason or another, Drude did not get to sail on September 15. In August she was in Copenhagen, where she saw Mrs. Anderson and where she may have had a visit with the Bjørnsons, for in a letter to them in September she speaks of her great pleasure at having seen them. Some weeks seem to have intervened, for she apologized for not having written before, elaborately explaining that she had hitherto thought of Bjørnson as her kindred spirit, but she had come to see that Karoline Bjørnson also was, and she could not think of one without the other. She was writing to tell them of a visit she had made to Gausdal the day before. This experience had been something she had dreaded, but it had turned out to be delightful. Climbing up the hill to Solbakken, the house she had left five years before and which had not been occupied during the interim, she found the trees had grown so much that the house was almost hidden among white-stemmed birches. "It was so still, almost like an enchanted castle," she wrote. "And that's the way it has stood since we left, with all our memories playing around it undisturbed." Looking at the house, she had thought of all the hopes that were buried there. In full view of the place, she had found a spot to sit in the wooded area and had written to Kristofer. As she wrote, the feeling came on her that not a single one of their hopes had been buried or crushed, but that they were very much alive on the other side of the world.[56]

That mood seems to have stayed with her during the fall months after she returned to Minneapolis. In late November she wrote to Mrs. Anderson, who by that time had returned to Madison. Since coming home Drude had been very busy, but she could not remember a time since she had first arrived in America when she had felt so well and full of energy. Every day she worked with Kristofer from nine in the morning until two. With the coming of cold weather, she had to keep watch over the stoves, but the children had been well all fall. They had no extra people in the house, and found home most pleasant when the family could be by themselves. Sometimes at night she felt very tired, but after a good rest she felt vigorous and energetic again. "You can see everything is going well and we are content."[57]

Janson was equally happy to have her home. The following spring, as he was looking forward to another summer in Brown County, he wrote Bjørnson that he was glad Drude would again be with him in that paradise. Yet, during her absence, he had been amazingly productive. He had prepared the first issue of his monthly, finished his labor novel, then called *The Mysteries of Minneapolis,* and had written a short story, "A Riddle" (En gaade). He had also found his writings the focus of a controversy among the Icelandic settlers in Manitoba, Canada—although in this case Janson himself was only indirectly involved. Bjørn Petersen in Winnipeg had become interested in Unitarianism and had given lectures in communities near that city. To further his work, he had translated several of Janson's sermons into Icelandic. This action roused the Reverend Jon Bjarnason, an Icelandic Lutheran pastor, to write a refutation that he sent to *Budstikken*, thus briefly drawing Janson into dialogue.[58] Janson was naturally pleased with Petersen's spontaneous show of interest, and he succeeded in securing for the Icelander financial help for missionary work among his countrymen. Describing the group in the *Christian Register*, Janson said that the people of Iceland were descended from the noblest blood in Norway. They had preferred a life of freedom on a rough island to one of subjection under a Norwegian king. Their descendants in Manitoba were poor, but they were people of rare intelligence and lovers of literature. And in Iceland they had had what Janson called "a prophet of Unitarianism" in an eminent scholar and liberal theologian, Magnus Eirikson.

By the time Janson came to write this article in September, 1887, his church in Minneapolis had been completed on the outside. It was as imposing a structure as anyone could wish. With red brick walls resting on a foundation of massive gray stone, the building rose to a height of some forty feet at its peak and was ornamented with a towering steeple and elaborate porticos at the main entrances. But the interior had to be finished, and money was running short. As he had done so many times in the past, Janson sent out an appeal in the *Christian Register*: "It is long since you heard something from me, Mr. Editor; and your readers feel already safe, I suppose, to take a long breath and say: 'God be praised! Now Mr. Janson is at rest: he was always begging!' But no,—here he is, as usual, representing his work and his wants; and if therefore anyone suspects this article of ending like a Methodist service by sending round the collection box, let him beware of it, and jump to the next page."

He had three congregations, he continued, for the one in St. Paul had been incorporated. His books and pamphlets had been distributed all over the United States, and he had launched his monthly. The opposition had calmed. But the congregation in Minneapolis needed $1,500 to complete the interior of the church. More than that, according to their agreement with the loan fund, they must begin to pay back the borrowed money in two years, that is, by 1889. "If anyone has $100 to spare and would give it for lathing, plastering and wainscoting in the Minneapolis church we would be happy." The lecture room in the basement was being used, but the previous Sunday people had to be turned away for want of space. "I feel it distressing to be compelled to send people off and continue to do so for two years because we are not able to finish our church hall."[59]

7

Saamanden and Christian Socialism

ON A rainy Sunday morning in October, 1887, the Reverend George Batchelor, western agent of the American Unitarian Association, visited the two Unitarian societies in Minneapolis. In both places, he was surprised to find mostly men present, something unusual in the long-established Unitarian churches in New England. The preponderance of men had been especially noticeable in Nazareth Church. Batchelor had come in toward the end of the service but in time to witness a baptism and the admission of new members—and to hear the martial strains of the closing hymn, "Forward! Forward!" Coming from so many young male voices, it was enough to make one's blood tingle, he thought. He reported that after the service Janson was so busy taking subscriptions for his new monthly, *The Sower* (*Saamanden*) that he had no time to visit with his friends.[1]

The rain, Batchelor conceded, might have had something to do with the small number of women present. No one else has mentioned a lack of women at Janson's Sunday morning services—but, so far as the membership in the Minneapolis congregation is concerned, Batchelor's observation represented the true state of affairs throughout the years. In the beginning, Janson had been sure he would eventually attract more women, once they understood that they would be given the same voting rights as men, but this opportunity never seems to have been much of an inducement. Janson was to complain that Cupid was his greatest opponent. When a young man in his congregation became engaged to an orthodox girl, one of the conditions of the marriage often was a return to the Lutheran fold. In a reminiscent article written some twenty-five years later, a charter member, A. Grinager, stated that the congregation had been made up of young people, mostly men, who were honorable, open-minded, and intelligent, but that none of them was rich.[2]

Even though new members were taken in, formal membership seems always to have been small. For one thing, the Norwegian population in the city fluctuated, as immigrants, after being in the city a year or two, saw opportunities elsewhere—a chance to get some land or a place where a particular trade was in greater demand than in Minneapolis—and left the city. This shifting meant that Janson's income from the congregation was often very small. Writing to Bjørnson late in 1888, he was to say that the more energetic and able moved away, leaving only the poor behind; so what he received from the congregation on Sundays was twenty dollars a year at the most.[3] This fact also meant that the burden of building the church, which demanded so many bazaars and programs, rested primarily on Janson and Drude: they supplied the ideas, coached the performers (for plays and tableaux), designed the decorations, and superintended the work.

Yet, for three and a half years—from the autumn of 1887 to the spring of 1891—Janson was to have a tranquil life, perhaps his happiest years in America. His St. Paul congregation was already incorporated, and within the next few years he was to organize two others. His reputation as a supporter of labor also grew. He became a member of the executive committee of the Minneapolis Farmers' Alliance and, after 1888, a staunch advocate of the Populist party. Even the hostility of the Lutherans showed some crumbling. He established friendly relations with Adam Dan, a Dane, and with Lars Heiberg, a Norwegian, both strong church leaders. An even greater achievement was to persuade Professor F. A. Schmidt, the triumphant leader of the Anti-Missourians (who was by then, ironically, the colleague of Professor Sven Oftedal at Augsburg Seminary) to take part in a series of theological debates in Nazareth Church. On these occasions, both sides observed all the courtesies—which everyone agreed was much better than the old system of thundering anathemas from the distance. And the evidence is strong that it was Janson who caused the first bill for the abolition of capital punishment to be introduced into the Minnesota state legislature. It did not pass—actually it did not become law until 1911—but it was Janson's parishioner, Hans P. Bjorge, who at Janson's persuasion, started the ball rolling in 1891.

Yet an environment that was bracing for Janson gradually became more difficult for Drude. With immigrants pouring into the city every year, he was always assured of a church thronged with people, most of whom greatly admired the preacher even if they were not won over to the cause he espoused. With so little opposition from the orthodox, he could bask in his adulation. It is significant that after 1887 most of the criticism Janson received in the press came from his friends.

With lecturing and three congregations to serve outside the Twin Cities, Janson was often away from home making rounds to places where he was warmly received and applauded. At home he was often concerned with relieving the distress of the many who came to him for help. No one doubted the genuineness of his concern—least of all Drude—but with more indigent persons coming into the city every year, the misery about the Jansons seemed endless, and she felt that she could not cope with it. When they themselves felt financial stress, the burden of economizing fell largely on her. She had a large family to care for, and hardly a winter passed when someone was not sick. To an extent, Janson saw this situation, for he often wrote Bjørnson that Drude's life was by no means easy, but he seemed to fail to realize that while his efforts got recognition, she had no such rewards. All of this was to make her increasingly dissatisfied with living in Minneapolis.

2

None of this was on the horizon, however, when Drude returned from Norway in the fall of 1887. At long last, Janson could put out his monthly, an accomplishment she had anticipated as eagerly as he. The magazine was to have keener competition than would have been the case four years earlier, for the city with its swelling Norwegian population now had a number of Norwegian-language newspapers. These included a daily, the *Minneapolis Daglig Tidende*, published by Thorvald Guldbrandsen. This editor also was to take over *Budstikken* the next year, continuing it as a weekly. *Fædrelandet og Emigranten* had been moved from La Crosse to Minneapolis, and Christian Rasmussen had transferred his *Illusteret Ugebladet* from Chicago to Minneapolis, where he also established a book publishing firm. All these papers circulated beyond the confines of the city, but even so, Janson's *Saamanden* was to find readers in Minnesota, Iowa, Illinois, Michigan, North and South Dakota, Nebraska, Montana, Texas, Wisconsin, and California, and in Wyoming and Washington territories.

Saamanden's name evoked memories of Henrik Wergeland, the

young poet and humanitarian who had carried seeds in his pocket, scattering them wherever he found a fertile spot. Printed on pulp paper, about five inches wide and eight long, every issue contained thirty-two pages. On the cover was a small picture of a man throwing out seed as he strode along the countryside. Its motto was expressed in four words: Freedom, Truth, Love, Progress. Through the years, the format remained the same. From the beginning, it had a social orientation which became stronger as time went on. During the first year, it made no mention of politics, but by 1889 it was championing the Populist party.

The magazine offered a great deal for the money: it cost ten cents a copy, or by subscription, a dollar a year. Invariably it began with a poem followed by a lecture or sermon that might take up half the issue, but the content was informative and readable. For the very first number, Janson wisely chose his "Jesus and the Jews," which had gone through a long testing on the lecture platform. His purpose was to show that the Jews in Christ's time were hoping for a political messiah who might relieve them of the Roman yoke; they did not understand the teachings of Jesus that first one must look within his own heart and command himself. They were appalled at his breaking Jewish customs such as keeping the Sabbath, associating with tax collectors and the like, and his insistence that all men—non-Jews as well as Jews—were the children of God. All these innovations led them to cry for his crucifixion. Based on historical sources as well as the Bible, the sermon pictures a whole milieu: the bloody but able Herod, the Pharisees, artisans as well as Biblical scholars—stern in their observance of Jewish law, but patriots, highly respected by their fellowmen. It deals with the Essenes, ascetics living in a monastic community, vegetarians, total abstainers from alcohol, like Jesus stressing the inner life.

Some scholars, Janson remarks, have thought Jesus to have been a member of this group. It discusses the Sadducees, archconservatives, aristocrats, from whom the high priests were chosen. The article is developed from specific instances and anecdotes. One may not be able to finish reading it in one sitting but, after one is through, he feels he has learned something that tempers his judgment concerning the crucifixion. In the same volume, Janson ran a series on the early life of Jesus, a translation of the work of the Reverend W. C. Gannett. Since the Bible has very little about the childhood of Jesus, Gannett had relied on historical sources, including the Apocrypha, and the articles describe the houses, schools, and everyday life of the Jews at the time.

Saamanden's scope was wide. There was no corner of the world it did not cover. Labor conditions were discussed as they existed in Belgium, England, Norway, France, even in East Corea (Korea). Religious tolerance was a key principle with Janson, and readers of his magazine found that one must not only accept other denominations but regard the non-Christian religions with respect and even reverence. His "Mohammedanism and Christianity" was to quote many noble precepts from the Koran and later to explain why the Muslims were making more converts in Africa than the fragmented Christian sects. From the *North American Review,* he translated the debate on Christianity between two Chinese, Wong Chin Foo and Yan Phou Lee, concluding that the Christian Yan Phou Lee had not adequately answered the charges of his non-Christian opponent. Ramabai Dongre of India was in this country raising money for her school for child widows in India. She had not joined any denomination but independently characterized herself as a "Hindu-Christian." The article "Hindu Women," which appeared in *Saamanden,* was a lecture Janson had given to raise money for her cause. In a later issue, one was to read the happy news that she had left the United States with $50,000.

Book reviews and biographical sketches also appeared in the publication. Its tone was serious but never heavy, and now and then a bit of dry humor entered in, as when one reads that Mrs. Elizabeth Rogers, president of a district of the Knights of Labor in Chicago, was a knight of labor in a double sense, for at thirty-nine she was already the mother of twelve children. For the first year of his magazine, Janson drew material from more than twenty sources, including a few Norwegian and Danish journals and Norwegian-language papers published in this country; the majority of his sources, however, were American periodicals, especially Unitarian publications. This variety meant arduous translating.

Saamanden had four regular departments. "Labor Issues" reported on such matters as child labor, working conditions in factories, the sad plight of the Negro more than twenty years after the Civil War. Another, "The Status of Women" (Kvindesagen), drew much of its material from the *Woman's Journal,* the organ of the American Women's Suffrage Association. The achievements of women in fields normally restricted to men were frequently mentioned, not only of those entering such professions as law and medicine, but also of women who had been licensed to drive locomotives or operate steamboats. From time to time, one reads of Mrs. Annie Jenness Miller, the dress reformer—among other things the implacable foe of the corset. In one instance, the case of a woman in politics is described. When male pranksters put the name of Mrs. Suzanne Salter on the roster for mayor of Argonia, Kansas, with the intent of making her a laughing stock, the women of the town rallied to elect her. Later one reads that she proved a very good mayor, closing the saloons and getting the gamblers and roustabouts to leave town.

"Arbeidsmarken," almost a literal translation of *Unity's* "Notes from the Field," was devoted to church news, such as state and regional conferences, the establishment of new congregations, and instances of orthodox clergymen going over to the liberal ministry. "Letters and Answers" shortly became a potpourri, readers besieging Janson with requests to define pantheism, to tell whether there was any truth to the rumor that Victor Rydberg, Bjørnson, and Robert Ingersoll had recanted, and to give the origin of such rituals as baptism, confirmation, and the eucharist. While many of the letters in the magazine were commendations of Janson and *Saamanden,* now and then a doubting Thomas emerged. In the second issue, Knut Tone of Gilman, Iowa, advanced the argument that prayer was superfluous as God was both omniscient and all-loving. There was no point in plaguing Him, Tone reasoned, saying that one must at least expect Him to be as compassionate as oneself. He indicated that his own philosophy was epitomized by what had been found on a tombstone:

> Here I lie, Abraham Buskerod,
> Have mercy on my soul, O God
> As I would do, if I were God
> And you were Abraham Buskerod.

In the translation, the spelling of the name has been slightly altered to preserve the rhyme. The original reads:

> Her ligger jeg, Abraham Buskerud,
> Forbarm dig paa min Sjæl, o Herre Gud
> Som jeg vilde gjøre, hvis jeg var Gud
> Og du var Abraham Buskerud.

It took the issues of October and November, 1887, to satisfy Tone, chiefly by arguing that prayer benefits the petitioner because it fills him with the spirit of God. When one prays for the comfort and well-being of one's fellowmen, he discovers that the love of God is as great or greater than that of a human father who cherishes the requests or confidences of his children.

3

One of the selections in the first volume of *Saamanden* created something of a sensation. The signature "D. J." made it fairly safe to assume that the author was Drude. The article dealt with the aftermath of the hanging of the anarchists in November, 1887, after unsuccessful appeals for clemency to Governor Richard J. Oglesby of Illinois, to the Illinois Supreme Court, and to the United States Supreme Court. It ran in two installments. Entitled "A Minister's Courage and His Persecution (Prestemod og presteforfølgelse), the first part dealt with a sermon by the Reverend John C. Kimball of Hartford, Connecticut, in which the minister declared that the condemnation of the accused men was unjust, because it was a response to popular hysteria and had resulted in making martyrs of the executed persons.

This was bold talk at a time when the word *anarchism* was anathema. Instantly, Drude reported, Hartford was in an uproar; newspapers vied with one another in attacks, not so much on the sermon as on Kimball personally; he was reviled as an agitator, anarchist, and a menace to law and order. Pressure was put on the congregation to dismiss the minister, and those who showed any sympathy for him were threatened that they too would be exposed as anarchists. Kimball suffered every kind of harassment, even to having his mail opened and examined. Finally, his parishioners were forced to call a meeting to decide his fate. After a prominent editor in the community had pointed out the danger of having such a doctrine as anarchism defended from the pulpit and had urged members to show their support of law and order by discharging Kimball, the minister was permitted to speak. In a gentle and forbearing tone, he said that he had spoken out of conscience and could not retract anything.

Drude had established Kimball as a heroic figure—a lone man steadfastly holding his ground before his angry accusers. In a brief postscript, she told the result of the meeting, giving the account a new twist: "The congregation stood the test. The women saved it. Kimball was retained by a majority of ten votes. Supporting him were twenty men and twenty-nine women. Against him were thirty men and nine women."[4]

Even with *Saamanden* as their main outlet, the Jansons continued to write for other papers. Both were to discuss the new Norwegian school of Bohemian literature, Drude in Norway's *Nylænde* and Janson in the Danish women's magazine, *Kvinden og Samfundet.* In the latter and also in *Budstikken,* Janson wrote that he was glad the subject of marriage was coming up for honest discussion, but the frank, realistic treatment of sex in current novels disgusted him. Reading them, one might assume that a young man never thought of a woman except for sexual purposes, he said, citing Lauritz Druse in Garborg's *Men* (Mannfolk) as an example. He had himself spent six years in Kristiania as a student, where he and his friends—not all of them theological students—never so much as thought of visiting a brothel. One thing that safeguarded a young man's morals, Janson thought, was being in love, for then he idealized his beloved and would do nothing that might taint their relationship. He deplored the lack of interest in religion among young people in Norway, sadly adding that the church was to blame. He did think it would be a good thing if women came to marriage better informed on nature's purpose in bringing the male and female together.[5]

This condemnation does not seem to have been strong enough for *Folkebladet.* A few weeks later, the city newspapers reported a discussion about divorce held at a Liberal Ministers' Association meeting. Rabbi Iliowizi, deploring the increase of broken marriages, had advocated stricter laws. Janson had disagreed. Some couples, he argued, were basically so incompatible that it was impossible for them to achieve a harmonious marriage, and in such cases they should be permitted a divorce even if no infidelity or mistreatment was involved. This point of view *Folkebladet* found disgraceful, saying that Janson seemed in sympathy with the Bohemians in Kristiania who married and remarried every few years.[6]

Folkebladet, although it was no longer edited by Oftedal, on another occasion, was to bring up the old charge that Janson maligned—if not the Norwegians—at least the Lutherans. Minneapolis was in the midst of a furious debate over whether or not public places of amusement should be open on Sunday. Janson wrote in the *Morning Tribune*: "Being a European and reared in the Lutheran church, I do not understand this war. I have grown up with the idea that Sunday especially was a day when all public places of amusement should be kept open." *Folkebladet* could only urge that he go back to the Catechism, where it is made clear that Lutherans should refrain from dancing, plays, and frivolous entertainment.[7]

The following spring, Drude was to take *Budstikken* to task for a review it gave the International Women's Congress held in Washington, D. C., in March, 1888. The women, according to the paper, had dealt with too many subjects. Worse than that, Mrs. Elizabeth Cady Stanton had told a group of United States senators that they had the power to bring about a settlement of the women's suffrage issue, and, if they did not, the women would stretch out their hands to dissatisfied elements in the country. This statement must mean that the women would ally themselves with the anarchists and Socialists and communists, the editor of *Budstikken* said, concluding that, if the women could not hold better congresses, they should stay home and care for their children.[8]

Drude's answer, coming a month later, seems to have cowed Jørgen Jensen, the editor. He printed it on the second page of the paper, using front-page space to explain that he had received her well-written article. He then went on to respond to her points, so that the reader probably would read his defense before he got to Drude's letter. Many others, Drude declared, had been offended by *Budstikken's* review of the congress. She had long realized that Scandinavians in America did not value their women highly, but that anyone should take such an attitude toward the world's noblest and most gifted women, she had not anticipated. The *Budstikken* article was sorrowful evidence of how backward the Scandinavians still were, all the more disappointing in a paper which claimed—usually with justice—to be the spokesman for progress and development. The better American papers had been full of praise for the congress.

Did the editor understand, Drude demanded, the great backlog of work, the efforts spanning forty or fifty years, that had been necessary before such an international congress could even meet? All that while, women had been fighting prejudice, derision, and snobbery both from men and from members of their own sex. Although they still had not attained full citizenship, they now had won many rights previously denied them. By arranging such a congress, Americans had shown themselves admirable. The Scandinavians alone chose to treat the meeting with derision, an attitude that brought them little honor.

If the editor had been annoyed, Drude said bleakly, because the women talked, what had he expected them to do? Sit and look at one another? He had been particularly unfair to Elizabeth Cady Stanton, who had worked so devotedly for the cause, implying that she was willing to start a revolution because she had made it clear women wanted the same political rights as men.

What Mrs. Stanton had said to the senators, Mrs. Janson added,

195

had been this: "You have the power to settle the question, but if you won't, women can use other means—can stretch out their hands to dissatisfied elements in the United States." This stand, Drude maintained, was not a threat but a warning. Had Mrs. Stanton said she would appeal to the monopolists, Drude would have found it more alarming. All in all, the *Budstikken* article had made it clear that women could not get together for serious talk without having men suggest that they would be better employed staying home and caring for their children. The less responsible a man was, the more readily such phrases fell from his lips. Apologizing that she had been late in sending her protest, Drude explained that it had been delayed because of illness in her home. With a touch of acid, she added that she hoped it would be accepted because she had first "cared for" her children.[9]

In defending his article, Editor Jensen also turned to plain speaking. Mrs. Janson had said that the better American papers had praised the congress, but this view depended on which might be considered the better ones. He had drawn his material from the *St. Paul Globe,* which had condemned the congress much more severely than he. True, it had been called an international congress, but the number of women coming from Europe might be counted on one's fingers. And, among the American delegates, there were blue stockings and cranks, "with which America is so richly endowed." If Mrs. Janson had been disturbed that he, so many miles away, had called the congress a fiasco, he might remind her she had not been any closer.

The editor certainly did not think women should have sat and looked at one another, but they certainly should have restricted themselves to fewer matters. As it was, they had discussed too many. He was frankly amazed at Drude's defense of Elizabeth Cady Stanton. When the latter had said that women would stretch out to reach dissatisfied elements, who else could she have meant except anarchists, Socialists, and communists? The editor considered this kind of revolutionary talk quite properly a "threat," even though Mrs. Janson chose to call it a "warning." While he agreed that monopolists were America's greatest enemies, he did not want women allying themselves with anarchists. "We have no sympathy with anarchists, communists, and Socialists, even though we have sometimes explained their theories for the education of our readers."[10]

The Jansons did not press the matter, but some months later items in *Saamanden* suggested that Editor Jensen had been gravely mistaken. One reads that the Reverend Moncure Conway had been present at sessions of the congress and had come away astonished. "I remember the bygone days in the capitol when I listened to the oratory of Webster, Clay, Corwin, Seward, and Benjamin," he said, "and not since then have I heard such forceful, eloquent, and statesmanlike speakers as those of the women's congress." Another article reported the attendance of Mrs. Ormiston Chant, a distinguished delegate from London. A descendant of the famous orator Edmund Burke, she was said to have inherited her forebear's talent for speaking. She had remained in this country after the congress to lecture, and she, too, had experienced the derisive treatment Drude had spoken of. She told of former friends cutting her on the street, and on one occasion—at a social function—an imposing man had actually spat on the front of her dress.[11]

4

If Jensen had no sympathy for Socialism, anarchism, and communism, Kristofer Janson was not ready to dismiss them so completely. His own Socialism, certainly in the period 1887–88, was somewhat ill defined. His sympathy for the cause was aroused by his attraction to a "classless society"—although he never used the term. (If he had read Karl Marx, he was never led to discuss Marx's theories.) Like the other advocates of the social gospel, Janson wanted to bring about a leveling through the principles of Christ, changing those who were thus far Christians in name only into actual Christians. His weekly discussion meetings were almost exclusively devoted to social issues. Anarchism had been his subject in December, 1887, shortly after the executions in Chicago, and thereafter, through the winter and spring, he provided such topics as "Should Immigration Be Stopped or in Some Way Restricted?", "Women's Suffrage" (coming shortly after the international congress had been held in Washington, D. C.), "Socialism and Its Relationship to the Theories of Henry George," and "What Is Capital and Is It Productive?"[12]

Among those making their way to Janson's meetings week after week were some intelligent, highly articulate young men. Knut Hamsun, back in the city in the fall of 1887 after a summer's work in the Dakota wheatfields, was regular in attendance and usually ready with incisive comment. Although he seems to have found Janson's grasp of social problems superficial, he agreed with him on the Chicago anarchists; after the executions, Hamsun wore mourning, a black bow on his lapel. Krøger Johansen, a journalist newly arrived from Norway,

197

was usually at the discussions, lively and alert. A man of multiple talents, he worked as a cabinetmaker in a furniture factory until 1888; at that time Gudmund Johnson started another Minneapolis weekly, *Normanna,* and established Johansen as its editor.[13] Occasionally Fritz Gellerup, the anarchist, put in an appearance. It was he who led the discussion on the relationship of Socialism to the theories of Henry George, and it seems there were other times when Janson invited him to take part. Before his death in an accident in 1891, Gellerup's reputation as a radical seems to have extended far beyond the boundaries of Minnesota.[14]

Janson's Socialist friend, Svein Moe, who had been a leader in the group putting out *Den Nye Tid* a few years before, had gone to Los Angeles but was keeping in touch with developments in Minneapolis. In 1887 the city was shocked by the brutal murder of a streetcar driver by a thief who got no more than twenty dollars. The horror was compounded when it was found that the suspect, Peter Barrett, was only sixteen years old. In a time of increasing crime and disorder, people were understandably concerned that lawlessness was extending down to those who were hardly more than children. Peter had not come from an impoverished home; his parents were said to have been moderately wealthy. They were hardly exemplary citizens, however; it was alleged that they had made their money from "blind pigs," in the illicit trafficking in liquor.

In January, 1888, as Barrett's trial was going on, Janson was to use his case as a point of departure for a sermon, "Our Boys" (Vore gutter). It was a common-sense appeal for better moral training in the home and more concern about what children might be up to, the kind of observation that occurs to many only when they are alerted to the problem by some shocking event. *Budstikken* printed the sermon, and it made interesting reading because of the examples the minister gave of his own experience with youthful ruffianism. He told how his sons had been taunted because of their nationality when they had first begun school, their persecutors following them in groups and sometimes throwing stones. An American boy, Janson said, rarely risked an encounter with a single opponent, fist to fist, but commonly formed a gang which tormented one or two victims. Once when one of his sons had been injured by a rock, Janson had gone to the father of the guilty young ruffian, who shrugged the matter off, saying he never interfered in boys' quarrels.

Another time, a group of youngsters climbed up on the Janson house and amused themselves by pelting passersby with stones. When the minister found out what was going on and ordered them off, they answered him insolently, finally running over to the next lot, defiantly telling him they could do as they liked, as they were no longer on his property. He said that his sons had used their spending money to buy a variety of pigeons, which other boys came first to admire and later to steal. After an attempt to break the lock on the barn where the birds were then kept, they returned later to cut a hole in the door. When one of his sons found out who the thief was and reported the matter to the police, he was told they had too much to do to bother about pigeons.[15]

All of this seemed to convince most readers of the sermon that such boys were in need of better training and a tighter rein; the Socialist Svein Moe in Los Angeles objected to Janson's conclusions. In two letters to *Budstikken,* he argued that hoodlumism among boys was traceable to the evils in society, to hunger and need. Parents could not teach their children anything better because they had had no opportunity to learn it themselves.[16] This was nonsense, Janson retorted. To be sure, there were grave social wrongs which needed correction, but, even if these were to be remedied, that would not halt crime unless children were taught in their homes the difference between right and wrong. Advising Moe to be patient until his new novel came out, Janson concluded benignly with "Greetings from a friend."[17] If the wrongs were corrected, Moe answered, crime would exist for a time but merely as a vestige of the old order. Once the injustices spawning crime were wiped out, there would be nothing to encourage its growth. An individual can develop morally only when he is free from economic oppression; conscience is formed by social circumstances. "Can a tramp living miserably make choices—'know' the difference between right and wrong or have a 'conscience'?"[18]

Generously, Janson allowed Moe the last word. Even when he disagreed with people on particulars, he had a warm sympathy for all those who railed against injustices suffered by the workers. In the coming years, he was to eulogize both Fritz Gellerup and Marcus Thrane, and it is possible that he had already used Svein Moe for his model of the ardent Socialist in his still-unpublished labor novel. For the most part, the topic of Socialism did not enter into his Sunday evening readings although he did open the 1887–88 season with Zola's *Germinal.* Thereafter, he chose selections from Russian and French authors—Dostoevsky, De Musset, Feuillet, De St. Victor, now and then interspersing some comments on Garborg and Kielland.[19] In the spring of 1888, he delivered a sermon, "Jesus as a Labor Leader," in English. As "Jesus som arbeiderfører," it was published in *Saamanden* in February, 1890; in reading it, one suspects Janson of forcing the material to comply with his thesis. Although we are told that Jesus as a carpenter knew the trials of the working class at first hand—and that he thundered most against the rich and hypocrites—half of the sermon deals with the fair and equitable Jewish laws on the ownership of land. He cited the provisions for adjustment of inequities in the sabbatical and fiftieth jubilee years, the author having some difficulty in accounting for the Jews also tolerating slavery. His purpose was to show that even the best laws will not safeguard against injustices unless the spirit of brotherhood pervades the whole of society. The latter part of the sermon deals with how the apostles practiced a voluntary communism, thus being true followers of the master. On the whole, the argument for Jesus as a labor leader is a weak one—a fact which may account for Janson's saying that one could not expect a simple carpenter to build up an organization comparable to that of Henry George or of the Socialists in the nineteenth century.

5

Yet the fall and winter of 1887–88 were not completely overshadowed by social concern; there were lectures, concerts, plays, and social festivities. Knut Hamsun, hopeful of living on his summer's savings while he devoted himself to literature, was giving a series of lectures on Ibsen, Bjørnson, Kielland, and other Scandinavian authors. Although Janson did what he could to publicize the lectures, Hamsun's audiences tended to be small.[20] On January 22, when Hamsun's subject was Kristofer Janson, the latter took Hamsun's strictures in his stride, but *Budstikken* reported that many of the minister's friends were irritated at the judicial air with which Hamsun had censured Janson's writing. Hamsun had said that it was high time Janson abandoned his style of writing for an ill-defined class of common people by expressing the simplest meanings in the simplest way. Janson should leave that to those who could do no better; he should respond to the new trends in Europe and recognize the artist as the one who sees through the foibles of his age and exposes them. Hamsun thought that Janson should improve his diction, choosing words with deeper emotional overtones; the critic went on to say that the day of romantic poetry was over. All of this disappointed the newspaper's reporter, who felt that Hamsun should have handled his subject more circumspectly and with greater thoroughness.[21]

Some three weeks later, Hamsun was to be a featured speaker at a *lutefisk* supper given by Nazareth Congregation. The completion of the church had been proceeding at a snail's pace. In January, 1888, the stained glass windows of the main sanctuary had been put in place and the floor had been laid, but work on the structure seems to have been sporadic, stopping whenever money ran out.[22] Every effort was made to make this supper a gala event; the advertisement in *Budstikken* promised that the evening would unfold like a play:

Act I: *Ludefisk* with butter, potatoes, and *flatbrød*
Act II: Piano solo by Professor Gustavus Johnson
           Speech by Knut Hamsund
           Song by Mr. Thomsen
           Scene from *Peer Gynt*—in costume—by Krøger Johansen
           Ludefisk talk by Kristofer Janson
Act III: Coffee, cake, small talk, and music
All these delights—gratis — after payment of fifty cents admission
                    —Peter Kitchenmaster (Per Kjøkenmeister)

There was to be additional comedy. Somehow or other Knut Hamsun became lost and spent several hours wandering through city streets until at ten o'clock he found his way to the church. All the better for the experience, he told of his wanderings, saying that he had finally caught a whiff of *lutefisk* and thereafter could trust his nose to bring him safely into port.[23]

Olive Fremstad, later a diva with the Metropolitan Opera Company, was making her living by giving music lessons in Minneapolis. In February, she appeared in concert, assisted by Professor Gustavus Johnson, J. E. Gjesdahl, and Kristofer Janson, who read a poem by Jørgen Moe; all of this was warmly applauded in *Fædrelandet og Emigranten,* which declared that Miss Fremstad had improved greatly since her previous concert.[24] Shortly afterward, *Gjenboerne* (The Neighbors), a play by the Danish author Jens Christian Hostrup, went into rehearsal. Advertised as "en stor forestilling" (a great presentation), it had a cast of fifteen characters and was directed by Janson, who also was to give a talk on the playwright and the play before the performance began.[25]

Soon Knut Hamsun, who was now determined to return to Norway, delivered a lecture sharply criticizing America, with special reference to the only American city he really knew. This was too much for Janson. On Sunday evening, April 22, he dispensed with his usual

201

literary reading to deliver "A Defense of Minneapolis—an Answer to Mr. Knut Hamsund." So far as Hamsun was concerned, this was labor lost, for the following year, from Denmark, he published a book in which he made a violent attack on American culture, drawing his illustrations liberally from Minneapolis.[26]

During the late spring, Janson lectured and attended church conferences, staying close enough to Minneapolis to get back for weekends.[27] As he was to relate in his autobiography, his Sunday schedule was heavy—morning services in Nazareth Church at eleven o'clock, St. Paul services at four in the afternoon, and the Sunday evening readings in Minneapolis at eight o'clock. Once in a while, he had a substitute speaker for the latter, as when Mrs. Nellie Anderson gave a talk on "The Principles of Christian Science" on May 13.[28] One Sunday evening, Drude gave a lecture, and, on another occasion when Janson was hoarse, she delivered his Sunday sermon. Two of his daughters, aged thirteen and ten, took part in a short play on a Sunday evening for a church festival.[29]

Good news came from Norway; Bjørnson offered to buy Solbakken, the Janson home which had stood vacant for so many years. The Jansons had long wanted to dispose of the property and—as Drude said—would have sold to any buyer, but they felt a sentimental attachment to the house and were comforted to learn that Bjørnson planned to make it his home for his declining years. Writing on June 1, 1888, to accept the offer, Janson had no thought of leaving America. Even a vacation seemed out of the question for the next few years, until he had found a man capable of taking over during the interim. Bjørnson had suggested that Sweden might be ripe for Unitarianism, if the right man—such as Janson—went to promote it, but Janson did not find the proposal attractive. From what he had observed, he felt that the Swedes were either fanatically orthodox or else indifferent to religion and fond of card playing and conviviality around the punch bowl. Nor did a vacation in Norway seem especially appealing. Whenever he let himself dream, he thought of a world cruise—when Drude and he were old—that would take them to Japan, to India where he would visit his friends in the Brahmo Somaj sect, and then to Palestine, Syria, Greece, and Italy. He had been fascinated by the reports of the Reverend Arthur Knapp, whom the American Unitarian Association had sent to Japan; were he a younger man, Janson declared, he would certainly go there as a missionary.[30]

Even so, he was content with his lot. He was looking forward to the summer in Brown County and glad that Drude would be with him and not in Norway, as she had been the previous summer. But the vacation was still a month off. In the meantime, he was to make a lecture tour along Lake Michigan, incidentally "doing a little spying for the Unitarians." He was to mention this trip in both his letter of June first to Bjørnson and in the note that followed it on June sixth. One can only speculate that, as a director of the Western Association, he was checking to see that missionary funds were not going to those who confined themselves to preaching ethics to the exclusion of Christian theism.

A few days later, Drude was to write to Mrs. Rasmus B. Anderson in Madison. Professor Anderson had been home on vacation from his duties as minister to Denmark and was to take his family with him on his return to Copenhagen. Drude wished Mrs. Anderson a pleasant journey, glad that she at long last would have a year when she would have her whole family about her after the lonely winter she had endured while her husband had been in Europe. Drude's buoyant mood of the fall before had worn thin. As was so common in her letters, she began with an apology: she should have written before, but she had been so busy there was not a moment left over for letter writing. She had felt frozen all winter; when the spring came, the children had had the measles, and, since that time, there had been so much unrest and trouble that she hardly had the energy to drag herself across the floor. But she was looking forward to a peaceful summer in Brown County and glad to send Mrs. Anderson the news that Bjørnson was buying their house in Norway.[31]

Even as she wrote, the Jansons were deep in plans for a gigantic (*storartet*) bazaar to be given the following autumn, from September 30 to October 8, in Harmonia Hall. Every evening a new elaborate program would be given, replete with clever speeches, music, plays, and tableaux. There would be a dime museum (modeled after those of P. T. Barnum) in which the public would be promised a view of wonders of the world (to be hoodwinked by a play on words), but the exhibits must be carefully planned so as to amuse and not embitter the customers. It would feature popularity contests and straw elections, but the greatest drawing card was the magnificent first prize—a parlor set already purchased from Bradstreet, Thurber and Company in the Syndicate Building on Nicollet Avenue. During the week of June 10, this furniture was on display in the company's show window.[32]

By the time the Janson family set out for Brown County, they had a new worry. Eilev, their second son, had not been heard from in weeks. Kristofer wrote to the sheriff of the county in California which

203

included Eilev's last address, but that official could give them no clue concerning the whereabouts of the young man. The Jansons tried to comfort themselves that, while Eilev was an adventurous eighteeen-year-old, he was also remarkably levelheaded. Yet the uncertainty was to etch a groove of anxiety for them during the month of July, and Janson wrote Amandus Norman of his uneasiness. Finally in August, Eilev wrote. He was in British Columbia, then a wilderness, where he had been shooting bears, wolves, and other wild game. In their relief, the parents were to urge both of their sons to return home to settle down to earnest training for their future. Ivar was persuaded and did come back later that fall, but Eilev wanted to work and save money through the winter, promising that he would return to Minneapolis in the spring.[33]

During the summer, Drude began work on her second novel, *Ensomhed* (Loneliness), which dealt with life on the Minnesota prairie. Janson was busy reworking a story originally written by Amandus Norman during the year he had been the minister's student. Laid in the area about Reynolds, North Dakota, it is a realistic tale of a simple but heroic immigrant woman who grubs a living from the land in spite of such misfortunes as having a drunken and errant husband and fighting prairie fires. For some reason, Norman never wanted to acknowledge even being co-author: Janson was to publish it in 1889 as *Et arbeidsdyr*. In July his two character sketches, entitled "Old Synnove" and "Birte," came out in English in the *Christian Register;* they later appeared in Norwegian in his *Paa begge sider havet.* Janson also wrote a short play, "Fint og grovt" (Fine and Coarse), and a satirical tale of two rival small towns called "Potterville and Perryville."[34]

6

Yet it was his reading of two important books by well-known authors that summer which was to affect him deeply, to furnish him with subjects for sermons, and to provide some of the excellent material one finds in volume two of *Saamanden*. Both books, dealing with the religious life of the layman, were widely read at the time. By contrast, any of the articles then appearing in Unitarian journals, with their forced optimism, seem shallow and, like some of Janson's sermons, too simplistic. Hamsun was never able to find his way in Janson's Unitarianism, and even Amandus Norman, committed though he was, complained in his early months at Meadville that the religion expounded at the seminary was too bland; it needed a little salt water or a bit of Dakota blizzard, he wrote to Janson. At his Brown County retreat, Janson first read Tolstoy's *A Confession* and its accompanying *What I Believe.* Then he turned to Mrs. Humphrey Ward's *Robert Elsmere,* today hardly more than a period piece. Of course, this novel was more meaningful in an age when one person's defection to liberalism could produce a crisis in a marriage or a family, a situation which had occurred among the Norwegian Unitarians, even in Brown County.

In any age, Count Tolstoy's account of the religious crisis which radically altered his life would be arresting. A member of the Russian nobility, wealthy, in good health, and world famous because of such works as *War and Peace* and *Anna Karenina,* Tolstoy came to an impasse in his life while he was still under fifty. "Suddenly my life stopped. I had no more desires. I knew there was nothing to desire. The truth is that life was absurd. I had arrived at an abyss and I saw that before me was only death," he wrote. In despair, he began a search for some unifying principle that would give meaning to life. He began with the beliefs of the Russian Orthodox Church and later examined other sects; he was revolted by their condemnation of one another and by their tolerance of war. Observing that peasants seemed to have a faith that gave purpose to their lives, he turned to the source of that faith, the Gospels, learning enough Greek to study the early versions of the New Testament. From this study, he was to reject the dogma of the divinity of Christ and to work out his own set of Christian principles, drawn primarily from St. Matthew. For Tolstoy, to believe was to act: he lived as a peasant, made his own boots, and spent part of each day in such manual labor as chopping wood and plowing land, having signed away his property. In *What I Believe,* he delineated his creed in "five commandments": not to judge or bring others to judgment, to allow no divorce after the consummation of a marriage, never to take an oath, not to resist the evil-doer regardless of the provocation (nonviolence), and never to harbor enmity against any other nation or race, and thus never to consent to go to war.[35]

Janson was to herald Tolstoy's philosophy as a devastating blow to orthodoxy—and indeed, on the surface, the Russian's simple Christianity seems remarkably like what Janson had been proclaiming, with the exception of references to the asceticism of Tolstoy's later life. "A Russian Count and His Conversion" was to be the second sermon Janson delivered in Minneapolis during the 1888–89 season, and in February, 1889, this article appeared in *Saamanden;* it is so painstaking a retelling of *A Confession* that it retains much of the poignance of the original. He followed this later with sermons on each of Tolstoy's rules of life, although in these he was not to report on the Count's investigations of the biblical texts so much as to use the great author's views as a point of departure for his own thoughts on each subject. These also appeared in *Saamanden,* in four installments, Janson combining the last two of Tolstoy's commandments. The Sunday he preached on divorce, Anne Romundstad was so impressed that she summarized the sermon in a letter to her fiancé, Johannes Skørdalsvold, then in Europe. She concluded concerning Janson, "Han talte vakkert" (He spoke beautifully). In spite of his point of view in this sermon—as before, freely permitting legal separation or divorce but prohibiting remarriage—he was to reverse himself some years later in his lectures "Marriage and Divorce" (Aegteskab og skilsmisse).[36]

Mrs. Ward's *Robert Elsmere* deals with a clergyman in the Church of England happily married to Katharina, a deeply religious woman who shared his labors with a consecration equal to his own. While working on a theological treatise, Robert Elsmere begins to have doubts about the rightness of the dogma of his church and is further influenced by a neighbor. Eventually, he must confess to his wife that a change has taken place in him. Her devotion to the old doctrine—in particular to the divinity of Jesus—is such that she cannot possibly follow him. They separate, and Elsmere finally dies, alone, in the London slums, where he had been working as a liberal minister.[37]

Janson's sermon concerning the Elsmeres appeared in *Saamanden* in January, 1889, shortly after he had delivered it. In the article as published, he briefly summarizes the story and goes on to mention other instances of such religious conflicts, citing the crisis Bjørnson had gone through to which Janson had been a witness, the situation of a couple in Minnesota, and—in tribute to Drude—that of the Jansons: "I was so fortunate as not to have an orthodox wife. There was a time in our household when our roles were reversed, for my wife was Robert Elsmere and I was Katharina. She had to endure (as it must have seemed to her) a dull, orthodox husband, and I suffered in having what I thought was a heretical wife. Now when I read the pompous, heavily theological letters I wrote her and my sermons from that time—some of them printed—it is as if I were looking into a completely strange face—for I do not recognize myself. Thus my conversion to reason from theological brain-spinning was different from that of Robert Elsmere—indeed quite the reverse, the basis of happiness in our home, for it brought my wife and me together so we could work for a common cause."[38]

At the close of the summer, just before he left Brown County, Janson had written to Amandus Norman at Meadville. He said that he had revised Norman's story, calling the new version "Et arbeidsdyr," adding he would read it in Minneapolis but make no mention of Norman since that was the young man's wish. He also told Norman that he had discovered a Dane, a former folk-school teacher in Michigan, who had been arrested in Denmark because of a lecture he had given in the folk school on the French Revolution. Janson had engaged him for the winter to serve as "a kind of personal curate" (*kapellan*).[39]

7

It was to be a hectic fall. The bazaar, beginning on September 30 and extending through October 8, required the help of all the Jansons and culled talent from organizations and individuals throughout the city. The Normændenes Men's Chorus and the Norwegian Turner Society performed; the mayor and other prominent men in Minneapolis and St. Paul gave speeches; a "Professor Diedrich Menschenschreck" convulsed audiences by satirizing politicians (appropriate in an election year).[40] The Dime Museum was said to be especially inventive; in the popularity contests both the winners and the runners-up made admirable showings, and the straw voting revealed the usual false prognostications. There were multiple theatrical offerings: an act from Holberg's *Jacob von Tybo,* a scene, "Colonel Lutken Teaches His Servants to Dance the Minuet," from Janson's *Vore besteforældre* (Our Grandparents), such skits as "Peter Tramp's Homecoming" and "Ole Fet's Meditations," a tableau from Dybbøl's *Beleiring* (Siege), and one concerning David and Goliath. Only in the latter was there a slight irregularity. Holger Faurschou, a Danish policeman, a man of gargantuan proportions, was Goliath and the fifteen-year-old Arne Janson was David. Costumes had been rented. At the last moment, Janson was alerted by a hoarse whisper from Faurschou; the pants of his costume were too small. Desperately Janson rummaged about in the wardrobe, finally coming up with a clown costume that was big enough.[41] Attendance was good throughout, except for Tuesday, October 2, when it was thought the fact that the city primary was being held was responsible for a slackening off. But the bazaar cleared about $1,500,[42] and in the November *Saamanden* Janson reported "hopefully the church might be finished."[43]

Hardly was the bazaar over than Janson began a series of twenty campaign speeches in Wisconsin, urging the re-election of Cleveland and dealing largely with the president's proposals for the reduction of the protective tariff. Long a critic of the tariff, Janson had been engaged by the Democratic National Committee. Returning to Minneapolis one weekend in mid-October, he was surprised to find that he had been nominated as a Democratic candidate for the school board. At once he inserted a notice in the papers that for many reasons he must decline, grateful as he was for this show of public confidence.[44] Meanwhile during these busy months, he had to cut corners in *Saamanden*. In the September issue, "Letters and Answers" was omitted altogether, and in the October number one finds only the letters, all of them expressions of thanks for the magazine, no doubt chosen because they required no comment from him. Material for that issue is drawn from only five sources, most of it coming from the *Christian Register*. The short articles, usually set up in columns, appear in larger print than usual, as if an effort had been made to fill up space.

The Democrats lost on both the national and state tickets. A few weeks after the election, Janson was to deliver a sermon entitled "The Presidential Election and the Campaign before the Religious Tribunal." Although it was never printed, one can guess its content from what Janson wrote to Bjørnson shortly afterward. With the Republican victory, the millionaires could exercise a tyranny the like of which the world had never seen. Secure from European competition because of the protective tariff, the capitalists would continue to form combinations for the complete control of all commodities, raising prices and lowering wages with a free hand because of the continued influx of immigrants. "If the Republicans do not take the spoon in the other hand," Janson wrote, "they will be getting this country ready for a social revolution."[45]

In 1888, Janson seems to have chosen to support the Democratic party as the lesser of two evils; Cleveland had not advocated the abolition of the protective tariff which Janson found so indefensible but had merely suggested its curtailment. After the election, Janson had personal reasons for being disillusioned with the Democrats. He was supposed to be paid $300 for his campaign speeches in Wisconsin; by mid-December he had written twice to ask when this fee would be forthcoming, and to say that he had not received so much as a reply.[46] At first, one finds it surprising that in December—a month after the election—Janson printed the platform of the Minnesota Farm and

Labor party in *Saamanden,* the one that had been adopted the previous August. For all its fine rhetoric, the Minnesota Farm and Labor party in 1888 had collapsed before it got off the ground.

This splinter group had been an affiliate of the larger Union Labor party. At the time it adopted its platform, it nominated Ignatius Donnelly as its candidate for governor, promising to raise a campaign fund of $3,000. This backing never materialized. By October, Donnelly withdrew from the race, throwing his support to Merriam, the Republican candidate. As a result, Donnelly was hired by the Republican State Committee to make speeches, much as Janson had done for the Democrats.[47] A new political party always needs time to gather momentum; in the beginning, weaknesses in its organizational structure are more or less to be expected. Whether Janson reasoned in this way or not, the insertion of the Farm and Labor party's platform in *Saamanden* marks the beginning of his allegiance to what came to be popularly known as the People's party.

The preamble of the platform stated that other political parties were controlled by rings which operated in the interests of the monopolists. The population could be divided into two classes—the producers and the nonproducers. "Shall the people receive the fruits of their own labor or shall the nonproducers reduce them to slaves?" was the main issue. From the national government, the new party demanded freer money without the intervention of banks, the abolition of land speculation, a revision of the tariff so that all commodities necessary to life were on the free list, government control of both passenger and freight transportation, and federal operation of the telegraph and other means of communication. Among the demands made on the state government were the adoption of the Australian (secret) ballot, equal suffrage for women, safety regulations for factories and shops along with inspections, laws forbidding corporations to hire private detectives, weekly pay in legal tender, and an eight-hour day.[48]

8

During the fall of 1888, two articles concerning Janson came out in Europe—one in Kristiania's *Verdens Gang* and the other in a Danish periodical, *Ny Jord.* Neither dealt in any way with Janson's political activities, but both were to give on-the-scene estimates of the man. The second—written by Knut Hamsun—was the more comprehensive and certainly the most influential in this country.

The *Verdens Gang* article was written by Henrik Cavling, a journalist who later was to treat extensively of Scandinavian life in America. In November, 1888, he had visited the Jansons, informing himself about Unitarianism and attending services in Nazareth Church. His article in *Verdens Gang* dealt first with the feud going on in the Synod on grace. Cavling was set to wondering why leaders in that church organization should risk a serious rift over what—to an outsider—seemed like intellectual hairsplitting. While the shepherds were quarreling among themselves, Cavling was to say metaphorically, there was danger the wolf might take the sheep—especially if the wolf happened to be so gifted a man as Kristofer Janson. He found Unitarianism so benign a religion, and indeed so perfectly adapted to Janson's nature, that it almost seemed that the doctrine had been invented for him. Even as a young theologian in Norway, he had been suspect, Cavling continued, citing an instance when the young student had delivered a sermon with Pastor Lars Oftedal seated in the church busily writing throughout the delivery. When it was over, the pastor presented Janson with the evidence—no less than twenty-seven instances of heretical teaching. And the liberal preacher had hardly bettered himself by coming to Minneapolis, for there he had encounted Lars Oftedal's brother, Professor Sven Oftedal, who, along with his Conference brethren, looked upon Janson as a disruptive spirit.

Cavling was to describe Janson as a tall, broad man with a blond beard and large, expressive eyes, who bore more of a resemblance to a Grungtvigian folk-school teacher than to a clergyman. His sermons were not pontifical, but his thoughts were clothed in imaginative, poetic language, and he was not averse to bringing in humor that might cause the congregation to burst out in laughter. "On occasion, in the midst of a sermon," the journalist wrote, "He might sing, and then one does not know what to admire most, his delightfully clear voice or his eyes that seem to warm the room, more eloquent than a thousand voices. At such a moment Kristofer Janson's power is daemonic: the faithful can forget heaven in admiration of the pastor."[49]

Hamsun's article had the thrust of an expertly driven hypodermic needle: it found the vein right away. Janson had overreached himself; in attempting to be all things to all men, he was limited in the time he could spend on any one idea. The result was a superficiality that impaired him as a writer and took the edge off his work as a social reformer. Hardly an issue or new movement came to the fore that escaped Janson's attention. Yet he never examined any of these matters thoroughly; he was eclectic, selecting this and that feature which attracted him and incorporating them into his system. His information was drawn from the few newspapers he read, and the result was that, while his interests were wide, they lacked depth and his arguments were often faulty.

Hamsun dismissed Janson's Unitarianism as a kind of Turkish faith "with an odor of mysticism." His sermons, following the American fashion, gave a practical interpretation of religion, dealing with the questions of the day—"politics from the pulpit," illustrated in every way with anecdotes, statistics, excerpts from the newspapers. As a speaker, he was masterly. Every Sunday, in a buttoned Prince Albert coat, he stood before his audience, manuscript in hand. Without any fire or brimstone or other oratorical flourishes, he spoke with an engaging earnestness, keeping his large audience completely absorbed for an hour.

A thoroughgoing idealist, Janson gave of himself unstintingly. He was a minister, occasional speaker, traveling lecturer, writer, editor, and a member of many organizations. The demands made upon him by the American Unitarian Association were not oppressive, but the Scandinavians in America, especially those of his congregations, besieged him with their problems, expecting him to have an answer for everything. Yet, Hamsun went on, Janson's lack of effectiveness as a minister and social reformer lay in the man himself. His love of mankind exceeded his understanding of it. He was too fair, too gentle, too good: "Janson's gift is not that of a leader; he has a fine lyrical talent of childlike delicacy. In his hands statistics become poesy, references edification. He lacks the logical mind that can keep track of all the complicated threads of an issue and the bass in his voice that can thunder. In the midst of battle, you cannot hear him, only see his handsome, noble form stand before you. As a leader he lacks the cold boldness necessary if one is to dig his claws into an opponent and the fire in his speech that can brand. Janson cannot inflame or brand; he warms. To be a leader one must be able to dominate, and Janson cannot; he can gladden and help but he cannot strike. He is a physician at a warrior's post."

As a writer, Hamsun said, Janson had more than twenty volumes to his credit. While some were better than others, his work showed little development. Janson always walked along the same path. His books were as broad and as uniform as the prairie—from which they emanated. Yet on this point Hamsun was more indulgent. True enough, all of Janson's work, even the latest, was diffused with a summery mildness. But possibly one day—before it was too late—Janson would come forth with something great, "the work of art we await." His

211

earlier writings indicated that he was one of literature's delegates. "He can, if he will; give him time!" Janson was yet young (he was forty-seven), and there were youthful ideas germinating within him. That was as far as Hamsun could go. "But today he is the noblest public personality among the Norwegians in the West—a lonely delicate flower on the North American prairie."[50]

This appraisal was hardly more than damning with faint praise, but Janson was to thank Hamsun for it in such a manner as to give the critic a twinge of conscience. On December 26, 1888, Hamsun wrote to the Danish writer, Erik Skram: "I had a letter from Kristofer Janson today; he thanked me in a letter that glowed with goodness because I ripped him apart (*skælt han ud*) in *Ny Jord*—placing glowing coals on my head."[51] Years later, in his autobiography—then over seventy and the victim of a stroke—Janson spoke of his gratitude: Hamsun had been the only one to subject his writing to critical analysis.[52]

Before Hamsun's article came out, several in America had intimated similar thoughts about Janson—chiefly that he jumped to conclusions too fast; after its publication, one begins to find these sentiments in the newspapers. Yet, in respect to Janson's superficiality as a social reformer, one must add that he was very much the child of his time. In his *Rise of the Social Gospel*, Hopkins says that very little of a practical nature came out of the clergymen's agitation, and Dombrowski was to point out that the Christian Socialists had more in common with Edward Bellamy and Henry George than with Karl Marx. They thought of Socialism in sentimental and somewhat vague terms in keeping with their ideas of brotherhood. Such matters as surplus value, the class struggle, and economic determinism were largely ignored.[53]

9

The names of the Protestant valiants—Gladden, Converse, Rylance, Newton, Huntington, Silcox, Bliss, and many others—are found in *Saamanden*. They were Presbyterians, Swedenborgians, Congregationalists, and Episcopalians. One often reads in Janson's magazine of Father Edward McGlynn, the staunch supporter of Henry George, of Rabbi Solomon Schindler and other Jewish clergymen, and of Felix Adler and his Ethical Culture Society. These men were advanced in their social views, and so they tended to belong to the liberal wings of their respective denominations. After the formation of the Society of Christian Socialists, Janson frequently drew material from the *Dawn,* edited by William D. P. Bliss, but up to October, 1892, the American minister who seems to have influenced him most was the Reverend Hugh Pentecost.

Janson mentioned Pentecost first in *Saamanden* early in 1888, remarking on what courageous, truth-loving ministers must endure from their orthodox congregations. The Reverend J. C. F. Grumbine had to leave his church because of his support of Henry George, and the Reverend Hugh Pentecost had been forced out of his pulpit in Newark. "In a recent number, the *Nation* had the temerity to ridicule these men and the cause they serve," Janson wrote indignantly. In his farewell sermon, Pentecost had explained his difficulties candidly. No one had had any fault to find with his theological views, which were liberal, but hardly more so than those of many of his fellow Congregationalists. Orthodox leaders had objected, however, to his defense of Henry George, to his speaking under the auspices of the Anti-Poverty Society, to his political activity, to his criticism of the church for its indifference to labor, and to his insistence that all men, church members or not, were the children of God. The straw that broke the camel's back was his charge that the Chicago anarchists had been murdered. Pentecost had no regrets; he was tired of preaching for the rich and would organize nondenominational churches in Newark, Brooklyn, and Boston.[54]

Neither Hopkins nor Dombrowski refers to Pentecost; he is not included in Bliss's comprehensive *Encyclopedia of Social Reform,* published in 1908. In the late 1880s, *Unity* mentioned him frequently, and Louis F. Post, in his biography of Henry George, *The Prophet of San Francisco,* says that Pentecost underwent the same kind of persecution from his denomination that Father McGlynn suffered from his superiors. Post relates that Pentecost was one of the principal speakers at a banquet given by the Anti-Poverty Society to celebrate the launching of Henry George's *Standard.* This writer credits Pentecost with coining the word "Churchianity," an epithet leveled mostly at American Protestantism for its indifference to the needs of the working class.[55] After establishing liberal congregations, he began putting out pamphlets containing his sermons, soon enlarging them to a magazine, *Twentieth Century,* to which such persons as Edward Bellamy and John W. Chadwick contributed.[56] In a reminiscent volume, *The Ardent Eighties,* Gregory Weinstein, a Russian immigrant who came to be closely identified with Felix Adler's Ethical Culture Society and various reform movements, briefly characterizes Pentecost as an attractive personality and a seductive speaker, but one who "promised to bring the millennium on this earth in too short a time."[57]

From reading *Saamanden,* one is impressed with the theological similarities of Janson's doctrine and that of other socially oriented clergymen, not only those in other denominations but also those of other faiths. In the second volume of *Saamanden,* beginning with the November, 1888, issue, he presented translations of five lectures delivered by Rabbi Solomon Schindler of Boston. This formidable task was not done by Janson but by Kristian Baun and is of such magnitude as to suggest that Baun might have been in Janson's employ and that he might be the Danish folk-school teacher who had run afoul of Danish authorities because of a lecture on the French Revolution.

Rabbi Schindler occupied the pulpit of Temple Adath Israel, a Jewish Reformed congregation, in Boston. A German by birth, he had immigrated to the United States some time after the Franco-Prussian War and had served in New Jersey before coming to Boston. Occasionally he had articles in the *Christian Register,* and, according to Benjamin O. Flower, he was a man with great originality of thought whose sermons often appeared in Monday morning papers, even though his views were displeasing to more orthodox Jews. He was sympathetic to the ideas of Henry George and later was to be a pioneer in the Nationalist movement, which espoused a brand of socialism derived from Edward Bellamy's *Looking Backward.*[58]

Saamanden's remarkably interesting series had the general title "Messianic Anticipations." In a footnote to the first lecture, Janson wrote, "Although we Christians are much too prone to overlook the literature and the development of the Jews, we must go to them for information on the Old Testament and its ideas. These lectures ... have interested me greatly and I hope they will others. It is good for us to know what the Jews have thought and believed about their Messiah, since we have been wont to say 'Jesus was the Messiah'—as if that closed the subject."

One sees that Janson found in Schindler's discussion a confirmation of his own views. According to the rabbi, the anticipation of a messiah among the Jews was political in origin, not religious. (Janson held that the Jews turned against Jesus because they were looking for a leader to relieve them of the Roman domination and that the treachery of Judas Iscariot stemmed from such a disappointment.) The rabbi was in agreement with Janson on the verbal inspiration of the Bible. He doubted that the gospels in the New Testament had been written by Jews, and, in respect to the miraculous conception of Jesus as well as the supernatural details surrounding his birth, he called attention to such phenomena having previously been ascribed to Buddha, much as Janson had done. In the third lecture, subtitled "The Carpenter's Son," the rabbi's description of Jesus is similar to that often given by Janson, although the rabbi questions the importance of Jesus as a preacher, saying he is not mentioned by such historians of the period as Josephus or Justus of Tiberias, nor is he named in the Talmud.[59] Much of this lecture is a protest against blaming the Jews for the crucifixion. Rabbi Schindler says that the accounts given in the gospels reveal such an ignorance of Jewish laws that he could only conclude they came from Grecian writers, not Jewish.

In the fourth lecture, "Judaism, the Mother, and Christianity, the Daughter," the rabbi, like Janson, insists that reason must have a central place in religion. He rejects the statement of one of the early church fathers, *"Credo, quia absurdum est"* (I believe because it is absurd). Janson had prophesied that the world would one day have one religion. The rabbi did not go that far, but he predicted that Judaism and Christianity would eventually be united. In its development, Judaism had continually placed greater emphasis on reason, and, in the rabbi's words, Christianity was moving "backward to reason," a process begun by the Reformation and in modern times reaching its highest point in Unitarianism. He was to give Christianity credit for having civilized and thus united the Western world, something the Jews could not have done because of their parochialism, nor the Greeks because of their self-sufficiency. However, before Judaism and Christianity could be united, the Christians would have to give up their idealization of Jesus and therefore no longer look upon him as Christ. Both sides, he said, would have to break down the prejudice (the rabbi spoke of it as "race prejudice") that had kept Jews and Gentiles apart. His fifth lecture, "A Real Messiah," is an account of Bar Cochbar, the leader of the insurrection against the Romans (A. D. 131–135), who at first was so successful that he compelled the Romans to evacuate Jerusalem. He was proclaimed king and had coins minted bearing his name. After the war spread all over Palestine, fifty towns, as well as many villages and hamlets, came into the possession of the Jews. He was finally defeated by Hadrian's general, Julius Severus; the Holy City was razed to the ground, and the date, 135 A.D., marked the dispersion of the Jews. According to the rabbi, Cochbar was the kind of deliverer the Jews of Jesus' time had anticipated—an interpretation which coincided with that of Janson.

215

In December, 1888, Janson wrote to Bjørnson. Things were going well in every respect, he said, except the economic. He had sold his house on Nicollet Avenue and bought a new one only a few blocks from the church, but he was going to have a hard time meeting payments because his money was tied up in a lot he owned in Minneapolis and in land Ivar had bought in California. If Bjørnson should happen to have any extra cash and be able to send the last payment on Solbakken, Janson would be grateful, but otherwise he thought he could manage, given a little time. Ivar had returned and was busily studying history and natural science. Eilev had gone back to San Francisco, where he was a conductor on a cable car, but he had promised to return home the following spring, when both boys must seriously set about preparing for their future.

Janson's labor novel had gone the rounds of publishers in Norway and was at the time in the hands of a Danish firm from whom Janson had heard nothing. It had been a hectic fall, with campaigning and the bazaar. Although the latter had been profitable, it had meant untold work. Drude had overexerted herself in preparing for it, and that, along with all her work in getting the children's clothes ready for school, had made her life anything but pleasant.

"Do you know anything about Pastor Hugh Pentecost?" Janson asked Bjørnson. "He is a man for you. He shares your point of view completely, the questioner's standpoint. There is a boldness and freshness in what he says, which are so blessedly un-American. Excerpts from his speeches often appear in *Saamanden*."[60]

216

Drude as a young woman

Drude Krog Janson
Portrait by Kristian Ross in Rome, 1880

Nazareth Church in 1889

Nazareth Church in old age

Nora Free Church near Hanska and cottage where the Jansons lived

Parsonage of Nora Free Church in 1906

The Janson house on Nicollet Avenue, Minneapolis

The Janson Family

Left to right: front row, Borghild, Arne; second row, Drude, Signe, Ivar, Ingeborg, Kristofer; standing behind, Eilev.

Kristofer Janson in old age with members of his family in Denmark

Left to right: Louise Bentzen, Borghild with child, Drude, Signe with child, Kristofer Janson, Viggo Forchhammer; in foreground, sons of Forchhammer.

8

Literary Critic
and Author

IN FEBRUARY, 1889, the Jansons moved into their fine new home at 1419 Ninth Street South. In northern climates, people do not ordinarily change houses in the dead of winter. We do not know what induced the Jansons to do so; the most likely speculation would be that a purchaser of the Nicollet Avenue property was eager to acquire possession.[1]

While their new house could hardly be called a mansion, it was a very commodious two-and-a-half-story frame structure with such ultra-modern conveniences as central heating and gas lights. Ivar was at home to look after the furnace in Janson's absence; at last Drude was relieved of making the rounds to see that the stoves were kept going as she had done in the Nicollet Avenue location. If she had found the moving an ordeal, she recovered quickly, for on Sunday evening, March 2, she delivered a lecture in the church, her subject being "Should Women Take Part in War?" Janson had written Bjørnson that she would soon "take hold seriously" in her preaching. The lecture had been advertised well in advance.[2]

The new dwelling, located a scant three blocks from the church, provided room for entertaining fairly sizable groups. It was set back on a gently sloping lawn, some thirty feet from the street, with its main entrance on the south side, and it was equipped with an oblong porch. On the street side, it was ornamented by a bay, a series of four windows projecting out and with the glass set into wooden scrolls at the top. Inside, the rooms with their nine-foot ceilings were light and

217

airy. A broad stairway led to the second floor, where Janson set up his study in the large front room.[3]

Shortly after they were settled, the Jansons entertained the church *Kvindeforening* (Women's Society) and soon its musicales were given there. Their social circle was increased by the addition of Jacob Fjelde, the thirty-year-old sculptor, who had come to this country two years before and had lived briefly in Chicago before going on to Minneapolis. Unlike the painter Haakon Mellvold, who had to struggle for even a meager living, Fjelde seems to have been an immediate success. In January, 1889, *Illustreret Ugeblad* reported that he was overwhelmed with orders, having completed busts of Mayor Ames, Mrs. Albert Scheffor, Congressman Snider's wife, Professors Sverdrup and Oftedal, and many others. The *Minneapolis Sunday Tribune* carried a feature story on the young man, "A Peep at a Studio," in February, saying that he was the only sculptor in the Northwest and probably the only one between Chicago and San Francisco. Among his many orders were those of the Jansons—a bust of Kristofer and a medallion with the profile of Drude. These were to be in plaster instead of the marble with which Fjelde ordinarily worked.[4]

Late in 1888, Drude's second book, *Ensomhed* (Loneliness) had been published in Minneapolis. It was a somber tale of the Minnesota prairie, in which both a father and his son (the central character) were driven to suicide. Although reviewers were agreed that Mrs. Janson had talent, they were hardly more than lukewarm in their estimate of the book. It did not arouse the interest that *A Saloonkeeper's Daughter* had, largely because people did not recognize Drude's models as they had in the earlier book, but also because the novel seemed too unrelieved a tragedy.[5]

2

In February, news of Knut Hamsun filtered into the city. *Illustreret Ugeblad* reported that he had given a series of talks in Copenhagen before the University Student Association on cultural life in modern America. Copenhagen papers gave interesting accounts of these appearances, the Minneapolis weekly continued, and the young author had been complimented by Georg Brandes. Hamsun had also written an article on Kristofer Janson in *Ny Jord* and had written a sketch entitled "Hunger," which had awakened favorable attention.[6] Actually, some people in Minneapolis had heard the story. Janson had read it late in

December, 1888, at that time respecting the author's wish for anonymity and announcing it only as "Hunger, a Tale of Kristiania."[7]

Soon Hamsun's lectures were incorporated into a book, *Fra det moderne Amerikas aandsliv*. On Sunday evening, May 5, Janson reviewed the book for his reading, and thereafter, in one way or another, he was involved with the volume for the rest of the year. It was an audacious piece of work, arising out of Hamsun's frustration after two attempts to make his way in this country. Yet, in spite of its exaggeration and open malice, it was and is a highly amusing book, and readers today will find that on rare occasions—and on minor matters—Hamsun hits the target.

The theme of the book is that America's god is money. Hamsun asserts that the country has been populated by the riffraff of Europe, who came for material gain. Crossing the ocean makes a man no better, and, as far as his descendants are concerned, a man cannot be more than the son of his father. American literature is flaccid and puritanical, for it is almost criminal to describe the naked leg of a chair. Hamsun could except a bit of Hawthorne, Bret Harte, and Poe, and he respected Mark Twain, designating him as "that bleak pessimist." It is the newspaper reporters who reveal the shifting scene with accounts of murder, scandal, and violence that daily scream from the papers. The theaters, he continued, have realistic stage settings, but they characteristically shift scenes with all house lights on. The farce is the most popular play; the country has a few good actors, but when a European drama is presented (for example, Ibsen or Sardou) it is sure to be emasculated. Furthermore, attending the theater can be very unpleasant, for those sitting on the first floor are regularly showered with cigar ashes and nuts from the oafs in the balcony. Americans are hostile to foreigners. Sarah Bernhardt has made American tours, but she is not highly regarded because she had a child born out of wedlock.

Hamsun declared that the idea of American schools being free is a fiction. All citizens are taxed for them every time they drink a glass of water or buy a pound of meat. Millions are spent on these schools, but they are not worth a fraction of the cost. Arithmetic and bookkeeping are well taught, for they represent true American values, and the schools do a thorough job of teaching American history and deifying George Washington, but the other subjects (in excessive numbers, including even philosophy) are taught through teachers' harangues, blends of all possible odds and ends. A strong moral and religious influence hovers over the classroom. A boy caught throwing a spitball would be forced to get down on his knees to implore Jesus to forgive him.

Time and again, Hamsun refers to the execution of the Haymarket anarchists to point up the travesty of American justice, saying that the men were put to death for the ideas they held rather than any overt act. American art is crude. Whitman's rhapsodic poetry the critic finds formless and incoherent. He is more respectful of Emerson, judging him to have an underdeveloped psychological sense and an overdeveloped moral one. American churches are pleasant places with stained glass windows, resounding organs, carpeted floors, and luxuriously padded pews. They have polished doors and polished people—particularly the women. Some men attend, either because they are politically ambitious or because it is shrewd business to be in the good graces of the church. The sermons are like those in Norway in not being at all enlightening but unlike them in being highly entertaining, usually containing anecdotes, witticisms, and citations from the newspapers. Hamsun often chose to attend church rather than the theater, even when he had a free ticket in his pocket, for in church one was safe from cigar ashes.[8]

The book has many hilarious anecdotes. A man named Pearl Johnson, Hamsun says, wrote a book on free love. It was all theoretical, for, with the exception of his mother, the wretched man did not know a single woman by name. He was at once clapped into prison—but he adds, American women commonly practice free love. Let a husband be gone three or four months—without writing or sending money to his wife—and the wronged woman will sob out her story to a judge who will sympathetically grant her a divorce. According to Hamsun, the ovewhelming number of divorces in America are granted on complaints of women.

Worse than that, Hamsun goes on to say, American women do not want to bear children. Early in the marriage, they might consent to one or two, but by the time they are in their early thirties, they want to be through. They use various contraceptives, and, those failing, they could always find doctors to perform abortions—an open practice according to Hamsun. Should this fail—for some women might be so careless as to postpone seeing the physician—she must bear the child. But, Hamsun continues, one could understand her chagrin, for she would be unable to hold an office in a women's congress. However, most women are not careless and therefore have plenty of time for churchgoing and attendance at congresses.

America is overrun with churches. Minneapolis and Copenhagen were about the same size (Hamsun makes comparisons of the two frequently throughout the book), but Minneapolis had 146 churches to Copenhagen's 29. In America, ministers are privileged people who get 10 per cent discounts in stores and ride the trains for half fare. They are frequently hired to give campaign speeches. Soul-saving takes fairly extensive training; a theological course at a university takes three years. In contrast, a medical course may take only one. Hamsun was willing to admit that there were some good medical schools in America as well as distinguished doctors, but he points out that there were "colleges" where a diploma was forthcoming after four months, citing the official report of the Illinois State Board of Health for 1888.

Yet, in spite of its many churches, crime is rampant in America. None of it requires any cleverness or finesse; it is all raw brutality or stealth. Hamsun cites the case of a bank cashier named Scoville who removed $500,000 from the bank vault and took a fast train to Canada, where he was safe from United States authorities. When a government agent followed him there, to tell Scoville that he might keep a third of the loot and return to this country a free man, the embezzler considered the matter, but, after consulting his wife, he shook his head. As Hamsun puts it, "Mrs. Scoville, who was virtually the same as Mr. Scoville, had said no to America."[9]

Janson could not let all these criticisms pass without protest. Reviewing the book in his church was not enough: he wrote four long articles for *Budstikken,* the series running from June 26 to July 17. Norwegians in America would have no difficulty in judging the book, Janson said, for they were acquainted with actual conditions, but it could do considerable mischief abroad. He conceded that Hamsun had grounds for criticizing American materialism, its prudery, its undeveloped taste in art, its import tax on books and cultural objects, but he objected to Hamsun's singling out various obvious idiosyncrasies and oddities in America without making any effort to get to the wellsprings of life in this country. These sources of power were the American democratic institutions with their capacity to educate; they would not be affected by the "ignorant and unfounded comments of Hamsun." Likewise, Hamsun had leveled his attack on the whole of America, whereas his own experience had been extremely limited, a fact which forced him to draw his examples mainly from Minneapolis and North Dakota.

Together with his criticism of the hostility of Americans to foreigners, Hamsun had ridiculed their boastful, noisy patriotism, saying that the mere mention of Washington or Lincoln caused a theater audience to burst into applause. Janson saw in that only a wholesome, spontaneous demonstration of love of one's country. Hamsun had sneered at the Minneapolis Atheneum for not having Schopenhauer and Hartmann on its shelves, but, in its materialistic zeal, for having stocked itself with patent reports. Janson was to remind him that it was not a public library but a private collection, generously open to the public for what use it might make of it. Having a sizable family and thus being well acquainted with both the public and private schools, Janson doubted that such a thing as sending the spitball-thrower to his knees could have happened more than once; he thought a teacher might have a class sing a hymn on occasion, but otherwise he knew that any religious teaching was a dischargeable offense. If elementary pupils in America were ignorant of Norway, one might find comparable ignorance in European schools. Hamsun had said that, in this country, neither high school teachers nor their students knew that Norway had had the telegraph since 1883, and that grade school pupils did not know that there was a Norway—they did know that there was a Scandinavia, which to them was Sweden

In his discussion of journalism, Hamsun had omitted all mention of magazines dealing with political issues and literature, such as the *Nation*, the *Twentieth Century*, with its liberal articles on religion, or Henry George's the *Standard*. Janson doubted that such things as a cigar ash cascade coming from the gallery happened in the best theaters. He was particularly aggrieved at Hamsun's comments on American women. He could not condone abortion, but the fact was that they knew more about the physical laws of the body than did Scandinavians and could limit their families, something that met with Janson's approval. He had said on other occasions that couples should not have more children than they could adequately care for, deploring the ever-growing families among parents already impoverished or those in which one of them was ill, often with tuberculosis. On personal grounds, Janson could testify that Hamsun's perspective was clouded by bias. He had lived a year in Janson's home, and yet when he wrote his article on Janson, he had not given his host's ministry due weight, neglecting the fact that this was what Janson considered to be his vocation. Hamsun, quite simply, was prejudiced against religion. Janson earlier had praised the volume's charm for its sprightly anecdotes and wit. He closed on the same note: "In spite of these obvious faults, the book is so sparkling, so delightfully written, and reveals such a fine stylistic talent that one must hail it as having great promise for the future."

222

Throughout the summer, *Budstikken* printed comments from readers about Hamsun's work. Fritz Maurer found it disgusting, revealing Hamsun's bitter grudge against this country.[10] Fritz Landgraff said Hamsun and Janson had such completely different natures that one could not expect them to view America in the same way. Hamsun had, indeed, given a dark picture,[11] but Janson, for his part, could not bear to have American institutions criticized.[12] Late in August, *Budstikken* carried a bristling exchange between Ferdinand Fredrikson and Janson. Although Fredrikson censured Janson on several matters, he was most disturbed about the minister's comment that Scandinavians lacked the knowledge to use contraceptive measures, insisting it was not ignorance but moral rectitude that restrained them. Janson was condoning "child murder."[13] Irritated, Janson retorted that he was as much opposed to the aborting of a fetus as anyone, and when Fredrikson insisted on prolonging the discussion with arguments that any kind of birth control was morally wrong, Janson did not reply. Thus disputes on Hamsun's book quieted down for a few months—until Janson's labor novel was published.[14]

3

Meanwhile other events were happening. In the winter and spring, Janson confined himself largely to Norwegian writers for his Sunday evening readings. Kielland's *The Professor* (Professoren) was especially popular because it had been such an unusually interesting book.[15] Janson had read Ibsen's *The Lady from the Sea* at his meetings in December, but, in spite of his interpolations, audiences often felt Ibsen's plays were too obscure, and even Luth Jaeger greeted the announcement of the reading of one more Ibsen drama with the comment that it would probably turn out to be another riddle. Janson delivered an address on "Henrik Wergeland and His Times" in Grand Forks, North Dakota, that was said to be so masterly that the Wergeland Society (Foreningen Wergeland) in Madison, Wisconsin, invited him to give it at its Seventeenth of May commemoration.[16] In a letter to *Illustreret Ugeblad*, the Scandinaviske Arbeiderforening, a working men's organization, thanked Janson for his efforts to put the cause of labor before the public, saying that his efforts had counted for more than theirs.[17] The St. John's Day celebration (St. Hans fest) had attracted such a crowd that people had had to stand in the corridor and out on the sidewalk awaiting their turn to enter.[18] All of these things were largely routine—pleasant ones to be sure—but they were dwarfed by the two great happenings of the spring: Eilev's arrival home, and the spontaneous emergence of the Underwood, Minnesota, congregation—an organized group which called Janson to be its minister.[19]

Eilev was nineteen—a tall, handsome fellow, relishing his triumphant return as an explorer of the wilderness and as a metropolitan resident, who had worked for the better part of a year as a cable car conductor in San Francisco. Sixty years later he was to chuckle over the memory of that homecoming: he brought with him a tidy sum in savings, and for the occasion he had bought a smart new suit, one with a fashionable cutaway coat. As his mother was to write Bjørnson two years later, he had a will of iron and had already decided on his future career. He was going to become a physician and surgeon. He would study throughout the spring and summer, take entrance examinations, and enter the University of Minnesota medical school in the fall. It seemed such a good plan that Ivar decided to do the same, though their father cautioned them that they were setting their sights too high. They could try it, but they had been away from books for several years, and it would take more than a few months' study to pass the rigorous examinations. In the meantime, the parents were happy over the prospect of having both sons with them for some years to come.[20]

At the time Underwood, Minnesota, was hardly more than a clearing in the woods; it had a railroad station, three stores, and a few houses. However, thirty people in the community subscribed to *Saamanden,* and Janson was inclined to think the paper had been the actual missionary. The town was not ordinarily on his lecture route; Janson usually chose bigger places, nearby Fergus Falls or Rothsay, some twenty miles away. He did, however, have an earnest admirer in Otto Nilsby—a young man who had spent three years preparing for the Lutheran ministry at Augsburg Seminary, had withdrawn because of his interest in Janson's teachings, and had later persuaded his parents to his point of view.[21] He had been instrumental in forming a group; when it had thirty-two members, it had elected officers, choosing as president Hans P. Bjorge, a man already prominent in the Farmers' Alliance and soon to be a member of the Minnesota House of Representatives. Other officers were Nilsby, John Trondson, John O. Kalstad, Anna O. Kalstad, and Josefa Medjaa. Either just before this election or immediately after, they invited Janson to visit them, the result being the formation of the Free Christian Church of Underwood. Because the village had no building large enough to hold more than forty people, they at once raised money to build a town hall seating two hundred.

They began in May and arranged things so expeditiously that the building was dedicated early in July. Adopting the same motto as that of Nazareth Church, they immediately announced that the building would be available for all religious groups as well as for other meetings and community get-togethers. Janson promised to visit them at least once very other month, but otherwise Otto Nilsby took charge of services and was superintendent of the Sunday school. Janson was able to report the formation of this new congregation at the Western Unitarian Conference in Chicago in mid-May, and, when the Minnesota Conference was held in June, his report was said to have stirred "the latent missionary zeal in all hearts."[22]

Saamanden, of course, did not always meet with the success it enjoyed in Underwood. In its May issue, Janson printed messages from protesters. "Stop *Saamanden,*" Ole Tanum of Sioux Falls ordered. "Such literature is a disgrace to the Norwegian people in America." Another writer, whose name Janson withheld, pleaded that the minister change his ways, not only for his own sake, but for those he was misleading. "You speak of freedom," he wrote earnestly, "but it is only freedom to be fettered, hands and feet, in the service of Satan." It may have been more than one article that brought on these objections or pleas, but possibly the last straw had been a new series Janson had begun in the April issue, "Jesus' Spiritual Brothers." The first lecture dealt with Buddha; Janson introduced it by saying that the liberals accept no books of divine revelation—neither the Old Testament, the Persians' *Zend Avesta,* the Hindus' *Veda,* nor the Mohammedans' Koran. Likewise, they held that there were no "chosen people"; God has no stepchildren but is the loving father of all men. He then related the legends on the birth, life, and death of Buddha.[23] The series was comprehensive, continuing for years and coming to include not only such early figures as Lao Tse, Marcus Aurelius, and Origen, but also moderns, such as George Fox and John Wesley. All these men and all the scriptures—Persian, Hindu, Muslim, Jewish, and Christian—were to be revered. Every religion, Janson maintained, is a rainbow stretching from earth to heaven.

Possibly Ole Tanum was getting too much of Hugh Pentecost, for *Saamanden* was peppered with excerpts from his *Twentieth Century.* In volume two, one finds that Pentecost's religious views are strikingly similar to Janson's: he does not accept the tyrannical Jehovah of the Old Testament as the father of mankind, nor the verbal inspiration of the Bible, nor the divinity of Jesus.[24] Yet most of the excerpts in the second volume of *Saamanden* deal with Pentecost's social views. He

225

was enough of an extremist that *Unity*, in March, 1889, felt called upon to defend him, saying: "Though a radical reformer, he is as far as possible from being a red-handed revolutionist. His cordial and manly bearing make his visit a pleasant memory."[25]

From *Saamanden,* one concludes that Pentecost was first and foremost a single tax man, and even to the left of the movement of Henry George, for he wanted to abolish all private ownership of land. In writing of the anthracite industry, he said that few companies owned the mines and a half dozen railroads pulled the coal to market—a monopoly that cost the consumer one third more for every ton of coal. The coal was in the earth; the rights of the mining companies were not those of owners. The state had the obligation to prohibit the plundering of the public. He would have the state collect a tax of $2.25 per acre of coal and have the federal government operate the railroads as it did the post office.[26] He was bitter about the indifference of Catholic and Protestant churchmen to poverty. The pope had criticized the materialism of the age, said Pentecost, oblivious of the fact that he and other churchmen had created that evil. It was the lack of material things that brought Socialism, nihilism, and communism into being. The pope was an educated and polished man who had never known poverty. Methodist clergymen drew Pentecost's scorn for their attempts to prohibit the Sunday paper from going through the mail, to forbid dancing, and to keep women from wearing bird plumage on their hats. These ministers apparently had nothing to say about the number of people huddled together in cheap lodging houses. Sometimes, he foresaw an idealistic, anarchistic society. First, the private ownership of land must be abolished, then a cooperative republic would be formed, and finally all force (statutes) could be done away with—then anarchy, which was brotherhood, would prevail. The single tax movement, nationalism, and anarchism were steps in a desirable progression.

4

On February 18, 1889, the Society of Christian Socialists was formed in Boston. Janson followed the movement with great interest. A few months later, the Christian Socialists published a statement of principles which had been adopted on April 15. He was to cover these developments in the June, 1889, *Saamanden.* He traced the Christian Socialist movement back to England, where it had been the brainchild of Charles Kingsley, F. D. Maurice, and others. Although the English society had had a short life, it had lasted long enough to spread—

though by another name—to France, Germany, Norway, Italy, and Austria. At long last, an organization had been formed in America, by twenty persons—nine ministers, nine laymen, and three women (one counted twice). They crossed denominational lines, ranging from orthodox Baptists and Episcopalians to liberal Unitarians and Universalists. The Reverend W. D. P. Bliss was president and A. G. Lawson, secretary. Janson translated their statement as adopted in April:

Declaration of Principles of the Society of Christian Socialists

To exalt the principles that all rights and powers are gifts of God, not for the receiver's use only, but for the benefit of all; to magnify the onesidedness of the human family, and to lift mankind to the highest plane of privilege, we band ourselves together under the name of Christian Socialists.

We hold that God is the source and guide of all human progress, and we believe that all social, political and industrial relations should be based on the Fatherhood of God and the Brotherhood of Man, in the spirit and according to the teachings of Jesus Christ.

We hold that the present commercial and industrial system is not thus based but rests on economic individualism, the results of which are: 1. That the natural resources of the earth and the mechanical inventions of man are made to accrue disproportionately to the advantage of the few instead of the many. 2. That production is without general plan, and commercial and industrial crises are thereby precipitated. 3. That the control of business is rapidly concentrating in the hands of a dangerous plutocracy, and the destinies of the masses of wage earners are becoming increasingly dependent on the will and resources of a narrowing number of wage-payers. 4. That large occasion is thus given for the moral evils of mammonism, recklessness, overcrowding, intemperance, prostitution, crime.

We hold that united Christianity must protest against a system so based, and productive of such results, and must demand a reconstructed social order, which, adopting some method of production and distribution that starts from organized society as a body and seeks to benefit society equitably in everyone of its members, shall be based on the Christian principle that "We are members one of another."

While recognizing the present dangerous tendency of business towards combination and trusts, we yet believe that the economic circumstances which call them into being will necessarily result in the develop-

227

ment of individual character, will be at once true Socialism and true Christianity.

Our objects, therefore, as Christian Socialists are: 1. To show that the aim of Socialism is embraced in the aim of Christianity. 2. To awaken members of Christian churches to the fact that the teachings of Jesus Christ lead directly to some specific form or forms of Socialism; that, therefore, the church has a definite duty upon this matter, and must, in simple obedience to Christ, apply itself to the realization of the social principles of Christianity.[27]

Early in July, as the Jansons set out for Brown County, carpenters were hammering in the interior of the Minneapolis church, promising to have it ready for dedication in the fall. With the exception of the girls, who had household chores, each member of the family had a special project lined up for the summer. Arne, a responsible sixteen-year-old, was showing promise as a violinist. He must keep up his practice, taking care, of course, to keep out of earshot of those who were writing or studying, but that was no problem, for through the week he could have the church to himself. With their sights on medical school, the two older boys allowed themselves only one diversion—a little hunting now and then. Drude was to begin another book, while Kristofer worked on *Sara*, a novel largely centered in Chicago, for which he must consult such volumes as Campbell's *Prisoners of Poverty* and Nelson's *The Slave Girls of Chicago*. The elder Jansons were determined to study Nationalism, the type of Socialism described in Bellamy's *Looking Backward*, which derived its name from the nationalization of all industry as described in that novel. Clubs were being formed all over the country, patterned after the first one in Boston by Edward Everett Hale, Francis Bellamy (the brother of Edward), Frederick A. Hinckley, James Yeams, Philo W. Sprague, and Rabbi Solomon Schindler. Indeed, the Society of Christian Socialists had been organized largely by Nationalists.

The Jansons were to read *Looking Backward* and to supplement it with *The Co-operative Commonwealth* by Laurence Gronlund, which had come out in 1884; this, the Jansons had heard, was a theoretical presentation of the principles found in Bellamy's book. Gronlund was a Dane, whose name had been anglicized from Grønlund. He was a close associate of the Reverend W. D. P. Bliss, and in 1895 was to organize the American Fabian Society.[28]

It was a happy summer. Early in August, Jenkin Lloyd Jones tried to entice Janson to a meeting at Jones's summer home in Illinois, but the Minnesotan would have none of it. "You are lovely & Jenkin Lloyd Jones," he wrote, "but if your tongue was that of a nightingale and your countenance that of an angel and your grove at Helena valley a paradise, you should not be able to allure me from my safe resthold here." He sent greetings to "all of you queer Unitarians" who said they wanted a rest but continued to hold meetings and plan new work.[29] Writing to Bjørnson, he was rhapsodic about life in Brown County. The family was living like natives on the Sandwich Islands, wearing not much more than the proverbial fig leaf, although he doubted that the natives lapped up as much cream as the vacationing Jansons. The children were jubilant, storing up strength for school. Ivar and Eilev hoped to enter medical school in the fall, plans their father thought were too ambitious, for they had worked as common laborers for the last couple of years and Eilev had even hunted wild game in British Columbia. "It was a miracle that he had escaped with his head," his father commented.

No one in Norway or Denmark wanted to publish Janson's labor novel, *Behind the Curtain* (Bag gardinet). Furthermore, he had found out that he had three—only three—subscribers to *Saamanden* in Norway. That fact certainly showed how popular he was in his native land; it hardly tallied with Bjørnson's assertion that Scandinavia was ready and waiting for Unitarianism. In America, however, his religious work, his real vocation, was progressing slowly but surely. At long last, he could dedicate the Minneapolis church, and he spoke of the new congregation in Underwood, saying that his experience there was the happiest in a long time.

Social problems, he told Bjørnson, were demanding more and more attention. Bellamy's *Looking Backward,* nothing more than an argument for state socialism in novel form, was the great sensation, and Nationalist clubs were being organized everywhere. "As a minister, I shall take part in this. What good does it do to preach love of God and man when our fellow creatures are poor, freezing, and hungry? And the present system of free competition, motivated by greed, will ruin itself in the long run just as it ruins all good in human beings. Take money away so it is impossible to buy as much as a glove, and people's greed will change to something nobler. What shall I do with all my poor who cannot find work in the winter—strong, fine men who go unemployed? That grieves me more than you know. . . . I have so little to share with them." He added that it was the Scandinavians who suffered the most. Great expanses of land lay unused because speculators were waiting for prices to go up, and in the meantime there were people who longed to settle on it if they only could.

Drude's book, *Ensomhed* (Loneliness), had been published, and Kristofer thought that it was good. Currently she was working on another, something her husband did not know much about, except that it had a heavy, sorrowful theme. Her first novel had been translated into Dutch and was appearing in one of the best papers in Holland, he jubilantly reported.[30]

5

When September came, Ivar and Eilev decided to stay in Brown County until October 1, when they would try their luck with the university entrance examinations. If Janson was disappointed that his sons would not be present at the dedication of the church on September 8, he made no mention of it, for, as Eilev said later, his father hated coercion and had even been permissive about his sons' attendance at Saturday school. For both him and Drude, the building of the church had been wearying. Actually the $1,500 made at the bazaar the year before had not been enough. The gallery or balcony, designed to accommodate a hundred people, still was not finished; the final painting of the ceiling and walls had been done by four young men of the congregation, working in their spare time—and the pews were still not paid for. The Jansons knew that they faced another bazaar.

Nevertheless, the church was beautiful. As Janson described it in *Saamanden,* the place was light and friendly, thanks to the expert work of the quartet of painters. The woodwork had been stained a light oak, and the pews were of solid cherry. Variegated light streamed through the six arched, stained-glass windows on either side of the building. For the dedication, the church was decorated with flowers and greenery. The auditorium, which could comfortably seat six hundred, was packed to the doorway. In addition to Janson, the Reverend Henry M. Simmons of the First Unitarian Society took part in the ceremony, and the choir of his church sang several numbers. The Reverend August Dellgren of the Swedish Universalist Church brought greetings from his congregation.

In September, *Saamanden* carried a brief description of the dedication, and *The North*, an English-language weekly newly established in Minneapolis, also had an article on it. This paper was published by Luth Jaeger and his father-in-law, Colonel Hans Mattson, the former serving as editor. The congregation was small, Jaeger wrote, since most

Norwegians were Lutherans. However, because of the theological discussions held at Nazareth Church, some of the orthodox broke away from their old religious moorings to turn to Unitarianism. There were also immigrants, "more or less imbued with the spirit of religious unrest characteristic of the intellectual life in the old country." Jaeger, who was himself a Unitarian, had been an ardent supporter of Janson in the days of the latter's lecture tour and during the early years of his ministry. However, by 1889, he questioned some of Janson's ideas on social reform. Speaking of the immigrants who had joined the Nazareth congregation, he said: "They naturally drift into Mr. Janson's church, his personal charm, his radical if not always thoroughly digested views of man and society, and his ever responsive sympathy attracting them and holding them fast under the spell of his individuality."[31]

By this time the Jansons had heard from Bjørnson. The letter has not been preserved, but, from Janson's response, it is clear that the poet was wondering whether the minister was going overboard on social reform. Bjørnson was getting *Saamanden*, and since he had been alerted to read Pentecost, he was possibly finding some of Janson's liberal utterances alarming. "Don't be afraid," Janson wrote him reassuringly. "My ideas are securely on the ground." Mixing his metaphors, he went on, "I am borne on the stream of the times. . . . It is good to ride on top of a great world-wave that is sweeping forward." He was completely absorbed in Socialism, he added, saying that for a long time he had been sympathetic but before he could not take part in it seriously because he had not had time to study it sufficiently. During the summer, however, he had given it attention and had become convinced. He spoke of the Christian Socialists, of the *Dawn,* the journal of that society, and of the Nationalist movement. For the following Thursday, he had scheduled a meeting in his church to be conducted in English; Mr. Edwards, editor of a Minneapolis-based magazine, *Reason*, and Mrs. Kate Buffington Davis, a handsome young matron who was very enthusiastic about socialist ideas, would speak. The Sunday after that Janson would deliver a sermon entitled "Thy Brother's Blood Calls to Me from the Earth," in which he would lash out at millionaires who oppressed workers cruelly while they themselves were sheltered by the law.

Janson went on to say that he had sold the vacant lot he owned. Now he possessed no land other than the lot his house stood on, and he could thunder against land speculation with a clear conscience. But he was worried about money. He had a payment of over $7,000 to make on his new house the following June, and he wondered whether it would be possible to get the 2,000 crowns still due on Solbakken. (Bjørnson had transferred the property to his son Erling, who had recently married.) And Janson had had nothing but bad luck with his labor novel, *Behind the Curtain*. The manuscript was now in his hands, and he had decided to have it printed in Minneapolis at his own expense.

Bjørnson was, at the time, involved in a bitter dispute wth Christopher Bruun, Janson's old colleague at the Vonheim folk school. No one had treated him so poorly as Bruun, Janson was to write, but nevertheless it grieved him that Bjørnson and Bruun should have this falling out, for, in spite of old wounds, Janson could not bring himself to doubt Bruun's integrity. He wrote briefly of the family, remarking that Drude was "a summer child." She really lived during the time she had the sun, birds, and flowers. When she returned to town and had to deal with cooking, clothes, school, and all other chores, she withered up (*skræmper sammen*) and lost her joy in life. At the time, she also had a cold.

Drude was to complete the letter: "It is not true I wither up. That's a big lie. I couldn't help smiling when I read it, and for that reason I am sure it is not true. I have been so careless as to catch a bad cold, and when that happens, I get cross and act as if heaven and earth were afire." True enough, she resented a return to the city with all its slander and coarseness, which always reached them, no matter how hard they tried to keep away from it. There was loneliness and loneliness. The country had a wonderfully rich nature, the colors and beauty always changing. In the city were only the disgustingly dusty streets.

She had put her whole soul into her writing, Drude assured Bjørnson. If the book she was working on was a failure, she would give up. She had also studied Socialism during the summer. Both she and Bjørnson could rejoice in what would come in the future—not right away, of course— but their children would live to reap the benefits. Bjørnson must not smile at this and say that she was a foolish dreamer. He must study the possible reforms, and once he had thought them over, he would be as inspired as she. When one lived in a great nation like the United States, one saw the necessity for a change. She had long realized that the social system was bad; she had read *Progress and Poverty*, but while Henry George had made a great contribution, one could not stop there. When Bjørnson had read *Looking Backward*, if he were interested, they would send him Gronlund's *The Co-operative Commonwealth*. She had read the two books in that order, Gronlund filling in the gaps in socialist theory after she had read Bellamy. On the Bruun matter, she was in full agreement with Kristofer. Bruun, she thought, had sunk from being an apostle—though, unfortunately, a small one—to being a simple party man. Both the Jansons were eagerly looking forward to Bjørnson's new book, *Paa Guds veie* (On God's Way).[32]

By this time, Fjelde had completed the bust of Kristofer and the medallion with Drude's portrait. He had not succeeded with Janson, according to Luth Jaeger, for he did not get a good likeness, but he had been more fortunate with Mrs. Janson.[33] At the time, an exhibit of pictures from Norway and Denmark was also on display, one arranged by the Norwegian Art Association. Earlier, Americans had criticized some of the pictures as being too small; the previous spring Janson had published a long article in *Budstikken* on the collection, saying that it was very good with the exception of a few pictures. Americans have poor taste in art, Jaeger was to write in *The North*, echoing the earlier judgment of Hamsun and Janson.[34]

6

Saamanden was now beginning its third year. As one might expect, the magazine carried a review of *Looking Backward*. As a work of art, not much could be said for it, Janson reported. Few books had aroused so much attention; the reason was that the novel contrasted conditions in the late nineteenth century with those of the year 2000, when Julian West awoke from his hypnotic sleep of over a hundred years. In the interval, the state had become the sole employer; everyone worked and all shared in the wealth produced. With poverty abolished, crime had all but disappeared, and the cultural level of the nation had risen. "The book attempts to show," Janson wrote, "that the principles of state socialism not only sound good in theory but they can be practically realized." He advised those who wanted a more scholarly spelling out of the theory to read Laurence Gronlund's *The Co-operative Commonwealth*. For the masses, *Looking Backward*, with its story line, was more palatable, and one could already see the results in the Nationalist clubs being organized across America.[35]

In the third volume of *Saamanden*, social reform is stressed more than in earlier issues. One feels the contagion of Bellamy's book. In this novel, Julian West, marveling at the transformed conditions, asked Dr. Leete (the physician who had revived him) whether human nature had changed. It had not, the doctor answered, but conditions had changed, and along with them the motives of human action. The nineteenth century had been dominated by selfishness, and in industrial production selfishness is suicide. Competition, the instinct for personal gain dissipates energy, whereas cooperation is the secret of efficient production. In *Saamanden*, one finds "Economic Facts" by Mrs. J. C. Falls, president of the newly established Sociological Association of America. With an impressive array of statistics, she pointed out that, while the number of millionaires in the United States had increased, the income of laborers and farmers had steadily declined. Every seventh person, she continued, was either living in poverty or receiving charity, whereas increasing numbers of women and children were working in factories. During the previous ten years, the population of New York state had increased by 24 per cent, while crime had risen by 38 per cent. "It is obvious," she concluded, "that competition has reached a point where it is seriously damaging the social fabric, and if civilization is to be carried forward to newer and greater efficiency, it is imperative to bring about co-operation between capital and labor."[36]

Frequently the sermons in the third volume of *Saamanden* deal with the need for social reform. Janson's "Thy Brothers' Blood Calls to Me from the Earth" never appeared in the paper, but it is found in his 1892 collection of sermons, *Lys og frihed*.[37] The sermon gives a historical development of man's inhumanity to man, beginning with Richard Arkwright and spelling out in relentless detail the misery wrought by the factory system in England. Continuing, it shifts the scene to America in 1889, with gripping evidence of a similar unhappy situation. The title comes from the Old Testament account of the murder of Abel by Cain. Unfortunately, in the opening paragraphs of the sermon, Janson digresses on the contradictions found in the Bible, a departure extraneous to his theme.

An early fall issue of *Saamanden* was also to carry a brief item by H. Tambs Lyche on the growing popularity of Socialism. (Lyche, enthusiastic in his support of *Saamanden,* was to contribute an article on Lao Tse for the "Jesus' Spiritual Brothers" series in the November issue.) Two years before, Lyche had written, the subject of Socialism had been virtually taboo in polite society. In the spring of 1889, he had attended the annual Unitarian convention in Boston. Tremot Temple had been filled to capacity with the finest people of Boston, who had listened to Edward Bellamy's lecture on Socialism, interrupting with applause every radical statement the author made. He had been followed by an Episcopal minister, the Reverend W. D. P. Bliss, president of the Society of Christian Socialists, who had glowing words of praise for such men as Karl Marx. "If this is the trend, what will the next two years bring?" Lyche wondered.[38]

Following the meeting on Nationalism at which Edwards and the dynamic Mrs. Davis had spoken, Janson announced that his weekly discussion meetings would be given over to Nationalism, examining it point by point. For the next issue of *Saamanden*, he was to translate a sermon by an orthodox minister, the Reverend J. B. Silcox, using it as the lead article. In his "The Church and Social Reform," Silcox, who won prominence in both the social gospel and the Christian Socialist movements, says little that Janson had not said before. One could be thankful, he remarked sarcastically, that the sun and moon were hung up so high, for otherwise greedy monopolists would attach meters and charge so much for each ray. He was to point out—as Janson did later—that the Bible was a radical book. Were he an atheist who hated Christianity, Silcox declared, he would read the Bible in the marketplace as a means of inflaming the masses.[39] As fate would have it, the publiction of this sermon was to cause Janson a bit of embarrassment. It contained three verses of Thomas Hood's "Song of the Shirt." Janson had seen a Dano-Norwegian translation of the poem in *Nylænde*, and, in appropriating three stanzas, had neglected to give the source. Later when Bjørnson publicly declared that Janson had made an excellent translation of Hood's poem, the minister urged him not to mention the matter again.[40]

In October—to their parents' surprise and delight—Ivar and Eilev passed their entrance examinations to the University of Minnesota medical school. By this time, both Kristofer and Drude were deep in preparation for the church bazaar, which was to run from October 27 to November 4. Shortly before it opened, *The North* commented on the activities of "this irrepressible congregation which by hard and uphill work has been able to raise one of the finest Scandinavian church edifices in this city."[41] A trifle less elaborate than the one of the year before, the bazaar was otherwise similar; it cleared $800, two hundred more than the original goal. In addition to Janson, *The North* reported, credit for its "grand success" was due to Mrs. Janson, Christian J. Haug, and H. Hasberg.[42]

Shortly after the bazaar, Janson was invited to Hudson, Wisconsin, where a group of forty-four were ready to organize a Unitarian congregation.[43] Although he was pleased with this turn of events, his satisfaction would have been greater had he not been so worried over family finances. The new house was costing more than he had anticipated. He was still getting the $2,000 allowed him from the beginning by the American Unitarian Association, but as it had been promised only until his congregations were able to support him, he had doubtful moments when he wondered how long it might continue—rather than any hope that it might be increased. To meet household expenses, the Jansons took in eight boarders, making the winter of 1890 an especially grim season for Drude.[44]

Late in 1889, Janson's labor novel came off the presses of the Rasmussen Printing Company in Minneapolis. A hard-cover book printed on heavy pulp paper, it sold for a dollar. *Illustreret Ugeblad* urged its readers to buy copies for Christmas gifts. Possibly it was fortunate for Janson that the novel was not reviewed until after the first of the year. In *The North*, Luth Jaeger dismissed it as below Janson's usual standard. The reviewer for *Budstikken* said the novel contradicted everything Janson had said in his criticism of Hamsun's *Fra det moderne Amerikas aandsliv*.

Janson had intended his book as a novel of protest against the exploitation of the worker—in this case, the immigrant—by the American moneyed class. Its secondary theme was the unfortunate status of women. Its final title, *Bag gardinet* (Behind the Curtain), implies that back of the facade of a civilized, Christian society stands a ruthless power structure indifferent to the misery it inflicts on the poor. The characters are native Americans and Norwegian immigrants. James Plummer is a philanthropist, a leading citizen and prominent church member. His elegant house on Seventh Avenue South is well staffed with servants, and he maintains a fine equipage complete with liveried coachmen. He owns remunerative business property on Nicollet Avenue and is engaged in many enterprises in which he is a take-it-or-leave-it employer. A "smart" man, Plummer's rise to power has included arson and the illegal apppropriating of timber from the Wisconsin forests. He had fathered a son by an Indian woman, sending them both packing when he met a young seamstress who became Mrs. Plummer. As the novel opens, they have two grown children, a daughter, Fanny, and a son, Frank.

There is only one cultivated person in the Plummer household—a maid, Agnes Pryts, who, along with her mother, Mrs. Wilhelmine Pryts, had been forced to leave Norway to escape the creditors of the girl's financially irresponsible father. Agnes shortly escapes the Plummers: as an eleventh-hour substitute for a pianist engaged to perform at a Plummer soiree, she so impresses the guests that she can thereafter give piano lessons, providing a modest, comfortable home for herself and her mother.

Her place in the Plummer household is taken by her friend, Dina Nilsen, whose father as well as her brother Arne are in Plummer's employ, to be fired and blacklisted in the course of the novel. Daniel Nilsen, the father, is an ardent Socialist who frequently writes articles for the papers, for a time escaping Plummer's vengeance because of his skill as a worker. Though kindhearted, Nilsen is irascible and bitterly resentful over having damaged his hearing in the Plummer railroad shops. The other Norwegian to play a leading part is Linner, once a prominent attorney in the city as well as a brilliant violinist. He is an alcoholic wreck, who lives in a room above the saloon where he performs nightly on the violin, with liquor as his payment.

The novel is primarily Dina Nilsen's story. Young Frank Plummer tries unsuccessfully to seduce the girl. One night, after she had been out in a chilling wind, he offers her a glass of strong wine. Innocently, the girl takes it, and, while she is unconscious, the young man violates her. When she tells her father that she is pregnant, Nilsen orders her out of his house, without waiting to hear the circumstances. She is befriended by a kindly American couple, Dr. and Mrs. Walters, who are instrumental in bringing about a reconciliation between father and daughter. When Nilsen tries to bring suit, no lawyer in the city will prosecute a Plummer. Finally, Linner heroically pulls himself together and wins the case, the jury allowing Dina $15,000. The effort is costly for Linner; soon afterward he has a stroke and dies. When the Plummers appeal the case—getting the elder Plummer's half-Indian son to perjure himself that he had spent a night with Dina—the former verdict is reversed. Dina drowns herself in the Mississippi, and her father, maddened by grief, revenges himself on the Plummers by hanging himself just over the front door of their magnificent residence. The plot has a curious epilogue: Dina's death so torments Frank Plummer that he shoots himself at her grave. As the novel closes, James Plummer grieves over his son, musing, "He had too much of what people call heart—and conscience does not go—does not go—in business."[45]

Janson was deeply offended by the *Budstikken* review. In saying that the author had contradicted his criticism of the Hamsun book, the critic had added insult to injury by implying that such a thing was typical—"a Janson sequence." Finding Nilsen and Linner the most effective characters, the reviewer had dismissed the Plummers as types to be found in any country. The good people in the novel were Norwegians, he said, adding drolly that he did not object to Janson's portraying good Norwegians, but he did not think he should do so at the expense of another nationality. What he found most plausible was the jury's granting Dina $15,000, saying that American juries were likely to do that when a woman was involved and especially if her attorney was a good speaker.[46]

At the time the novel had been read in Nazareth Church, Andreas Ueland had reservations about it, which he disclosed to Rasmus B. Anderson in a letter: "He [Janson] has really one fault and that is that he jumps too easily to conclusions. His writings concerning this country may be true as far as the Scandinavians are concerned, at least to a great extent, for there he has had opportunities to know, but generally he has made up his mind about Americans too soon, and therefore often makes mistakes. I think you will agree when you see something that he has now finished but which has not been published."[47]

Janson, of course, never saw this letter, but he felt that the *Budstikken* charge of contradiction made him sound like a weathervane. Defending his novel, he said that he drew his characters and situations from what he saw in the life about him. The kindly Walters and the unscrupulous Plummers were typical Americans, and he had intended the Walters to be a foil for the businessman. Certainly he had shown both Linner and Nilsen to have faults, even though they were Norwegians. In criticizing Hamsun's book he had defended America against categorically sweeping charges. That did not mean that he thought the nation had no faults; his novel had not attacked American institutions but the corruption and rottenness that had invaded those institutions, even the courts.[48]

One could mention other faults in the book. Janson spends considerable time relating how the Plummers entertain a bogus French count, spurred on by the prospect of marrying their daughter to a nobleman. While this part of the plot is meant to highlight the superficiality and cultural simplicity of the Plummers, it is based on such a comedy of errors as to tax one's credulity. Too frequently characters go into long harangues: Dr. Walters on the status of women, Nilsen on Socialism, and Linner on the evils of alcohol. Yet the novel has some memorable episodes, among them Mrs. Pryts's Christmas party and the courtroom scene in which Linner addresses the jury.

There can be no question that Janson honestly felt the novel to be a true representation of life in Minneapolis. Some of the characters and incidents used can be positively identified; in other instances, they are so strikingly similar to those found in the area at the time as to rule them out as pure invention by Janson. Mrs. Pryts, Agnes, and Dina were modeled after his sister-in-law, Mrs. Wilhelmine Behr and her two daughters. The circumstances that caused Mrs. Behr to leave Norway were identical to those of Mrs. Pryts in the novel. Linner is similar to Jacob Seeman, an attorney who was at one time regarded as the most brilliant violinist in the Middle West but who gradually became pauperized because of alcoholism. Janson was well acquainted with a woman who worked to get support for Bethany Home, a refuge for unmarried mothers, and this person seems to have been his model for Mrs. Walters. A legend is still alive in western Wisconsin of a millionaire lumberman whose background seems similar to that of Plummer—even to the Indian consort.[49]

Janson had sent a copy of his novel to Bjørnson, saying that the latter, who had been in the Middle West, would understand it, though it might be "too local" for most Europeans. Although Bjørnson had sent the Jansons his *Paa Guds veie* (On God's Way), Kristofer and Drude had received no letter, and Janson wanted reassurance that the money due on Solbakken would reach him before June, when he would have to meet a payment of between seven and eight thousand dollars on his new house and take out a new loan. However, he was grateful for Bjørnson's novel, which revealed that it was deed rather than creed which determined who walked in the ways of God. Janson was sure it would be a great help in his work; he had already read it in the church where people had listened fascinated, although Janson felt that some of the subtleties escaped them. He had admired Bjørnson's speech in defense of the strike of women workers in a match factory in Kristiania; he had printed a generous excerpt from it in the December, 1889, *Saamanden*, and he wondered what Bjørnson thought of Janson's new Christmas hymn in the same issue.

8

Ivar and Eilev seemed to be doing well in their medical studies; they were diligent students. "Say what you like about America," Janson wrote, "the opportunities here for young men are superior to those in Europe." The *wanderlust* was out of their systems; the boys would be at home with the family for at least another three years, for both hooted at the idea of marriage before they had finished their course.

Janson's work was going well: more and more Scandinavians were being attracted to Unitarianism through *Saamanden*. Writing on a Wednesday morning, he said he would take a train to Hudson, Wisconsin, where he would lecture until Friday. He would be home over the weekend, preaching in Minneapolis and St. Paul. The following week he would go to Underwood, Fergus Falls, and Rothsay. Bjørnson could visualize it by imagining that, if Janson were in Norway, he might have one congregation in Kristiania, another in Trondhjem, a third in Bergen, and a fourth in Christiansand. Actually Janson had six congregations. He was counting Fergus Falls where he had been invited by a newly formed Free Christian Society, as a letter published in the January, 1890, *Saamanden* indicated. However, for one reason or another, this group was never incorporated into a congregation.

He dwelt on his financial problems. Drude was doing all she could; they had sixteen people at the table every day. She was created for more intellectual stimulation than she received and less drudgery, he reported sadly. She was often tired and longed for the time when they might leave America.[50]

He had too much to do, he told Bjørnson, for, in addition to his pastoral duties, he was an author, bookseller, and editor. Even so, he had taken on additional work. One of his colleagues, the Reverend Joseph Henry Crooker, had written a book, *Jesus Brought Back*, which so impressed Janson that he planned to translate the whole of it, running it serially in *Saamanden* and later publishing the translation as a book—with the author's permission, of course. As a social reformer, he must continue to thunder at the inequities of the times. The paper also carried his sermon, "How Shall We Reconcile Our Society with God?" In it he quoted a passage from the Epistle of James, a favorite with social gospel clergymen, for, as Janson said, it seemed an ominous warning to capitalists, land speculators, and bankers:

Go to now, *ye* rich men, weep and howl for your miseries that shall come upon *you*.

Your riches are corrupted, and your garments are motheaten. Your gold and silver is cankered; and the rust of them shall be a witness against you, and shall eat your flesh as it were fire. Ye have heaped treasure together for the last days.

Behold, the hire of the labourers who have reaped down your fields, which is of you kept back by fraud, crieth: and the cries of them which have reaped are entered into the ears of the Lord of sabaoth.

Like the Reverend J. B. Silcox, Janson found the Bible a radical book: "Doesn't that sound like the rumbling of a Socialist pamphlet today? Is it not thunder in the air—the prophecy of revolution? . . . There will come a day of retribution for rich men in which the innocent will suffer with the guilty if present conditions between capital and labor, the rich and the poor, prevail much longer. The Socialists work to solve these problems, so intricate and involved that all the institutions and laws in this country are bound up in them. Say what you will about the Socialists and the methods they use, one thing you will have to admit—that the majority of them mean well and are driven by the need to reconcile society with God."[51]

240

Throughout the year, the columns of *Saamanden* included news of the labor situation around the world. Thankfully America had some clergymen with a conscience—the Episcopalians in the East. Janson hoped that the Lutheran ministers would read of their activities and reconsider what role they themselves should play. Because shopgirls often had to work twelve to fourteen hours on days before holidays, the Episcopalians were campaigning to have all stores close at six o'clock on such days. Some firms had already agreed to this reform, the first being a Japanese company. (It was not the first time "heathens" had shamed the so-called Christians.)[52] From England, the Reverend John Burns, a Methodist minister, had reported that laborers were showing great enthusiasm for organizing themselves; gas workers, dock workers, bakers, and others had won significant victories.[53] Pastor John Brown of New England said that the mills in his part of the country were paying their workers starvation wages.[54] Father Edward McGlynn, in commenting on the pope's remedy for poverty, had declared bitterly that His Holiness seemed to have his eyes in the back of his head, and wished that that great office might go to a young man with the ability and force to make the position what it had originally been intended to be.[55]

Farmers were being victimized too. An earlier issue of *Saamanden* had reported that, on both sides of the Red River, there was cheating in the grading of wheat. Under the inspection system used, it was judged two grades below what it rightfully should have been, and there was little doubt that the elevators and railroads were conniving to oppress the farmer.[56] Some months later one reads that the Associated Charities of Minneapolis and St. Paul had sent George Brackett to study farming conditions in Dakota. No one, he found, lacked the necessities of life, but the farmers were the prey of loan sharks, paying as much as 80 to 100 per cent interest. Brackett was working to organize a trust company which would make loans in Dakota at 10 per cent a year.[57] Janson himself was a member of the Minneapolis Farmers' Alliance, and in June, 1890, was elected to the executive committee of the local unit.[58]

Although *Saamanden* was not mentioned, Janson came up for brief comment in *Current Literature*, published in New York City. The article was not signed, but the style suggests it was the work of Hjalmar Hjorth Boyesen. *Budstikken* promptly reprinted it: "Among the Norwegian authors who have settled for life in the United States is Mr. Kristofer Janson of Minneapolis. He is a Unitarian minister and his sermons, or rather lectures, never fail to attract the highly educated part of the

Danish-Norwegian population of the Twin Cities. At the same time he is a well-known and popular lecturer among the Scandinavian working-men, and few understand better how to address this class of people. As an author he has pictured the unhappy lot of the majority of immigrants coming over here devoid of knowledge in regard to climate, people, and language of the United States, and, although some of his sketches are very somber, they have, nevertheless, that attraction for the readers which truth will always command. Mr. Janson lives on the outskirts of Minneapolis and his house is the centre of the Scandinavian circle in Minnesota."[59]

At the time this article was printed, a Swedish Unitarian society was being organized in Minneapolis. Axel Lundeberg (he was not ordained until later) was a graduate of the University at Upsala, and had come to the United States some two years before as a journalist. Attracted to Unitarianism, he had spent some months at Lombard College in Galesburg, Illinois, before he moved to Minnesota. Janson was glad the American Unitarian Association was supporting Lundeberg's efforts in Minneapolis.[60] Naturally *Folkebladet* did not share this view, deploring the extent to which Yankee money was being used to proselyte among the Scandinavians. The paper enumerated the missionaries mournfully: the Baptists had the Norwegian Ween Olsen, the Presbyterians, the Swedish Evert Nymanover, the Universalists, the Swedish August Dellgren, the Unitarians, the Norwegian Kristofer Janson, and now they had added the Swedish Axel Lundeberg.[61]

Lundeberg was to begin much as Janson had done, giving free lectures—"Some Thoughts about the Bible," and "Is Unitarianism Free-thinking or Atheism?" Meanwhile Janson told Bjørnson that he could report only good things from his mission field: his fortnightly visits to Hudson were drawing a full house every time; in Underwood interest was as lively and flourishing as ever; in Fergus Falls, after the organization of the Free Christian Society, people had to be turned away for lack of space; and in Rothsay the hall had been packed. One thing that had helped had been that the orthodox had begun to try to refute the arguments for Unitarianism. However, people seemed to want to hear both sides, which was a step forward, better than the blind prejudice that had prevailed earlier.

But the winter passed into spring—and Janson still had not heard from Bjørnson. By March 31, he could wait no longer; the big payment on his house was only two months away. He was in an irritable mood. "I have sent you two letters without getting an answer in spite of the fact that I dealt with business matters concerning Solbakken, and I am worried things will not be settled in time. Move your lazy body to your desk and gladden your property-poor friends with your illegible scratches." He let loose on other things that taxed his patience. Norway must be full of crazy people, eternally in a dither about one thing or another, he wrote. First it was the girls who packed matches, then the warship, he said, referring to disputes in Kristiania. Now comes the great furor over Gunnar Heiberg's play *Kong Midas*. It was ridiculous the way they carried on about that, acting as if it were a great national issue. Bjørnson could hardly have appreciated this, for the play was considered to be an attack on him. It had been denied a presentation at the National Theater and was given at the Tivoli in Kristiania, where noisy demonstrations broke out nightly between the defenders of Bjørnson and the supporters of the play.

Janson had other news which could hardly have cheered Bjørnson. A pirated edition of *Paa Guds veie* had come out in Minneapolis. "I don't believe it will hurt either you or your publisher," Janson wrote serenely. "What with the protective tariff and other skulduggery, the imported edition costs two and a half dollars, too much for the poor souls in America who want to read the book." The dollar edition would gain Bjørnson many more readers and strengthen his rapport with his countrymen in America.

When Janson turned to family matters, he was less waspish. The two older boys had passed their first examinations in medical school admirably; their parents were proud of them. Arne was stringing up and was a lively, diligent lad. Through the winter, the children had had their share of minor illnesses; Borghild suffered still from a light case of rheumatic fever. Janson had too much to do and too many worries, but he was thankful he was well. Drude took life too hard. Janson would be relieved when he could send her and the children out to Brown County for a rest. Bjørnson must tell all the news of his family—and get the rest of the Solbakken money from his son Erling and send it when he answered Janson's letter. "You will thus do me a great, great service. You know the mortgage on my house falls due in June."[62]

10

Up to this time, the newspapers had said virtually nothing about Janson's Spiritualism. Occasionally, he had dealt with the subject in a sermon as he did in St. Paul in April, 1889, when his title was "Has Spiritualism Any Influence on Our Religious Life?"—but these lectures were never reviewed.[63] He had not discussed the matter in his paper. However, communication with the dead is mentioned briefly in his

Easter sermon which appeared in the April, 1890, issue of *Saamanden*. It occurs in dreams or visions (*syner*), he said. But the sermon was directed mostly at materialists who held that one lived on only in his descendants, a barren prospect according to Janson, one unworthy of God and contrary to all religious teaching from the dawn of history.

At about the same time, *The North* came out with an elaborate front-page story of a seance that had been held at Elim House, a hotel owned by a John Mattson at the corner of Fourth Street and Eighth Avenue South. Mattson had invited sixteen–eighteen persons to be present, among them N. P. Olson, an employee of the paper, who wrote the story. The guests included both men and women, among them Kristofer Janson, Axel Lundeberg, O. E. Erickson, and Dr. H. M. Toll, a Swedish physician who had recently come to the city. Mrs. Toll was also present, and Mrs. Mattson is mentioned, but beyond that none of the other women were named. A certain Mr. Pigeon also had been engaged as a medium; he was described as a pleasant, healthy-looking man who was known for his "powers and abilities."

The seance was held in the Mattsons' private parlors. In one corner of a room a temporary cabinet had been improvised by using quilts and blankets. This was inspected by the guests, who also examined the floor of the room above and the ceiling of the basement below. When everyone was satisfied, the medium went into the cabinet taking with him two cane bottom chairs, a guitar, a small dinner bell, a slate and slate pencil. He seated himself in one of the chairs, placing the other so that it faced him. The other articles were put in a corner of the cabinet. The guests formed a semicircle extending from one corner of the cabinet to the other. The place had been darkened by removing the lamp to an adjoining room, with the door between slightly ajar to allow a faint shaft of light to enter. Although it was customary to bind the hands and feet of the medium, the company decided against this, feeling that it might "cause suspicion." Instead, it was agreed that whoever was called in to occupy the other chair would control the medium's hands and feet. In a short time, the heavy breathing of the medium assured the others that he was in a trance.

What then took place was to confound Olson and many of the others. As they kept their eyes on the curtain, a snow-white hand appeared moving up and down for a few seconds; it disappeared and then returned, plainer than before. Kristofer Janson was called into the cabinet. He later explained that he sat facing the medium, holding the man's hands and securing the man's legs between his own. Everyone was surprised to hear the guitar playing and the bell ringing. When asked if he still held the medium's hands and feet, Janson replied that he did, saying that he felt hands patting his forehead and pulling his hair and beard. The patting could be heard outside the cabinet. The bell, being vigorously shaken in first one corner of the cabinet and then in another, appeared outside the curtain, being held by a small delicate hand. "The wrist and part of the arm were visible," Olson wrote. "What seemed to be the sleeve of a night shirt with a wristband about an inch wide covered the extended arm. Neither of the two men wore sleeves of that kind."

As they were called into the cabinet, other guests had experiences similar to those of Janson: one woman was grasped by the arm while the bell was rung directly in front of her face; Mrs. Mattson saw the dim outline of a luminous being and at the same time a hand and a foot were visible outside the curtain. While Mrs. Mattson held the medium's hands, the pencil was heard to move across the slate. After reading the inscription, the guests led the medium out of the cabinet. Three chairs were arranged in a row. Janson took the center one with the medium on his left, and Mattson on his right. Soon the foreheads of all three glowed with a steady phosphorescent light, "resembling in character the aurora borealis." There were other strange phenomena: the guitar back in the cabinet began to play and presently appeared at the opening in the curtain about two feet above the head of Janson and several feet from where the medium sat. At one time, two iron rings, less than a foot in diameter, were produced, examined by the company and found to be solid. A handkerchief was tied on one to make the two immediately distinguishable. Janson sat holding one of the medium's hands while Mattson had the other. The rings were handed into the cabinet; the curtain shook slightly and in an instant one ring circled the medium's wrist and the other was on Janson's left arm. Janson said that he was positive he had not relinquished the medium's hand. Olson concluded his article by saying, "The psychical manifestation was sought for its own sake. There was no point in deception. What was seen was seen by all present."[64]

Some four months later, *Budstikken* was to carry a brief account headed "Is Kristofer Janson a Spiritualist?" It was a curious item, for the information in it had come by a circuitous route. Someone in Minneapolis had written a letter to a paper in Norway, declaring that Janson was a warm supporter of Spiritualism and that he had accepted its claims almost without qualification. Seances were frequently held in his home, the correspondent wrote, and the subject was often discussed at well-attended meetings at his church, "where one can hear a most bizarre blending of reason and unreason."[65]

Nowhere else does one find any mention of such meetings being held, but Janson was having seances conducted in his study. Although Drude does not seem to have been opposed to this in any way, she was, at the moment, more interested in Theosophy, often discussing its principles with Mrs. Davis. According to Mrs. Dina Behr Kolderup, "It was Spiritualism upstairs and Theosophy downstairs." Eilev Janson remembered being present while the two women discussed Theosophy, in particular the "laws" of dharma and karma.[66]

11

However, while the seances had some notoriety, they were in no way lessening Janson's interest in social reform. The liberal ministers of the city, concerned over American Protestantism's neglect of the working class, were holding a series of evening meetings in the Bijou Theater on Washington Avenue for those who never otherwise set foot in a church. Besides Janson and Simmons, Universalist and Swedenborgian ministers took part, and, in *Saamanden*, Janson reported that the meetings had been well attended.[67] He also kept readers informed about developments in Nationalism and Christian Socialism, but he was finding it embarrassing to report concerning the Minnesota Farmers' Alliance.[68] A bitter feud had broken out between Ignatius Donnelly of the state executive committee and R. J. Hall, president of the state Alliance. Rather than air that conflict, Janson chose to give more constructive news: the great growth of the Alliance in Kansas, whose members had sent a list of their grievances to their representatives in Congress; the promise of "industrial cooperation" among members, exemplified by Dakota farmers banding together to buy machinery; the resolution of the 30,000 Minnesota members condemning the United States Supreme Court for decisions that enabled a packing house to make almost a two million dollars yearly profit while farmers got low prices for their livestock.[69] Not until August could he urge support for the Alliance's state ticket in the fall election. By that time, a compromise candidate had been nominated for governor, Sidney M. Owen, editor of *Farm, Stock, and Home*, the largest agricultural paper in the state.[70] He was a very fine man, in sympathy with Nationalist ideas, Janson assured his readers, adding, "Those of us who do not want to be slaves of the rotten old parties will support the Alliance ticket with all our might."[71]

In April, 1890, word came that Marcus Thrane, the long-time crusader for the rights of labor, was dead. He was, of course, also a notorious church-baiter. Although his target had been the Norwegian Lutheran clergy, Janson had found his ridicule of religion in his *Den gamle Wis-*

consin bibelen (The Old Wisconsin Bible) offensive. Such allusions as Janson had made to Thrane previously had been reproving. The latter had wanted to tear down institutions without having any constructive program to offer in their place. In the spring of 1890, however, Janson held memorial services for Thrane, and his eulogy was later the lead article in *Saamanden*. Thrane's friends were grateful for this; a year later when they organized a memorial service for him in Chicago, they invited Janson to be one of the speakers. He was not able to attend, but he sent a long message to be read at the service.

For his work as a pioneer in the labor movement in Norway, Thrane has since received full recognition. In 1949, the Norwegian government had his body moved from Eau Claire, Wisconsin, to Oslo, where it was buried with appropriate ceremonies. He had been the first to organize a labor union in Norway and had been imprisoned there for eight years before coming to America in 1863. At his death, he had only a small circle of friends, but Janson had found him to be a true follower of Jesus. He had heard Thrane say that organized religion was man's greatest enemy, but this bitterness, according to Janson, was the result of the treatment Thrane had received in Norway. Thrane, he said, was not a labor leader but an agitator. Once he had fomented discontent, someone else had to take over to direct group action. Nevertheless, such men were needed: the masses must be aroused by repeated alarms. "That was Thrane's work. It was a long protest against tyranny—political, economic, ecclesiastical—in which he was always faithful to the idea of his youth: the gospel of brotherhood."

Drawing on what Thrane's son had said about his father's last years, Janson said that when the old man was so frail he could no longer speak before crowds or write his satirical pieces, his chief delights were children and flowers. Janson closed with an apostrophe: "The blessings and love of children will carry you to those light realms whose very existence you doubted. And here on earth, whenever men who are struggling for a cause rally under the banner of Scandinavian martyrs, your name will be mentioned as one who has broken ground for the new seed. Whatever weakness or imperfections that may have characterized your work will be forgotten. What will be remembered is your struggle for freedom, equality, and brotherhood. Men will hope that what was a driving force in you will also move in them: love for one another."[72]

Shortly after he had written this eulogy, Janson heard from Bjørnson, who sent the last payment on Solbakken. Janson could breathe freely: he was now in a position to negotiate a new loan on his Minneapolis house.

247

9

A Stressful
Fiftieth Year

ON THURSDAY, May 22, 1890, Drude Janson was in Brown
County, sitting outdoors, writing to Bjørnstjerne Bjørnson. With her
pad propped up on her knee, a bottle of ink beside her, she was to
explain how she had been released from Minneapolis more than a month
ahead of the regular schedule. The Jansons had discovered that the
school their four younger children attended was unsound and had withdrawn them. Since it was so close to the end of the school term, they had
closed their house in the city—as far as social activity was concerned—
and she and the four had made their way back to Brown County.

Back on her beloved prairie, she reveled in the scene about her,
describing it to Bjørnson: a magnificent sky overhead, trees in foliage,
sheep grazing, swallows darting back and forth from the eaves of the
church, and the grasshoppers and other insects chirping in gladsome
song. Nature meant more to her than ever before. That and books compensated her. "I am so completely fed up with Minneapolis, Bjørnson—
O God, how tired I am of it," she confessed. "That's too bad when one
must live there, but I cannot help it." All winter she had been so miserable that she could not write him, for he could see through any disguise
she might attempt. Then came his scathing letter to Kristofer. Bjørnson
was so right: Drude was not created to keep boarders. Nothing on earth
could induce her to do it again. The very thought of it made her shudder.

Did Bjørnson remember what he had written? It didn't matter, but
she felt as if she could kiss him for every word—for his understanding
of her. That gave her courage to believe in herself. "And if I dare do
that, nothing else matters; then, creating my own world, I can live

248

patiently in Minneapolis *for a time*." (She had underlined the words.) Living as she had been doing had been intellectual suicide, but the next year she would have her own room where she could read and work. She had just sent off two stories to Hegel, the publisher. Both were tales of the prairie and very sad. "But I can't help it, Bjørnson—life affects me that way—here anyhow."

She was glad all the ado about the play, *Kong Midas*, had not affected Bjørnson's ability to work. As she saw it, Heiberg had meant to satirize Bjørnson in the character Ramseth, but the result had been nothing more than a caricature. Kristofer had read the play before a Sunday evening audience, as he did all new books from Norway; he had had about 150 present the first night, less than half of whom returned to hear the second half. But, of course, the sophisticated Kristiania-tone of the play had been algebra to them.

Kristofer had enjoyed himself over the epithets Bjørnson had lavished on him in the letter, Drude wrote satirically. She felt both *halleluja-pige* and *hjernekikker* (hallelujah-girl and brain-peeper) were very appropriate.[1] Kristofer, she explained, was oblivious to everything but his ministry: "He goes about his work regardless, glowing with faith, and it makes no difference to him if he is in Minneapolis or the furtherest Sandwich island as long as he can preach his gospel and get people to listen to him. He involves himself in all their sufferings, goes among all those poor souls and listens to their misfortunes and tries to be father confessor and comforter to them—but I can't, for I am a child of the world with yearnings outside of his wretched flock in Minneapolis. He would find it so wonderful to have a wife who could share his work and go about as a sister of mercy and bride of the Lord. But I can't be that, and I am so tired of hearing of need and misery."

It was not that Drude was indifferent to conditions in America which, she assured Bjørnson, were much worse than those in Norway. They gripped her and she felt one hardly had the right to speak, think, or write about anything else until people had their eyes opened to how intolerable things were, but she could not go about as the tender comforter, much as she might admire those who could. To Bjørnson, she defended Socialism: "We have a large, beautiful room in our house which we will not need next winter. If I were to suggest to Kristofer we turn it into a hospital, he would be beside himself with joy—but that Drude will not do—deliver me! But on the larger issues I agree with him completely, and if I could get you to accept Socialism, I would shout hurrah so you could hear it in Norway. Wherever I turn, whether it be in the esthetic, religious, or social area, everything is affected by this hor-

249

rible Babylonian mismanagement. Call it a dream, but it is a dream that has given life meaning for me, one that secures the future of my children and grandchildren and is necessary for the development of the world, and I assure you without it we will descend into chaos. If you lived here two years, you would agree with us—no, *you* would not have to be here that long."

As if cheered by Socialism, Drude went on to report a happy event. "Think of it, I have at long last found a friend—I think I dare call her that, for as you know there are not many here I care about—the first since I came to Minneapolis." The friend was Kate Buffington Davis, an American from the East. She had been the secretary of the first Nationalist Club in Minneapolis and a directing force for the movement in the city. Most Americans, from what Drude had observed, were narrow-minded and pretentious. Like Mrs. Davis, Drude was enthusiastic over the Nationalist movement: "I go to the Nationalist meetings and am a Socialist." During the summer she intended to study Darwin's *The Origin of Species* and *The Descent of Man*. However, she was sure she would never accept "the survival of the fittest" as a natural law. Instead, it was the boldest and greediest who survived—the ones who did not see or hear the suffering of others—and the gamblers, for there was no other way of regarding those who traded on the stock market.[2]

On the face of it, Drude's remarks about Kristofer were hardly more than what many another wife might say about her husband at a time of irritation, especially when she knew she had the sympathy of the person in whom she was confiding. Yet years later, both Eilev Janson and Mrs. Kolderup were to say that the rift between the Jansons began when Drude lost interest in her husband's work. Although both Janson's son and Drude's niece censured Drude, they felt some qualification about doing so. If she was tired of hearing of misery, they acknowledged they at times had felt the same way, suspecting that Janson, who could not resist an appeal for help, was often taken advantage of by those who besieged him. Even members of the congregation could view his charitableness with trepidation. The late Mrs. Marie Stoep—a sister of J. C. Huseby, the last president of the congregation—revealed to the author that, at one time, the treasurer of the church had left the city abruptly, taking with him the funds of the congregation. The church officers wanted to report this act to the police, but Janson would not permit it, saying, "It's too bad he should do that, for he was basically so fine a person."[3]

When she wrote to Bjørnson, Drude was in no way planning a revolt. At the beginning of the following year, the church school program was changed to Sunday morning before the regular services, and she was in charge of the music. She continued to manage the mailing out of *Saamanden*, and, for its fourth volume, she was to translate a long sermon by James Freeman Clarke. Yet, faithful as she was in these duties, she continued to urge Janson to find a successor and formulated plans for their escape from Minneapolis.[4]

During May and June, 1890, while Drude and the children were in Brown County, Janson remained in Minneapolis. In the spring, the paintings of Vassili Vasilievitch Verestchagin were on exhibit. According to Michael Bryan's *Dictionary of Painters and Engravers*, Verestchagin is today thought of as the most famous of Russian painters, if not technically the best.[5] Janson was deeply impressed by the exhibit. He preached on "Art as an Educator with Reference to Verestchagin's Work." This sermon gave vivid descriptions of scenes from the Russo-Turkish War, of the agony of Jesus, and of Mohammedans at worship. It was published in the May, 1890, issue of *Saamanden*. Later in the summer, as Janson finished his novel *Sara,* he imagined his heroine having the benefit of seeing the Verestchagin pictures. In June, Janson's church gave its annual St. John's Day festival, which seems to have met with the success of the previous ones. He was also following the activities of the Norwegian Lutherans with great interest as three formerly rival groups consolidated to form the United Norwegian Lutheran Church in America. The three were the Conference, the Norwegian Augustana Synod, and the Anti-Missourian Brotherhood, the latter a splinter faction which had broken away from the Norwegian Synod over the dispute on predestination. In *Saamanden,* he was to speak of this union as a hopeful sign, saying that he hoped the new church might grow in tolerance to the point where it would "welcome us Unitarians as their Christian brethren and acknowledge that we too work for God's kingdom on earth."[6]

2

Janson had not been long in Brown County for his summer vacation when he received a message from Hjalmar Hjorth Boyesen requesting him to write an article on Norwegians in the United States for *Cosmopolitan*, a national magazine for which Boyesen was an editorial adviser. His first choice for the assignment had been Rasmus B. Anderson, never, it seems, with any high hopes that the latter would accept. In his letter to the former minister to Denmark, Boyesen said that he would ask Janson if Anderson did not care to write the piece.[7] Remembering the previous winter's financial hardship—when Drude had slaved over a houseful of boarders, Janson could not afford to pass up such an offer. In mid-August, while he was at work on the article, he was himself the subject of an extended profile by Oscar Gundersen published in the *Minneapolis Søndag Tidende* on August 17, 1890; another version appeared in *Budstikken* at approximately the same time. It was a perceptive piece, one that can bear comparison with Hamsun's earlier article in *Ny Jord*. Gundersen's judgment of Janson did not differ radically from Hamsun's; it is also strikingly similar to that of modern critics who have surveyed the whole of Janson's career.

At the time, Gundersen was just under thirty years old, a bookkeeper in Chicago, who had emigrated from Norway in 1882 when he was twenty-one. A precocious young man, he had already spent some three years in a Methodist theological school in Kristiania. In America, once he found a way to make a living, he devoted all his leisure time to study and writing. In the course of time, he produced a volume of poems and a book on Emerson (in Norwegian), both of which he published at his own expense. He was thoroughly at home in German, could read French, and apparently had made appreciable progress in Greek; later, it was his custom to read a chapter of the New Testament in the original in lieu of attending Sunday morning services. Before his death in 1941, he had contributed to virtually every Norwegian-language newspaper and magazine published in the United States. His literary contributions won him rewarding friendships, but only once was he paid for his writing—an article in English on Kielland which he wrote for a Chicago morning paper.[8]

Gundersen had written for *Saamanden*. In the second and third volumes, his "En engelsk bibelkritiker" appeared in three installments. This was a free interpretation of the ideas of Matthew Arnold.[9] It was printed without comment by Janson and never aroused any response from readers, who quite possibly found it too esoteric. Although Gundersen had a readable style, the articles have allusions to such figures as Pascal, Sainte-Beuve, and Taine. His "Fremtidens religion" (The Religion of the Future), printed in the June, 1889, *Saamanden*, argued that many of the ideas of the liberal Christians, as well as those of the orthodox, were headed for extinction. He found the aim of the liberals to bring back Christianity to its original simplicity somewhat absurd: men of the nineteenth century could not view the world as people had done almost two thousand years before, nor was it desirable that they do so. He predicted that belief in an anthropological God and in personal immortality would in time not be generally held.

252

In his "Kristofer Janson: A Critical Review," Gundersen character-ized the minister as a man who came to reason by way of the heart. He preferred the idyll, a trait of character that kept him apart from the intellectual stream of the late nineteenth century. Bjørnson had also been slow in feeling the impact of discoveries in the natural sciences, Gundersen thought; the poet's religious crisis had not come until the late 1870s, even though *The Descent of Man* had been published in 1871 and *The Origin of Species* twelve years earlier. Yet, having re-ceived the message, Bjørnson went the whole way. Janson had also briefly toyed with the new learning, but when he saw where it would lead, he turned homeward. In the age of Darwin, one finds Kristofer Janson serenely reading Theodore Parker.

Were he to choose a religion, Gundersen went on, he would certainly prefer Janson's liberal Christianity to the shallow freethinking of such men as Robert Ingersoll. Even so, Unitarianism was an outmoded philos-ophy, a vestigial remnant of early nineteenth-century rationalism. It em-bodied the idyll, and that is why it appealed to Janson. The man had no understanding of the natural sciences nor any real historical sense. His refusal to accept the miracles of the Bible was not grounded on empirical evidence but on the assumption that it would be unworthy of God to violate the physical laws He had established. For a time, Janson had been influenced by Hugh Pentecost's anarchistic views, but this belief had been superseded by Socialism, which Americans, with their prejudice toward anything that smacks of Europe, preferred to call Nationalism. Janson's Nationalism was not based on any research but on the wishful fiction of Bellamy

Although Janson's writing showed some originality, Gundersen be-lieved that he was not a *digter* (poet), merely a poetic talent. Lacking both the intuitive psychology of Bjørnson and the reflective psychology of Kierkegaard, Janson either has his characters declaim or does it for them. In his fiction, he was at his best when he held himself to a half-satirical vein. He was not capable of irony. As a man of feeling, he was better in verse than in prose. Bjørnson had said that he was the best Scandinavian hymn writer since Grundtvig, and Gundersen felt that the hymn was the best vehicle for a man of feeling. When Janson was in the right mood, the results were indeed pleasing, but when he was not, the hymn seemed rather flat. All too often, God and Janson seemed too much hand in glove.

Gundersen could only regret Janson's Spiritualism, a belief the critic regarded as the great humbug of the age. Then he revealed where he felt Janson's greatness lay: "Let this unpleasant impression be banished;

253

let me see Janson as the preacher in the original meaning of the term. His noble form stands before us proclaiming his warm faith that God is our father who 'has no stepchildren,' that 'all men are brothers' and we must work tirelessly to make all this a reality. We are no longer speaking of lyricism and rhetoric. . . . Here is pure will and kindliness of heart, above all, goodness: 'All religions are witness to man's need for communion with God, a magnificent rainbow bridging earth and heaven where God's love glows in the refracted colors.' We are moved by his goodness. We forget the egotism and other externals and are uplifted by the moral idyll he presents and feel ourselves close to tears. Back of the inspired preacher looms the image of the Son of Man who two thousand years before stood on the shores of Galilee and pleaded, 'Love one another!' "[10]

The prominence given this article in two Norwegian papers would seem to indicate that the immigrant community was becoming more sophisticated; a few years before articles on Janson were either vituperative or extravagantly laudatory. Judged on a cultural basis, it was a notch or two above Janson's "Norsemen in the United States," which was to appear in the fall of 1890 in *Cosmopolitan,* a breezy and informative piece also containing critical comment. Janson began with the Vikings, briefly mentioned a Norwegian colony in New Jersey in 1624, before going on to the Quaker immigration of 1825 following the work of Cleng Peerson and Knut Eide. He described the hardships of those who had come before the Civil War, naming the places where they had settled, and concluding by saying of the Norwegians generally: "They are considered a hardy, honest, industrious class of people, where the saloon has not exerted its baneful influence upon them."[11]

Janson described Norwegian participation in the Civil War, saying that his countrymen were to be found in virtually every Western regiment, noting that the Fifteenth Wisconsin, made up of Scandinavians, distinguished itself on many battlefields, especially at Chickamauga, where its commander, Colonel Hans Christian Heg, was killed. He wrote glowingly of the achievements of this regiment: " 'I think I shall have to send my Fifteenth Wisconsin,' General Sherman used to say when something risky was to be done."

In discussing the religious life of the Norwegians, Janson explained that the Lutherans were divided into six rival groups, correcting this with a footnote which referred to the recent formation of the United Church. As he had done before, he spoke of their contentiousness: "The Norwegian is a born controversialist. He likes to discuss, to twist words, to push arguments, to indulge in hair-splitting definitions; and as the religious field is the only one in which he feels himself at home he gives free vent to his fighting spirit in his ecclesiastical controversies. A Scandinavian Lutheran church convention offers a tragi-comical sight. It is held in mediaeval style. No quarter is given to the slightest heresy; wholesale condemnation, the stake and eternal damnation await the sinner that goes astray. The Bible is considered a great arsenal of doctrinal weapons and projectiles. The combatants launch Biblical thunderbolts against one another. Moses and David and the prophets are made Viking chiefs who brandish their swords with delight: and when one of the parties is about to be pushed to the wall, its ministers command a charge of bayonets along the whole line with St. Peter and St. Paul as standard-bearers. The inspiring words of command, the smell of powder, and the smoke of burning heresies stir up the farmer. He feels his importance as a crusader: the fanaticism of his leaders influences him and he considers himself a sentinel of God's kingdom on earth, whose holy duty is to resist and repulse all those modern innovations that come and ask for admission in the alluring guise of 'progress.' "[12]

Janson mentioned that there were also Methodists and Baptists among the Norwegians, going on to speak of his own Unitarian movement which had six congregations and had erected a handsome church in Minneapolis. He sketched the careers of such distinguished Norwegians as Rasmus B. Anderson and Hjalmar Hjorth Boyesen, and named a number of educators, lawyers, clergymen, and merchants before going on to an extensive account of the various newspapers and their influence. Only Knute Nelson had reached eminence in national politics. Norwegians often appeared on state ballots, but their activity was hampered by the animosity the Norwegians felt toward the Swedes. If they could overcome this lack of political unity, the Scandinavians, Janson thought, might have a dominant influence in Minnesota and at least hold the balance of power in Wisconsin and the Dakotas. The article, nine pages long, was illustrated with photographs of Professor Georg Sverdrup, Rasmus B. Anderson, Hjalmar Hjorth Boyesen, Consul P. Svanoe, and Kristofer Janson.[13]

3

In September, when the Jansons returned to Minneapolis, Drude discovered that her friend, Mrs. Kate Buffington Davis, had also been writing. Mrs. Davis' short story, "A Daughter of Lilith and a Daughter of Eve," was to appear in the *Arena* in January, 1891. Henry Steele Commager, in his *The American Mind*, has identified the *Arena* as the original muckraking magazine, saying that its pages were open to "Populists, Socialists, and heretics of all kinds." This periodical was published in Boston by Benjamin O. Flower, whom Commager has characterized as "half crackpot, half genius."[14] Only on rare occasions did Janson excerpt material from the *Arena* for *Saamanden*, but the Eastern magazine had some distinguished contributors; among them were Dr. Alfred Russel Wallace, Helena Modjeska, Elbert Hubbard, Edward Everett Hale, Dion Boucicault, Hamlin Garland, Rabbi Solomon Schindler, Minot J. Savage, and Helen Campbell. By present-day standards, Mrs. Davis' story would be judged sentimental. It relates how a young man was lured into marriage by a daughter of Lilith only to realize his mistake when he later met a daughter of Eve. Mrs. Davis was certainly a prominent figure in Minneapolis. Somewhat later *The North* carried a biographical sketch of her, describing her as "a woman of commanding presence, large, well proportioned, with the stamp of individuality on her handsome, sympathetic face." She had, the article continued, a strong inclination toward mysticism; this might have been dangerous had it not been that Mrs. Davis was so well endowed with common sense. She seems to have been a feminist as well, for in 1892 when she became editor of the *Housekeeper*, a magazine published in Minneapolis, she assembled a staff made up entirely of women.[15]

Janson also admired Mrs. Davis, and, as mentioned before, she had spoken in his church on occasion.[16] At the time, he was rejoicing that Johannes Skørdalsvold had decided to join Nazareth Church. The two had been on friendly terms for years, and indeed the only time Janson had received sympathetic treatment in *Folkebladet* had been the period during which Skørdalsvold had been its editor. He was a graduate of the college division of Augsburg Seminary, and, since that institution was not yet fully accredited according to American standards, he had taken a bachelor's degree at the University of Minnesota. A dedicated temperance worker during his student days at the university, he had operated a coffee shop as a means of combatting the saloon. In 1889 he had toured Europe, sending back to *The North* a report of an interview he had had with Henrik Ibsen; the dramatist had said that he had several friends in Minneapolis, among them Kristofer Janson.[17] Skørdalsvold's decision seems to illustrate what an act of valor it required for an immigrant to become a Unitarian. He had made up his mind in the summer of 1890 and had written to Janson in Brown County. "I have no doubt your choice will bring you suffering and possibly financial loss," Janson had responded. Whether or not the choice had been a wise one would depend on the inner peace and security it brought Skørdalsvold.

256

"One's happiness in life," the minister said, "depends on being true to one's ideals and pursuing the truth—in any event that has been my experience."

Skørdalsvold's announcement had come as a surprise and a great joy, Janson revealed, not only for the pleasure the former's presence in the congregation would bring, but because he represented the progressive and thinking young people of Minneapolis and was therefore a herald of things to come. Janson immediately named Skørdalsvold superintendent of the Sunday school, to be organized that fall. More than that, he wrote that he was counting on his friend for help in the discussion meetings and with the social gatherings sponsored by the church. At the time, Janson had already decided that the meetings dealing with special topics would begin with an examination of the Alliance party, and he was to urge Skørdalsvold to do a little preliminary work. "Stump as much as you can for the Alliance ticket and keep people from becoming drunken swine," he wrote.[18]

Janson himself was prepared to do his bit for the Alliance party in *Saamanden*. He purposely waited until the October, 1890, issue to have political material in the hands of his readers just before the election in November. Both the Republican and the Democratic parties had outlived their usefulness, he wrote. The Republicans, once the champions of abolition, were now controlled by the moneyed interests; they were ready to crush the farmer and the laborer, as the passage of the McKinley Act testifies. The Democrats, no longer imbued with Jeffersonian democracy, held out promises of tariff reductions merely as a bait; such reforms as they had made in the past were negligible. The Alliance party would take government out of the hands of politicians and place it in those of the people. This action was urgently needed: farmers from Maine to the western boundaries of Dakota were being driven off their homesteads as sheriffs came to foreclose, and they were finding themselves empty handed after years of toil. Strikes had become the order of the day in the cities. A great storm was brewing that would lead to civil war in the country—and the fact that so far there had been no bloodshed made the situation no less threatening.

The Alliance party proposed a ten-point program which included land reform requiring that holdings of speculators be put in the hands of actual settlers. Under the new laws raw materials—oil, coal, metals, lumber—would pass from private hands into the control of the state. The monetary system would be overhauled, allowing for adequate coinage and breaking the hold Wall Street had over the secretary of the treasury. Child labor would be abolished and the period of compulsory school

257

attendance lengthened. Women would receive equal pay with men for equal work. All labor disputes would be settled by arbitration; interest rates would be lowered; the protective tariff would be removed from necessities. To reduce political corruption, the Australian secret ballot would be adopted.

No one, Janson told his readers, expected all these reforms to come at once; it was a program for gradual change. Even if one were not in accord with the Alliance party on every one of these issues, he could see that the leaders were sensitive to the prevailing discontent in the country. Although critics were prophesying that the Alliance party was doomed because it lacked money, here was a chance for the people to demonstrate love of one's country and their conviction that their fellowmen would prevail over the power of wealth.[19]

As it turned out, the results were gratifying. Victories in Minnesota did not match those in Kansas and Nebraska, where the Alliance won control of both houses of the state legislatures, but in Minnesota, as in South Dakota, the party came to hold the balance of power, making a very respectable showing in its first attempt to figure as an independent political unit. Actually, the election of 1890 gave the Republican party its first major reversal in twenty-five years. In the Fifth District, it sent Kittel Halvorson to Congress and Ignatius Donnelly was elected to the state senate. Although Sidney M. Owen did not win as governor, he drew almost 25 per cent of the vote, commanding so much support that William R. Merriam, the Republican candidate, barely nosed out his Democratic rival with 40 per cent of the ballots cast.[20]

4

Vitally interested though he was in the Alliance party, Janson did not give it all his attention. He was ready with goodly fare for his Sunday evening readings: another chapter in Hamsun's novel *Hunger*, his own novel *Sara*, and Drude's latest story, "Sort Himmel" (Black Heaven), which, accidentally or not, had the same title as the last chapter of Hamsun's book on American cultural life. But that fall Nazareth Church was to reach out to a wider public by periodically offering Sunday afternoon concerts, the performers being the most talented musicians in the Twin Cities. On these occasions, Janson dispensed with services in St. Paul, his congregation there being encouraged to attend the concert. The first was given on October 5 with Gustavus Johnson, Olive Fremstad, and Heinrich Hoeval on the program. The last named, a violinist, was to play an impressive part in the musical history of Minneapolis, and was later the first concertmaster of the Minneapolis Symphony Orchestra. The concerts shortly became famous, drawing music lovers from all over the area.[21]

These were part of Janson's program to bring *skjønhed i livet* (beauty into life). Many a time he was to bemoan the limitations, the ignorance, of Norwegian immigrants, but there were also times when the Americans presented a problem as well. Since he had begun holding services in St. Paul in the fall of 1886, he had used the basement of Unity Church, and now and then when his congregation gave a program, they rented the same place for the evening as well. For four years, this had been an agreeable arrangement. To be sure, the St. Paul Unitarians, fearful of what their neighbors might think, had asked that Janson's Sunday evening programs include no theatricals, a stipulation to which Janson had agreed. Then late in November, 1890, the trustees of Unity Church refused further use of the basement on the ground that Janson's Sunday evening programs had featured waltzes and mazurkas.

Wounded, Janson reproved the trustees on several matters. To them he addressed a letter: "You name the Waltz by Chopin as an objection; but we did not dream of, that the trustees of Unity church were so ignorant of musical affairs as not to know, that Chopin's waltzes and mazurkas are *not dancing music at all* [italics Janson's], but classical music played on all your so-called sacred concerts by Danz orchestra and others. Our entertainment was for the purpose of getting means to pay our obligations to you for hall rent, as the collections taken will not cover them. We are nearly compelled to use Sundays, because we cannot on any other evening expect a decent crowd. Our people are mostly poor toiling working men. When they come home on weekdays after 12 hours incessant toil weary and dirty, they do not feel like to attend any entertainment. But Sunday is their day for rest and entertainment, if their wealthy employers (strict Sunday observers of course) do not force them to work that day with threats of discharging. We feel sorry that our brother-Unitarians now will throw stones in our way and hamper us in our honest efforts to support ourselves. We have so much of a fierce opposition to meet from the orthodox flock, that we thought that sufficient. This your refusal will partly break up all our entertainment. We had already sold 50–60 tickets round in the city, when your thunderbolt came. The president of our society had to hurry round during the service last Sunday in order to get another hall and now we have to post a man at your door, chasing people, who will come, off to a little hall down on Seventh street. We did not imagine, that it was such a matter of significance, whether we remained a few hours longer in your hall on Sunday afternoon or not. But we have to obey and turn our audience on the street again.

"What is the sorest point to me nevertheless is not the refusal in itself, but the weak and narrow standpoint you have chosen on the Sunday question. Your secretary says in his letter, that you 'do not wish to offend the feelings of those, who think waltz music inappropriate on the Sabbath.' But is it not your duty as Unitarians, who have broken the letterworship of your forefathers and got a purer idea of God and Sunday worship—to protest against those old ideas, which will represent God as a crabbed and cross grandfather, who wishes the Sunday to be a vinegar-day, where laughter and innocent merriments and all, that make the soul happy and refreshed shall be forbidden? Did our great master from Galilee wish 'not to offend' the feelings of the Pharisees and their victims on the Sabbath? No—he violated their Sabbath observances time after time, and when they objected he taught them and us 'that the Sabbath was made for man and not man for the Sabbath.'

"I wanted to see the Unitarians courageously side with their master on this point and not, like the orthodox Puritan church, with the Pharisees. You have chosen the contrary, and you have of course your free will to do so. But so long, as I can breathe I will side with my master and hurl all the invectives I can against hypocrisy in whatever form it appears.

"I feel badly, that we are so poor, that we cannot be independent, else we would not any longer darken your threshold. But be assured, that this will be the last time we shall apply for the use of your basement outside the service. And untill we can secure a place of worship of our own, we have to go to your hall with that bitter feeling, that we are only a tolerated nuisance not a band of brethren.

In sadness,
Yours, Kristofer Janson."[22]

5

Yet, if Janson was irked with the St. Paul Unitarians for what he considered their craven adherence to a Puritan Sabbath, he was even more annoyed to find so many Norwegians prejudiced against Spiritualism. Actually, what most distinguishes volume four of *Saamanden* from its predecessors is that, for the first time, this topic comes to be freely discussed in its columns. Janson was not, strictly speaking, responsible for this change; readers questioned him on the subject. From October, 1890, to the end of the year, the correspondence columns of *Saamanden* dealt with virtually nothing else. The first query came from a subscriber in Chicago who wanted Janson to explain when life ended. Could one put any faith in the claims of Spiritualists, he asked, and, if so, where could he make contact with them?

Life never ended, Janson assured the correspondent. He could cite two kinds of evidence, probabilities and facts. It did not seem reasonable that this life—full of trouble and sorrow as it is—could be the only one given us by a just God. All religions, pagan as well as Christian, subscribed to a belief in the immortality of the soul. In the material world, one saw that matter was changed but never destroyed. Yet these were only probabilities. The Spiritualists could give concrete proof that those who had departed this life still lived and could, under the proper circumstances, communicate with those on earth.

Unfortunately, Spiritualism had attracted charlatans. Janson warned that any seances where admission was charged were suspect. The meetings that he had attended were held in private homes including only friends and acquaintances. No professional medium was present, but one person in the group served in that capacity, making no claims or prophecies about what would take place. Under such circumstances, Janson had received messages both from those he had known in this life and from strangers, and these were of such a nature that he could not doubt their authenticity. If the writer wanted to study Spiritualism, Janson advised him to call on Colonel John Bundy, editor of the *Religio-Philosophical Journal* at 92 La Salle Street in Chicago, adding that the editor made it his business to investigate those who made extravagant claims and to unmask the fraudulent.[23]

The following month Janson printed a letter from Atwater, Minnesota. The writer and his family were delighted with *Saamanden*, so much so that when they had finished a number they sent it to the man's father in Kongsberg, Norway, from where they received a liberal paper in return. They sometimes found that the latter publication included articles reprinted from *Saamanden*, citing Janson's discussion of the place of reason in religion and his articles on Tolstoy. But the Atwater writer was troubled about Janson's Spiritualism. People in that community generally regarded it as humbug. They had heard of a case in Chicago in which a medium had claimed he could call forth any spirit on demand and had swindled any number of people before he had been exposed. Some local individuals in Atwater were talking of canceling their subscriptions to *Saamanden*; the writer was passing this information on to Janson because he did not want to see the magazine damaged. He had also consulted his father in Kongsberg on the matter and reported that, much as the latter admired Janson's insistence on reason in religion, he found Spiritualism mysterious and unreasonable.

The Atwater letter exasperated Janson. He could not understand, he wrote in reply, how Christians could be so prejudiced against Spiritualism when the Bible actually was full of it. So far as dissatisfied subscribers were concerned, he declared that he had generally kept the discussion of Spiritualism out of *Saamanden*, but that he surely had a right to reply when he was questioned about it. Much of the intolerance concerning the subject was traceable to unscrupulous frauds who took advantage of bereaved persons. No one on earth could call forth a spirit, he insisted; the medium was merely the instrument of such spirits as chose to use him. Once the medium was out of a trance, he could remember nothing of the messages he had conveyed. Yet the fact that charlatans operated did not condemn Spiritualism any more than quack healers discredited the science of medicine. Rather than turning to ridicule, people who had not bothered to give the matter serious study should honestly admit that it did not interest them and that they knew nothing about it.[24]

Normally letters in *Saamanden* were signed "N.N.," an abbreviation for the Latin *nescio nomen* (name not known), unless the person specifically wanted his name to appear. Such a writer was Olav Haugtrø of Sioux Falls, South Dakota. He liked the monthly, saying it was the only readable Norwegian religious paper in the country. However, there were times when he was confused about Janson's views. Surely, if he believed communication with the dead to be possible, the editor of the magazine must also accept the miracles of the Bible. According to Haugtrø, this life was enough of a bitter comedy without being followed by another with earthbound ties. No one knew whether there was a life in the hereafter, Haugtrø asserted, nor, while he was alive, did he have any means of finding out. He also differed with Janson on the existence of a personal God and on the forgiveness of sin; in spite of these differences, however, he wished Janson well and hoped his work would prosper.

Such amenities did not mollify Janson. He disliked the tone of levity in Haugtrø's letter. Unwilling to give Spiritualism serious attention, the writer had done what people had done through the ages whenever a new idea presented itself—they turned to ridicule. In believing that communication with the dead was possible, Janson was under no obligation to accept the miracles of the Bible. Messages from the dead were not supernatural but completely natural, and one day science would be able to explain the phenomenon.[25]

Up to this time, Janson's sermons apparently had contained no more than casual references to Spiritualism. On the first Sunday in November, 1890, however, he expressed views that seem to have been generally accepted by Spiritualists of the time. Although the sermon, "Hvem er Guds engle?" (Who Are God's Angels?) was never reviewed in the press, Janson later included it in his collection of sermons, *Lys og frihed*. Previously, he had been inclined to give angels short shrift, regarding any mention of them in Scripture as poetic embellishments, not to be taken literally. He seems to have been mindful of this as he began his All Saints' Day sermon, for he says that the materialism of the age may have caused men to dismiss angels too summarily as figments of the scribes' imagination. Conceding that this might be the case in certain instances, he goes on to point out that many cases of angels appearing before men are found in both the Old and the New Testament. He draws his illustrations from the days of the patriarchs down to the angel who delivered Peter from prison, to the one who warned Paul of the impending shipwreck, and to those who appear in Revelations. Who were these beings? Special creations of God? That was possible, but Janson had come to regard them as beings who had once lived on earth. He had three reasons for this view: in scriptural accounts they appear as human; when they manifest themselves in the present day, they come as a relative, a friend, or someone beloved; and they declare that they are the spirits of human beings released from the bonds of the flesh.

Though unseen for the most part, these spirits are about us at all times, responsive to the word and even the thought of living persons who call upon them, Janson continued. Some are good and others evil; each person chooses, by the kind of life he leads, whether he will be attended by good or bad spirits. All children have guardian spirits, benevolent ones as long as the child does not fall into bad practices or consort with evil company. Then the good spirit will be supplanted by the evil.

Janson cited instances of how spirits, speaking through a medium named Mrs. Conant, told how closely they felt themselves bound to their loved ones. He told of other spirits who regretted some of their acts while on earth and sought to help those they had previously injured. Messages conveyed through a man named Home revealed that even the good angels or spirits were by no means perfect and that they must work for their own further development.[26] They felt a magnetic attraction toward the earth and were ready to comfort and advise. Some might think it unfortunate that those beyond must still be concerned with the troubles of this world, but Janson found it logical. If one were to ask any father or mother whether he or she preferred an afterlife in which he sang songs of praise or was in close contact with his family and friends, Janson was sure every noble person would say, "Let me be with my own, even though I must at times grieve over their lot."[27]

Some twenty years later, Benjamin O. Flower, editor of the *Arena*, was to publish his *Progressive Men, Women, and Movements of the Past Twenty-Five Years*. In discussing Spiritualism, Flower quotes Professor Joseph Rhodes Buchanan, whose ideas seem strikingly similar to Janson's: "The Christian Spiritualists accept the teachings of the Sermon on the Mount and the Bible phenomena. Indeed, they insist that the Bible is full of Spiritualism, from Genesis to Revelation: that nothing is emphasized more positively, clearly, or convincingly than the return, under certain conditions, of spirits who had once dwelt in the flesh. Thus Moses and Elias on the Mount of Transfiguration were so real and tangible to the Apostles that they suggested to their Master the building of three tabernacles, one for Moses, one for Elias, and one for Christ and the Apostles. The liberation of Peter from the prison in Jerusalem, and the apparition that announced to St. Paul the coming wreck of the vessel on which he was sailing to Rome, are merely two of numerous incidents illustrating this fact. Again, the Apostle John clearly emphasizes the verity of spirit return when he says, 'Believe not every spirit, but try the spirits whether they be of God.'

"Furthermore, as showing that in the opinion of the canonical writers, the angels constantly appearing throughout Holy Writ were disembodied spirits that once lived on the earth, we find that in the last chapter of Revelations, when the author of the book falls down to worship before the feet of the Angel who showed him the things, the Angels says, 'See thou do it not, for I am thy fellow-servant and of thy brethren the prophets.'

"The Christian Spiritualists hold that the Bible clearly teaches that the spirits of the dead, both good and bad, under certain circumstances, influence the lives of mortals, and that the only way to be safe and secure from the possibility of evil influences is to be positive against evil thoughts and not give them attractive power; that Jesus was constantly casting out evil spirits who had taken possession of unfortunate mortals—mortals who probably were not necessarily bad, but who were negative."[28]

6

Committed as Janson was to Spiritualism, his own religious tolerance, nevertheless, was always in evidence. The fourth volume of *Saamanden* (1890–91) contains his "General Booth and the Salvation Army," commemorating the twenty-fifth anniversary of the founding of that organization in England. This article was followed later by a shorter one on the Salvation Army's important work in America. He had Otto Nilsby of Underwood translate Robert Ingersoll's "Heresy and Heretics," a piece that took up more than two thirds of an issue. Inclusion of the Ingersoll article was not prompted by the impending heresy trial of a Presbyterian minister. Ingersoll described the theocracy that Calvin had established in Geneva, spelling out in detail the treatment he had given Servetus and others. To this was appended a note from Janson to the effect that Ingersoll's lecture was one-sided, but that his facts were straight, and, to an extent, his indictment against the Calvinists might be made against the Lutherans as well. H. S. Rikstad, one of Janson's proteges at Meadville, contributed a sympathetic account of the Ethical Culture Society, which reads as though its author might have attended meetings of the group and even interviewed Felix Adler.[29] From Norway's *Verdens Gang*, Janson excerpted an appreciative article on the work of the St. Joseph Sisters in Kristiania. His series "Jesus' Spiritual Brothers" dealt with Epictetus and Mohammed.[30]

In later years, Janson's contributions to the *Christian Register* became infrequent. This fact is reflected in the opening of his article printed in a late 1890 issue: "We are still living and living well." The church in Minneapolis had been completed. Average attendance was 400, but at times the seating capacity of the new church was taxed to the utmost. All of his congregations outside of Minneapolis were doing well with the exception of the one at Fergus Falls, where progress was slow. He had lengthened his lecture route and had received additional invitations to places in Wisconsin, North Dakota, and Minnesota. He was glad two Norwegian students at Meadville would soon graduate and would thus be able to help him. One of them, Johannes Brauti, had served at Underwood and Fergus Falls the preceding summer, proving himself to be very capable.

The opposition Janson now encountered was "not so fierce." Once in a while, a correspondent to *Saamanden* sent in a caustic letter, but these were usually expressed in such a manner as to appear ridiculous. There had been other minor incidents: he found himself the object of a newspaper story because he had publicly referred to a Lutheran pastor as "brother." From another pulpit, a minister had said Janson's congregation had "built a temple for the black Satan." However, people in general were not in sympathy with expressions such as these, finding them unjust.

By the end of 1890, the Swedes had their own Unitarian society under the leadership of Axel Lundeberg. Janson and Lundeberg would soon invite their orthodox brethren to take part in a series of meetings at which they would discuss their religious differences. He could think of no better evidence of the changed spiritual condition of his countrymen than the many appreciative letters he received from Massachusetts, Minnesota, Dakota, Illinois, Washington, Texas, and cities in Norway.[31]

Shortly after he wrote this report for the *Christian Register*, gas lights were installed in Nazareth Church. They were used for the first time for the sacred concert given on December 28.[32] The church was as modern and well equipped as any in the city. Looking forward to the new year, he was confident that Nazareth Church would soon be the gathering place for Norwegians from all over the city. The weekly discussion meetings were to be given over to religious debates with an orthodox team headed by no other than Professor F. A. Schmidt.

At the time, there was probably no man more in the public eye among the Norwegian Lutherans than Professor Schmidt, and probably no one with more personal experience than he with the various synods and their affiliates. A German, he had been on the faculty of Concordia Seminary in St. Louis, the theological school of the German Missouri Synod. After the Norwegian Synod had affiliated itself with that body, Professor Schmidt had taught at Luther College in Decorah, Iowa, and, when the Norwegian Synod had established its seminary in Madison, Wisconsin, he had become one of its faculty. It was he who precipitated the *naadevalget* (or predestination) dispute, and who came to lead the dissident group known as the Anti-Missourians, which in 1887 had severed its ties with the Norwegian Synod. He had also been one of the leaders in the formation of the United Church, which had designated Augsburg as its theological seminary, so that he had become the colleague of Professors Sverdrup and Oftedal. No evidence exists that these two men took part in the debates or even attended. However, by that time, relations between them and Professor Schmidt were already strained by criticism the latter had made about Augsburg. This friction created a situation which was later to result in the two professors withdrawing from the United Church to form the "Friends of Augsburg," a group that ultimately led to the formation of the Lutheran Free Church.[33]

In the debates, Professor Schmidt had the assistance of his theological students from Augsburg. Beginning in January, 1891, the meetings were held on a weekly basis, continuing into April, all of them in Nazareth Church. For Janson, the mere fact they were ever convened was something of a triumph. For years he had been trying to draw the orthodox into a discussion, and the subjects were the very ones he had previously dealt with in his treatise, "Is Orthodoxy Right?": the verbal inspiration of the Bible, the atonement by the blood of Christ, eternal punishment, the existence of a personal devil, and the light God has given for man's guidance.

According to *The North*, Nazareth Church was packed week after week for the debates. Editor Jaeger, remarking that the orthodox had previously refused to take part in any such discussions, praised Professor Schmidt and his students from Augsburg for "bravely and openly defending their side" and for encouraging the leading members of the various orthodox churches to attend.[34] Only once during the series was their continuation threatened. At the close of the meeting on March 23, Janson announced that the following week members of the audience would be allowed to take part. This brought a protest from Professor Schmidt in the form of an open letter printed in *Budstikken*. The professor objected to what he termed a "free for all," feeling it would be an invitation to heretics to vent their enmity toward the Bible and the God of the Christian church. He was, however, willing to continue as they had in the past, saying that he felt such discussions were of benefit to those interested in religious truth.[35] When he stayed away from the following open gathering, Janson wrote him that the meeting had been conducted in a decorous manner in spite of the free exchange of opinion. He was, however, eager to have the professor return and suggested that each side choose three representatives as speakers for the following session, an arrangement he hoped would meet with Schmidt's approval.[36] Janson's right-hand man throughout had, of course, been the Reverend Axel Lundeberg.

After the series of debates was over, Janson was both pleased and disappointed. In *Saamanden*, he was to write that they had stimulated popular interest in religious issues; after each meeting, as the audience walked down the steps of the church, they were discussing matters brought up during the evening. Furthermore, Nazareth Church gained fifteen new members at the end of the debates. He found, however, that the orthodox were hard to deal with in religious discussion. When the verbal inspiration of the Bible had been the issue, they had insisted on quoting Biblical passages to support their view, wholly ignoring the fact that whether or not such passages were divinely inspired was the central point. Confronted with contradictory passages, they would sometimes admit that they could not explain the differences, but by the following session, having had a week to ponder the matter, they would come forward with elaborate rationalizations. Often they evaded direct questions, resorting to emotional appeals to the audience to be true to their childhood teachings. Worst of all was the attitude that they had taken toward

Biblical scholars, impugning their motives by saying they wanted to undermine religion.[37]

7

While the debates were going on, Janson was deeply disappointed at the defeat of a bill to abolish capital punishment in the Minnesota state legislature. It was House File 222, introduced by Hans P. Bjorge of Underwood. According to Halvor Moen of that community, Bjorge later told a group of friends—Moen among them—that he had introduced the bill at the instigation of Kristofer Janson. Shortly before the twenty-seventh session of the legislature was to convene, Bjorge had called on Janson in Minneapolis. When the minister urged his friend to introduce legislation for doing away with the death penalty, the latter, who had hitherto given the matter no thought, remonstrated that he was totally unprepared. Janson swept his objections aside, saying that he would provide the material. Accordingly, on February 2, 1891, Bjorge introduced "A Bill for an Act to prescribe the punishment of murder in the first degree." It was referred to the judiciary committee and reported back to the House on February 7. On February 12 and again on February 26, the House constituted itself a committee of the whole, and on the latter date the matter was indefinitely tabled; this meant that its fate was sealed so far as that session of the legislature was concerned.[38]

"The sad news has come to us that the attempt to abolish the death penalty in Minnesota has failed," Janson began in his lead article, "On the Death Penalty" (Om Dødstraffen) in the March, 1891, *Saamanden.* His argument took up about a third of the issue and was not so much a valedictory for Bjorge's effort as a call to renew the attack. For those who could quote Biblical passages that God demanded a retributory justice, Janson could cite others to the contrary, notably the Fifth Commandment and Ezekiel 23:11 to the effect that the death of an offender was not pleasing to God, but rather that the individual should change his ways and continue to live. State executions were even worse than such crimes as murder or lynching, Janson said, for the latter were committed in moments of passion, whereas the death penalty was handed down in cold deliberation. The psychological punishment it inflicted on the condemned was inquisitorial, for a long period always elapsed between the sentencing and its execution. No evidence existed that fear of punishment was a deterrent to crime. Furthermore, public hangings—then the practice in Minnesota—brought out the basest instincts in man, and Janson reminded readers how people had stood in line for hours in order to witness the execution of Peter Barrett, a teenaged boy, a year before. He pleaded that the idea of retaliation be abandoned and that prisons be made places of rehabilitation.

During the time Janson had been concerned with this reform and with the religious debates, Drude had found another woman friend, one different from Mrs. Kate Buffington Davis, but in her way as talented and colorful. She was Mrs. Valborg Hovind Stub, the wife of Professor Hans Gerhard Stub of the Norwegian Synod. She was living in Robbinsdale, a community to the northwest of Minneapolis, where the Norwegian Synod had established its seminary after moving from Madison, Wisconsin. Mrs. Stub was a singer. Until the summer of 1890, she had not appeared in the city, having spent the previous year and a half studying voice in Weimar and Paris. An attractive woman, she had married Stub, a widower, in Norway in 1884. The marriage had taken place a short time after she had completed a tour of German cities, where she was said to have attracted favorable comment from Franz Liszt. From *The North*'s review of her first concert in Minneapolis, one learns that she used her mezzo-soprano voice with sound musical intelligence, intensity, and dramatic force, all of which caused the editor to judge that she had talents rightly belonging on the stage. Some time after this concert, Mrs. Stub established a studio in the Century Piano Company Building in Minneapolis, and it appears that she was popular with her voice students. From all accounts, she did not particularly relish the society she found in Robbinsdale. According to Mrs. Kolderup, she was lonely and unhappy, often visiting Drude Janson to "escape the ladies' aid in Robbinsdale." Dr. Bernard Sorose—whose father, Professor Wilhelm M. H. Petersen, was one of Stub's colleagues at the seminary—has said that the Robbinsdale community of professors and their wives regarded Mrs. Stub as something of a showpiece, sometimes referring to her as Stub's *stasplag*. It is clear that the husband did not approve of his wife's association with Drude Janson.[39]

Music was soon to become Drude's absorbing interest, prompted not so much by her friendship with Mrs. Stub as by the entrance into the Janson orbit of a young violinist, Claude Madden. On Sunday afternoon, March 29, 1891, Nazareth Church gave one of its sacred concerts at which Madden, then twenty-three years old and recently arrived from the East, was one of the performers. The Jansons were quick to recognize him as a man of extraordinary talent. After the concert, they invited him to accompany them home where the personable young man was to impress them even more. He played the piano delightfully, could improvise, and had, on occasion, composed. To Drude he seemed more European

269

than American, for he disparaged American cultural standards, saying that he was hopeful that he could go abroad the following year for study. Soon he became a frequent visitor at the Jansons, taking over the violin instruction of their son Arne. In the summer, when the family went to Brown County, Claude Madden was invited to live in their house, Drude feeling that he would exert a beneficial influence on her two older sons, whose medical studies required that they remain in the city during the summer.[40]

8

In time Madden, the Jansons, Mrs. Stub, and others were to form a musical colony, the members collaborating with one another. Claude composed music for lyrics written by Kristofer, and Mrs. Stub made the selections part of her repertoire. When Madden composed music for the violin, Janson wrote prose descriptions of the story programmed into the music. Yet while Janson could join in all this exhilarating creative activity, it touched only peripherally on Nazareth Church, and there is some evidence that, as early as the spring of 1891, the minister was having some misgivings about what had developed. On May 5, 1891, he celebrated his fiftieth birthday. The May *Saamanden* was to print his poem, "On My Fiftieth Birthday" (Paa min femtiaarige fødselsdag), in four quatrains, on its title page. He had been, Janson concluded, a most fortunate man, and, confident as he was of eternal life, he could look forward to the future with hope, blessed by the spirit of God. Twenty years later, he was to use the same poem to commemorate his seventieth birthday, making only the minor change of fifty to seventy in the first verse. Generally descriptive of the vicissitudes of his life, the poem follows an alternating pattern, speaking of reverses and compensations. It began:

> Fifty years—bruised by the world's harm,
> Fifty years—borne in Our Father's arm,
> Fifty years—warmed by love's steady glow,
> Fifty years—strengthened by sorrow and woe.[41]

In the same issue, Janson thanked all who had remembered him on his birthday, saying that gifts of flowers, letters, and verse had streamed in throughout the day. In the evening, the women of Nazareth Church had held a reception for him in the church parlors and had presented him with a hundred dollars to which friends both inside and outside the congregation had contributed.[42] *The North* also reported that this had been an extremely pleasant event with about a hundred and fifty people present. In his acceptance speech, Janson reviewed his years in America, saying that the secret to a serene inner life lay in remaining true to one's ideals. Never before, he said, had he felt so strong and sound in body and soul. In view of the circumstances, the remark was ordinary enough, but it was one Janson was later on to make increasingly—and it seems defensively—during his last troubled year in America.[43]

During the spring of 1891, Janson had a dream which, he has said, had a profound effect on him. In his autobiography, he has related that, as he slept one night, he dreamed that Jesus entered the room, dressed in a long white garment and wearing a crown of thorns on his head, the latter so embedded in the flesh that drops of blood stained his garment. The figure gazed at Janson compassionately and then moved as if to leave. In the dream he rose from the bed and, clasping the figure at the knees, entreated, "Master, do not leave me thus!" The figure lifted Janson up, embraced him, and placed the crown of thorns on his head. For days thereafter, he was in something of a state of rapture, during which time poems about Jesus virtually flowed from his pen. Later these formed the content of his *Jesus-sangene*, published in 1893. Yet so absorbed was he in the experience at the time that when Sunday came he had no sermon prepared. He related the dream to his congregation, going on to read some of the poems and to comment on them, later saying that many persons had assured him that the readings had been better than a sermon.[44]

Minneapolis papers friendly to Janson made no mention of the event, but the story traveled by word of mouth, and versions of it appeared in various Scandinavian papers. Janson did not refer to it in *Saamanden* until later in the summer and then only in his correspondence column in answer to questions from a reader in Winnipeg, Manitoba. A Swedish paper in that city, so the correspondent wrote, reported that Janson had had a vision of Jesus in which the apparition told the minister that he was pleasing to him, whereupon Janson was reported to have knelt down in worship of Jesus. In return, the figure embraced Janson and placed the crown of thorns upon his head. A local minister had made reference to this happening in a sermon, the writer added, saying that it would be desirable to have Janson's word whether there was a grain of truth to it and also to the rumor that Janson had more than once been subject to such visions.

It was remarkable, Janson answered, what a hubbub the event had aroused, garbled accounts having appeared in so many papers. He assured the Canadian reader that it had been a dream occurring at night, and he then related it, omitting however the crown of thorns incident which was to appear in his autobiography. There had been no worshipping. From the accounts in newspapers, one might think Kristofer Janson was becoming insane, he wrote, but he could assure readers that his sleep was ordinarily sound and that he was most certainly not "accustomed to having visions."[45]

There can be little doubt that in his original version Janson had said that the crown of thorns had been placed on his head. Here the imagery is arresting. Although dreams may have more than one interpretation, there is common agreement that they arise from some deeply seated concern of the psyche. One can only speculate why he, even in a dream, should attach to himself this symbol of excruciating suffering. The event took place some months before Drude was to give him a shattering blow, and the possibility exists that he had some haunting fears of what the future might bring.

9

Yet, on the surface, all seemed to be well with the Jansons. Kristofer appears to have had no difficulty in getting his novel *Sara* published. It was distributed by Alb. Cammermeyers Forlag in Kristiania in 1891. While both the miserable conditions of the working class and religious orthodoxy play an important part in the book, its major theme is the emancipation of women. Sara had begun life in a Wisconsin farming community dominated by the Hauge Synod. Her parents, industrious and frugal, are prosperous people, but theirs is a cheerless household. Her father, kindly and sympathetic, accepts his religion with Spartan endurance; her mother, though not cruel, is so dour that Sara had never been able to develop any affection for her. Suspicious of the public school, Sara's parents had first taught her at home, but eventually the Hauge Synod had established its own school, where Sara had the companionship of other children, especially Peter Hanson, who brought her into contact with a freethinking tailor, a merry individual who possessed a number of children's books which the youngsters could read surreptitiously. However, for other reasons, the schoolmaster made a victim of Peter, who ran away, leaving the lonely Sara with the thought that, if things became unendurable, there was always "Peter's way."[46]

Some time elapses before Sara tries to escape. After confirmation, her formal education over, she works at home until she is married to Abraham Jensen, the local minister, the union an arrangement between him and the girl's parents. All of this she accepts docilely as the natural order of things. Some time later, Thomas Falk, a Norwegian artist, comes to

272

be a guest in their home; among other things, he paints portraits of both the pastor and Sara. During the sittings, Sara discovers Falk's religion to be broader than hers and that he believes "a woman belongs to the man she loves." He pays her a little incidental courtship, and when he goes, leaves her a Danish translation of Hugo's *Les Misérables*. Despite Sara's efforts to keep her reading a secret from the pastor, he discovers it and throws the book in the stove. Facing a rebellious wife, he is at a loss to account for the change from her former docility until her parents suggest that Sara may be pregnant and therefore behaving erratically. This diagnosis—which is false—transports the pastor but brings Sara to the realization that she can never willingly bear his child. When the chance comes, she takes a train to Chicago, where she seeks out Falk and confronts him with, "Take me. I'm yours." When Falk summarily orders her back to her husband, she rushes blindly out on the street. Toward evening, she chances to meet her old schoolmate, Peter, who finds her lodgings for the night and eventually locates work for her. These events comprise the first half of the book.

In Chicago, Sara gets to know the odorous, filthy tenements where the poor must live, the sweatshops where girls sew at piecework, sometimes making as little as $1.30 for a week's work, the prison-like factories whose unguarded machinery can cripple or deform workers, the streets thronged with ragged, emaciated persons tramping from place to place in search of work. After Sara has had her own dismal experiences, Peter suggests that she consult Lizzie, whom he innocently describes as working nights. When, one morning, they arrive at the clean, habitable flat that Lizzie has provided for herself and her aged mother, Sara is agreeably surprised, only to have her misgivings confirmed when Lizzie arrives wearing gloves and carrying a parasol. Alone with Lizzie, Sara hears the girl's bitter account of how she had learned that only through prostitution could she provide an adequate living for her mother and herself. In time Sara gets to know of the dishonest foremen who extort fees for hiring workers. When her Irish friends, Pat and Bridget, carry out a family murder-suicide pact, Sara realizes the hopelessness of employees who are blacklisted. To assure the reader that these dismal conditions and events were not exaggerated, Janson provides a footnote indicating that he has drawn his material from such books as *Prisoners of Poverty* and *The Slave Girls of Chicago*.

Sara's deliverance comes not by her own efforts but by the fortunate intervention of Mrs. King, a wealthy and benevolent American woman. After Sara has found tolerable conditions in a Marshall Field workroom, she is the victim of an epidemic and is sent to a hospital, where she arouses the sympathy of Mrs. King. Hired as the widowed woman's companion, she soon becomes more like a daughter. With Mrs. King's help, she is able to arrange for Lizzie to find lucrative work as a seamstress and to have Peter sent to a technical school. The world of music, art, and literature opens for Sara; she attends concerts, sees the Verestchagin exhibit during its Chicago showing, and becomes a member of the Ibsen Club, a study group similar to the Emerson and Browning societies. Accompanying Mrs. King to Europe, she is awed by the beauty of Rome. There she again meets Falk, without embarrassment, for Sara has become a poised young lady and recognizes her infatuation for the artist to have been merely a substitute for her youthful longing to know the world of music, art, and literature. By this time, Falk is too limited for Sara. She has no interest in belonging to the cultural elite who turn their backs on the millions who are deprived of all the advantages of life. Happily, she finds that another of Mrs. King's circle, Henry Brown, shares her views on social betterment. Brown proposes, but Sara feels that all thought of marriage is out of the question. On her return to the United States, she attempts to set up schools for children and women in Norwegian immigrant communities, all of which end in failure largely because of the intervention of local ministers. When the train on which she is returing to Chicago is wrecked, Sara discovers among the injured passengers her husband, Pastor Jensen. She takes him back to their old home and nurses him until he dies. Then, not waiting for the funeral, she again departs for Chicago, wiring ahead to Henry Brown that she is free. Now she will marry him. As the novel ends, Brown introduces Sara to the contractor he has engaged to build their new house on Lake Michigan. The contractor is her old schoolmate, Peter Hanson, by this time the head of his own firm and happily married to Lizzie, having overcome the objections that she had raised because of her past.[47]

As a novel of protest, this picaresque tale, with its many coincidences and neatly contrived conclusion, is too diffuse to be effective. Janson might better have restricted himself to working conditions in Chicago; the chapters dealing with that subject are the best, and in their harsh detail somewhat similar to the writing of Upton Sinclair in *The Jungle*, which was to be published about a decade later. With some exceptions, the characterization is weak, for even Sara is too idealized to make much of a mark as an advanced woman. Bold as she is in breaking conventions and decrying the intellectual suicide forced on women in Norwegian immigrant communities, she otherwise demonstrates a selflessness that would do credit to a medieval saint. Although Janson seems to have had large audiences when he gave readings from the book, its publication caused no stir in Minneapolis.

10

Some time during 1891, Janson printed a pamphlet containing two lectures on labor conditions. The first, "Why Is the Present Social Order Untenable?", was followed by "Do We Have a Better System to Replace the Old?" Indifferent to Gundersen's criticism that his social views relied too heavily on Bellamy's sentimental novel, Janson drew his material for the lectures from *Looking Backward*, Gronlund's *The Co-operative Commonwealth*, and the sermons of Hugh Pentecost.[48] In the first lecture, Janson declares that the only fair social system is one based on brotherhood, assuring everyone, regardless of race or color, the same treatment. Competition, he says, leads to the usurpation of such natural resources as land, forests, and mines by a few; it means that those who succeed do so only by ruining their rivals; it breeds war by allowing luxury and ease to the few at the expense of the many; it creates antagonisms between the haves and the have-nots, leading to violence and ultimately even to revolution; and it necessitates child labor and makes women hardly more than chattels.[49]

All this Janson had said before; the second lecture, more original, consequently makes more engaging reading. As he sees it, all wealth and the management of industry and commerce must be under state control. Work must be demanded of every person, who in turn must be given enough to assure a comfortable living. He might be guaranteed an annual income, although Janson thinks it preferable to dispense with money altogether and to issue credit coupons redeemable at government storehouses supplied with all kinds of consumer goods. This system would not reduce life to a monotonous level, Janson argues, for one may use his coupons as he chooses. His house (actually owned by the state) might be simple or elegant according to the number of coupons surrendered for rent. He might elect to keep a carriage and horses, or, being otherwise inclined, to have a sailboat. Coupons were not to be of cumulative value: they must be used up during the course of a year.

All department heads would be chosen by vote of their fellow workers; if proven incompetent, they would be deposed in the same way. Since some kinds of work are more strenuous than others, persons engaged in arduous labor would have a shorter work day. Necessary tasks that are dangerous could be assigned to volunteers, Janson thinks. He says that such jobs have an attraction for some people and suggests that they might be compensated for by national awards which would be prestigious but which would in no way upset the distributive system. According to Janson's plan, however, work requiring great physical effort would be performed by the young. All children would be required to complete the elementary school, most of them at the age of fourteen or fifteen. They would then engage in what Janson calls a work-discipline program for three years, doing manual work at a time of life when their physical strength is at its peak. Because all youth would enter this service, no opprobrium would be attached to physical labor. At the end of the period, each young person could choose a profession or trade for his life vocation and receive the necessary training, provision being made at certain stages for those who had made the wrong selection and thus needed to be reoriented.

Under this equitable system, the nation's economy would boom, according to Janson. For one thing, workers would be highly motivated, knowing that they were contributing to the common good rather than to the enrichment of a rapacious employer. Furthermore, the new system would effect great economy by eliminating the duplication necessary under private enterprise in which rival companies manufacture the same goods. All the barriers keeping women from various trades and professions would be abolished. As the equal of men, they would be encouraged to enter any kind of work for which they were mentally and physically qualified. Hospitalization and health care would be available to all; special programs for the handicapped would insure them a fruitful life. By building theaters and concert halls in every community, the state would encourage people to make a worthy use of their leisure and thus in time develop a cultivated, enlightened society.[50]

Possibly Janson prepared these lectures for publication during his summer sojourn in Brown County, as he ordinarily relegated such matters to his months in the country. He did write a novelette, *Du er kjød af mit kjød* (You Are Flesh of My Flesh). That he should choose to write about a love triangle was ironic in view of developments shortly to follow in his own household. Upon his return to Minneapolis in the fall, this short novel was to serve as one of his first evening programs, heralded by an announcement in *The North* that it was based on a true incident. After the reading, the paper reported that many in the audience had glowing things to say about it, "ranking it among Mr. Janson's best productions."[51]

The origin of the tale is not hard to find, for Janson had spoken of it in the lectures that grew out of his tour of 1879–80. Aagot Field, an immigrant girl working in a factory, narrowly escaped scalping when her long braid of hair was caught in the machinery. When the physician called to attend her asked for volunteers to supply skin grafts, the Norwegian factory hands held back, but two young Americans offered themselves. In Janson's fiction they are of Irish descent, the Patterson brothers. Both fall in love with Aagot, but Jack, the elder, withdraws when he learns of his brother's feelings. He had promised his dying father to look after Jim, and he is a man always true to his word. Grateful to both, Aagot is drawn to Jack, but she marries the younger brother when she thinks the older to be indifferent to her. Both she and Jack languish under this arrangement, and he finds it so intolerable that he decides to go away. While paying a farewell visit to the girl, he confesses his real reason for leaving, all of which brings the two into an embrace—and Aagot offers to go with the man she loves. Coming upon them as they are in each other's arms, the enraged Jim shoots them both and then disappears. When an innocent man is being tried for the murder, Jim, heavily disguised, appears in court, asking to be heard. Revealing his identity, he confesses, and then, before a packed courtroom, uses the same revolver to end his own life.[52]

This novelette was Janson's last work of fiction while in America.

10

Fascinated by
Spiritualism

ALTHOUGH Kristofer Janson did not leave America until September, 1893, his departure and his decision not to return were precipitated by what happened late in 1891. At that time, Drude asked to be free from their marriage. Much as she had before revealed her attachment to Knut Hamsun, she told Janson she was in love with young Claude Madden. Some three years later—after the impending divorce of the Jansons had become common knowledge—Janson briefly described the break to Bjørnson: "Do you remember how you often teased her that one day a Spanish skipper would come and carry her off? Well—the Spanish skipper came—that is the whole story. She asked for her freedom and she got it, for I had to respect her grounds and we had to settle it in accordance with our commonly held principles. For twenty-four years I had courted that woman in vain."[1]

Yet, at the time, Janson was to undergo so agonizing a period that the analogy of the crown of thorns hardly seems inappropriate, inviting the speculation that Janson's dream concerning the apparition of Jesus of the spring before might have been based on a presentiment. Faced with the dissolution of his home and the loss of his work, he tried to carry on with his ministry, to advocate social reform through political channels, and—if it were possible—to absorb himself all the more in Spiritualism.

Of course, the public was not aware of the changed relations of the Jansons. Drude's declaration came in November or at the latest early in December, 1891. From later letters of both Kristofer and Drude, as well as those of Drude's niece and a friend of Janson, one gets an approximation of the series of happenings in the eventful fall of 1891.

278

2

On the surface, the church season seems to have begun very much as usual. Janson read, in addition to his own novelette, a more polished version of his *Jesus-sangene*, the poetic cycle inspired by his dream of the previous spring, then followed it with Kielland's *Jakob* and with Shakespeare's *King Lear* (in Norwegian translation).[2] In the early fall Nazareth Church gave another fair, and while this one does not seem to have been as elaborate as its predecessors nor as well publicized, it netted the congregation $420. In St. Paul, Janson had moved his services from the Unity Church basement to a hall on Arcade Street, probably as a result of his difference with the church trustees, but the shift allowed him freedom to present the waltzes and mazurkas of Chopin whenever he chose. When *The North* conducted an inquiry on whether married women should be permitted to teach in the public schools (then forbidden), Janson responded that he considered them more fit than the unmarried, especially if they had children of their own.[3] In mid-November he preached a sermon, "Var Henr. Wergeland en Unitar?" (Was Henrik Wergeland a Unitarian?), which was justly praised. For, whether one agrees with Janson's conclusion or not, he gave a sensitive and comprehensive interpretation of Wergeland's magnificent epic, *Menneske*. It was the lead article in the December, 1891, *Saamanden*.

After the happy summer in Brown County, Drude was buoyant, as is evidenced by her letter to Bjørnson in October. She was sorry she had not written before, regretting especially that she had not congratulated the poet on his Seventeenth of May address at Gjøvik, which she found a beautiful testimony to liberal Christianity. However, her apologies seem no more than social amenities, for it is obvious she was eager to report on her own household.

They had never had it so good, she wrote. Kristofer's work was growing, with new openings appearing everywhere. Several orthodox ministers, Methodists and others, had written him for advice and help. He was considering a lecture tour to the west coast the following winter, when he would visit those clergymen and possibly find a successor for himself among them. He was beginning to think of severing his connections in America. The American Unitarian Association had many new missionary ventures and was putting pressure on the older ones to be self-supporting. The new Western secretary was a very exacting man, who insisted on prying into every little thing.[4] He was critical of Janson's social views and would very likely prejudice the American Unitarian Association against him. Thus it was only a matter of time before Kristofer would leave, and Drude, for her part, was glad of it. He had accomplished a noble work by laying the basis for a liberal religious movement that would bear great fruit among the Scandinavians in America, but there was no point in his spending his life in the New World. He could continue *Saamanden* elsewhere if he chose, and he needed a richer cultural environment. In America he had given everything and received nothing, and in the long run the strain was bound to leave its mark on him.

They had a plan. In another year their two elder sons would complete their medical course. They would practice a year in order to make a little money. The following spring the family would go to Norway, where they would board the girls with Drude's sister Kitty. The boys would explore Europe; Kristofer could make a lecture tour, and when it was over, he and Drude would travel about in Europe and later decide where they wanted to live permanently.

Their children were all they could wish. Eilev had led his class all through his medical studies. He was engrossed in his work and would, without question, make an unusually fine doctor. Ivar was also a good student, but his interest in medicine was not as deeply grounded as that of his brother. He was a dreamer with a fine poetic nature, having inherited Kristofer's disposition as well as his lyrical gift. During the summer he had blossomed out, writing poems almost daily. The Jansons could not judge his diction well as the poems were in English, but they were good, revealing a personality struggling to find its form. What had done more than anything to develop Ivar's nature was the life the Jansons had lived in recent months and the companionship they had enjoyed.

3

The spring before they had met a young American violinist from New York. During the summer months he had lived in their house, and the two older sons had heard music all day. The young man was Claude Madden, a lively and highly gifted person. Having him as a companion had transported the boys into another world. Madden was barely twenty-three but mature beyond his years. He considered the Janson house his home and would do so as long as he remained in the city. Thus the whole family had had the benefit of his company. The Jansons had found others who shared their interests—a German family living close by whom they saw almost daily and a few American families. Every Saturday or Sunday the group gathered at the Janson house where they enjoyed the most delightful music. Thus they lived in a world of their own—outside of Minneapolis—which was wonderful after all the sterile years.

The next year Madden would go to Germany to study and give concerts, Drude continued. With his gifts, he was sure to have a great future. More than anyone else, he reminded Drude of Bjørnson, and thus she had liked him all the more. For that matter, he was fascinated by Bjørnson, often gazing at the Jansons' bust of him and continually questioning Drude about the poet. They had planned to meet Madden in two years—at Aulestad, Bjørnson's home, for the musician wanted to go to Norway after the Jansons were there. Drude was sure Bjørnson would greatly enjoy meeting him.

Their girls were becoming as tall as their mother, Drude wrote, with the exception of Ingeborg, but she was (and Drude briefly turned to English) "the sweet good mother of the family—so good! so good!" Borghild was the most original, and Signe, a bit reserved and fine, was the princess. Arne was completely a boy, mischievous and undeveloped. He attended high school and studied the violin.[5]

In the days that followed the writing of this letter, at least parts of their family's plan crystallized. Janson made arrangements for a lecture tour beginning in January, 1892. The clergyman in the West in whom he seems to have been most interested was the Reverend John L. Ericksen, pastor of the Norwegian-Danish Methodist Episcopal Church in Portland, Oregon. Virtually every issue of the fifth volume of *Saamanden* contains some mention of this man. The September, 1891, number has an account of an Ericksen sermon, "The Religious Tendencies of Our Times," in which he so deplored the superstition, ignorance, and prejudice found in the old dogmas that one might guess that his departure from the Methodist church was imminent. The October *Saamanden* reported that this was indeed the case and that Ericksen was entering the Unitarian ministry. In the November issue one learns what a zealous worker Brother Ericksen was. He had organized a Unitarian congregation that already had formed a society for women and another for young people, accomplishing all this in spite of the persecution that invariably follows a new movement. During Kristofer Janson's visit to Portland in January, Ericksen would be formally installed as a Unitarian minister.[6]

In other respects, *Saamanden* was to deliver its usual quota of good reading. The September issue opened with a charming poem by the Reverend Adam Dan, a Danish Lutheran pastor. Janson had translated Henry M. Simmons' *The Unending Genesis* and was to run this serially from September through February, using the title "Studier over skabelseshistorien" (Studies on the History of Creation). In September he included an account indicating that Bellamy's theories were proving to be practical for they were in operation in the Amana colony in Iowa.[7] All through the fifth volume, one reads of Spiritualism, mostly in the correspondence columns, where much of the discussion centers about the experiences of Ivar Langland, who had witnessed the curing of disease by the laying on of hands and had frequently communicated with spirits who inspired and advised him.[8] Janson, who had kept Spiritualism out of the first three volumes of *Saamanden*, no longer was reluctant to discuss it. In an earlier issue, one reads that the recently deceased archbishop of Mexico had been a believer in Spiritualism but had lacked the courage to declare himself publicly. Apparently Mazzini had been one, too, for in the same issue appears an account of a letter he had written to Jane Welsh Carlyle in which he told of the comfort he received from his beloved dead.[9]

Later—in a letter to Bjørnson—Drude was to admit that "the Spanish skipper had come," but charged that Janson's Spiritualism had brought it all about, for his absorption in the subject had so unnerved her that she felt the ground disappearing beneath her feet.[10] In his *Life Story*, Rasmus B. Anderson says that Janson's congregation had become displeased with his advocacy of Spiritualism and had lost confidence in him, but Anderson does not pinpoint the time that this became evident.[11] However, it is evident that Luth Jaeger was grieved over Janson's Spiritualism. On December 6 the minister's sermon was "The Laws of the Other World." Three days later, *The North* commented on the sermon: "Rev. Kristofer Janson regaled a small portion of his last Sunday forenoon audience and disgusted the greater number of it with as rank a spiritualistic sermon as the most rabid believer of that shadowy faith could wish for. This is the second time in less than a year that such a thing has happened, and there is a feeling of sorrow and disappointment among those who love him best that his eminent gifts and brilliant pulpit powers should be diverted into such channels. The laws of this world are hard enough both to make and live up to, why then waste precious moments on speculations as to those of the next?"[12]

Yet, a week later, *The North* was to express its admiration for Janson's great abilities and those of Claude Madden. On December 13, a concert was given in Nazareth Church, one which *The North* spoke of as "sacred," although much of it was secular music. Madden and Professor Gustavus Johnson had played Beethoven's *Kreutzer Sonata* for violin and piano, and each had contributed a solo. Janson and G. W. Ferguson had sung solos, and the Swedish Quartette had performed. A highlight of the concert had been Madden's rendition of two original compositions for the violin, "A Lyric Poem" and "Polish Dance." Jan-

282

son read his prose poem, "Violin Strings," which the paper declared to be "a gem of its kind . . . recited in his most felicitous manner." Madden's compositions had been "marked with the strong individualty of the author," and the prose poem, according to the paper, gave "a key to the language of the violin and is a production of marked originality and delicate beauty."[13]

4

At approximately the same time that Drude had broken with Janson, another person came to live in the Janson household. She was Louise Bentzen, engaged as Janson's secretary and the tutor of his daughters. Just under thirty, she was a Norwegian born in Nordland who, with her father, had migrated to the United States as a young woman. She has been described as five feet six or seven inches in height, stockily built, with large, heavily lidded eyes and a great wealth of hair which she wore braided and wound about her head as a coronet. Conversant in German and English as well as Norwegian, she was well equipped for editorial work on *Saamanden*. Dina Behr Kolderup, who also came under her instruction, has said that Louise was a very good teacher. She was also a medium, and, from many accounts, extraordinarily endowed with psychic powers. Eilev Janson, who liked and admired her all his life, later recalled that Louise had "said some amazing things." His sister, Ingeborg Janson von Streng, reported that Louise possessed a sixth sense, impossible to describe in ordinary terms. Drude has written that she was at first greatly impressed by her.[14]

Louise Bentzen had not been at her duties long when Janson left Minneapolis on January 4, 1892, on his lecture tour. His itinerary included towns and cities in Iowa, the Dakotas, Montana, Colorado, Idaho, Utah, Oregon, Washington, and California. For the most part, he was to lecture in Norwegian, but here and there an American audience awaited him. In Seattle, the Unitarian Parish Union was offering a winter series of lectures, one of which was to be Janson's "Bjørnstjerne Bjørnson." On February 14 he occupied the pulpit of the Oakland, California, Unitarian Society; later he was to deliver his "East of the Sun and West of the Moon."[15]

A few days after his departure, Agnes Behr, then living in St. Paul and working in the office of the deputy collector of internal revenue, spent the weekend from Saturday until Monday in the Janson home in Minneapolis. Shortly afterward, on January 12, she wrote her sister Dina, then visiting in Chicago. It was a candid, girlish letter—among other things advising Dina how to encourage a young man to invite her to the theater and to hire a carriage, "if he has any sense and cash." Agnes also described her weekend at the Jansons. At the time, she wrote, all were taken with Louise, whom Agnes described as "one who sees spirits." Agnes thought Miss Bentzen was given to strong fantasy, and characterized her as "obviously a sister of Kirsten's maid once upon a time." Louise, Agnes continued, told many strange tales and it was amusing to listen to her. The letter concluded: "And I don't believe she is lying."

In a light vein Agnes revealed that Claude Madden had been the Sunday evening speaker at Nazareth Church. She wrote in English: "Claude preached about 'The Responsibilities of Men.' If he had only written it down it would have been good, but as it was, it was a little mixed up. But he stood their [sic] as though he were old in the business, and spoke of marriage and everything else. There were very few people though."[16]

One evening, Agnes wrote, they had sat around the fireplace in the Janson house and had sung all their old favorites to the accompaniment of their guitars, but they had not attempted "I Spaniens land," for that song was the special property of the two missing members, Dina and Uncle Kristofer. Eventually Agnes made reference to Drude's relationship to Claude Madden: "I opened Aunt Dina's letter and, as I guessed, there lay a letter to Tante [Drude] and a card for me. Tante was very wounded that Aunt Dina said she hoped Tante was not Madden crazy any longer."[17]

5

Janson was gone for two and a half months, returning to Minneapolis near the middle of March. The February, 1892, *Saamanden* carried an account of his experiences. Conditions on the west coast were much as elsewhere: the few liberals who struggled against prejudice were generally regarded as freethinkers and "children of the devil." Many young people, bored with humbug, had abandoned religion altogether, ridiculing ministers and churches, while they turned to the worship of the American golden calf, money. The majority trod the old paths, subservient to their ministers, who had discovered the ignorance of the masses to be their best assurance of keeping people under the yoke.

Janson had found himself regarded as the greatest scoundrel "in two shoes." Ministers had warned parishioners against attending his lectures, even those on historical or esthetic subjects. In one community the placards advertising his addresses had been systematically removed immediately after they had been put up. A minister had engineered this strategy, Janson discovered, adding that the man had been a Methodist and not a Lutheran. An amusing incident occurred when Janson was delivering his lecture on "Henrik Wergeland and His Times." A curious fellow had ventured to attend, although he did so with a bad conscience. During the program, a slight earthquake occurred, causing the building to shake and the windows to rattle. As soon as the tremors subsided, the man made a plunge for the door, certain that the quake had been sent as a warning to him.

Janson wrote from Portland. He gave a heartening account of the progress of the Scandinavian Unitarian church, and in the same issue reported that the Reverend John L. Ericksen had been formally installed as a Unitarian minister on this occasion, the Reverend Earl Morse Wilbur giving an address in English and Janson one in Norwegian. The new congregation received good support from the American Unitarian church in the city, one of the finest congregations in Portland, served by two ministers, T. L. Eliot and Earl Morse Wilbur. Its membership included the most intelligent men of the city, and the congregation was foremost in philanthropic work. It maintained a reading room, heated and comfortably furnished, which was open every evening of the week.[18]

On Sunday evening, March 13, shortly after he had returned to Minneapolis, Janson was honored by a reception in Nazareth Church. According to *The North*, every seat was filled, with the aisles crowded and the back of the church basement occupied by people standing. Claude Madden, Gustavus Johnson, Dr. Clarence Strachauer, and Miss Mamie Helm, all a part of the intimate Janson circle, furnished the music. The front platform was decorated with potted plants—roses, lilies, hyacinths—placed there by friends. Among the flowers, Janson found the message, "Welcome home. We rejoice in your return. [Signed] Many friends." Janson read the note aloud as an introduction to his brief (and as one might interpret it now) rather somber address. He compared his work, at home as well as everywhere else—so *The North* reported—to that of Henrik Wergeland, who kept garden seeds in his pocket, scattering them wherever he found a fertile spot. Janson said he would spend his life scattering the seeds of love, peace, and faith in whatever is good. He knew that the orthodox looked upon him as the most depraved of men, but he predicted that one day the masses would see he had been right and would thank him when he was no longer among them. *Saamanden* also carried an account of the reception.[19]

At the time of his break with Drude, Janson had moved his personal belongings to a small room on the second floor. When he was at home, he spent much of his time in his study, a large room at the head of the stairs; there people came to discuss their problems. It seems that even when he was having a troubled time, he was never too preoccupied with his own worries to bestir himself to help others. Occasionally these acts of kindness came to be a part of the public record. Thus, in its December 30, 1891, issue, *The North* reported that a man known as Oscar Wedel had died in a barn in Albert Lea, Minnesota, nine days before. He had been a member of the prominent Wedel-Jarlsberg family in Norway, the paper reported, adding, "In later years he was a heavy drinker, and efforts to reclaim him, particularly by Rev. Kristofer Janson have proven only temporarily successful." In the spring of 1892, Janson printed in *Saamanden* a letter from a man who had been injured at his work and had been bedridden for a year. He was twenty-eight years old, the father of a family, and though somewhat improved, he would be a cripple the rest of his life. He had written the Arctander law firm to ask about the possibility of getting compensation from his former employer and had been advised to let the matter rest. The man was a Lutheran, he wrote, but he felt that Janson would not refuse advice to a man of a different faith. From the reply, one learns that Janson had gone to the Arctander firm in Minneapolis to investigate the case but could report only that the lawyers, much as they personally felt that the man was entitled to compensation, had found the details of the accident so unclear that they saw no chance of winning were they to bring the matter to court.[20]

Shortly after Janson had returned from the West, he wrote Bjørnson in response to a letter the Jansons had received the preceding November, which had gone unanswered for four months. Neither of the Jansons, it seems, was ready to disclose the changed relationship, and, in his letter, Kristofer avoided any mention of it, only once betraying any bitterness toward Drude. He may have had another reason for postponing writing: Bjørnson had written that he had heard the Jansons had accepted Spiritualism, something the poet declared to be completely alien to him. Ordinarily, Janson dismissed such statements in short order, but with Bjørnson he was more circumspect. He began by virtually denying his Spiritualism but later came to admit it. It was a disgrace, he wrote, that neither he nor Drude had written before, but he at least must be partly excused, for he had been on a lecture tour of more than two months and in his absence work had accumulated.

Bjørnson deserved a good scolding for an expression he had used in his letter, Kristofer went on. Had the Bjørnsons become Mormons, improbable as that was, he would never have said he felt "wholly alienated." Besides, Bjørnson certainly did not believe the absurd accounts about Janson appearing in the newspapers; Janson had just sent a brief article to Kristiania's *Verdens Gang* to straighten matters out. He was no more a Spiritualist than was a certain friend of his, namely Bjørnstjerne Bjørnson. Then followed lengthy quotations from Bjørnson's *Kongen* to the effect that men's ancestors, in spirit, hover about to inspire and encourage. That was exactly the case, Janson contiued, that the unseen were always about, ready to aid and inspire. Bjørnson must be man enough not to be annoyed by all the humbug that invariably associates itself with a great movement, and Spiritualism in all its purity and beauty Janson regarded as something great, giving comfort to those who would otherwise despair. Not that he had needed such comfort, for he had always believed in one's development beyond the grave, but now he had become all the more certain of it, having received messages from his beloved dead. Drude was annoyed that just because Janson interested himself in the subject she should do the same. She had thought that Bjørnson knew her well enough to realize she went her own way and was not diverted by anyone just because he happened to be her husband or friend.

Janson wrote briefly of his family, saying that Drude was at the time engrossed in music, for they had a musician living in the house who would be leaving for Germany in six weeks. Arne was to make the violin his career and would be sent to Germany the next year if the Jansons could afford it. Kristofer himself was preaching, holding discussion meetings, editing *Saamanden*, preparing a volume of sermons for publication, and struggling in every way, for he felt he still had his best years before him.

Janson was disturbed that Bjørnson was involved in legal processes. Such things brought only trouble and expense and embittered one's life. "What do I care if idiots call me a traitor and blasphemer so long as God does not?", he wrote. "His judgment seat in my own conscience is the only tribunal I am concerned with. I go my way and do what I think is my duty and let them scream and thunder as much as they choose. . . . It is better to suffer wrong than to retaliate." Then, aware that Bjørnson might find all this sententious, Janson added, "Now I can see you have turned your head to ask if the inner-mission sermon is not soon over."[21]

6

At the time this letter was written, Drude's affair with Claude Madden was perhaps over; it was at least nearing its end. Publicly Kristofer seemed to be on the same terms as before with Madden, happy to collaborate with so brilliant an artist. On March 27 Claude gave his last Minneapolis concert in Nazareth Church, and some three weeks later he appeared with other musicians at the Hotel Aberdeen in St. Paul. In its review of the latter, *The North* reported that Madden had taken part in presenting a Beethoven trio for violin, viola, and cello, mentioning his playing of a solo. As an encore, the account went on, he had used one of his own compositions, "A Russian Legend," for which an English text, in keeping with the music, had been written by the Reverend Kristofer Janson.[22] One reads that Madden had also composed music for Janson's lyrical poem "Mellom rosor" (Among the Roses), which Mrs. Valborg Hovind Stub had sung with great effect. The paper also announced Claude Madden's impending marriage. In the company of his fiancée, Miss Johanna Holtzermann, and her mother, he had left the city to take passage for Europe. The couple would be married in Germany, and the musician had said that he planned a visit to Norway the following spring.

Yet if Janson's public image changed very little, privately he was a lonely man. There were, of course, no angry scenes in the Janson house. Dr. Eilev Janson was to say later: "Mother and Father always had the highest respect for one another," and, if one allows a brief period of bitterness, there is little reason to doubt the son's judgment, unconventional though their behavior might have been. Eilev's sympathies, however, were with his father; he remembered his concern for his father and seems to have felt a measure of relief that Kristofer could find companionship in Louise Bentzen. More and more, Janson was drawn to the young woman, not only, it seems, because of her intelligence, her gifts as a medium—important as they may have been—but also because of her interest in his charities and his social concerns.

Of Louise's background little information is available, and none at all on her life in Minneapolis before she came into the Janson orbit (we do not know how she made her living or who her friends were), but it is certain that she knew of the Jansons' estrangement and the circumstances that had produced it. That she should be attracted to Janson is hardly to be wondered at. He was a few months short of fifty-one, a handsome, vigorous man, his beard lightly threaded with gray and his hair touched at the temples. Bereft, he needed comfort. That was the interpretation of Janson's daughter, Ingeborg, who, in reference to Louise, wrote in 1934, "That remarkably gifted person came into Father's life simply because he *was lonely*; Mother's strong nature sought *other* ways, interests, and friends than Father." [The italics are in the original.][23]

Perhaps the eventuality of another woman's coming into Janson's life had never occurred to Drude; in any event, his deepening attachment to Louise seems to have escaped her notice. Some time before the church season closed in June, 1892, she implored Janson's forgiveness and asked that he take her back as his wife. According to Peter Ydstie, when Janson told her that he had found a woman who was able and willing to be his co-worker, Drude at first accepted the decision with good grace and only later developed an antagonism toward Louise and sought to blacken the younger woman's character. Afterward, in a letter to Bjørnson, she wrote that, when she realized the part she had played in bringing about his domestic debacle, she tried to do everything she could to make restitution.[24] It is likely she made reference to more than the public record reveals, but in the spring of 1892 she was to take part briefly in Kristofer's work. In April, *The North* reported that Janson had read the first two acts of a play by Drude.[25] Without giving its title, the paper remarked: "The production, while hardly original in its conception, is of undoubted merit and contains many strong and fine features." It dealt with social conditions, having as its heroine a young girl reared in luxury who awakens to the realization of the misery found among the poorer classes.

For the forthcoming issue of *Saamanden,* Drude contributed a long article entitled "Verdens martyrer" (The World's Martyrs). Read today with the knowledge of her anguish during the last year in America—all the greater because of her realization that she had brought it on herself—one finds the piece poignant. She begins by retelling a scene from Dostoevsky's *The Brothers Karamazov,* which leads to a discussion of willing and unwilling martyrs, the victims of an unjust society. She pictures the bleak poverty of immigrant life in pioneer settlements and the misery found in cities, saying that when injustice becomes too great, the system will destroy itself and a better one will take its place. As the evils of society arise from ignorance, so do the mistakes of individuals, for people act without realizing the consequences of their deeds. How often, she writes, one hears people say, "If I had known what I know now, I should not have acted as I did." Yet she concludes that it is through such experiences one becomes a responsible person, climbing a ladder toward a finer self.[26]

7

All during this time, when the domestic affairs of the Jansons were becoming increasingly tangled, *The North* was running a succession of articles on Kristofer by his Swedish colleague, Axel Lundeberg. Beginning in March, shortly before Janson had returned from the west coast, these pieces were drawn from a lecture Lundeberg had delivered the previous December, the first of his series on Scandinavian authors. It is a bit ironic that, in his autobiography, Janson was to express his gratitude to Hamsun for the *Ny Jord* article, saying that the latter had been the only one who had tried to understand and present both his religious and literary work before the public. It is unlikely that Janson had forgotten either the characterizations of him by Gundersen or Lundeberg's efforts to interpret him, but, writing in Norwegian, he hungered for the attention of critics in Scandinavia and never got it. Perhaps he felt that he had been subjected to a little too much analysis on the part of local pedants writing in provincial papers in America.

Lundeberg's discussion of Janson as an author would have justified such a feeling. The reviewer had nothing to say that had not previously been said by Hamsun and Gundersen, except perhaps his comment that living in America had not been to Janson's advantage as a literary man. Norway, Lundeberg declared, was the "cradle of modern classical literature." The American West offered little stimulation for a writer; everything was as monotonous as the endless prairie. Material interests predominated. Politics was not, as in Norway, inspired by the noble love of liberty and independence but was a "slave in Mammon's dirty service." Taste and artistry had not been developed to the same extent as in Norway. Janson himself had faithfully mirrored American crudeness in his novel *Behind the Curtain*.[27]

Lundeberg simply nibbled at Janson's theology. Himself a "radical Unitarian of an independent character," as he characterized himself on another occasion, he could not see how Janson could escape a contradiction on the problem of evil when he argued that God was the creator of all things, thus making Him also responsible for evil. Nor could Lundeberg fathom his doctrine concerning prayer, that one should not ask God to break His natural laws for the convenience of the petitioner, but should confine himself to asking for spiritual blessing. No reasoning man could accept this, the critic said, because thus asking for anything was forbidden. Lundeberg apparently assumed that, if the blessing was not already present, one could not, according to Janson's doctrine, expect supplication to produce it. He also questioned Janson's concept of Jesus as the perfect man and the unattainable ideal. "No, the idea of human perfection has not been reached; it is not to be found behind us," Lundeberg wrote, "but before us and it will perhaps once be reached." More than that, Janson still clung to an anthropomorphic God—not by incarnating Him in human form but by investing Him with such human qualities as love and wisdom. Nature considers only the whole, not the parts, the writer continued. Love is a relationship between persons and therefore cannot exist between God and man. Science has yet to identify what that relationship is.[28]

For Janson the man and for what he had created in Nazareth Church, Lundeberg had the highest praise. The religious and sociopolitical discussions held in the church had broadened the outlook of the Scandinavian population in the city; the concerts and musical entertainments were the best Minneapolis had to offer. In his Sunday evening readings through the years, Janson had elevated public taste, for as a reader he was the equal of anyone to be found in America and vastly superior to anyone in the West. The social events sponsored by the church were such that one felt proud to bring his friends to them.[29]

Janson was a gentleman in the best sense of the word, the Swedish minister continued. "When, upon my arrival in Minneapolis, I visited Janson in his home, then on Nicollet Avenue, and saw the tall man with the beautiful features and bright eyes, he reminded me more than anyone else of John, the apostle of love."[30]

Yet Janson's personality was such that he inspired a kind of idolatry, Lundeberg maintained. As for the followers, the critic said: "He has become a little god to them, whom they worship as the orthodox worship Christ. Janson thus has put an end to the Jesus worship but he has not been able to prevent that, contrary to his own will, in its place has risen a Janson worship." There was too great a gap between Janson and his hearers. One always heard about Kristofer Janson, never about the Norwegian Unitarian church. Should the minister leave, no one was qualified to take his place. And Lundeberg regretted Janson's Spiritualism: "He also has preached his spiritualistic dreams from the pulpit and so strong is the magnetic power of his influence that he has converted quite a few to his shadowy faith. It is to be hoped that Janson himself before long will see his mistake."[31]

8

By the time this criticism was printed, Spiritualism had served as the theme of a discussion in Nazareth Church. On April 25, Janson had prefaced the program with a lecture, "Er materialismen en ven eller en fiende af liberal kristendom?" (Is Materialism a Friend or Enemy of Liberal Christianity?), which was to be the lead article in

Saamanden the following fall. One of the alarming developments revealed by the religious debates or discussions of the previous year,
Janson began, had been the materialism prevailing among the Scandinavians, especially the Swedes. When a member of the audience declared this life to be the only one and that all else was mere speculation,
the statement was greeted with applause. Orthodoxy was no threat
to liberal Christianity, for, by clinging to its medieval doctrines, it
would die out, for soon no one would accept it. Materialism, however,
posed a real danger: if a person denied God and a developing human
spirit, he was more likely to give free rein to his animal nature. Janson was not accusing all materialists of loose morals, but he was
pointing out that they lacked the guidelines of religious persons. In
this lecture, Janson's purpose was not only to reveal why he believed
in God and personal immortality, but to show that such a belief was
reasonable.

Since the natural world, in which lower forms of life develop into
higher ones, is governed by immutable laws, one must assume a great
lawmaker or God. Speculation about who created God is pointless,
for that is not and never will be amenable to human reason. The materialist does not, of course, deny that the world is regulated, but he
insists that its pattern is that all plants and beings have come into life,
matured, and died. Man, in common with all other organic matter,
lives on only in his descendants. True enough, man does live on in
that sense, but also as an intelligent, developing personality. Surely if
life in this world consists of gradual change to a higher type, it is
reasonable to expect this process to go on after death. Materialists
might object that the development is too slow, that God might better
have created man perfect in the first place, but Janson felt that would
make life colorless and without meaning.

Thus he quixotically evaded the question about what point there
might be in this long struggle for perfection, if one in the end were to
find that his existence is without color or meaning. The materialist
points out that doctors, in dissecting a human body, have never found
any evidence of a soul; he insists that personality is the product of the
nervous and digestive systems. But he ignores the unseen, which is
just as real as whatever is perceptible by the senses. Here the Spiritualist can meet the materialist on the latter's own terms: he has incontro-
vertible proof that the so-called dead persons live on as intelligent
beings. Scientists were coming to accept Spiritualism, among them
Darwin's co-worker, Alfred Russel Wallace, who had experienced mani-

festations through a medium, a ten-year-old girl, under circumstances that excluded all possibility of either fraud or hallucination.

Since Spiritualism produces the only evidence that the materialist will accept, Janson felt that Christianity should be grateful and support the new movement instead of ridiculing and reviling it. Thankfully, some ministers were being receptive. A Pastor Thornton, eleven years before, had advised an assembly of clergymen in Newcastle, England, not to close their eyes to a religion that might prove to be sent by God, and the royal chaplain of Holland, Herr Rewile, had openly acknowledged his acceptance of the faith, and wisely so, Janson thought, for the truths of Spiritualism constitute the church's most powerful weapon against positivism.[32]

By the time this lecture was delivered, Janson's long-awaited collection of sermons, *Lys og frihed* (Light and Freedom) had come out—$1.50 in paper and $2.00 in hard cover. Through the years, Janson had been planning the volume, preserving for it the sermons that he felt were his best. Although they are not arranged in chronological order but rather in accordance with the orthodox church calendar, the book opens with "Under What Banner Shall We Christians Assemble?", Janson's evocative rallying call which he had delivered in the fall of 1882 upon his return to America with his family. For the most part, the sermons are developed from Biblical texts, but for some the minister also turned to literature and legend, as in "Dr. Jekyll and Mr. Hyde," "St. Christopher," "Ygdrasil's Ash," and the popular "King Hodding's Journey," which he had given in English as often as in Norwegian. A few, such as "The Meaning of the Eucharist for Us" and "The Liberal Trinity," are clearly partisan, expounding Janson's Unitarian theology. Some reveal his trust in Spiritualism, as do "What Is Death?" and "Who Are God's Angels?". Many express his social concern; the most powerful of these is perhaps "Thy Brother's Blood Calls to Me from the Earth." Over all, one finds that the light and freedom indicated in the title come from responding to the God within each of us, by being a Christian in deed through following the shining example of Jesus.[33]

9

By the spring of 1892, several of Janson's young protégés were already in the ministry, while others were nearing the completion of their training. Herman Haugerud, who had served an American congregation in Puyallup, Washington, for several years, was leaving for further study at Harvard. Johannes J. Brauti was the resident minister at Underwood and also served Fergus Falls, Battle Lake, and Tordenskiold, all in Minnesota. Still a student at Meadville as well as a contributor to *Saamanden*, Hans L. Rikstad was to be employed during the summer months by the Minnesota Unitarian Conference; he held meetings in New London and Paynesville. In June, Janson's former pupil, Amandus Norman, graduated from Meadville; on that occasion he delivered an address entitled "The Relation of Material Prosperity to the Permanent Welfare of a Nation." Earlier he had thought of taking up his ministry in Reynolds, North Dakota, in the area where he had first settled in coming to America. Janson had sometimes affectionately called Norman the "Red River Valley apostle." However, Norman, on his graduation, hungered for further study and decided to spend the following two years at Harvard.[34]

Unitarianism was continuing to make inroads among the Icelanders. The Reverend Bjørn Peterson had a well-established congregation in Winnipeg. Another congregation had been organized at Gimli, Manitoba, a community some fifty miles north of Winnipeg, by the Reverend Magnus J. Skaptason.[35] The circustances of its founding were so unusual that the new church at Gimli became a focal point of interest at the Minnesota Conference's semiannual convention held at Nazareth Church on June 15 and 16. Skaptason had been a Lutheran pastor. At a meeting of his synod he had announced that he no longer found the doctrine of an everlasting hell acceptable, a statement which led to his soon being forced out of the synod, together with a number of his congregation who had chosen to follow him. At the meeting of the Minnesota Conference, the Reverend T. B. Forbush gave an account of the lively dispute going on in Gimli, over the more liberal group's occupancy of one of the church buildings. This was followed by Janson's reading of a letter he had recently received from Skaptason thanking him for books and saying that Icelandic Unitarianism was closer to that of the Norwegians than to that of the Americans.[36]

Unfortunately, not many of the Icelanders in Manitoba and North Dakota could read Dano-Norwegian, but those who could would relay the content of what they read to others. Their basic principle, the Canadian minister wrote, was love of God and of one's neighbor. They did not accept the idea of everlasting punishment nor the verbal inspiration of the Bible. Although Skaptason had never publicly denied the divinity of Christ, he had preached that all human beings are the sons and daughters of God and that Jesus was the Saviour because of his teachings and example, not as a result of his death on the cross.

As the church season drew to a close, Ivar and Eilev Janson received their medical degrees from the University of Minnesota. In Minneapolis, a movement was afoot to establish kindergartens in the city. In a June issue, *The North* reported that the movement had had "another field day" the previous Sunday, when a meeting had been held at the Lyceum Theater at which Charles B. Gilbert, superintendent of the St. Paul public schools, Mrs. Kate Buffington Davis, Miss Hattie Twichell, and the Reverend Kristofer Janson had been the principal speakers. In the course of the discussion that followed, he had offered the kindergarten association the use of the vestry of his church for a school for small children, should it be decided to establish one in that part of the city.[37]

A week later the church closed for the summer. The Jansons, accompanied by Louise Bentzen, left for Brown County. For everyone but Kristofer, it was to be the last summer on the prairie.

11

The Trauma
of Divorce

VERY LITTLE of a factual nature is known about Janson's activities during 1893, his last year in America. Newspaper mention of him became so rare as to seem ominous. This abrupt change is especially noticeable in *The North,* the lively weekly that prided itself on its comprehensive coverage of Scandinavian activities. Yet even after Janson's church services began in the fall of 1892, the newspaper carried notices of them only now and then. Editor Jaeger's attitude toward Janson had altered. He had adopted a satirical tone, often wording his comments as if to imply that the minister was no longer to be taken seriously. Occasionally *The North* contained statements in which Janson was not named but which seem to contain covert allusions to him. One was printed in the issue of August 10, 1892: "Spiritualism is making numerous converts among the Norwegians of this city, and there are several for whom it seems to be easy to fall into trance."

If the items from the newspapers and *Saamanden* were the only available sources concerning Janson, the record would be fragmentary indeed. Some years later, however—after the terms of their divorce had been agreed upon—both Kristofer and Drude described their last year in America in letters to Bjørnson. At about the same time Peter Ydstie confided to his friend Torkel Oftelie his version of what had brought the Jansons to an impasse. Finally in 1897—the year in which the divorce became final and Kristofer and Louise Bentzen were married—Drude published an autobiographical novel, *Mira,* spelling out the humiliation the heroine endured when another woman, a medium,

296

entered the household. In certain paragraphs, the language in which Drude described Louise to Bjørnson in her letters is identical to that she used in portraying Ernestine Helsing in the novel.[1]

From these personal sources, we get some idea of the tensions Janson was under and the experiences that kept him buoyed up. His home life was, of course, strained. Although he tried to keep up outward appearances, rumors circulated in the city, with Drude figuring as the wronged wife and Louise as the brazen intruder. Old members of the congregation were grieved over the situation, and some of them left the church. However, Janson's Spiritualism also had its drawing power, and, as a result, his following grew rather than withered. Through his occult investigation, he felt he had come to know God's plan for the universe, and this belief bolstered his faith in his mission. He had not, however, forgotten his commitment to social betterment. The events of the last year can best be told by first dealing with the record taken from the press, then from the letters, and, last, from Drude's novel.

In Brown County, it had become Janson's practice to hold confirmation exercises the last Sunday in August, just before he returned to Minneapolis. Living in the country only two months of the year forced him to concentrate his religious instruction during that time, meeting with the confirmands twice a week. Much of the rest of the program was scheduled into the Sunday service when the congregation gathered for the day on the hill. In his earlier years, with a whole congregation to educate, Janson had also included adults, assembling all outdoors; the children and young people sat on the grass, the older folk on chairs, the entire group forming a semicircle around Janson as he interspersed gospel readings with song. Most of the parents were of farm stock from Toten and Gudbrandsdal in Norway, who commonly spoke their native dialects, a speech piquant and pleasing to Janson.

In the summer of 1892, Louise Bentzen was one of the teachers in the Hanska church school. "She was a moody, changeable person," one of her pupils, Minnie Running, has recalled. Minnie, who was the daughter of one of the carpenters who were carried through the air along with the Jansons during the tornado of 1883, seems to have been a diligent student who became one of Miss Bentzen's favorites. But one day there was no pleasing the teacher. When she directed a question at the girl, Minnie answered promptly. "That is correct," said Miss Bentzen, adding severely, "but you need not express yourself so crudely." The girl was so confused and wounded that she never forgot the incident. The teacher, as was her custom, had spoken in *riksmaal,* or Dano-Norwegian, and Minnie had answered in the dialect commonly used in her home. On that particular day, the peasant speech was enough to set Miss Bentzen on edge.[2]

What prompted her irritation we shall never know, for unlike Kristofer and Drude, Louise left no personal testimony of how she felt then or during the troubled months that followed. Yet, even by the summer of 1892, she must have been having an uncomfortable time. This was not because of Drude, who—from all accounts—was at the period trying to steel herself to accept the situation. All the younger Jansons, with the exception of Eilev, regarded Louise with mounting antagonism.[3] Ivar in particular resented her and came to look upon her as a schemer who had taken advantage of circumstances to gain influence over his father.[4]

It is unlikely that anyone living that summer in the little red cottage was happy. It was an unproductive season for Janson's literary work; that fall he seems not to have had any harvest of new stories or a novel for his readings when he returned to Minneapolis. Even his long-promised cycle of poems, *Jesus-sangene,* was not ready for publication. During the summer months he had been the victim of a malicious trick, and, although this happening had no direct bearing on his domestic affairs, it may show that, by certain persons, he was regarded as a somewhat ridiculous figure. A subscriber in Chicago had ordered *Lys og frihed* which Janson had sent. On receiving the book, the man wrote that his pleasure in getting it had been destroyed by the pretentious, self-glorifying letter that had accompanied it. Janson was stunned: he had sent no letter. Soon he found out what had happened. The book had arrived while the recipient was away from home. In his absence, someone else had opened the package, inserted a letter of his own composition, and resealed the package, leaving no evidence of tampering. According to Janson, the letter, headed with his Minneapolis address, had begun in a vein so similar to his own style that he acknowledged it as a clever imitation. But the writer had gone off on a tangent, devising grandiose statements to the effect that a few Christs still walked the earth and Janson considered himself one of them. The forger's letter concluded: "I am the truth. Kristofer Janson." Reporting this in *Saamanden,* Janson indicated that he wished to warn readers to be skeptical about any strangely worded messages claiming to have come from him. "If it has happened once, it can happen again," he said.[5]

Bad news came from Portland, Oregon. The newly organized Scandinavian Unitarian congregation had demanded the resignation of its minister, John L. Eriksen, and Janson found the action to be justified.

What the offense may have been we do not know, for in the August, 1892, issue of *Saamanden* Janson reported only that Eriksen had been unworthy of his trust, having revealed himself as a Unitarian in word but not in deed. To encourage the stranded congregation to keep going, Janson urged that it choose leaders from among its members, using for their meetings material from *Saamanden* and *Lys og frihed*. "This blow was unexpected and has hit me hard," he wrote.[6]

One cannot tell what long-range plans Janson may have had for Eriksen. The two had been in correspondence for some time prior to Janson's going to the west coast. This clergyman was the only orthodox minister among the Norwegians to shift over to Unitarianism, and he was an engaging man. It is just possible that Janson had thought of him as his own substitute in Minneapolis for the year he would be in Norway. At the time—and for more than a year thereafter—Janson clung to the hope that his future with Louise might lie in America. He would make his lecture tour and terminate his marriage to Drude while he was in Norway. Then he would return to America and eventually marry Louise. He realized that his position as a divorced and remarried clergyman might create difficulties, but he reasoned that they would not be insurmountable once it was known he had been the injured partner in the divorce action.

Budstikken had been silent on Janson all through 1892. (From an editorial published the following spring, one concludes that the editor had no more use for Spiritualism than had Jaeger.)[7] Thus it seems surprising when its Aungust 24 issue gave prominent place to a poem dedicated to Janson, "Til Kristofer Janson." At first it may also appear strange that the poem was written by Oscar Gundersen, the bookkeeper-savant of Chicago, whose analytical article on Janson two years earlier had revealed the man as out of touch with the intellectual currents of the time, as a second-rate writer, and as so naive he was the ready dupe of Spiritualism. Yet it is also true that Gundersen had found Janson personally a noble man, who, by his example and by the moral earnestness of his preaching, put one in mind of Jesus. It was this side of Janson that Gundersen's poem exalted.

One can only guess how the verses came into being. Janson was so kindly and generous a man that even the sharpest of his critics could find themselves humbled by the man's magnanimity. In one of his letters, Hamsun confessed to feeling shamefaced on receiving Janson's thanks for the dressing-down that Hamsun felt he had given him in *Ny Jord*. Possibly Gundersen's poem was the result of a similar twinge of conscience. The year before, the thirty-one-year-old Gundersen had published at his own expense a small book of poems, *Stemnings-billeder* (Pictures of Moods), which Janson had reviewed in *Saamanden*. After his severe criticism of Janson, Gundersen may have been surprised at what the minister had written about his poetry. Gundersen, Janson had written, was a cultivated young man, the kind he liked to find among the Norwegians. In religion, Janson went on, the book's author had not found a spiritual home, for he was a questing soul who had been greatly influenced by Matthew Arnold's *Literature and Dogma*. Janson would like to see a young man more optimistic than Gundersen's verses revealed him to be, but what critic could presume to dictate what a poet should express? Here and there, Jansen found minor fault with Gundersen's diction, but he concluded by heartily recommending the book, urging readers to buy it to help the talented young writer to publish more.

Janson was touched by "Til Kristofer Janson." Presumably he was not the regular reader of *Budstikken* he had once been, for he did not know about the poem until the following winter. He reprinted it in the February, 1893, issue of *Saamanden*. In thanking Gundersen, he explained that he did not ordinarily print tributes to himself unless the author expressly asked that he do so, but Gundersen's poem had merit because of its beautiful portrait of Jesus.[8]

In the fall of 1892, the Jansons returned to Minneapolis, but the newspapers give no indication of whether services were held in Nazareth Church on either September 4 or 11. *The North* did report them for September 18. From *Saamanden*, one finds that Hans L. Rikstad, the Meadville student and frequent contributor to the paper, preached for Janson on September eighteenth. The following week, *The North* had one of its rare notices. If this finally cost Jaeger a pang, he restrained himself, for he printed the announcement without comment: "At Nazareth Church the Rev. Kristofer Janson will give his views on whether, before assuming the bodily shape in which we now inhabit the earth, we have lived on this planet and whether we are to return after death."[9]

We do not have this sermon, but when Janson departed for Norway a year later, he had already announced that he would deliver a lecture there on the same subject as well as one which seems closely related, "Concerning Spiritualism, Its Significance and Dangers." Thus not more than a few months could have elapsed between the composition of his sermon of September 25, 1892, and the lecture on the same subject delivered in Norway. The latter contains a thoroughgoing explanation of how the process of reincarnation works, intelligence Janson had received from spirits through a medium. His lecture on Spiritualism was to contain another apocalyptic revelation—God's master plan for His creation. Referring to this as "evolution's great law," Janson explained that higher forms of life evolved from the lower in the physical world and that the same process was going on in the spiritual world, where beings advanced from sphere to sphere until they ultimately reached the perfection that made them one with God.[10]

2

Much as Janson seems to have found comfort and a sense of exhilaration from what he learned in seances, he continued to work for social and political betterment on this earth. In the fall of 1892, he was deeply concerned over the up-coming presidential election, when the newly formed People's party was taking part in the contest. Although the papers gave no indication of it, he seems to have preached on the subject early in October. His sermon was printed in that month's *Saamanden*: "How Should a Christian Vote in the Coming Election?" This act climaxed a long effort on Janson's part: he had supported the Populist party from its very inception.[11]

Earlier, *Saamanden* in a four-page spread had told of a meeting to be held to organize "the great Reform-Party" on February 22, 1892, in St. Louis. Attending would be representatives from the Farmers' Alliance, women's suffrage organizations, labor unions, temperance societies, "Greenbackers," antimonopolists, and other reform groups, large and small. All were dedicated to breaking the existing power structure and "giving the country back to the people." Janson had translated the program for the meeting and had also published in his paper Frances Willard's proposals for women's suffrage. He had prefaced all this by "The Call," in which he translated from the preamble to the program, a document written by Ignatius Donnelly:

"We meet in the midst of a nation brought to the verge of moral, political, and material ruin. Corruption dominates the ballot box, the legislatures, the Congress, and touches even the ermine of the bench. The people are demoralized. Many of the States have been compelled to isolate the voters at the polling places in order to prevent universal intimidation or bribery. The newspapers are subsidized or muzzled, public opinion silenced, business prostrate, our homes covered with mortgages, labor impoverished, and the land concentrated in the hands of capitalists. The urban workmen are denied the right of organization for self-protection; imported pauperized labor beats down their wages;

301

a hireling standing army, unrecognized by our laws, is established to shoot them down, and they are rapidly disintegrating to European conditions. The fruits of the toil of the millions are boldly stolen to build up colossal fortunes, unprecedented in the history of the world, while their possessors despise the republic and endanger liberty. From the same prolific womb of governmental injustice we breed two great classes—paupers and millionaires. The national power to create money is appropriated to enrich bondholders; silver, which has been accepted as coin since the dawn of history, has been demonetized to add to the purchasing power of gold by decreasing the value of all forms of property as well as human labor, and the supply of currency is purposely abridged to fatten usurers, bankrupt enterprises, and enslave industry. A vast conspiracy against mankind has been organized on two continents and is taking possession of the world. If not met and overthrown at once, it forebodes terrible social convulsions, the destruction of civilization, or the establishment of an absolute despotism."[12]

Janson's excerpt was longer than this quotation. He admired Donnelly's statement and was later to translate additional sections of it in *Saamanden*, using an extended version which the politician had prepared for the nominating convention of the People's party held in Omaha on July 4, 1892. In the August, 1892, number of *Saamanden*, Janson's report on the meeting is confined to the Donnelly document along with a statement that it had been enthusiastically accepted by the convention.[13] In the next issue of the paper, he quoted the *New Nation* to the effect that the new party was winning over many of the nation's newspapers. He said that in Colorado the formerly Republican *Greeley Tribune* had swung its support to the People's party, and in less than a month sixteen other papers in that state had followed suit. The same shift of allegiance was happening in Nebraska, Texas, South Dakota, Missouri, Iowa, and indeed in other states.[14]

This was the background for Janson's sermon on the election of 1892. One is hardly surprised by the inclusion of the long excerpt from Donnelly's preamble. Detractors had sought to dismiss it as exaggerated political propaganda, Janson said, going on to remark that, if the charges made there were only half true, they should be enough to rally Christians to the new party. Janson believed all of these charges to be true, saying that the People's party would hardly find it wise to launch its career with lies. As evidence that Donnelly had not misrepresented conditions in the country, Janson cited instances of unrest and disturbances in Pennsylvania, Illinois, Idaho, and Montana.

302

The People's party stood for the principles of Jesus, Janson thought. Like other parties before it, it too might in time become corrupt, but in 1892 it gave the Christian his only option, regardless of how he might feel about its candidates or the particular features of its program. Nowhere in the sermon did Janson mention the nominees for president and vice-president, James B. Weaver and James G. Field, and in this omission he may have reflected general sentiment, for Donnelly's biographer has said that the People's party convention delegates displayed more enthusiasm for their platform than for their candidates.[15]

The new party did quite well in the election. Its candidate for president received twenty-two electoral votes, the first time since the Civil War that a third party had had a voice in the electoral college. In his *The Populist Revolt,* John D. Hicks records that the new party elected about ten to the House of Representatives and could count on a number of other Congressmen who owed their election to political deals of one kind or another. In Kansas, Colorado, Nevada, Idaho, and North Dakota, the People's party drew 48 per cent or more of the popular vote. Three states—Kansas, North Dakota, and Colorado— elected Populist governors.[16] Kansas best supported the new party. The state went for Weaver, elected the entire Populist state ticket, and won five of seven seats in Congress. In Minnesota, the Populists held the balance of power in the state senate and sent one representative to Congress.[17] Only the cumbersome nature of the Minnesota ballot prevented the Populist electors, whom the Democrats had endorsed, from winning.[18]

3

It was just at election time that a change took place in the Janson household. Both Ivar and Eilev had been practicing medicine in the city. Ivar had decided to stay in Minneapolis permanently and had opened an office in the New York Life Building, but Eilev had been restless, hoping to find a place where a young man might have more of a chance. One day he heard that Astoria, Oregon, had a sizable fishing colony made up of Scandinavians. On the strength of this information, he left for Oregon on November 4. It turned out to be a fortunate move, for in the course of a few years he built up a good practice.[19]

The departure of Eilev was reported in *The North,* but one reads nothing of his father. *Saamanden* appeared regularly but served up no chatty morsels on the activities of Nazareth Church and its minister. Then, in mid-December, one finds a bitter allusion to Janson written by his Unitarian colleague, Axel Lundeberg. As one might expect, it dealt with Spiritualism. Lundeberg had been one of those present at the seance held in Elim House some years before. In *The North,* he wrote that most of the participants, with the exception of one or two, had regarded the phenomena as examples of sleight of hand, even though the observers had not been able to explain how these tricks had been brought about. Lundeberg had recently come upon a book, *The Bottom Facts Concerning the Science of Spiritualism* by John A. Truesdell. Explaining that the author had been a medium for twenty-five years and thus was in a position to give a full account of how such feats as those at Elim House could be achieved, Lundeberg first gave a detailed resumé of Truesdell's book. He then concluded: "I recommend the above to the perusal of everyone who is sufficiently unprejudiced to be able to view this question from an unbiased stand-point. I have been present when a man whose great influence ought to be used for a better purpose has directed poor, ignorant Scandinavians to such fraudulent tricksters as the one here exposed in order to learn the truth at the expense of their reason and at the cost of perhaps their last dollar. I do not blame anyone who is sincere in his conviction, as I know this man to be, but I think his influence ought to be counteracted unless we want to see our countrymen veiled in medieval darkness."[20]

Lundeberg's strong statement drew no response. Even at Christmas, no mention was made in *The North* of either Janson or Nazareth Church. In the January 18,1893, issue the paper announced that Janson would read Ibsen's *The Master Builder* the following Sunday evening. Jaeger commented: "The occasion to hear him read and interpret the latest Ibsenian riddle should not be missed." In this case, it may well be that Jaeger's sarcasm was directed at Ibsen rather than at Janson.[21] Two weeks later the paper reported that Janson's reading for the following Sunday night would be "Mother's Hands" by Bjørnson, and that on Monday evening the subject of the discussion meeting would be "Is the Protest of the Socialists against the Existing Order Justified?"[22]

Another long interval follows in which one reads nothing of the Jansons, but on March 8, 1893, *The North* announced that Mrs. Kristofer Janson, her three daughters, and her youngest son would leave for Norway in a month, to be joined by Janson in the fall. The following week the paper reported Janson's resignation as minister of

Nazareth Church, to become effective the following September.[23] Apparently Jaeger was no longer close to sources of information within the congregation, for in his March 22 issue he had to publish a retraction: "Our remarks in last week's issue anent Rev. Kristofer Janson prove to be somewhat misleading. The reverend gentleman has not resigned, as stated, but merely asked for a leave of absence for one year, the same to take effect next fall."

The same paper contained a review of Arne Janson's farewell concert on the violin, asserting that the young performer had lived up to all expectations. The following week his father was represented by a brief mention. His sermon for the confirmation services the previous Sunday had been spoken of very highly, the paper reported, adding that "even members of orthodox churches [were] going so far as to admit there was nothing seriously objectionable in it." The paper announced that Nazareth Church had granted Janson a leave of absence for one year beginning in September and that it was likely a student at Meadville would be engaged as his substitute. A week later Jaeger reported Drude's departure in an article entitled "Off to Europe." It was an epitaph for an era: "Mrs. Drude Krogh Janson and her four youngest children left last week for Norway where the daughters will remain with relatives while Mrs. Janson and her son Arne in the fall intend to go to Germany to enable the latter to pursue his musical studies.

"The departure will be deeply felt by a number of friends who at different times have enjoyed the hospitality of Mr. and Mrs. Janson. For several years Saturday evenings at their homestead were surrendered to an ever shifting, but always interesting, circle of friends. Names such as Mrs. V. H. Stub, Miss Burdick, Gustavus Johnson, Schlachter, Hoevel, Madden, Harwood, Fjelde will be readily recognized in this connection. At these gatherings were rendered classical and modern music of the highest order. The beautiful songs of Schubert generally sung by Mr. Janson himself to his wife's accompaniment; overtures and sonatas by Beethoven, Mozart, Mendelssohn varied with the stirring music of Chopin, and an occasional echo from Sclav composers, and finely executed pieces of Grieg, Gade, Kjerulf, Selmer and other Scandinavian masters. Then as an interlude, a cup of most delicious tea served daintly by the young ladies of the house; a bit of original poetry, set to music by Claude Madden, for instance, and a recitation—to say nothing of the quiet corner talks and animated discussions.

"There will be a tinge of sadness mingled with the memories of those delightful gatherings, but we hope that the God speed which in behalf of many friends we extend to Mrs. Janson and her family, may be turned into a welcome back sooner than now expected."[24]

From the little information we have of the five months that Janson remained in America, it seems that he was at times hopeful he would be able to return after a year in Norway. But sometimes he was clearly gnawed by doubts that he would be able to arrange it. On April 8, a few days before Drude's departure, he wrote Amandus Norman, then completing his year at Harvard Divinity School: "Read this through thoughtfully and reply after you have given it careful consideration. This fall I shall go to Norway, presumably to be away for a year," he began. He explained that he had been granted a leave by his congregation on the condition that he find a substitute, and his choice had fallen on Norman as the person with the greatest inspiration, the most positive faith. The congregation in Minneapolis had blossomed out with many new members, young men and women, Janson said, adding that he would find parting from them hard. He summarized what Norman's duties in Minneapolis, Hudson, and Brown County would be, predicting that they would give the young man valuable experience for the time when he would take up his long-planned ministry in the Red River Valley. *Saamanden*, Janson wrote, would be in the hands of someone else who would, of course, welcome Norman's advice and help. All these responsibilities would begin the first Sunday in September. He added that the salary would help Norman pay off some of the debt he must have incurred during his years of study.

Years later Norman was to publish this letter and others that he had received from Janson. In the one mentioned here, Norman deleted parts, a fact suggesting that Janson may have confided the state of his domestic affairs.[25] However, in tone the letter seems genuinely cheerful, and in that respect it contrasts with remarks he made in May at a church conference in Menomonie, Wisconsin. Speaking on religious work among foreigners, Janson said that immigrant groups should be served by a preacher who could use their native language. Foreigners who come to America as adults learn slowly, he said, and are never at ease when listening to a sermon in English. He understood exactly how they felt from his own experience; he was never as deeply affected by an English speech as by one in Norwegian. In listening to English, one had to strain so much to get the meaning, and even then it seemed cold and bare. "If I stayed here a hundred years, I would never be Americanized," he said. "The rules of society, of politeness, the mode of thinking, reasoning, speaking, and writing are of another kind. They are against my nature, my education, my customs. I may love and admire many Americans, but I will never become one of them. You cannot deprive the leopard of its spots."[26]

In May and June, notices of Janson's services appeared more regularly in *The North* than during the previous seven months. The issue of May 10 announced that Amandus Norman would replace Janson for the following year, and, as the spring wore on, the paper carried accounts of concerts and entertainments and of Janson's exchanging pulpits with the Reverend Henry M. Simmons. On June 25 the season closed with Janson preaching on "True and False Authorities."[27]

At least once during the summer—on July 9, 1893—Janson wrote Norman from Brown County. No one, he declared, could entice him away from that delightful place, but he would be happy to have Norman visit him, and it would give the young man a chance to get acquainted with his future parishioners. However, if Norman found traveling to Brown County out of the question, Janson supposed that they could take care of their business by correspondence, which would settle the ordering of events for Sunday, September 3. On that morning Janson would deliver his farewell sermon, and in the evening he would ordain Amandus Norman, being assisted in the latter by his colleagues Simmons, Forbush, and Crothers. Once that ceremony was over, Janson added facetiously, Norman would be able to baptize, perform marriages, and travel half fare on the trains.[28]

The events of September 3 followed this planned order. Janson's sermon, entitled "The Salvation Army," also became the lead article in the next issue of *Saamanden*. In it Janson used the well-known religious organization by that name as a point of departure, urging people to profit by its example of raising the fallen and eradicating ignorance, tyranny, and intolerance. This, he said, was essentially what he had been teaching through the years. To what extent he had succeeded only time would tell. In any event, he was sure of one thing: he had personally won the love of many. He saw it shining in their eyes that morning and felt it in their warm handclasps. He hoped this affection would grow and be accompanied by confidence in him so that, should it be necessary, they could say: "We know Kristofer Janson would never do anything unworthy; we know him too well, and that is final." At the time, he knew that not everyone had such trust. There were those whose feelings toward him could be corroded by doubt and slanderous gossip.

As he continued, he became somewhat defensive: "It is my earnest

307

intention to return in a year, unless conditions should make that impossible, and if you, when the time comes, want me back. The world lies before me, thank God, so Minneapolis is not the only place where I can preach. I know I have my best, my strongest years ahead, my finest thoughts, most glowing expression; I have never felt so inspired as now, and I hope I still have a little to tell the world, and have something worth reading in my sermons and books."[29]

That day Janson's *Jesus-sangene* was on sale for the first time. Dedicated to the Scandinavian young people "who aspire and fight for an ideal," the book contained 126 poems which Janson had arranged into 45 sections under such headings as "The Fig Tree," "Jesus in Gethsemane," and "Resurrection"; most of the selections centered about events in the life of Jesus. Not all were new: three had been in Janson's *Salmebog* in 1883, and six others had been included in various issues of *Saamanden*. Janson's dream about Christ, which had aroused so much attention some years before, was the subject of "Consecration," which appeared directly after the introduction. In the poem, the wearing of the crown of thorns comes to symbolize the suffering and persecution of all who strive to be Christ's followers.[30]

Although the ordination of Amandus Norman took place in the evening as planned, it was obscured by Janson's leave-taking; it received only brief mention in *The North* and *Saamanden*.[31] On Wednesday evening, September 6, a farewell reception for Janson was held in the basement of Nazareth Church, the event filling the place to capacity. The rooms had been decorated by the young women of the congregation. Peder Ydstie had written a commemorative poem which had been set to music and was sung by Klara Kristopherson. Speeches by Mathias Eidnes, the editor of a liberal Norwegian paper, Amandus Norman, and O. Tandberg, president of the congregation, followed. Janson, who had already received $60 from Brown County and $25 from Underwood, was given a purse of $85, gifts he found to be very generous, considering the hard times. That night he spoke of how his career as a reformer, beginning when he sought to get recognition for *landsmaal,* had led to ever-widening fields. He had come to that stage of development where he realized the whole of creation was linked together by a great chain of being, wherein all things were united from the minutest grain of sand to the greatest spiritual power. He had never felt more inspired nor more capable of work than at that very time, and he hoped that when he returned he would have many years to work among his countrymen in America.[32]

Janson left Minneapolis for Norway on Monday, September 11, 1893. His departure was reported by *The North* but not accorded the long valedictory which Jaeger had written for Drude. Louise Bentzen became the editor of *Saamanden,* then entering its seventh year. The format of the monthly remained the same, but, with Janson gone, it lost some of its sparkle. Sometimes old sermons were printed, one from as far back as 1884. After the September issue, much of which may have been prepared by Janson, the correspondence column no longer appeared, although this omission was in part compensated for by letters from Janson which appeared from time to time until the spring of the following year. Financially, *Saamanden* does not seem to have been flourishing. In an advertisement for *Jesus-sangene* in the September issue, Janson referred to the many careless subscribers who had not bothered to send in payment. By the end of the year, the situation does not seem to have improved, for then Jakob Meyer, who was acting as Janson's business agent, reported that 430 subscribers were in arrears.[33]

The November, 1893, *Saamanden* on its opening page carried a poem by Janson, "On Board," in which the wide reaches of the sea with the vaulting sky overhead cause the author to reflect how the love of God carries each of His children to eternity. The same number contained the first letter from Janson, a sprightly piece that told of enthusiastic audiences which greeted Janson's attack on the old dogmas with thundering applause. Janson felt that Norway offered him a great field in which to work—if the Scandinavians in America had no use for him any longer. The young people in particular were weary of orthodoxy; all they lacked was a leader. Gratified that his lectures aroused so much interest—the one on the future of Scandinavians in America always drew smaller crowds—Janson wrote that he had more invitations than he could accept.

In the same issue appeared a letter from L. Heiberg, a Lutheran minister, thanking Janson for *Jesus-sangene,* which the pastor had found uplifting even though his theology and that of Janson differed greatly. Accompanying the letter was a verse tribute of seven stanzas, entitled "Greetings to the Author of *Jesus-sangene*." As in the case earlier with Gundersen's criticism, the pastor's gracious words came some months after Janson had reviewed his *Brogede blade* (Multicolored Leaves) in *Saamanden,* commending Heiberg for dealing with the burning questions of the day in a forthright manner.[34]

In December, Janson wrote in his letter from Norway: "Now the

309

music has begun with a full orchestra!" He had met with opposition: ministers preached against him, tracts denouncing him were printed, letters reviling him in one way or another descended upon him. These attacks he referred to with good humor, except to comment that ignorance and fanaticism existed in Norway as well as in America. One anonymous writer declared that Janson should be run out of town; another thought he should be sent to Siberia; a third addressed him as "Herr Hottentot." The state church theologians behaved exactly as Janson had predicted they would: instead of meeting argument with argument, they dismissed what Janson had to say as "vulgar and flat rationalism." In Flekkefjord he had not been able to rent a hall, and he had come very near not getting one in Haugesund.

True enough, he had also received letters of encouragement, but he knew lonely moments in Norway. Many of his old friends were now estranged because of their disapproval of his religious views. He missed the backing of a respected, well-developed organization such as he had had in America. Having written this, he concluded that he was, after all, a "sower" and that God would bring forth a harvest in due time. He still had an extensive itinerary to follow in Norway, after which he expected to go to Sweden and Denmark.[35]

Four months later, in May, 1894, Janson wrote: "I have now made one of the most crucial decisions of my life, to remain in Norway and not return to America." Some eleven years before, he had written that no one in Norway had any interest in the religious views he represented, but now the situation had changed, and he saw a promising field before him. The young people especially were searching for something new, and this had led them in many directions—toward materialism and Spiritualism, and into ethical societies. Although this fermentation was promising, it was too diffused. What was needed was a leader, a man of sympathetic understanding, who could unite the various groups on a broad common ground. This Janson hoped to do, and he also saw opportunities to help people understand what he considered to be the true value of Spiritualism. In mountain communities in the north, he had found people interested, but unfortunately they were too absorbed in psychic phenomena to appreciate what the movement had to offer in uplifting man's daily life. In the west and south of Norway, he met people skeptical about Spiritualism and inclined to dismiss the whole idea as humbug, but in Kristiania there was a society with a hundred members, a number that was far too small for the population of the city. Janson had also encountered many persons who publicly assumed a supercilious attitude but who had privately questioned him about his views and seemed eager to hear of his experiences.

Turning to the religious situation in America, Janson did not find it promising. The third generation of immigrants would grow up speaking English and would affiliate with American congregations. Prospects of recruiting members from immigrants yet to come did not seem bright; these people were generally poor and ignorant and already so indoctrinated with state church teachings that only a few would dare to break away from the old dogmas. It had been hard for him to leave his congregations in the New World, especially Nazareth Church, where he had worked so long and hard, but he felt it was his duty to remain in Norway, adding that it would be cowardly for him to return to America because of the financial support assured him there. This was the core of his message, although he touched on his future in Norway, predicting that the state clergymen would eventually tolerate him when they saw that he intended no proselytizing but merely to gather around him those who had already broken away from orthodoxy because of their convictions.[36]

The June, 1894, issue of *Saamanden* also contained a letter from Janson, but this communication dealt with his experiences in Denmark, from where he was writing, and made no mention of America. Later in the summer, in the number which rounded out volume seven of the magazine and was the last issue to be published in America, Janson addressed readers in a full-page announcement. *Saamanden* would be continued from Norway, volume eight beginning the following January. Janson hoped his American readers would continue to subscribe to the monthly and would get others to do so. In the future, payment for *Saamanden* would have to be made in advance. From past experience he had found that to be the only sound policy, for at the time of his writing approximately 400 subscribers were still in arrears. Then, as the last sentence in his leave-taking, he wrote: "I have taken the greatest risk in my life, to destroy my bridges behind me and to depend wholly on the Norwegian people. I hope I shall not be disappointed."[37]

4

If *The North*'s treatment of Kristofer's departure was somewhat cool and disappointing, the newspaper's account of Drude's leave-taking had not revealed her bitter personal feelings. The depth of her suffering at the time was made clear when she later wrote to Bjørnson:

"Kr. wanted us gone—he hated to look at me, who, he thought, was the cause of his misfortune, and at the same time he implored me to write a letter in which I said I was unwilling to return to America so he could get a divorce on that." She had written no such letter, she declared, nor had she at that time consented to a divorce. Yet she knew that her situation was desperate: all she could expect at best was that a separation from Janson would act as a cooling-off period which would make him see that a reconciliation was, in all practical ways, the best solution. Thus, hoping against hope, she steeled herself to face her sisters, especially Dina. She wrote that she felt half crazed by the time she arrived in Norway. She never mentioned the fact, but it could not have helped matters that the twenty-fifth anniversary of her marriage to Janson, on May 22, was then only a few weeks away.[38]

Drude was forty-six years old, brown-haired and slender. Peder Ydstie has said that when conditions were right—when she was in the company of a person she admired and she was dealing with something in which she was deeply interested—she could be extremely engaging. Ydstie was Janson's friend, but he appears to have had no hostility toward Drude. Instead, he seems to feel that, if she later acted shabbily, she had been unduly influenced by others, notably by her son Ivar and certain members of the Nazareth congregation. It was Ydstie's opinion that the failure of the Jansons' marriage came from irreconcilable differences in their two natures. He was emphatic that Kristofer's interest in the occult had nothing to do with it. He wrote in the margin of one of his letters: "It was not Spiritualism that was the point of contention with the Jansons but their different moral views on relations between the sexes."

Ydstie said that Drude had a "Hjørdis-nature," referring to Ibsen's imperious heroine in *Hærmændene paa Helgeland* (The Warriors at Helgeland). In this play, Hjørdis would have as her husband the one who was the bravest of the warriors, and, according to Ydstie, Drude would choose a man who would add lustre to her name. She had married Janson when he was a promising writer, anticipating that literary fame would come with the years. Instead, Janson had chosen to bury himself as a preacher on the Western prairie, becoming deeply involved in his work and relatively indifferent to the fact that his literary reputation in Norway was fading. She had never felt drawn to Janson's parishioners, the writer continued, adding that she was too honorable to pretend something she did not feel. In the same way as she had recognized the literary ability of Knut Hamsun, she had admired

312

Madden's musical talent. The young violinist had an attractive personality, and he was quite naturally affected by the admiration of so charming a woman as Drude. All that Ydstie could readily understand. What puzzled him was that Drude could delude herself that a man some twenty years her junior would want to attach himself to her for the rest of his life. When Drude learned what Louise Bentzen had come to mean to Kristofer, she responded generously, saying that she was glad to have played a part in helping him find this woman. It was only the influence of others that later caused Drude to blacken Louise's name.

In his letter Ydstie wrote that in the divorce settlement Janson had allowed himself to be the scapegoat and was resolved not to reveal Drude's indiscretions to a scandal-hungry public. For her part, Drude had regretted her slander of Louise, and so the Jansons had reached an amiable settlement.

Drude stayed in Norway until the fall of 1893, when she and Arne went to Dresden, leaving the girls with Drude's sister Kitty. At about that time Kristofer arrived in Norway. Throughout the autumn and the following winter, they exchanged letters. With all the persuasion she could muster, Drude later wrote, she asked that they might again establish a home where they would be man and wife—at least in the eyes of the world—for the sake of their children, Janson's work, and his good name. Still very bitter, Kristofer wanted a divorce, asking that Drude make a clean breast of her part in the breakup. This she consistently refused to do, later explaining to Bjørnson that such an admission would not be the truth in the light of what had happened afterward, presumably a reference to Janson's relations with Louise Bentzen. While the Jansons were in the midst of this correspondence, Drude received a letter from Louise, pleading that Drude consent to a divorce. By this time, Drude wrote that she was overcome with weariness and gave in, warning Kristofer that she would take no responsibility for whatever might follow. This was the situation that determined Janson's decision not to return to America.[39]

During their period of strain, neither of the Jansons communicated with Bjørnson. They were obviously reluctant to bare their troubles before one who had been the warm friend of both. Not until February 1, 1895, did Kristofer write to the poet. The month before, he had organized a congregation in Kristiania, calling it Broderskabets Kirke (The Church of Brotherhood). This was the letter in which he was to say that "the Spanish skipper had come." He did not, however, discuss his domestic affairs until he had given a pathetic account of his own recent experiences in Norway. He was writing more than half a year after the Jansons had reached their divorce settlement, and as Ydstie had said, the husband had become the scapegoat. Kristofer told Bjørnson that he expected to remain permanently in Norway unless he was starved out. The autumn before, he continued, he had for a time completely lost courage, for he had lectured in the north, south, east, and west without being able to lay aside a cent for his family; he had barely made his own expenses. "The saintly people of Bergen demonstrated, and likewise the virtuous citizens of Kristiania. I am a fallen man in their eyes," he wrote. They had boycotted his lectures. When he encountered old friends on the street, they shook their heads and walked by him. In January he had begun his regular church services in Kristiania, and it looked as if he would be successful, for he had had as many as 700 in his audience. It was necessary for him to charge a small entrance fee, ten øre, and the sum thus accumulated was all Janson and his family had to live on.

Before turning to his marital troubles, he dwelt on his work saying that the years in America had developed him greatly: "If only this unfortunate family difficulty had not taken place; it has done great damage both to me and my work. Through the insane slander which has circulated, I have lost the confidence of many, and it will be years before I, with patience and love, can win them back, one by one. But I shall win them. I have lived through two purgatorial years which I would not want to go through again, but I hope I've come out whole. Naturally you have heard that at last everything is over between Drude and me—for good. The pitcher went to the well so often it finally came home without handles."

In his loneliness, Janson continued, he had found a woman who could and would be his co-worker, one who shared his interests and responded to all that was best in his nature. That should be something to gladden all his friends. But the world is so perverse in its ideas and morals, that it would prefer to see him a bleak martyr, a deceived husband, rather than a free soul who could raise the banner of hope and dream of a home where the husband and wife loved one another and really were one.

He had looked forward to the time when Louise, who had edited *Saamanden* for him the last year, would return to Norway, find some work in Kristiania, and act as his secretary. However, when she had come, the gossipers attacked her reputation like savage animals, and

314

people told Janson that, as long as Louise remained in Kristiania, he might as well give up all thought of his church services. For the sake of his work, he had felt it best to be cautious and give way; Louise had moved to another city and the following week she would go to Denmark. The slander had been so widespread that Janson could not appear on the street in the company of a woman, even a very old one, without the gossips weaving their tales. He found it bitterly ironical that he, who had always been so circumspect in regard to women, should now be regarded as a graceless philanderer, the prey of scandalmongers. Not that he minded for himself, he wrote, for such people would hurt themselves more than they would him. His greatest worry was making a living. He was hopeful his children would soon be able to take care of themselves. With the exception of Ivar and Eilev, who were practicing physicians in America, they were in Dresden with Drude, with whom Janson corresponded regularly. He had also taken over their full support.[40]

Some eleven months later, on December 28, 1895, Janson wrote again, acknowledging a letter he had received from Bjørnson while the latter was in Rome. In the meantime, he had published his pamphlet *Ægteskab og skilsmisse* (Marriage and Divorce) which included four lectures, tracing the history of marriage customs, advocating divorce when the partners wanted it, and favoring freedom to remarry. In this last, Janson had reversed himself. Years before in America, he had said that divorced persons should not be allowed to marry again, arguing that such a stipulation would keep people from contracting hasty marriages. In his letter Janson mentioned that he had sent Bjørnson the pamphlet and was eager to get his opinion of it. Although Janson noted that his family in Dresden was well and that his seventeen-year-old daughter Borghild had married, most of what he said concerned his efforts to eke out a living in Kristiania. He was the "shorn lamb," he wrote, ostracized by the "better people" of the city, and, as a result, was working among craftsmen and laborers. He still charged admission for his religious services, gave lectures interpreting the plays of Ibsen and Bjørnson, and—following his practice in America—delivered Sunday evening readings and held discussion meetings on Monday evenings.

Drude did not write Bjørnson until early in 1896. She was then living in Dresden with her four younger children. Although she now had been in Europe for more than three years, she had made no attempt to communicate with her old friend. From the circumstances that prompted this first letter, one gets a picture of a lonely, still-anguished woman, who felt somewhat unsure of her status with Bjørnson. One day she had a visit from young Peter Egge, who had said that he had just heard from Bjørnson and that the poet had instructed him that, if he saw Drude Janson, he should give her a kiss. For Drude receiving a message from Bjørnson was a sudden shaft of sunlight. She had not been so happy in a long time, she wrote. Often, in heavy and even terrified moments, she had longed to talk with Bjørnson, the one who always understood everything and had been a source of strength to her in the past. Yet perhaps the long silence between them had been for the best, she wrote, for, if the ordeals of life are to develop an individual, he must stand alone in his darkest hour. Her suffering had not crushed her; it had only destroyed the worst in her nature, and she hoped the new growth was better. She had learned to live for others rather than only for herself. She reported on her family, and then asked whether Bjørnson would do her the great service of having his publisher send her some of his works, for she was eager to have her children become familiar wtih them. In Dresden, they had only a few volumes, which she named, adding that Kristofer had kept most of his extensive library. That was her only reference to her husband.[41]

We do not have Bjørnson's responses to either Kristofer or Drude. Yet at this juncture—in answer to Drude's first letter—it is evident that he asked pointed questions about the Spanish skipper and in some measure expressed his awe at Kristofer's generosity.

Clearly apprehensive, Drude answered early in 1896: "You know *so* much—I must be permitted to say a bit more—not to lessen your admiration for Kristofer but to tell you a little about me and if possible have you understand a little better where I stood and where I stand. It is true the Spanish skipper came, but the conditions under which he came you do not know." As she described the situation, she had lived in so murky an atmosphere of seances and spiritualistic communications—phenomena that both attracted and repelled her—that she had lost all sense of reality, being in poor health at the time. At a moment when her resistance was completely broken down, "it happened," she wrote. Saying no more about her own affair, she went on to say it was just at that time that Louise Bentzen entered their home. "Can you imagine such a fateful conflict?" she wrote.

"O God, Bjørnson," Drude continued, "to this very day when I think of her, something stiffens within me. She is for all honorable people who know her—except Kristofer whom she has completely hypnotized—

a terror, a sphinx whom they can never fathom." Drude assured Bjørnson that she was not saying this to excuse herself, and she went on to relate that, when she saw how completely Janson was in the power of this young woman, she realized the enormity of her own wrongdoing. Then, she wrote, she did everything she could to make restitution, summoning all her energy to counteract Louise's influence, but she was struggling against a power she could not match. Of this crisis, Drude wrote, "I felt as if I could go into a primeval forest and never see the sun or know happiness again."

During this exchange, the Spanish skipper was never identified. Drude's letter drew a sympathetic response from Bjørnson; five days later, she wrote again, beginning, "Thanks, thanks—God bless you for believing in me—there is nothing on earth like having the trust of those one loves. When your letter came, I was happier than I have been in a long time." Drude gave a nightmarish account of her last year in America, one centering on Louise Bentzen's mesmeric power over Janson: "When she had obtained all, all power over him, and she realized I began to see through her, she in part cast off her mask before me and the children and we saw the animal claws protrude through the madonna guise she had assumed."

During that year, Drude continued, she had been saved from madness only through the comfort she derived from her sister and her friend, Valborg Hovind Stub. Louise, according to Drude, was wholly a creature of guile. "She was always the suffering martyr who fell ill with cramps and hemorrhage, frightening the life out of him [Janson] whenever a word had been said to her or about her to him; and at last he came to believe we had systematically set about to destroy him and he watched over her but otherwise heard nothing."

Up in Janson's study, Drude continued, seances were held in which spirits came to bless them, greeting the minister as a savior of mankind. The worst was the way in which Louise deluded Janson about the great roles he had played in other periods of history through reincarnations. While these sessions were going on, Drude and the children sat downstairs in terror. Drude had not attended any of these meetings, nor had she ever seen Louise in a trance, but on one occasion, Drude had secretly read entries in Janson's journal of seances, finding them, as she expressed it, "the most far-fetched absurdities one could imagine."

Yet Drude had thought that Kristofer might be saved if clear evidence was put before him that Louise was resorting to lies and intrigue.

The shock might kill him, Drude had reasoned, but even that was better than his being in the power of this malevolent woman. Getting the evidence was easy, for members of the congregation, grieved over the situation, agreed to confront Louise at a time when she would have no opportunity to prepare herself. Of the family, only Ivar was aware of Drude's plan. Everything went according to schedule. Drude had watched Kristofer, fearful of how he would be affected by the blow. He had smiled mildly, assuring the others that if Louise had said a thing was so, it must be true. The experiment had been a failure.

Finally Ivar had been successful in getting Louise to leave the house, Drude went on. At a time when Janson was not present, the young man threatened Louise that if she did not go willingly, he as a physician would have her committed to an institution for the insane. She went on March 8, 1893, according to Drude as "a persecuted martyr and heroine." Drude and her four younger children left for Norway on April 12. Yet in that month's interval, Drude wrote, they all breathed a little easier, even though Janson regarded his wife as his greatest enemy.

Under Louise's influence during that last year, Kristofer's nature had changed, Drude wrote. He became niggardly, and Drude had to use stealth to buy necessary articles of clothing for her family in preparation for the return to Norway. He seemed to have lost the power to reason logically and ignored everything that had happened in the recent past. He kept reminding his wife that at one time she had wanted her freedom and had liked Louise—and he constantly asked why Drude had changed.

In speaking of her correspondence with Kristofer just after he had returned to Norway, Drude explained to Bjørnson that relations between the two had been bitter, but that in recent letters he had been mild and friendly, more like his old self. Until recently he had sent them money earned from his lectures during his first winter in Norway. Later, however, he could make only enough to keep himself going, and Eilev had taken over the care of the family. He had a good practice, Drude wrote, and was a wonderful son and brother. By March, 1897, she noted, the divorce would be final and Janson would be free to marry Louise. She believed that he awaited the date with longing, but she and the family felt only anxiety and dread, hoping that some miracle would prevent the inevitable blow.

Drude warned that Bjørnson must not divulge that he had heard anything about Louise from her. That would only arouse the old bitterness again. When she had first arrived in Norway in the spring of 1893, she had thought of Bjørnson as the one person who might be able to open Janson's eyes. However, the poet had just left the country. When Drude later went to Berlin, Bjørnson was in Eisenach. To get there Drude needed three hundred marks which she did not have. "Had I *known* you could have saved him," she wrote, "I would have had to scrape up the money somehow—but he came to Norway—you went farther and farther south, and through letters you would not be able to reach him—it was as if fate drove the two of you farther and farther apart."[42]

In another letter, Drude dealt with the possibility that Bjørnson might "save" Janson. This message was written in February, and its subject matter is such that the year must have been 1896. She apologized for having written at such great length in her previous letter and for not having expressed herself more clearly. Bjørnson must not think she was trying to excuse her own conduct. Nor did she want him to believe that she was complaining about Kristofer; she was trying to make him realize how much he needed sympathy and help, for everything possible had been done to open his eyes. He had been hypnotized by Louise, Drude maintained, or had been sacrificed to some evil power that emanated from Louise. Above all, Bjørnson must not have any investigation of Louise undertaken. Sooner or later, news of it would reach Kristofer and cause his bitterness toward Drude and the family to flare up again. Especially was it important that he should never know that Bjørnson had obtained any information about Louise from Drude. What she had in mind was that Bjørnson would personally meet and converse with Louise, making his own judgment. Then through direct personal contact—by the sheer force of his personality—the poet might break Louise's spell over Janson. If that did not succeed, nothing would.[43]

Yet at the time—if one can judge from Janson's letter to Bjørnson—it seems that Janson's fortunes had risen a bit. He was still in Kristiania, from where he wrote in February, 1896, pleased that he was drawing appreciative audiences for his lectures. He had delivered four on successive Fridays, three of them on Bjørnson's *Over evne* (Beyond Our Powers) and the last on Bjørnson himself, one that had, among other things, recalled old days at Aulestad and Solbakken and had caused Janson a twinge in the process. The evening of his writing, he would begin on Bjørnson's *Kongen* (The King), and the following Sunday evening he would read *Sigurd Jorsalfar*. At the time, the king of Sweden and Norway had just taken up residence in Kristiania, Janson observed in a light-hearted vein, and thus it should be a very good time to read *Kongen* and proclaim republicanism. From his recent study of the play, he realized that something had previously escaped him—the extent to which Bjørnson had attacked the hypocrisy and humbug in the nation's institutions. To interpret the play properly for his audiences, he had to weigh every word, actually relive Bjørnson's own creative process; having done this, he felt he must thank Bjørnson for the drama, on his own and for the nation. He was moved by the author's courage and by his love of truth and of man, and proud to be one who fought for the same ideals, although it was true that the two were not in accord on religious matters. But as he finished his reading of the play, he would deliver a citation on Bjørnson, and this he included in his letter, saying that he did not want the poet to think he was "polemicizing behind his back."

The eulogy was long. Only at the end of his letter did Janson return to personal matters. Bjørnson had asked him whether he also had to support the woman he hoped to marry. By no means, Janson wrote. She was much too proud; she would starve before she would accept anything like that. Actually the situation was just about the opposite: it was she who had given him presents, to the point that he was almost ashamed. It had been she who had financed his trip the previous summer to Denmark, where they could be together for three delightful weeks at a place where Louise and the woman who employed her were guests. At Christmas Louise had sent him articles of clothing that he needed, garments she had sewed herself. Everything Janson could lay aside went to his family in Dresden, all of whom were well. In March there would be only one more year to go before his divorce was final. His work was proceeding; he was well and thankful.[44]

Two months later Drude was to write to Karoline Bjørnson, presumably in response to the latter's inquiries concerning Louise. This was not a subject Drude could deal with temperately. "She calls herself Louise Bentzen and comes from a wretched family among whom there is not *one*—so far as I know—who can speak the truth." According to the spirits, she has a more exalted name and is of better origin, and Kristofer believes that she is a swan descending to live among geese." Louise, Drude went on, was living in Copenhagen with a Fru Carstensen, who belonged to the Danish nobility and might even be a countess. Drude could describe the exterior of the house and knew its exact location, information she had obtained from her niece who had been in

Copenhagen the previous fall. Were the Bjørnsons to go there the first part of May, Louise would likely be there, but hardly later. Drude knew Kristofer was going to Denmark early in June, to be in the neighborhood of Vesterhavet, and there the two could meet. Kristofer would remain there all summer. Louise had arranged the whole thing, Drude wrote, and she had seemed to make friends all over Denmark, especially among wealthy people. Kristofer had been there the summer before, visiting at Tyen at a beautiful estate from where he had an opportunity to travel about. The mistress of the place where Louise lived had been known to say that Miss Bentzen was by no means a burden but an angel and that it was a blessing to have her in the house. "Yes, she is considered either an angel or a devil," Drude wrote, adding, "there seems to be no middle ground so far as she is concerned." Having written this, Drude again warned that the Bjørnsons must not in any way divulge that they had received any information from her. That would bring back all the old bitterness, she explained; it was so wonderful to have peace and not to shiver every time the mail came lest some new suffering lay in store for her.[45]

From his letter in the early fall of 1896, one finds that Janson had spent at least some of the summer in Denmark. He was writing Bjørnson from Kristiania, where he was concerned with the fortunes of Broderskabets Kirke. The Sundays had begun well, he wrote, with from 400 to 600 people present, but meetings on Tuesday and Friday were somewhat thinly attended. Yet, rather than being depressed, he seemed almost elated. For one thing, he had met Bjørnson in Copenhagen, a happy encounter after the two had not seen one another in some fourteen years. As guests at a social function, they could not, of course, indulge in any heart-to-heart talk, but their conversation had been long enough for the gracious Bjørnson to offer that, when he returned to Norway, he would deliver a lecture for the benefit of Broderskabets Kirke. This would be a prestigious thing for the congregation whom Janson described in language that awakens memories of early days in Minneapolis. "Our congregation," he wrote, "is mostly made up of humble people, who more often must be helped than asked to help. People with money feel themselves to be superior and cling to 'the establishment,' and the educated young adults are religiously indifferent and ignore my efforts—but they will one day come."

Bjørnson's lecture would also be a great financial help. While Janson had been in Denmark, the rent still had to be paid. The congregation had bought a piano—so necessary for meetings and social functions—on installments and had gone somewhat into debt. This would be hard to take care of in addition to their current expenses, but if Bjørnson would give them a lift, they should be able to clear 400 crowns—and Bjørnson would have the eternal gratitude of Broderskabets Kirke. "Let us know ahead when you will come and what you will speak on, so we can advertise," he suggested at the time. Janson was fifty-five years old, and he made passing reference to his white hair and beard, but his tone was confident. He was, he assured Bjørnson, one of the most fortunate of men, one of the Lord's blessed, and he would be wholly content were there not always about him so many who were unemployed and in need.[46]

5

Drude's hope that some miracle might finally save her marriage was not to be realized. The Jansons' divorce became final on March 24, 1897. Nine days later, on April 2, Kristofer Janson and Louise Bentzen were married.[47] That same year Drude published *Mira,* her thinly disguised autobiographical novel under the pseudonym Judith Keller.

Both Signe Janson Forchhammer and her brother Eilev were later to say that they wished the book had never been written. Drude's niece, Dina Behr Kolderup—who did not read the novel until the 1960s—thought the character Alf Winter to be a gross libel of Kristofer, and she wrote, "It made me boil!" Yet others—not so intimately involved and perhaps able to be more objective—have declared *Mira* to be the best of Drude's novels. Such a view is epitomized in Aschehoug's *Konversasjons leksikon*, in which *Mira* is said to be a moving and highly individualized work, valuable both as a picture of the times and as a human document.[48]

One readily understands the objections the Janson children might have to the book. In it the fortunes of Mira and Alf Winter are so similar to those of their parents that no one could miss the parallel. The fictional couple and their children live in two locations in Norway while Alf is a teacher, and then they move to a midwestern American city, where he is a minister. At first Alf finds among his parishioners arrogant and presumptuous people who had become wealthy, frequently as saloonkeepers. When they realize they cannot order Alf about, they drop out of his church and are replaced by persons of better character and manners, but they, too, are immigrants drawn from Norway's lowest classes, who can provide Mira with no companionship. Books and solitary walks become her only pleasures. She had resigned herself to a bleak existence until she meets a gifted young musician named Gerard. He is always in the throes of musical creativity, and he brings his ideas to Mira, saying that she is the only one from whom he can get understanding. For her part, Mira finds a new interest in life, but she is not blindly infatuated. She sees that he often does not finish a work because it is crowded out by a new flash of inspiration. She keeps these incomplete pieces of work and preserves them with the thought that he might return to them later. She realizes that he is indolent and has a taste for luxury, and that, if he is left to his own devices, he will be prodigal of his talent, but if he is rightly guided, he may turn out to be another Wagner. That is the role Mira envisions for herself, but at that point the young man is snatched away by a dowager, who is determined that he shall marry her niece and who has the power to carry out her intentions.

Alf Winter had met the young man and had also been impressed by him, so much so that for a time he stayed at home on evenings when Gerard called. Later, however, the lure of his occult studies had drawn Winter out to meetings where people told of their experiences with departed spirits and held seances. Mira had visited these gatherings on occasion but had been repelled by them. At one she had met Ernestine Helsing whom Alf greatly admired, saying that the young woman dedicated herself to errands of mercy—nursing the sick and comforting the dying. Just at the time the young musician is lost to Mira, Alf informs his wife that he knew Ernestine loved him and that he would like to have the young woman live in his home, where the children might benefit from her influence. He explains that he realizes his wife does not love him, and he hopes that at some later date he might marry Ernestine, but until such a plan can be worked out, he hopes Mira will accept the situation with good grace.

As the Winter household comes under the sinister domination of Ernestine Helsing, Mira and her children undergo experiences similar to those Drude had described in her letters to Bjørnson. She soon discovers that Ernestine is not the saintly person she is purported to be. When Miss Helsing realizes that Mira sees through her, she no longer pretends to goodness before the wife and children, and they see how evil a person she is. Mira discovers that Ernestine has an uncanny way of bringing out the worst in everyone she encounters. When Alf becomes fearful that she is being persecuted by his family in his absence, the devious young woman seems to enjoy heightening his anxieties, for she invariably falls sick just as he is about to return. Whenever he is home, nightly seances are held in his study, and these are attended by persons with strangely glistening eyes. While the seances are in session, Mira and the children sit below in the living room, where they hear hymn singing—and sometimes sounds that fill them with fright.

Alf's personality changes: he becomes niggardly, questioning Mira's every expenditure as if to insinuate that she is intent upon ruining him. All this Mira recognizes as the work of Ernestine. Deciding that her husband is too good to be the victim of this scheming woman, Mira waits for a chance to expose Ernestine before him. The opportunity comes. A Mrs. Hansen, a member of the congregation, is seriously ill. Ernestine immediately announces that she will keep a nightly vigil, and every evening departs to take up the watch, returning in the morning. One day she reports that the sick woman is greatly improved. As it happened, Mira meets Mr. Hansen on the street that same day, and on congratulating him on his wife's improvement, she finds that the lady has just died and that Ernestine Helsing has not been near her except for a visit at the onset of Mrs. Hansen's illness. This fact Mira reports to Alf, who retorts that if Ernestine had said that she had nursed the woman, she certainly must have done so. He adds that Hansen had chosen a poor way to repay a kindness.

Matters finally came to a climax when the Winters' oldest son sobs to his mother that he can no longer live under such conditions. The boy had previously threatened Ernestine, and while he had been unable to carry out his design, he had frightened her. The boy's weeping convinces Mira that she must act. She resolves to have a talk with Alf the next day. This results in the couple's separation.

Throughout the novel, Mira grieves that she has been the means of depriving her children of their home. The breakup of the marriage hardly seems much of a loss, for the heroine had rarely found it more than tolerable. Alf Winter is presented as a self-centered dreamer, so lacking in sensitivity that while the couple were engaged, he had sent Mira poems, not addressed to her, but to a previous love whom he had not been able to win for one reason or another. Early in their marriage, Mira had found herself harnessed with full responsibility for the management of the home and the care of the children. Whenever Alf had free time from his teaching duties, he was off traveling, departing as the birches began to bud and not returning until the snow lay on mountain ridges. Yet in those days, his wife had the stimulating company of the school community. Her intellectual awakening had taken place shortly after the birth of her first child, not because of her husband but under the tutelage of another teacher whose lectures she had attended.

It was this friend who had told Mira that she reminded him of a bird which does not know its own power before it has tried its wings. He was fearful that the monotony of everyday life would clip Mira's wings. Secretly she vowed that this would never happen. She is described as an impulsive, strong-willed woman, intent on living life to the fullest. To her love of nature, books, art and music had been added a curiosity about the outside world, and, for that reason, she had been willing and eager to go to America where Alf was to take up his ministry. Yet, at this point, the heroine confesses that she has violated the great law of the universe: she was living for herself rather than for others, an offense always punished until the lest vestige of selfishness is burned out. She admits that, although she had been scrupulous in caring for the physical needs of her children, she has made no effort to share their secret thoughts and aspirations.

Drude gave her novel the sub-title "A Life Story." It is a little work of only 170 pages, with the narrative completed twenty pages before the end of the book. Most readers are likely to skim this last section, finding it heavily moralistic. It is an account of a dream that Mira has after she has undergone her sufferings. Like the rest of the novel, this part reflects the author's theosophical leanings. With some fervor, she has declared that thoughts have creative energy, going on to explain that it had been the power of thought that had called the young musician into her life. In the dream, Mira finds herself guided by a mysterious old woman who announces that she has been drawn to Mira's side by her thought. In the course of the dream, Mira finds that reincarnation on this earth may be necessary before one's spirit is worthy of existence on a higher plane.

In the dream, Mira journeys over Europe and America by means of astral projection, a phenomenon ordinarily described in occult literature as the state of a living person who temporarily leaves his body while his spirit moves to some distant spot. The old woman is intent on pointing out to Mira man's inhumanity to man, and much of what she sees reminds us of the social ills Janson had preached and written against during his tenure at Nazareth Church. Thus Mira views acres of land lying fallow, the property of speculators, while homeless people search for a place to settle. She views the miserable living conditions of underpaid coal miners and later the luxuries of the marble palace where the mine owner lives. She sees persons in chilly attics and damp basements, and observes red-eyed women huddled over their sewing as their children cry for food. Soon she sees the bier of the coal mine owner and is able to follow his spirit into the misty land of the hereafter, to discover that it was this earth at a future time, a world in which the hostility between classes has become so great that it erupts into cataclysmic bloodshed, causing Mira to cry out. Suddenly the scene changes and Mira sees a field of white and red flowers, the latter signifying martyrs who had given their lives for the truth. The old woman explains that from them a new race would come to inhabit the earth, but only after it had been visited by flood, earthquake, pestilence, and fire. All things in the universe are related: evil in individual lives creates disharmony in nature. After describing this series of visions, Mira says that, although this was all a dream, she feels that she has had a glimpse into eternity.

As the book closes, Mira and her children are comrades without any secrets from one another. For them the past—even the scheming of Ernestine—has left no scar, and Mira feels rich in their love.[49]

One can only regret the bitterness that produced this book, for, in spite of its confessional tone, one senses that the portraits of Ernestine and Alf Winter spring from a deep hurt. Drude did not get much from her eleven years in America: for most of the time she had shared Janson's trials—from blown-down churches, the onslaughts of Sven Oftedal, and all the bazaars and other entertainments necessary to raise the walls of Nazareth Church. She had dreaded the harsh winters, knowing that every year would bring its quota of illness. Worst of all, she was lonely. Mrs. Kolderup has suggested that Drude's friendship with Valborg Hovind Stub resulted because both found themselves in an uncongenial environment. It is a bleak existence when one cannot find the company one enjoys, no matter how many worthies may be present.

12

The Verdict
of the Years

FOR SOME fifteen years after Janson's departure, Nazareth Church clung to a precarious existence, sustained by "hardly more than a score of earnest but rather poor men." This information comes from a brief piece of writing attributed to Johannes J. Skørdalsvold, which was found among the papers of Georg J. M. Walen, who at his death in 1948 had been the minister of Nora Church for sixteen years. The manuscript, a scant two pages, is partly typewritten and partly in Walen's handwriting. Two paragraphs were taken out of their original order and placed at the end. The article is entitled "The Free Christian Church of Minneapolis," with the words "By Skørdalsvold" directly under the title. Since many of the details given can be verified by data obtained from other sources, it seems a fair guess that the statement gives a reliable resumé of the history of Nazareth Church.

According to this account, Janson had not been gone long before trouble over Spiritualism was brewing in the congregation. On four evenings during the late winter of 1894—February 8, 15, 22, and March 3—the president of the congregation, together with selected members of the church, held seances in the basement of the building, ordering the janitor to keep everything secret. When the matter nevertheless became known, the congregation called a meeting for April 3 and, in the words of the manuscript, passed "a mild resolution of censure against the spiritists and their behavior." The writer goes on to say that the vote was 39 to 34, adding that this showed that the congregation was practically split in half. A month later, "the medium, Miss Louise Benson, and about 40 other members withdrew from the congregation."

327

These events were also reported in *Evangelisk Luthersk Kirketidende*. In an early spring issue, this organ of the Norwegian Synod told of dissension within Nazareth congregation, saying that O. Tandberg, the president, was a Spiritualist and that he and a group had held seances in the church, but that Amandus Norman was not a Spiritualist, and that it was likely that the congregtion would soon divide. In a May issue the paper printed the laconic statement: "Kristofer Janson's so-called congregation has split."[1]

"The Free Christian Church in Minneapolis" is not a polished piece of writing, and it is possible that it is an early draft or simply notes that Walen made from an original. In its present form, one finds the sources of the material added parenthetically as "Tidende" or "Christian Register." On occasion, the text is interrupted by such avuncular comments as "the most reliable information on any organization is looked for in the minutes of its meetings." Although it does not always seem that the writer was in possession of this church record, from time to time he produces figures. "On September 25, 1892," he wrote, "it was reported that 40 out of 192 members had paid their dues." In 1896 he said that the congregation had 64 members in good standing. It seems that through the years the total had fluctuated, but that there had always been a core of about 20 staunch supporters who could be depended upon.

One can feel for those twenty who bore the burden in the days after Janson had gone. "More than once," the author of the manuscript wrote, "the outlook seemed to get brighter but in a few months the work sank down to deadening drudgery." He tells that in 1900 the church in Minneapolis was remodeled to permit the minister and his family to live in the rear of the building, and then reports that six years later, on June 26, 1906, it was sold to a Jewish congregation for $8,000. Of this sum, $6,000 was turned over to the American Unitarian Association, which kept it as a special fund.. Later the interest on the money was used to finance a quarterly published by the Nora Free Christian Church. After the sale of the church building, the congregation rented small halls for meetings. The last pastor was H. A. Sather, who resigned on April 30, 1908.

"In a few years," the manuscript concludes, "the itemized business of the church was carefully settled. The church has not formally disbanded, but it has held no meetings for about 20 years and the understanding is that it is dead. The majority of members have joined the First Unitarian Society of Minneapolis."

The two paragraphs, earlier referred to as having been moved, appear on the second page of the manuscript. The first deals with the Spiritualist movement in the church and Janson's commitment to it. The second claims that the collapse of the congregation could be traced to Janson's divorce and his remarriage:

"A minority party stultifies its very life by moral delinquence. The great leader of the Norwegian Unitarians in America left his wife in America and married his former private secretary after his return to Norway.

"This was the load that finally smothered the Free Christian Church of Minneapolis, and it is a credit to the Norwegian Lutherans of America that they frowned upon this kind of an affair."[2]

These lines must have been written in 1928 or later. The last sentence seems to illustrate Skørdalsvold's forthrightness, a characteristic that won him the respect and trust of orthodox and liberals alike. All his life he kept the letter he had received from Kristofer Janson when he had decided to join Nazareth Church, and he remained a Unitarian for the rest of his days. Yet it was his conviction that the scandal following in Janson's wake had damaged the congregation. Nor was he the only one to believe this. Accounts of Janson's years in America written in this country commonly ended on a note of censure. In 1915, Rasmus B. Anderson, writing in his *Life Story* of his association with Janson, said: "But to this picture there is still a darker side. A woman who was a fanatical spiritualist, a Miss Benson, invaded the Janson home and his family was broken up. Without going into further details I may add that Kristofer Janson and his wife, with whom he for so many years lived an ideal life, were separated and Janson afterwards married Miss Benson."[3] O. N. Nelson, in his *History of Scandinavians and Successful Scandinavians in the United States,* was blunt in his dismissal of Janson: "With all his brilliancy, however, Janson did not seem to be well balanced. He became a Spiritualist, returned to Norway in 1894, was divorced, and married a medium."[4]

Janson left the ministry in 1898. For the rest of his working days, he was a lecturer for the Labor Academy in Norway. In his autobiography, he has said that members of his Kristiania church—like his Minneapolis congregation at first—had been willing to follow him as long as he attacked old institutions, but that they shrank back when he turned to constructive work. In his memoirs, Janson has chosen to omit all mention of his domestic difficulties, but from the little he says of his church in Kristiania, one concludes that the brave optimism

329

of his letters to Bjørnson about winning back people's confidence was never justified. Hamsun was probably right in saying that Janson loved human beings better than he understood them. Yet on one matter he seems to have made no mistake: that was in his choice of Amandus Norman as his successor in America.[5]

Although little is known of Norman's first years as minister at Nazareth Church, they could not have been other than a trial. One might wonder how he got along with Louise Bentzen. Except for the September, 1893, issue of *Saamanden*, in which his ordination and his taking part in the farewell reception for Janson are reported, he is never mentioned. Under Louise's editorship, the monthly became quite detached from the church, and while news items were included, they were never drawn from local sources.

Norman remained at Nazareth Church until 1896. At that time, he left the ministry for a short while to edit various Norwegian-language periodicals in North Dakota. Herman Haugerud succeeded him as leader of the Minneapolis church. This minister had broader experience than Norman, but like him he was an alumnus of Meadville with graduate work at Harvard. In 1898, Broderskabets Kirke in Kristiania called Haugerud to succeed Janson, and it was then that Norman returned to Nazareth to remain there until 1906, the year the building was sold.

In spite of this inauspicious beginning, Norman was to have a rewarding career in the Unitarian ministry. He had none of the platform brilliance of Janson and thus had not been able to give the Minneapolis church the drawing card it needed to keep its pews filled. But—as his friends have said—his sermons, if quietly delivered, were carefully worked out and rich in content.[6] During their years at Nazareth, the Normans, like the Jansons before them, spent their summers in Brown County, where the congregation was as stable as Nazareth was the opposite. In 1906, as Nora Congregation prepared to commemorate the twenty-fifth anniversary of its founding, the church leaders decided that the time had come to have a full-time minister. Their choice fell on Amandus Norman. To prepare for his coming, a spacious two-story house was built on the site of the little red cottage that had been occupied by the Jansons. During the years since the church had been founded, changes had taken place in the community. The Blessom farm, about a mile from the church, had been subdivided into lots to form the village of Hanska. In 1906 it had a population of seventy-five.

A friendly, outgoing man, Amandus Norman, like Janson before him, believed that a church and its minister must be actively concerned with the welfare of the community. The village had no library, but Nora Church had one and made its books available to the public. Under his guidance, the congregation erected a building in Hanska, which they called the Liberal Union and which all other groups in town, religious or secular, might use for meetings. He arranged that the community be on the itinerary of the University of Minnesota extension program for its winter series of lectures and concerts. On occasion, when groups of Norwegian immigrants appeared in Brown County, he conducted classes in English even though it was very rare that one of the newcomers showed any interest in Norman's Unitarian faith.

Apparently Norman could do nothing to keep the church at Hudson, Wisconsin, alive, but from time to time he visited Underwood. Dr. Charles H. Lyttle, in his history of Unitarianism in the West, has credited the survival of the Underwood congregation to Norman.[7] From 1914 until his death in 1931, Norman put out a quarterly, *Mere Lys,* which circulated in the United States, Canada, and Norway. Although others contributed, most of the articles were written by the editor. Not all were religious in character. At one time he ran a series called "Astronomy for Everyone," and during World War I he wrote detailed reports on the military movements of each of the warring nations. His discussions of religion tended to be speculative and were rich in allusions to Plato, Aristotle, St. Augustine, Herder, Lessing, Fichte, Pascal, Renan, John Fiske, and many more. The quarterly did not have the diversity of *Saamanden* but it had news items and an occasional letter from a subscriber and, all in all, it was interesting reading.

Once *Mere Lys* printed the greetings of Norman as representative of Det Nordisk Unitariske Forbund i Amerika (The Nordic Unitarian Association in America). Whether this organization included more congregations than those at Hanska and Underwood is not certain, but Norman's use of the word "Nordisk" suggests that there might have been other Scandinavian societies. Be that as it may, he also worked hard to strengthen his church's American ties. This was not a difficult thing to do, for Nora Congregation had had a strong bond with New England Unitarians ever since the tornado of 1883.[8] In 1908, when Nora Church was host to the Minnesota State Unitarian Conference, Norman and Dr. Frederick May Eliot organized the Minnesota Conference of Unitarian Young People. For the following fifteen years, this group, numbering about a hundred, met on Mt. Pisquah in three-

331

to five-day sessions, during which they were addressed by speakers from all parts of the United States and Canada. The young people lived in tents pitched on the church grounds and were fed in the Kaffe Stova (Coffee House) by the women of the congregation. In 1920 Meadville conferred the degree of doctor of divinity upon Amandus Norman. Dr. Eliot, later president of the American Unitarian Association, has said that the award met with acclaim from Unitarians across the nation.[9]

Nora Church retained affectionate ties with Kristofer Janson so long as he lived. In his autobiography, published in 1913, Janson said that this church had been his favorite, although in his letter of 1894—announcing his decision not to return to America—he had spoken of Nazareth Church as the one he would especially miss. However, by the time he came to write the story of his life, the Nazareth Church building had been sold and its members had scattered, and he might have reflected that the little congregation in Hanska, which never at any time posed a problem, was more to be valued than the spectacular one in Minneapolis, which always needed bolstering up.

Norman and Janson seem to have kept up some kind of correspondence, although it is not known how often they exchanged letters. In his first issue of *Mere Lys,* Norman reported that Janson, on hearing of his successor's forthcoming quarterly, recalled his own experiences with *Saamanden.* As if to give his old pupil his blessing, Janson wrote that, although *Saamanden* had meant hours of translating articles and correcting the spelling and syntax of letters from readers, it had been a labor of love.

2

As chance would have it, the last person in America to hear from Janson was his old friend and Brown County parishioner, Anton O. Ouren. He had written in response to a letter from Ouren which had followed a circuitous route before it finally reached him in Denmark in the spring of 1917, a few months before his death. The fall before, the Jansons—Kristofer, Louise, and Dag, their thirteen-year-old son who was severely retarded—had moved to Sønder Jernløse in Denmark at the urging of Janson's friend, Dr. Frederik Sandby, who had an addition built to his home in order to provide the Jansons with an apartment.

Janson's letter was in every way worthy of the "poet-preacher," as the Americans had liked to call him. As far as his own affairs were concerned, he had nothing but misfortune to report, but he was still so gallant and drolly whimsical that it is clear that—in spite of illness, bereavement, and financial difficulties—he had been spared the final indignity of a warped and altered personality.

"Old age—hm," Janson wrote wryly. He could not hope to return so interesting and newsy a letter as he had received. As Ouren would notice at once, his handwriting had become hardly more than a scrawl. His eyesight was failing, probably Janson thought, because of the diabetes from which he had suffered for several years. He could no longer read and must depend upon others for every letter and newspaper article. His walk had become a shuffle, and at seventy-six he was a far cry from the healthy specimen he had once been. He found it hard to concentrate, and he was so forgetful that there were times when it was as much as he could do to remember his own name.

Under such circumstances, it had been impossible for him to earn money lecturing. Since they could no longer afford to live in Norway, they had moved with all their possessions to Denmark. Hardly had they arrived when their beloved child Dag died. This had been so great a blow to his wife that she had been bedridden ever since with great emotional and physical suffering. However, she was beginning to sit up for a few hours each day, and she had, on occasion, taken a few steps; so it looked as if she would survive, but Janson thought her health would never be wholly restored.

He knew that Ouren was interested in the rest of his famliy. Ivar and Eilev were physicians in Seattle. They were fine boys and had helped both him and Drude. Indeed, all his sons and daughters were especially generous and good to one another. He spoke of their marriages and then reported that Drude and Ingeborg were in Kristiania, sharing the city's war-time misery; thus far, however, they had neither frozen nor starved.[10]

Janson died in Sønder Jernløse on November 17, 1917. Memorial services were held in Nora Church, and in Minneapolis Oslo Lodge, No. 2, Sons of Norway, gave a program dedicated to Janson with reminiscences of his many activities ranging from his lecture tour of 1879-80 to his later years as a resident of the city. Soloists sang several of his songs. Johannes Skørdalsvold spoke of Janson's steadfastness in holding to what he thought was right; Halvard Askeland recalled that he had delighted students at Augsburg Seminary during his lecture series. Lauritz Stavnheim, the principal speaker, in an address entitled "Janson som saamand" (Janson as a Sower), likened him to Wergeland, who had been persecuted in his day by the powers that be but who had come to be appreciated by later generations. Whatever one might think of Janson's views in respect to one thing or another, Stavnheim said, there was one fact that all good and honorable people must agree on: Janson was a noble person who sought to promote all that was fine and virtuous.[11]

Amandus Norman has said that he received letters from persons in various parts of the country urging that a subscription be started for funds to raise a monument in honor of Janson. It is not known who all of these people were, but on two occasions their letters appeared in print. One was from Siver Hage of Madelia, Minnesota, who wanted the monument to be erected on Mt. Pisquah, and he offered a hundred dollars as a beginning toward the subscription. The other came from Julius B. Baumann of Carlton County. He wrote to *Sønner av Norge,* the Sons of Norway monthly, after he had read of the memorial program given by Oslo Lodge. He suggested that the society might spearhead such a drive, saying that some years before it had erected a memorial to an orthodox minister whose services to the Norwegian-American community was not restricted to those who accepted the dogma of his church.[12]

For this purpose, Norman appointed a committee headed by Tor O. Dahl, a Minneapolis alderman, with Lauritz Stavnheim as secretary. However, as the group assessed the matter, they decided that the times were not favorable for such a project. The First World War was then going on, and people were besieged on all sides for money for this and that cause related to the conflict. The project was therefore postponed, and it never seems to have been activated again.[13]

The April-July, 1918, issue of *Mere Lys* turned out to be the most significant memorial to Janson produced in this country. Containing sixty-four pages, it was larger than most editions of the quarterly, with tributes to Janson in both prose and verse interspersed with his poems and his sketch "Blaaveisen" (The Anemone). Included were Norman's sermon, "Kjærnen i Jansons lære" (The Kernel in Janson's Teachings), Stavnheim's "Janson som saamand," "Ved Kristofer Jansons barre" (At Kristofer Janson's Bier), an account of Janson's funeral excerpted from the Danish *Protestantisk Tidende. Mere Lys* also traced the friendship between Janson and Norman by including the former's letters to Norman from January, 1885, to July, 1893. Only those written in 1893 had deletions.

Scandia, a Chicago publication, carried laudatory editorials about Janson and a number of articles by A. Grinager, one of the charter members of Nazareth Church. "Smaatrak fra Kristofer Jansons virk-somhed i Minneapolis" (Sketches from Janson's Days in Minneapolis) was the general title of the series. Some of Grinager's comments on the nature of Janson's congregation have been quoted before. Most of his pieces deal with the minister's kindliness and compassion. One told of Janson's officiating at a child's funeral on a Sunday. His Sundays were always crowded, for he had services in St. Paul late in the after-noon and then had to get back to Minneapolis for his evening reading. The funeral was to take place in the home of the bereaved parents early in the afternoon. Janson had brought a sandwich to eat after his regular morning service, and then he had proceeded to the house. The child had been stricken with what people thought was a strange malady, and they were fearful of contagion. When the appointed hour passed and only the parents and the child's aunt were present, the father finally said that they might as well begin. As was his custom, Janson had a carefully prepared address. This he delivered in full, speaking to the three people in attendance—so the grateful father told Grinager—as if he had a whole congregation before him.[14]

In another sketch, Grinager gave a dramatic account of a seance he had once attended with Janson. The medium was in a trance and in the course of the evening transmitted widely different voices from the dead. One was that of a woman with a command of excellent Swed-ish, who identified herself as a poisoner, who ultimately had been executed. Another, a man's voice, was coarse and rough; the presum-able possessor said that he had been a sailor who had died of alcoholism. He volunteered the information that he was miserable in his present state. "You must pray to God to help you," Janson is reported to have said, whereupon the voice retorted that that was more in Janson's line, and asked why didn't he do it. The minister then did pray so earnestly that all were moved. Grinager ended his piece by saying that, for all he knew, the medium might have been a fraud and the different voices trickery, but of one thing he was certain: Janson's was genuine.[15]

In the summer of 1931—almost fourteen years after Janson's death—another plan to memorialize him was briefly fanned into being. Nora Church commemorated its fiftieth anniversary. The event drew some 600 people; delegations came from Minneapolis, Underwood, Hudson, and other places, including Boston. In the tradition of Nora Church, it was a day-long festival, beginning with a service followed by dinner served in the Kaffe Stova, which required many sittings until all could be fed. In the afternoon, Amandus Norman read a paper entitled, "Kristofer Janson: As Man, Poet, and Religious Reformer." Not all the speaker's details concerning Janson's initiation into the Unitarian ministry were accurate. But this is understandable because they were not readily available. Janson himself had never spelled out this period of his life with any precision. What made Norman's address heartwarming were the scenes which his own memory produced. The address was a testimony of his devotion to Janson, as he readily admitted, saying: "Of course you may expect me to accompany the portrait of my predecessor and my best beloved teacher with all the sympathy I possess."

Norman had been very young when he had first caught a glimpse of Kristofer Janson. As a child he had once visited Vonheim Folk School in the company of an older brother. At that time, the school was at its best, Norman said; he went on to tell how he had sat on one of the back benches, weeping from excitement. What he saw and heard that day, in his words, "cast a spell" over him that lasted all his life. As he eulogized Janson, his voice rang with deep emotion: "Let us take a look in while the school is in session. The hall is filled with people, pupils, young men and women, farmers from the valley below, and strangers who paused for a day or two in order that they might hear and see what was going on at this *wonder-school* among the mountains. The door opens quietly, and Kristofer Bruun enters—a strange, slender, outlandish-looking figure of small stature, a great man, a dreamer of apocalyptic dreams, an Elijah among the mountains. With the prophet's dark hair falling in heavy curly waves down over his shoulders, this man who would tell the truth as he saw it, with utter impartiality, to pope, emperor, king or street gamin, was the prototype of the hero in Ibsen's great drama 'Brand.' He walks in quietly and sits down on a bench in a corner of the hall. Then Bjørstjerne Bjørnson enters, a man of gigantic frame, deep pentrating eyes, heavy eye-brows, finely chiseled nose, massive head crowned with a forest of coarse hair brushed back. He tears off his eye-glasses, wipes them in order that he may find his way among all these chairs and benches, and strides majestically through the hall, giving his right hand to one friend and the left to another until he comes to his chair in front.

"Again the door opens and Kristofer Janson rushes in—tall, rather slender, erect, athletic, large head covered with a mass of chestnut hair combed back, noble radiant face, smiling confident as a happy boy, saluting right and left; and I even thought he nodded approvingly to the observant little country urchin sitting with glistening eyes beside an elder brother, on one of the benches in a rear corner of the hall. When after more than half a century I try to visualize that assembly

336

of mighty farmers—many of whom were able to trace their lineage to worthy and valiant forebears of five hundred or even a thousand years ago, those noble, intelligent, shining faces, those steady, attentive eyes—then I feel like emphasizing that vague impression that I found myself in the presence of something potentially great and mighty—men and women whose mental bells had been set a-swinging, teachable pupils of their great masters; a group destined to lead in a great national awakening, to become one of the most consistently persistent advance guards of the New Freedom; one of the most vital and fruitful factors working for the advancement of orderly democracy, purposeful education.

"The school was really a mission station of that purposeful education in the central part of rural Norway, and there was present among these people a love of vital knowledge that perhaps made it unique in its time. There Kristofer Brunn lectured on—perhaps it was 'Abraham's Departure from His Sumerian Home' or 'The Wise Men from the East' or 'Barkakha the Son of the Sun'—while Janson relieved the effect of his ponderous Spartan eloquence with a couple of bright chapters from the book he was then writing. Then Bjørnson arose and began, 'Mr. Bruun, I cannot agree with you in what you said about those Eastern stories. . . .' Discussion followed, not only between these giants, but one after another the farmers arose in the hall and asked leave to speak. I repeat it: If one had been fortunate enough to be present at such a meeting at Vonheim or at its sister school Sagatun—a short distance from my old home—it was an experience never to be forgotten."[16]

In preparation for the address, Norman had reread the whole of Janson's work. His judgment of his friend was generally in accord with that of other critics: Janson was best as a lyric poet and writer of narratives. Norman conceded that Janson had not developed as an author, saying that he was more interested in working for the improvement of mankind than in writing books esthetically pleasing to critics. As Norman drew to a close he dwelt on Janson the preacher: "I loved Kristofer Janson for his great optimistic power and the hearty cheerfulness that characterized all he said and all he did. As the questions of his time appeared, he wove them into his program: the labor question, the cause of temperance, the cause of peace, women's suffrage and, above all, the cause of civilized religion everywhere at all times. In contradistinction to the poet Vinje who called him a priest in the church militant of Norway, I would term him a minister in the struggling

337

church of the Twentieth Century, where it is less the true faith than the upright life which saves men."[17]

In the audience there were many who had known Janson. Like Norman, they were in their sixties or older. That day, after Norman had finished speaking, the hope was revived of a suitable memorial for Janson. Spontaneously—so the *Christian Register* reported—a plan came into being to raise $25,000 for a Kristofer Janson Foundation, the money to be used to further liberal religion in the Northwest. Serving on the committee were J. C. Huseby, T. O. Dahl, N. J. Jensen, H. Pedersen, Louis Blegen, and Lauritz Stavnheim, with Amandus Norman as chairman. Norman's death a few months later, on November 14, 1931, may explain why the plan was never brought to fruition.[18]

3

Janson spent eleven years and seven months in the United States. Accounts dealing with his residence in this country conclude that his influence was slight. It is true that the number of professed Unitarians he left behind him was relatively small. Yet even in this respect he left his mark. After almost a hundred years, the Nora Free Christian Church flourishes, with its present membership the highest in its history. It still serves its immediate community, and its monthly church paper, *More Light,* is liberally sprinkled with such names as Becken, Haugan, Kjolstad, Korslund, Ouren, and Shelley (Sjele). It is the only Unitarian church in Brown County, and it draws members from New Ulm, Mankato, St. James, Odin, Madelia, and even more distant points. Undoubtedly it owes its longevity to many factors. Whatever the crisis, the congregation has always had its own able leaders. Amandus Norman's ministry was three times the length of Janson's. Nevertheless, it would never have been a Unitarian congregation had not Kristofer Janson met with its members on January 10, 1882, and, as he has said, "openly and honorably" told them where he stood.

Today "the hill' provides as impressive a view as it did in the days of the Jansons, or, for that matter, in the time of the Jesuit missionaries who preceded him by several hundred years. Below, on one side, are two adjoining lakes and on the other the prosperous farmland that has been carved out of the western prairie. As one might expect, many changes have taken place on the hill itself. The burial ground, long since incorporated into the Mt. Pisquah Cemetery Association, contains headstones going back to Janson's time, but, of course, there are many more—among them those marking the graves of two of its ministers, Amandus Norman and Georg Walen.

The cemetery lies behind the church, which, on the outside, appears to look much as it did in Janson's time. An annex, however, has been added, a place which houses the telescope that Norman bought in 1885 before he made his decision to follow Kristofer Janson into the Unitarian ministry. A few feet below the church and slightly to the south is the Jorgensen Museum, built from logs that formed the pioneer home of Ole Jorgensen, a charter member, who gave the address at the dedication of the parsonage in 1906. Originally the Kaffe Stova (the *landsmaal* name of the dining hall) was thirty feet to the north of the church, but since the erection of the commodious Fellowship Hall in 1964, the three buildings are connected.

About a hundred feet down the slope stands the parsonage, which, in keeping with stately houses of its period, has a rounded turret on the side. In this part, downstairs, is the minister's study, the decor of which suggests the history of Nora Church as it is usually presented. Along one wall are large photographs of Henrik Ibsen, Bjørnstjerne Bjørnson, Kristofer Janson, and Amandus Norman. Nearby on a bookcase is a bust of Ralph Waldo Emerson and across the room another of Theodore Parker. Commemorative booklets published by the congregation provide all this with a rationale, beginning with the social changes taking place in Norway during the 1870s and going on to describe how the Norwegian *banebryterer* (those who break down barriers) came to be linked with the New England Transcendentalists.

Through the years Nora Church and its adjoining buildings have been kept in excellent condition, and they have attracted visitors. In contrast, the structure that had been Nazareth Church stood neglected long after the Jewish congregation had ceased to use it. With its windows boarded up, its steps cluttered with dead leaves and other debris, the dingy red brick shell stood for many years securely on its high basement walls of stone, ironically impervious to high winds and storms. In length it covered most of the 150-foot lot on Twelfth Avenue South and Ninth Street, and it towered above neighboring houses, also much the worse for wear with flaking paint, sagging porches, and grassless front lawns. Then in the mid-1960s—as part of an urban renewal project—bulldozers moved in, razing the area. A high-rise apartment house for senior citizens has been erected where Nazareth Church once stood.

The Minneapolis building had been erected in a very short time.

339

When one recalls that Janson came to the city in December, 1881, to be missionary to the Scandinavians of the Northwest—most of whom did not know what a Unitarian was—and that before two years had passed his congregation had bought a lot at Twelfth Avenue South and Ninth Street, one sees that the man had not spared himself. In another two years, by November, 1885, the basement of the church had been dedicated, and shortly thereafter the edifice had been named Nazareth Church. By the following spring, the walls were up and the steeple in place, and, had it not been for the high winds on the night of April 14, 1886, the main sanctuary might have been finished that summer. The delay meant that it was not dedicated until September, 1889, allowing Janson only four years in his completed church before he left in 1893. One can understand his feelings when he announced his decision not to return to America. It was painful, he wrote, to part with friends and from his congregations—"especially from Nazareth Church where I have put in so much of my best work."

One might speculate on why Janson built such a large church, except that he always seemed to be in need of space to accommodate crowds. Throughout the years of his ministry, the newspapers told of people standing in the aisles, of halls crowded to the threshold, of late-comers turned away. Even in very large auditoriums, he could be easily heard, and one reason seems to be that his audiences sat in rapt attention, carried away not only by his vivid images and poetic diction but by the personality of the man and their trust in his goodness. Perceptive critics such as Hamsun, Cavling, and Gundersen might have some reservations about Janson's theology, but none concerning his character. It was Janson's surrender of that reputation that ruined his career in America and very likely cost him his vocation as a minister.

There is irony in the fact that Janson's defeat did not come from the Lutheran hegemony, which he challenged, but from the one person who had previously contributed so much to his success. There can be little doubt that Drude wrought much mischief, but in passing one must spare her a sympathetic thought, remembering that she had something to endure. Here we are not speaking of her appearance in tableaux and theatricals, her taking over the pulpit and managing a big household. She was gifted and strong-willed and presumably accustomed to admiration from girlhood. To her, Minneapolis was the last outpost of civilization, where she must waste her youth while Janson, with his great charisma, basked in the adoration of the public.

She was never to marry again. The fact that she became an object of pity as a wife rejected in favor of a younger woman must have been galling to one so proud and imperious as she. In the course of time, she and Janson came to be on friendly terms, but, according to members of the family, she was always somewhat reserved with Louise when the two occasionally met at family gatherings.

During Janson's years in America, it is likely that more people heard him than any other Norwegian minister. If the number who strayed from their original Lutheran faith remained small, this did not keep them from attending Janson's services and other programs. In addition to those who made their homes in Minneapolis, there were the many for whom the city was only a temporary stopping place before they made their way to rural Minnesota, Iowa, or the Dakotas. They often had memories of Janson, the *maalstræver* (champion of *landsmaal*) or had read his peasant tales and felt that they must not fail to hear him while they were in the city. In addition, Janson made lecture tours through the Midwest virtually every year, speaking in small towns to those who thronged in from the surrounding countryside.

He was proud of his ability to attract large audiences; his letters to Rasmus B. Anderson and to his Unitarian superiors are filled with reports of the large numbers in attendance. Possibly he was messianic, a man with an exalted ego who presumed that he spoke from God's point of view. At intervals through the years, various persons said or implied as much. In 1883, Pastor Th. Ylvisaker infuriated Janson when, in the course of a newspaper feud, rapidly growing more acrimonious, he declared that Janson's followers did not belong to Christendom but to Kristoferdom. Oscar Gundersen found in Janson's hymns that he and God operated too much hand in glove, but he said that one forgot Janson's egotism as soon as the man began to speak. Even Bjørnson castigated Janson as a "hallelujah girl"—so Drude has related—when he found out that, while Janson's congregations were increasing, his wife was taking in boarders. Drude had thought the poet's rebuke just, confiding to Bjørnson that Janson cared about nothing else so long as large audiences eagerly awaited him. Janson's colleague, Axel Lundeberg—before he became estranged over Janson's Spiritualism—complained that one never heard of Nazareth Church but always of Kristofer Janson; he went on to say that the minister was everything, the congregation nothing.

The romantic, filled with his inner vision, is generally known to be self-intoxicated. If this were true of Janson, one must add that the record reveals not the slightest hint of demagoguery. Instead, one reads of his gratuities to those who came to him asking for aid, of his efforts to reclaim drunkards and to get help for debt-ridden farmers. Some of

341

his contemporaries developed reputations for always pleading for money—notably Janson's adversary, Sven Oftedal—but such a charge never touched Janson. It is true that he appealed to the American Unitarians, especially when tornadoes destroyed his churches, and, in the case or Nora Church, that he received help beyond all expectations. However when Nazareth Church was blown down three years later, Janson did not fare so well. With the exception of his first plea for help, his requests for money were likely to be whimsical rather than emotional, and while they may have provided readers of *Unity* and the *Christian Register* with amusing reading, they do not seem to have brought in much cash. For that, Janson had been forced to undertake a lecture tour in the East.

At the time Janson began his ministry, American orthodoxy was being challenged, a conflict that brought on heresy trials, dismissals, and the like. Janson gave the Norwegian Lutherans in this country their first serious confrontation with liberalism. During his early years in this country, the various synods had been feuding among themselves for more than ten years. In the 1880s, the chief combatants were the two largest church bodies, the Norwegian Synod and the Conference. Bitter as this struggle was, it was a family quarrel concerning the interpretation of certain scriptural passages, the use of lay preachers, and whether to have a strongly centralized or a loosely federated synodical organization. No shadow of doubt, however, had been cast on the divinity of Jesus or the verbal inspiration of the Bible.

No one likes to be quarreling on all sides at once. It is perhaps understandable that the ministers sometimes panicked and expressed themselves absurdly in the face of the threat posed by Janson. The Synod ministers in Chicago found his use of drama to convey his message to be the final outrage, and Sven Oftedal declared that a religious dialogue with Janson would demean the Conference. In the long run, however, the Lutherans had little to fear, for Janson did not make Unitarians out of an appreciable number of Norwegians, and the scandal after his departure tended to discredit his movement.

Yet he may have influenced the Lutherans for all that—or at least may have predicted how they must conduct themselves in the future. Even while he was in Minnesota, some of the Lutheran clergymen softened their attitude toward him. As far as we know, Sven Oftedal never mellowed, but Professor F. A. Schmidt, Oftedal's colleague at Augsburg when it was the theological seminary for the United Church, found he could take part in a series of religious discussions with Janson at Nazareth Church during the winter and early spring of

1891. Janson was also on friendly terms with the Danish Lutheran pastor, Adam Dan, whose verse sometimes appeared in *Saamanden*—although it should be pointed out that Pastor Dan was a Grundtvigian, for the Lutheran state church of Denmark acknowledged that theological strain as well as the orthodox.

For its fiftieth anniversary number, *Unity* reprinted H. Tambs Lyche's defense of the Haymarket anarchists, finding comfort in the knowledge that the publication had been on "the right side." Much the same may be said about Janson. At times, one may feel that he pushed the metaphor of the sower a bit too far, that he may sometimes have indulged in self-pity, that he was not a practical man, and that his logic was at times specious—but on a great many issues his stand has stood the test of time. Of those who attended a program of Janson's congregation at one time or another, one cannot doubt that they were uplifted and enlightened by it. For them he opened up the delights of literature and music and encouraged the study of social and political problems. Coming from varied backgrounds—some of them from remote rural areas in Norway—they could learn and practice the social niceties in his church basement. It was his belief that wholesome recreation was a necessity, and for their entertainment he provided plays and tableaux, often drawing on the members of his own family and the Behr girls for actors. Beginning in September, 1887, he put out his monthly magazine, filled with interesting, informative articles, some of which provide good reading to this day.

Social reform moves slowly, as the status of racial equality in America will testify. Janson was not able to get the death penalty abolished in Minnesota in 1891, in spite of the brave efforts of Hans P. Bjorge, but twenty years later the measure did become law. It is also possible that the clergymen who preached the social gospel were not talking into empty air, for the Interstate Commerce Act came in 1887, the Sherman Antitrust Law in 1890, and the Populist victories in 1892. After the turn of the century, the cause of reform got greater support in the writings of the muckrakers.

Even in the sermons he delivered, Janson seems to have forecast a trend. On Sundays today the sermons of orthodox ministers are frequently broadcast over the radio, but it is extremely rare that one deals with divine retribution or eternal punishment. Instead, the love and compassion of God are emphasized. At present, clergymen recognize that, if the church is to be a viable force in society, it must speak out against the injustices of the day, and it is common for ministers and priests to follow in the footsteps of such men as McGlynn, Bliss, Pentecost, Huntington, and others whose activities Janson often referred to in *Saamanden*.

Janson's ideas on religious tolerance are now widely accepted. His enthusiasm for Spiritualism does not seem to have stood the test of time as well, for with the passing years the number of its adherents has declined, and the movement no longer has the endorsement of scientists like Sir William Crookes, Sir Oliver Lodge, and Alfred Russel Wallace.[19] Yet one must not be too quick to dismiss Spiritualism, for investigation is currently going on in the allied field of parapsychology. While it is true that the occult at the present time has caught popular fancy and resulted in bizarre rituals, some members of the scientific community accept the existence of extrasensory perception. According to Arthur Koestler, research in this field is being undertaken in American and European universities, with those of Russia in the lead.[20] It is interesting that a pioneer in this area, Dr. J. B. Rhine, has acknowledged a debt to Spiritualism: "The question raised by Spiritualism must be faced as one of science's greatest problems. The Spiritualist movement has aroused research interest in the issues, and great numbers of religious and scientific people everywhere will be interested in the final outcome. To a certain extent the problem of the existence of an accessible spirit world is just an outstanding aspect of the general question of the spiritual nature of man, or more broadly, of the presence of anything spiritual (or nonphysical) in the universe."[21]

Today the stories and novels that Janson wrote in America are more or less forgotten. The number of persons in this country who can read Norwegian with any degree of ease has diminished, and the plots and social problems of his narratives would very likely seem dated to most readers. However, his *Amerikanske forholde* could profitably be translated. Written about a century after St. Jean de Crevecoeur's *Letters from an American Farmer*, it bears a resemblance to that book. Crevecoeur's observations are based upon a much longer period of residence in America than Janson's. The French author tends to be more sentimental—but both men view America with romantic ardor, extolling the benefits of democracy.

Janson was the champion of labor in the days when corporations hired Pinkerton men to fire upon strikers and made use of labor spies and blacklists. He is a timely figure today for his advocacy of the equality of women. The women he reported on in *Saamanden* as running steamboats or driving locomotives are pioneers in those fields today as they were in Janson's time, but one realizes that he wanted more than political enfranchisement: he urged that women should have equal standing with men in the utilization of their talents.

Janson was a unique figure in Norwegian immigrant life. Poet and preacher he was, to be sure, but beyond that he was an agent of enlightenment. He illuminated the contemporary world, drawing from both faraway places and those near at hand so that the intellectual level he drew upon included such persons as Tolstoy, Ramabai, Verestchagin, Rabbi Solomon Schindler, Robert Ingersoll, Mrs. Humphrey Ward, Edward Bellamy, and Ignatius Donnelly.

To most of us—once we have satisfied the basic needs for food, clothing, and shelter—the world is a humdrum place, with each day monotonously similar to the one that preceded it. At intervals an individual arrives on the scene who can make it clear to us that the world is always new and always unfinished, and that it is badly in need of our best efforts if we are to hasten the day when inequities will be erased and the stranger be assured a welcome. It was this message that Oscar Gundersen, Marie Huseby, Lauritz Stavnheim, and many others heard from Janson. It is what Amandus Norman cherished in his old teacher and what he wanted to convey in his address for the fiftieth anniversary of Nora Church: "Few of those who did not have an opportunity to hear him can have any clear idea of what he gave us every Sunday morning at the Old Nazareth church in Minneapolis, or his never-to-be-forgotten public readings of the new Norse classics at the same place Sunday evenings. Mr. Janson was no theorizer. He had a perfect horror of the futile dialectics of Hegelianism—the dominant school of philosophy in Central and Northern Europe during the larger part of the Nineteenth Century. He was no systematic theologian. His great strength lay in his wonderful ability to absorb, to understand, and to reproduce vital things. He was a bearer of light and giver of life. Here the poet helped the minister to anticipate, to feel delicately what was right.

"Yes, a strange new life radiated from that stone basement at Twelfth Avenue South and Ninth Street, Minneapolis, on Sunday mornings during the Nineties. Usually every seat was occupied. All sorts and conditions of men came to listen. The preacher was filled with his subject, glowing flames rose from every line in his carefully prepared sermon, and a fellow-feeling for the rights of the suffering and submerged such as no other minister in these parts dared to express at that time. And we, who were young then, were entranced by all this goodness. We forgot all about the masterly eloquence, we forgot all about the egotism and selfishness out in the cold world, we were

345

lifted as on invisible wings to behold vistas of moral grandeur, and we had an unaccountable urge to weep and to vow to consecrate ourselves to do things that count."[22]

Notes and References

CHAPTER I

1. *Skandinaven*, May 13, July 5, 1879.

2. Egil Elda, "Kristofer Janson og den nationale bevægelse i Norge," in *Budstikken* (Minneapolis), November 5, 11, 1879; Hjalmar Hjorth Boyesen, "Kristofer Janson and the Reform of the Norwegian Language," in *North American Review*, 115:379–401 (October, 1872); *Decorah-Posten*, October 15, 1879.

3. The Norwegian folk schools, modeled after those established in Denmark by Bishop N. F. S. Grundtvig, were set up in rural communities to educate young adults. Students were taught the history, literature, folklore, and music of their native land. Instruction was given primarily by means of the spoken word rather than through books. For a comment, see Janson, *Hvad jeg har oplevet*, 177 (Kristiania, 1913).

4. *Norden* (Chicago), October 29, 1879; *Fædrelandet og Emigranten* (La Crosse, Wisconsin), November 18, 1879; *Budstikken*, January 13, 20, 1879, February 3, 10, 17, 1880. See also Erik L. Petersen to Rasmus B. Anderson, February 19, March 17, 1880; Anderson Papers, State Historical Society of Wisconsin, Madison.

5. Janson, *Amerikanske forholde*, 2 (Copenhagen, 1881).

6. Janson, *Amerikanske forholde*, 76.

7. Janson, *Amerikanske forholde*, 2.

8. Janson, *Hvad jeg har oplevet*, 176.

9. To this may be added the judgment of his children, Dr. Eilev Janson and Fru Signe Forchhammer, of Drude Janson's niece, Mrs. Dina Behr Kolderup, and of his granddaughter, Mrs. Elinor Janson Hudson. Comments about Janson have been drawn from interviews with the late Emil Hage of New Ulm, Minnesota, and Mrs. Marie Stoep of Minneapolis, and with Halvor Moen of Underwood, Minnesota, during 1960–62. Anderson's remark is found in *Life Story of Rasmus B. Anderson*, 300 (Madison, 1913). The portrait of Janson of about 1885 was supplied by Miss Mildred Ekeberg of Glenwood, Minnesota. It is a replica of one presented by Janson to friends in his congregation at Underwood, Minnesota. Portraits of Janson are in the possession of the author.

10. For a general account of the synodical strife, see E. Clifford Nelson and Eugene L. Fevold, *The Lutheran Church among Norwegian-Americans,* 1:245–253 (Minneapolis, 1960).

11. Janson, *Hvad jeg har oplevet,* 178.

12. Janson to Bjørnstjerne Bjørnson, September 5, 1879; Bjørnson Papers, University Library, Oslo. (The letter is dated simply "Friday the fifth"; in 1879, September 5 fell on a Friday.)

13. *Budstikken,* October 1, 1879.

14. Janson to Bjørnson, September 5, 1879; Bjørnson Papers. The words "Humbug lives!" were appended to the note in pencil. Janson, in thanking Bjørnson for this advance publicity, was acknowledging a favor which he was not to need on his next two departures from Norway for America, 1881 and 1882. Thus it is likely that Janson's note was written in reference to the newspaper article quoted above.

15. Boyesen's letters to Anderson are in the Anderson Papers. *Sigmund Bresteson* was published in Bergen in 1872. For Boyesen's article and review, see *North American Review,* 115:378–401; *Atlantic Monthly,* 30: 497–99.

16. Miss Woodward's letter is in the Anderson Papers.

17. Clarence A. Glasrud, "Boyesen and the Norwegian Immigration," in *Norwegian-American Studies and Records,* 19:24 (Northfield, Minnesota, 1956); see also Glasrud, *Hjalmar Hjorth Boyesen,* 72–76 (Northfield, 1963). Even the Reverend Erik L. Petersen, book reviewer of *Budstikken,* who apparently had his own reasons for disliking the Norwegian Synod, felt Boyesen's portrait to be grossly exaggerated.

18. For Janson's comments about his tour, see *Amerikanske forholde,* 15, 47, 55, 57, and *Hvad jeg har oplevet,* 182.

19. *Norden,* October 15, 1879.

20. Johs. B. Wist, "Pressen efter borgerkrigen," in *Norsk-amerikanernes festskrift 1914,* 88 (Decorah, 1914). In *Amerikanske forholde,* 94, 122, 149, Janson mentions situations that he later used for three stories: "En buggyprest" (A Buggy Minister), "En bygdekonge" (A Village King), and "Kvinden skal være manden underdanig" (Wives, Submit Yourselves unto Your Husbands). The last title is the one Janson gave the story when he translated it. In all of these stories clergymen figure prominently; *Præriens saga: Fortællinger fra Amerika af Kristofer Janson* (Chicago, 1885).

21. Janson, *Amerikanske forholde,* 140.

22. *Norden* (Chicago), October 22, 1879. Certain liberties have been taken in the translating. The original reads:

> Velkommen vær du norske Bror
> Til vore nye Hjem.
> Du kommer jo ifra vor Mor
> Med Hilsen fra den gamle Nord
> Med Minde fra vor Vuggesang
> Vor Vaar, vor Drøm, vor Sang.

23. The account of Janson's first lecture was taken from *Norden*, October 22, 1879.

24. All of these newspaper accounts were reported in *Budstikken*, October 28, 1879.

25. See pages 42–46, 81–83, 92, 95–99.

26. *Norden*, October 29, 1879; *Fædrelandet og Emigranten*, November 18, 1879. For the description of Janson's style of lecturing, I am indebted to Pastor Carl W. Schevenius, who got it from a member of the audience.

27. Bessie Louise Pierce, *A History of Chicago*, 3:429–35 (New York, 1957). Janson's judgment about the working people seems to have been a sound one. Social historians have since emphasized American Protestantism's neglect of the laboring classes in the latter half of the nineteenth century.

28. *Norden*, October 29, November 5, 1879.

29. *Budstikken*, January 30, 1880.

30. Janson, *Amerikanske forholde*, 89.

31. Janson, *Amerikanske forholde*, 81–83.

32. Janson, *Amerikanske forholde*, 83.

33. Janson, *Amerikanske forholde*, 134; A. Weenaas, *Wisconsinismen belyst ved historiske kjendsjerninger*, 93 (Chicago, 1875).

34. Janson's poem, "Din mor er død," written on the occasion of his mother's death, appeared in *Budstikken*, March 30, 1880. His letter to Bjørnson is in the Bjørnson Papers. By his home he meant Solbakken, the house he had built close to Aulestad during his days at Vonheim. Having severed his relations with the school, he expected to move when he found other employment.

35. Janson, *Amerikanske forholde*, 87.

36. *Fædrelandet og Emigranten*, November 18, 1879. The full stanza reads:

> Fram til Fridom, til alt som er godt
> ned med sit sleipt og laakt og raatt
> torka bort Taaror, elska bort Traas
> fram til den Gud som elsker oss.

37. Janson, *Amerikanske forholde*, 106.

38. Janson, *Amerikanske forholde*, 106.

39. *Budstikken,* November 5, 11, 1879.

40. *Budstikken*, January 20, 1880.

41. Janson, *Amerikanske forholde*, 46, 112–14.

42. *Budstikken*, February 3, 1880. The students' delight in Janson was recalled many years later by Hallvard Askeland, who had been at Augsburg in 1880, at memorial services held for Janson by Oslo Lodge Number 2, Sons of Norway, in the winter of 1918. The latter event was reported in *Minneapolis Tidende*, March 7, 1918.

43. *Budstikken*, February 10, 1880.

44. *Budstikken*, February 3, 1880.

45. Janson, *Amerikanske forholde*, 18, 48. For a review of Mrs. Livermore's lecture, see *Minneapolis Journal*, February 4, 1880.

46. Janson's *Amerikanske forholde*, 50.

47. Janson's itinerary was not published, however, in *Budstikken* on February 17. The previous week's issue had indicated that he would be in Alexandria on February 16 and in Fergus Falls February 18. The record of his movements has been compiled from his printed schedule as it appeared in the Norwegian-language weeklies. As he moved westward, occasional discrepancies in lecture dates occurred between announcements in the Chicago papers and those in *Fædrelandet og Emigranten* and *Budstikken*. In such cases, dates from the latter, which were closer to where he was at the moment, have been used. Janson's note to Anderson is in the Anderson Papers.

48. *Budstikken*, February 17, 1880.

49. Anderson Papers.

50. Janson, *Amerikanske forholde*, 85, 90–93.

51. Janson, *Amerikanske forholde*, 122; *Hvad jeg har oplevet*, 180.

52. Janson, *Amerikanske forholde*, 111.

53. For Janson's discussion of these phases of American life, see *Amerikanske forholde*, 17, 103, 104. He gave many illustrations of the fine character of Americans. An immigrant boy, hired to saw wood, had propped a primer against his sawbuck. Admiring this, some Americans promptly arranged for the boy to attend school. At times Americans attended Janson's lectures, even though they could not understand a word. When questioned, one would say, "Can't I be allowed to contribute 25 cents to a good cause?" Even when they were drunk, Americans behaved better than Norwegians in a similar state.

54. Anderson Papers.

55. *Decorah-Posten*, March 10, 1880.

56. *Decorah-Posten*, March 10, 1880.

57. *Budstikken*, March 23, 1880. The article in *Norden* was quoted in *Budstikken*, April 27, 1880.

58. See Janson, *Hvad jeg har oplevet*, 181, 182. For an account of the Channing memorial service, see *Unity* (Chicago), April 16, 1880.

59. Accounts of the lecture are in *Norden*, April 14, 1880, and *Budstikken*, April 20, 1880.

60. *Verdens Gang* and *Den Nye Tid* were published in Chicago. The *Verdens Gang* article was reprinted in *Budstikken*, April 27, 1880.

61. *Budstikken*, April 20, 1880.

62. Janson, *Amerikanske forholde*, 117. Janson calls the medium Mrs. Cora Ringwood. Chicago papers of the time give her name as Richmond.

63. Janson to Anderson, April 20, 1880; Anderson Papers. Janson learned that many Americans objected to Whitman's frank sexuality. "I talked to a fine aristocratic American woman about Walt Whitman and showed her one

of his boldest poems. She threw down the book, exclaiming, 'I find him disgusting!' " *Amerikanske forholde*, 68.

64. Anderson Papers.

65. This was an allusion to Janson's report of the Winchester incident, in which a coffin was said to have been removed from a Norwegian Synod churchyard and placed in a Conference cemetery.

66. "En tale om den rene lære" originally appeared in *Evangelisk Luthersk Kirketidende*, April 30, 1880. It was reprinted in *Fædrelandet og Emigranten*, May 4, 1880; in *Budstikken*, May 11, 1880.

67. *Budstikken*, May 11, 1880.

68. Janson, *Amerikanske forholde*, 11, 32, 33. Blanche K. Bruce served as United States Senator from Mississippi, 1875–81, while that state was still under Reconstruction government. During his term of office he entered debates on election frauds, Southern unrest, and civil rights. He fought for better treatment of the Indian, and advocated improvement of navigation on the Mississippi.

69. Janson, *Hvad jeg har oplevet*, 188; the card is in the Anderson Papers.

70. Janson, *Amerikanske forholde*, 63. The parenthetical comment is Janson's. The date of his visit has been established from a notation in Longfellow's diary for May 20: "Kristofer Janson, a novelist from Gausdal, called and stayed to lunch." Longfellow Papers, Houghton Library, Harvard University.

71. Janson, *Amerikanske forholde*, 58.

72. Janson, *Amerikanske forholde*, 62.

73. *Budstikken*, May 4, 1880. Whether or not Janson had delivered the address before giving it in Chicago, it seems that his ideas on the "pure teachings" had already crystallized when he came to America. In the list of lecture titles published by Professor Anderson in *Skandinaven* on July 5, 1879, number twenty was "Om 'den rene lære'" (Concerning the "Pure Teachings").

74. *Budstikken*, June 15, 1880. The article was reprinted from *Evangelisk Luthersk Kirketidende* of June 4, 1880. The fact that Janson denied the divinity of Christ, yet accepted him as the saviour, was to confuse Conference Lutherans as well as those of the Norwgian Synod. The same question was asked in the Conference's *Folkebladet*, December 22, 1881, after Janson returned to the United States. According to Janson, Jesus was a perfect human being who, by the example of his life and death, furnished a model for humanity to follow. Janson held the crucifixion of God to be an absurdity.

75. Anderson, *Life Story*, 299.

76. Janson, *Amerikanske forholde*, 121–57.

77. Janson may have been concerned with finances, but such fears proved groundless. Anderson reports that Janson's net proceeds amounted to $3,000; *Life Story*, 299. Janson did say that the tour was profitable but gave no details; *Hvad jeg har oplevet*, 190.

78. For some reason Petersen did not meet Janson during the lecture tour. On March 11, 1880, he wrote Anderson: "Give the enclosed photograph to Kristofer Janson from me. I never got a chance to meet him. When he was here, that was prevented by an unworthy trick of Synod big-wigs." On March 17 he again wrote: "Pastor Muus's yeomen go around everywhere telling people Janson did not want to meet me, that he did not consider me worthy, etc. The truth is that time after time I worked for him as much as my weak powers permit. . . . The way things are, it would relieve me to get Janson's own word that he wanted to meet me." Anderson Papers.

79. *Freeborn County Standard,* May 5, 1881.

80. Anderson's letter was dated September 8, 1881. After its appearance in *Skandinaven,* it was reprinted in *Folkebladet* (Minneapolis), September 22, 1881.

CHAPTER II

1. Kristofer Janson, *Hvad jeg har oplevet,* 190 (Kristiania, 1913); Dina Krog to Karoline Bjørnson, an undated letter, Bjørnson Papers, University Library, Oslo. Rasmus B. Anderson said that Janson "returned to Norway with fully $3,000 net proceeds"; *Life Story of Rasmus B. Anderson,* 299 (Madison, 1915).

2. Janson, *Hvad jeg har oplevet,* 192, 196.

3. Mrs. Dina Behr Kolderup to the writer, March 6, 1959; Brandes, *Levned,* 2:360 (Copenhagen, 1907).

4. Janson to Rasmus B. Anderson, July 18, 1881. Letters from Janson to Anderson here cited are in the Anderson Papers, State Historical Society of Wisconsin, Madison. *Et kvindesjæbne* was published in Bergen, Norway, in 1875, *Vore besteforældre* in Copenhagen in 1882. The portrait of Drude Janson is in the possession of Mrs. Betty Lou Nelson of Seattle, Washington, a great-granddaughter.

5. As Janson approached his home, Arne, then about seven, ran out to meet his father, his face beaming, and shouted, "Sigmund is dead!" Interview with Mrs. Elinor Janson Hudson, daughter of Arne Janson, July, 1965; Dr. Eilev Janson to the writer, July 4, 1959.

6. Janson, *Hvad jeg har oplevet,* 198.

7. Anderson, *Life Story,* 300.

8. Janson to Anderson, July 18, 1881.

9. Janson to Anderson, July 18, 1881. Johnson was a pioneer industrialist, founder of the Gisholt Machine Company. A biography of him by Agnes M. Larson was published by the Norwegian-American Historical Association in 1969.

10. *Skandinaven* (Chicago), September 13, 1881. The letter was reprinted in *Folkebladet* (Minneapolis), September 22, 1881.

11. Janson to Anderson, September 9, 1881. Excerpts from Norwegian sources here quoted have been translated by the present writer.

12. Janson to Anderson, September 9, 1881.

13. Anderson to Bjørnson, August 27, 1881; letters to Bjørnson here cited are in the Bjørnson Papers; microfilm copies of Anderson's letters in this collection are in the State Historical Society of Wisconsin. Aubertine Woodward's letters are in the Anderson Papers. *The Spellbound Fiddler* had appeared in Chicago in 1880.

14. *Skandinaven*, October 11, 1881.

15. Letters to Jones are in the Jones Papers, Library of Meadville Theological School of Lombard College, Chicago. Italics in the section quoted are Janson's.

16. *Skandinaven*, November 15, 1881.

17. *Christian Register* (Boston), November 24, December 1, 1881.

18. *Unity* (Chicago), December 1, 1881.

19. *Unitarian Review and Religious Magazine* (Boston), January, 1882.

20. *Skandinaven*, November 29, 1881. The other newspapers mentioned were quoted in *Budstikken* (Minneapolis), December 6, 1881.

21. *Fædrelandet og Emigranten* (La Crosse), December 6, 1881.

22. Anderson to Bjørnson, December 2, 1881. Italics are Anderson's.

23. Carl G. O. Hansen, *My Minneapolis*, 52 (Minneapolis, 1956).

24. Charles Howard Hopkins, *The Rise of the Social Gospel in American Protestantism, 1865–1915*, 79 (New Haven, 1940).

25. Hansen, *My Minneapolis*, 23, 51–54.

26. Hansen, *My Minneapolis*, 23.

27. Janson's denial was reprinted in *Budstikken*, August 30, 1881.

28. *Budstikken*, December 6, 1881.

29. Janson to Anderson, December 11, 1881; Simmons to Jones, December 12, 1881, Jones Papers.

30. Simmons to Jones, December 12, 1881; Janson, *Hvad jeg har oplevet*, 205; Janson, "The Scandinavians in America," in *Christian Register*, June 22, 1882.

31. Janson to Anderson, December 11, 1881. Italics in the letter are Janson's. The Lutheran church (and other orthodox Christian religions) accepted both the Nicene and the Athanasian symbols or creeds. Janson is here explaining that he was presented with a constitution suitable for a Lutheran church, not a liberal congregation.

32. Janson to Jones, December 12, 1881.

33. *Saamanden* (Minneapolis), November, 1893.

34. See E. Clifford Nelson and Eugene L. Fevold, *The Lutheran Church among Norwegian-Americans*, 1:224 (Minneapolis, 1960); S. Sondresen, "De norske kirkesamfund i Amerika," in *Norsk-amerikanerne*, 53 (Bergen, 1938).

35. Hans Nielsen Hauge (1771–1824), a lay preacher, brought about a religious revival in Norway despite persecution from state authorities.

36. *Folkebladet*, December 22, 1881.

37. *Folkebladet,* January 5, 1882.

38. Janson to Jones, December 19, 1881.

39. Anderson to Bjørnson, December 19, 1881.

40. *Budstikken,* December 20, 1881.

41. *Budstikken,* December 27, 1881.

42. Janson to Anderson, February 9, 1882.

43. Janson, in *Christian Register,* June 22, 1882.

44. The sermon is included in Janson's *Lys og frihed,* 70–78 (Minneapolis, 1892).

45. *Budstikken,* January 10, 1882.

46. *Budstikken,* February 21, April 4, 1882. A *husmand* is a tenant farmer.

47. Hansen, *My Minneapolis,* 58.

48. Ole Jorgensen, "Speech at the Laying of the Cornerstone of Nora Church Parsonage, June 24, 1906," in *Nora fri-kristne menighed,* 21 (Hanska, Minnesota, 1906), a twenty-fifth anniversary pamphlet. "Nora" is a symbolic term for Norwegian.

49. *Budstikken,* April 11, 1882.

50. Janson, *Hvad jeg har oplevet,* 207; Janson to Anderson, February 9, 1882.

51. *Budstikken,* January 31, 1882.

52. *Evangelisk Luthersk Kirketidende,* January 13, 1882; *Critic* (New York), January 14, 1882.

53. Janson to Anderson, February 9, 1882.

54. *Norden* (Chicago), November 20, 1881.

55. Janson to Anderson, February 9, 1882. On the Steensland-Anderson dispute, see Lloyd Hustvedt, *Rasmus B. Anderson: Pioneer Scholar,* 171 (Northfield, 1966). A loose translation of the French words would be, "What a noise over one omelet!"

56. *Budstikken,* February 7, 1882.

57. *Unity,* February 16, 1882; Anderson to Bjørnson, February 17, 1882.

58. *Budstikken,* April 11, 1882.

59. Janson to Jones, March 12, 1882. Italics are Janson's.

60. Janson to Jones, March 20, 1882.

61. Janson, *Hvad jeg har oplevet,* 251.

62. *Christian Register,* April 13, 1882.

63. Anderson to Bjørnson, April 18, 1882.

64. *Christian Register,* May 11, 1882; *Unity,* May 16, 1882; Western Unitarian Conference, Minutes of the Twenty-Eighth Annual Meeting, May 4, 1882, filed in Abraham Lincoln Center, Chicago.

CHAPTER III

1. A description of Fana Prestegaard and the arrangements for the Jansons' visit was furnished by Mrs. Dina B. Kolderup in letters to the author on August 12, 1962, and August 31, 1965.

2. The report of the visit of the Janson children to Damsgaard is taken from a letter by Dr. Eilev Janson to the author, dated November 23, 1958. Details concerning the mansion are drawn from Gustav Brosing, ed., *Det gamle Bergen*, 166 (Bergen, 1955).

3. Details concerning the festivities commemorating the twenty-fifth anniversary of the publication of *Synnøve Solbakken* are drawn from *Budstikken*, September 6, 1882; Janson's poem, "Til Bjørnstjerne Bjørnson," appeared in *Budstikken* on September 13, 1882. Janson gives an account of the event in *Hvad jeg har oplevet*, 199–202.

4. Janson to Bjørnson, August 13, 1882.

5. For a listing of Drude's translations of Janson's peasant tales, see J. B. Halvorsen, *Norsk forfatter lexikon 1814–1880*, 3:124–26 (Kristiania, 1892).

6. In *Hvad jeg har oplevet*, Janson relates how Bjørnson came to Janson's defense first by making clear to Drude the value of her husband's contribution to the school and to the whole community. Drude in her autobiographical novel, *Mira* (Copenhagen, 1897), credits her intellectual awakening to another man in the school rather than to her husband.

7. Allusions (usually facetious) to the Spanish skipper (*den spanske skipper*) are fairly numerous in the correspondence. See Drude Janson to Bjørnstjerne Bjørnson, April 9, 1883. In a letter to Georg Brandes dated August 17, 1883, Bjørnson wrote of how he had thought of Drude while creating the heroine of his play, *Geografi og kjærlighed*, going on to say: "Ah, Drude! I have lived in deadly fear that a Spanish skipper would come and take you.—Now I begin to believe that he can't." See Halvdan Koht, *Bjørnstjerne Bjørnson kamp-liv 1882–1884*, 2:97–98 (Oslo, 1932).

8. *Budstikken*, September 13, 20, 1882.

9. Janson's sermon, "Under What Banner Shall We Christians Assemble?", is found in his *Lys og frihed*, 1–9 (Minneapolis, 1893).

10. Charles H. Lyttle, *Freedom Moves West*, 163–178 (Boston, 1952).

11. Charles Howard Hopkins, *The Rise of the Social Gospel in American Protestantism, 1865–1915*, 124–26 (New Haven, 1940).

12. "Report from Kristofer Janson," in *Unity*, January 16, 1883.

13. Details of the early experiences of the Janson boys in American schools were furnished in Seattle by the late Eilev Janson in March, 1959; the description of Drude's first visit to Brown County was given by the late Emil Hage of New Ulm, Minnesota, in the summer of 1958.

14. *Budstikken*, October 3, 1882.

15. Janson, "Fra Amerika," in *Nyt Tidsskrift*, 2:22–37 (Kristiania, 1883).

16. *Budstikken*, December 27, 1882. The quotation is from *Unity*, January 16, 1883.

17. *Unity*, January 16, 1883.

18. *Budstikken*, January 24, 1883.

19. Drude Janson to Rasmus B. Anderson, February 20, 1883, in the Anderson Papers.

20. *Budstikken*, April 18, 1883. The sermon was printed in pamphlet form in Minneapolis in 1883.

21. Drude Janson to Bjørnson, April 9, 1883.

22. *Budstikken*, April 25, 1883.

23. Janson to Jenkin Lloyd Jones, n.d. Janson's comments on a forthcoming conference in Chicago would seem to place the time as the spring of 1883.

24. Janson to Rasmus B. Anderson, April 26, 1883.

25. Aubertine Woodward (Auber Forestier) to Rasmus B. Anderson, May 15, 1883. The minutes of the annual meeting of the Western Conference in Chicago, May 13, 1883, read: "Rev. Kristofer Janson gave a very interesting account of his work among the Scandinavians of Minnesota, of the force without and within to be encountered, and also of the draw-backs to his Sunday School work by reason of want of teachers who can speak the language. He spoke at some length of his Hymn Book now being published from which he hopes much as well as from the religious monthly he intends soon to start. At the close of his remarks he sang by request a Norwegian hymn of his own composition."

26. The Ylvisaker-Janson exchange appeared in the *Albert Lea* (Minnesota) *Posten* in the issues of April 20, May 4, 17, 25, and June 8, 1883.

27. The notices of the picnic of Janson's congregation at Lake Harriet appeared in *Folkebladet* on June 21 and 28, 1883. For an account of the controversy over *Folkebladet*, see Andreas Helland, *Georg Sverdrup*, 101–11 (Minneapolis, 1947).

28. Drude Janson to Mrs. Rasmus B. Anderson, June 18, 1883, in the Anderson Papers.

29. Anderson to Bjørnson, July 19, 1883.

30. Accounts of the tornado of 1883 are to be found in "Struck by a Cyclone," in the *Christian Register*, August 2, 1883. See also "Atmospheric Negations; or Truth Tried Through Tornadoes," in *Unity*, August 1, 1883, and Janson, *Hvad jeg har oplevet*, 208–11. In addition, the author used material sent by Eilev Janson on November 23, 1958.

31. *Unity*, August 16, 1883.

32. *Unity*, August 16, 1883.

33. Janson to Bjørnson, October 4, 1883.

34. Janson's account of his first meeting with Hamsun is found in *Hvad jeg har oplevet*, 219–20. The description of the Jansons' life in Madelia after the storm has been taken from "Kristofer Janson i Amerika: Brev til Verdens Gang," which appeared in *Verdens Gang* (Kristiania) on January 22, 1885. Though unsigned, the article must be the work of Knut Hamsun. In his research on Hamsun, Professor Harald Naess of the University of Wisconsin discovered the article and identified it as Hamsun's work.

35. The description of the Janson house at 2419 Nicollet Avenue in Minneapolis was supplied in March, 1959, by Eilev Janson and Mrs. Dina B. Kolderup of Seattle. Some details are drawn from "Kristofer Janson i Amerika," in *Verdens Gang*, January 22, 1885.

36. *Christian Register*, September 27, 1883.

37. Janson to Bjørnson, October 4, 1883.

CHAPTER IV

1. Janson, *Hvad jeg har oplevet*, 228.

2. On March 16, 1884, *Unity* quoted a correspondent on Janson's appearance in Sioux Falls, South Dakota, saying that his English sermon had been "spiritual, practical, and a poem in beauty." In its issue of May 22, 1884, the *Christian Register*, reporting on Janson's participation in a discussion, spoke of his "musical words."

3. Janson, *Hvad jeg har oplevet*, 124.

4. Olav S. Midttun, *Bjørnson og folkehøyskolen*, 21 (Oslo, 1954).

5. *Budstikken*, October 10, 1883.

6. "Kristofer Janson i Amerika," in *Verdens Gang* (Kristiania), January 22, 1885.

7. The original reads:

Hils Presten: Frihed til at tænke

er Menneskets Krav,

mod Himlen raaber det fra Jorden

igjennem Jesu Grav!

8. Illit Grøndahl and Ola Raknes, "Henrik Wergeland," in *Chapters in Norwegian Literature*, 63 (London, 1923).

9. Grøndahl and Raknes, "Henrik Wergeland," in *Chapters in Norwegian Literature*, 63.

10. *Christian Register*, November 15, 1883.

11. *Budstikken*, November 27, 1883.

12. *Verdens Gang* (Kristiania), January 22, 1885.

13. *Budstikken*, December 4, 11, 1883.

14. *Verdens Gang*, January 22, 1885.

15. Arthur M. Schlesinger, "A Critical Period in American Religion," in *Proceedings of the Massachusetts Historical Society*, 64:523–47 (Boston, 1932).

16. Janson's translation appeared in *Unity* on July 16, 1884. The original had been reprinted in *Budstikken* on June 1, 1884.

17. *Evangelisk Luthersk Kirketidende* (Decorah, Iowa), 11:74–75. The article was signed by A. Mikkelsen, O. Juul, N. C. Brun, J. Welo, and Chr. O. Brohaugh.

18. Miln was one of the ministers who had ordained Janson. According to Lyttle, in *Freedom Moves West*, Miln eventually became an Ingersollian. On leaving the Unitarian ministry, he seems to have had a brief career as an

actor. His departure from the Unitarian church seems to have disturbed Janson. In an undated letter to Jenkin Lloyd Jones, H. M. Simmons, Janson's Minneapolis colleague, wrote, "He [Janson] was pretty shocked over the Miln matter and has been anxious over what you would say about it in *Unity*." The letter is in the Jones Papers.

19. Janson, *Helvedes børn-Prædiken i dramaform* (Chicago, 1884).

20. Janson, "Kvinden skal være manden underdanig," in *Præriens saga*, 5–60 (Chicago, 1885). The English title in the text is the one Janson used when he translated the story from Norwegian.

21. J. Julson, "Lidt om Pastor K. Jansons seneste optræden her i Chicago," in *Skandinaven*, March 25, 1884.

22. "Hamsund" was the spelling Hamsun used during his first sojourn in America. When his "Mark Twain" was printed in *Budstikken* on April 27, 1887, the spelling was "Hamsun."

23. Knut Hamsund, "Hr. Dr. Julson," in *Skandinaven*, April 22, 1884.

24. Probably a reference to Janson's dispute with Pastor Th. Ylvisaker. The debate had finally pivoted on whether or not a passage Ylvisaker quoted was authentic. Janson held that Luther regarded it as apocryphal and ruled it out. The editor, who terminated the exchange, would not accept Janson's interpretation that "the Son of God" meant that Jesus was the child of God like any other human being, but he reprimanded Ylvisaker for using a disputed passage as an argument against an opponent.

25. "Bishop Grundtvig and the Peasant High School" appeared in *Scandinavia* (Chicago) in April and May, 1884. "Our Ancestors" was published in June, 1884.

26. *Unity*, January 16, 1884.

27. Janson to Rasmus B. Anderson, April 8, 1884, in the Anderson Papers.

28. *Budstikken*, April 15, 1884. According to *Budstikken* of June 14, 1884, Samuel Garborg's evening school was scheduled to open on June 18 of that year.

29. This information was supplied by the late Mrs. Marie Stoep of Minneapolis.

30. *Budstikken*, April 15, 1884.

31. *Budstikken*, April 22, 1884.

32. *Scandinavia*, June, 1884.

33. Lyttle, *Freedom Moves West*, 168. Chapter 13 of Lyttle's book, entitled "Is Unitarianism Only Christian Theism?", deals with the controversy up to the spring of 1884, when J. T. Sunderland succeeded Jenkin Lloyd Jones as secretary of the Western Conference.

34. Janson, *Hvad jeg har oplevet*, 229.

35. Lyttle, *Freedom Moves West*, 168–69.

36. *Christian Register*, May 22, 1884.

37. Lyttle, *Freedom Moves West*, 174. Four years later, on June 12, 1888, Henry M. Simmons wrote Jenkin Lloyd Jones: "I had supposed that one of

the best things in Unitarianism was its ability to harmonize differing opinions in one spirit but if it cannot harmonize two men whose principles are so high and whose real opinions are so nearly alike as Mr. Gannett's and Mr. Sunderland's, I do not know as it is worth keeping and [I] have been growing rather indifferent to it as of late." This letter is in the Jones Papers.

38. *Budstikken*, June 3, 1884.

39. *Christian Register*, June 19, 1884. See Paul Knaplund, "H. Tambs Lyche: Propagandist for America," in *Norwegian-American Studies*, 24: 102–11.

40. Many of the "confirmation talks" are still in existence, having been handed down from parent to child. The following is one from Brown County, delivered on August 26, 1888, using the text from Mark 10:15—"Verily I say unto you, Whosoever shall not receive the kingdom of God as a little child, he shall not enter therein." The minister called each child by name:

"Klara Bekken. You are the youngest member of the class today, and therefore I will speak to you of the child in your soul. When, as a baby, you were brought to baptism, these words were spoken over you: 'It is the child who opens the gates of heaven.' Today I repeat them and ask you to remember them. Protect the child within you; that is a treasure. We can grow out of much—clothing and shoes, childish books and games—but there is one thing we must not grow away from and that is a child-like confidence in God and all that is good. Just as you, when you were small, were rocked in the arms of your father and mother and felt so secure and happy that you reached out to embrace them, you must in your thoughts rest in the love of God, and, so to speak, put your arms about Him, our great Father. It is not easy to keep a child-like purity and innocence as one moves through life's cold stream, but you can do it if you will: God will help you. If you will preserve a child's confidence in God and live with Him through prayer; if you will meet all people with a smile and believe them to be more good than bad; if you will not let bitterness enter your heart but strive to be kind to all, regardless of how they might treat you, then you will have protected the child in your soul. God give you strength in this as you go on your way. In behalf of the congregation and myself, I ask God's blessing on you."

41. Although Janson at one time contemplated using the Lutheran communion service—along with an explanation that "This is my body; this is my blood" was to be interpreted allegorically—he came to work out a ceremony of his own in which the crucifixion was not an atonement for man but something to be remembered as the suffering and death of one who had taught that God is the loving father who wants men to regard one another as brothers.

42. Janson to Bjørnson, July 29, 1884. Janson barely mentioned the scarlet fever, but it seems that at least two of the girls were down with it. Nearly fifty years later, in a letter dated November 8, 1933, Drude recalled the time in a letter to her niece, Mrs. Kirsten Wennerblad of Seattle. It was her son

Eilev who had been her mainstay, she said. "I'll never forget how he, as a half-grown boy, watched with me over his sisters, sick with scarlet fever. Every night he took my place at their bedside so I could get some rest."

43. Hamsun, "Kristofer Janson i Amerika," in *Verdens Gang*, January 22, 1885.

44. Janson, *Hvad jeg har oplevet*, 221.

45. Peder Ydstie to Torkel Oftelie, n.d. Oftelie recalled that he had received the letter in 1894 or 1895; in the archives of the Norwegian-American Historical Association.

46. W. M. H. Petersen, "Unitariernes vildfarelsen i læren om synd og naade," in *Evangelisk Luthersk Kirketidende*, November 14, 21, 1884.

47. The *Independent*, November 20, 1884; *Unity*, December 6, 1884; *Evangelisk Luthersk Kirketidende*, December 18, 1885.

48. *Folkebladet*, December 9, 16, 1884.

49. *Budstikken*, December 23, 1884.

50. *Folkebladet*, December 23, 1884.

51. This correspondence is in the Anderson Papers.

CHAPTER V

1. O. J. Rollevson, "A Protest," in the *Minneapolis Evening Journal*, January 3, 1885.

2. *Folkebladet*, January 5, 1885.

3. *Folkebladet*, January 13, 1885.

4. The divorce proceedings of Mrs. Oline Muus against her husband, Pastor Bernt Julius Muus of the Norwegian Synod, were aired in the newspapers during 1879–80. Although the pastor was described as the tyrannical overlord of his household, no evidence was brought forth that he kicked or beat her as did the brutal Ola in Janson's story. Muus's lack of humaneness was illustrated by his refusal to send to town for a doctor after his wife had broken her leg and pleaded that he get a doctor to set the leg and apply or give her something to deaden the pain. Pastor Muus is said to have answered that the horses had worked hard in the fields all day and were tired. She must wait until the next day. "You must apply patience" (Du maa smør dig med talmodighed). Modern critics have assumed, like Oftedal, that Janson drew the material for his story from the Muus case. However, Janson's denial seems to be justified. In his *Amerikanske forholde*, which he wrote after his lecture tour of 1879–80, he tells of a case similar to that of his heroine, Emma, and also discusses the Muus case.

5. Janson, "Tilsvar til Sven Oftedal," in *Budstikken*, January 13, 1885.

6. "Et par norske farmerkone," in *Folkebladet*, March 3, 1885; Silo Sagen, "Pastor Oftedal og Pastor Janson," in *Budstikken*, February 3, 1885.

7. Possibly their delay in organizing churches was related to their distaste or disinterest in the synodical warfare, for they never seemed to be strongly partisan on church issues. One man said that some time prior to his con-

firmation in 1880, he had set out to walk some four miles to attend services and Sunday school at Our Saviour's Church, which belonged to the Norwegian Synod. On the way, he decided to vary his usual program by going to Trinity, a Conference church, for services. When they were over, he went to Sunday school at his own church, Our Saviour's. During the lesson period, the teacher asked who had attended services, later remarking that he had not seen the boy there. On being told by the boy that he had attended Trinity, the teacher was taken aback for a moment. Then shaking his head, he said reprovingly, "Those who desert their own congregation!" When the boy reported the incident at home, his father found the teacher's remark "nothing but foolishness."

8. The discussion club (Samtale Foreningen) was scheduled to hold its first meeting on January 17, 1885. See *Budstikken*, January 13, 1885.

9. *Unity*, April 18, 1885.

10. *Scandinavia*, April, 1885.

11. *Christian Register*, June 11, 1885.

12. *Christian Register*, July 23, 1885.

13. *Unity*, August 1, 1885.

14. Dina B. Kolderup to the author, February 4, March 6, 1959.

15. Eilev Janson to the author, November 23, 1958; Dina Kolderup to the author, February 4, 1959.

16. Dina Kolderup to the author, February 4, 1959.

17. On September 2, 1885, *Budstikken* announced that Janson's reading for the following Sunday would be "Den vilde rose i skogen" (The Wild Rose of the Forest), remarking that it was a new original story of the Indian wars in Minnesota. Aagot D. Hoidahl has said, "The story of the Indians, especially the Norway Lake episode of the Sioux War of 1862, is very well done." See her "Norwegian-American Fiction, 1880–1928," in *Norwegian-American Studies and Records*, 5:67 (1930).

18. *Minneapolis Morning Tribune*, October 15, 1885. On October 13 and 20, *Budstikken* printed Janson's sermon "Om temperance sagen og temperance bevægelsen i Amerika" (The Temperance Issue and the Temperance Movement in America).

19. *Folkbladet*, October 13, 1885.

20. *Folkebladet*, October 27, 1885.

21. *Budstikken*, November 3, 1885.

22. *Folkebladet*, November 17, 1885. Janson's salary was $2,000 a year. The board of directors of the American Unitarian Association had voted him a thousand dollars twice a year, normally in September and March. These arrangements were usually reported in the *Christian Register*.

23. Janson, "Til Folkebladet," in *Budstikken*, November 24, 1885.

24. *Folkebladet*, December 9, 1885.

25. *Budstikken*, December 24, 1885.

26. "En andet julebudskab til fordel for Pastor Janson," in *Folkebladet*, December 30, 1885.

27. *Budstikken*, January 17, 1886.

28. *Budstikken*, January 5, 1886.

29. Drude Janson to Mrs. Rasmus B. Anderson, November 21, 1885, in the Anderson Papers.

30. *Minneapolis Morning Tribune*, November 16, 1885; *Budstikken*, November 17, 1885. An account of the dedication appeared in *Unity*, December 5, 1885.

31. Janson to Bjørnson, December 11, 1885. One of Oftedal's "cohorts" appears to have been M. Falk Gjertsen, then pastor of Trinity Lutheran Church, the oldest Norwegian church in the city, and, so to speak, the "cathedral" of the Conference. Gjertsen seems to have attacked Janson from the pulpit. None of this reached the newspapers, but Mrs. Dina Kolderup has made repeated reference to Gjertsen's enmity in her letters (October 1, 1959, and January 19, 1961). Some eight years after Janson left America, Gjertsen was forced to leave the Conference because of circumstances too complex to report here. This brought about a rift in Trinity Church. Supporters of Gjertsen organized Bethany Congregation, calling Gjertsen as pastor. Gjertsen remained a Lutheran to the end of his life, but he never again had any synodical affiliation. Ironically, he became known as the "liberal" Norwegian minister in Minneapolis in the early 1900s—and in that sense inherited Janson's mantle. At a time when fraternal organizations met with opposition from the churches, he defended them, and otherwise gained a reputation for helpfulness and compassion. He supported the Sons of Norway when it was under attack from the Norwegian Synod. In 1915, the Sons of Norway successfully conducted a city-wide subscription to place a monument on Gjertsen's grave, a drive spearheaded by Norwegian Unitarians.

32. Janson's sermon, "Why Have We Called Our Church Nazareth Church?", later appeared in *Saamanden*, July, 1894.

33. Drude Janson to Bjørnson, November 17, 1885. Lucy Stone's voice was famous. "In appearance Lucy Stone was a little woman, with a gentle silvery voice which could quiet a violent mob," Betty Friedan has written in *The Feminine Mystique*, 81 (New York, 1963). On October 25, 1885, Janson delivered a sermon entitled "Should a Christian Woman Work for Votes for Women?" It was printed in *Budstikke*n, November 3 and 10, 1885. In *Hvad jeg har oplevet*, 229–30, he also mentioned the meetings which Drude described in her letter.

34. Drude Janson to Mrs. Rasmus B. Anderson, January 29, 1886.

35. Drude Janson to Bjørnson, January 29, 1886. On August 17, 1883, while he was at work on *Geography and Love*, Bjørnson wrote to Georg Brandes. In the comedy the leading character is a professor of geography so absorbed in his work he has time for nothing else. Not satisfied with being merely a household adjunct, the heroine leaves and stays away until the professor has seen the error of his ways. In his letter to Brandes, Bjørnson spoke

of the work as a play on divorce. Writers are really swine, he was to write
Brandes, saying he was taking one of his best friends, Drude, as his model,
a person who had never thought of leaving her husband. "Ah, Drude!" he
was to add, "I have lived in deathly fear a Spanish skipper would come and
take you.—Now I am beginning to believe he can't." See Halvdan Koht,
Bjørnstjerne Bjørnson kamp liv 1882–1884, 2:97–98 (Oslo, 1932).

36. Hansen, *My Minneapolis*, 115.

37. Andreas Ueland to Rasmus B. Anderson, March 28, 1886.

38. Ueland to Rasmus B. Anderson, February 4, 1886.

39. Janson, *Præriens saga* (Chicago, 1885).

40. *Budstikken*, January 26, 1886.

41. *Budstikken*, January 19, 26, 1886.

42. *Christian Register*, February 11, 1886.

43. *Budstikken*, April 20, 1886.

44. Some smaller buildings had been moved and had suffered minor damage, according to the *Minneapolis Evening Journal* of April 15, 1886.

45. Janson, *Hvad jeg har oplevet*, 218. By the time Janson wrote his autobiography, more than twenty years had elapsed since his Minneapolis church
had been blown down—the second such disaster to take place. He could then
reveal that the event gave a Conference minister the chance to observe, "It
is remarkable how much wind follows that man Janson." From Drude's letter
to Mrs. Anderson about the storm, one might guess the minister to be M.
Falk Gjertsen.

46. Drude Janson to Mrs. Rasmus B. Anderson, April 20, 1886.

47. Drude Janson to Bjørnson, n.d.

48. *Christian Register*, April 22, 1886.

49. *Christian Register*, May 6, 1886.

50. "We Are Orthodox," in the *Minneapolis Evening Journal*, May 3,
1886.

51. The *Christian Register* of May 13, 1886, quoted the remarks of the
clergymen from the *St. Paul Pioneer Press* and the editorial comment from
the Boston *Herald*, giving no dates for either.

52. *Christian Register*, May 13, 1886.

53. "Overtro og vantro," in *Folkebladet*, April 21, 1886.

54. *Christian Register*, May 6, 1886.

55. The *Unitarian* (Chicago), May 1886. *Unity*, in its issue of May 1,
1886, was to do its bit to dispel the notion that the destruction of Janson's
churches was part of divine vengeance, saying: "It is not because he is a
heretic and disturbs the peace of the Scandinavian heaven where the orthodox dwell but because he builds churches in a windy latitude that Bro. Janson
has been visited a second time by a cyclone and the upper part of his new
church, which was enclosed, but not finished, has been blown to splinters."

56. *Budstikken*, April 27, 1886.

57. *Budstikken*, April 20, 27, June 1, 1886.

58. "Report of J. T. Sunderland, Secretary of the Western Conference, Cincinnati, Ohio, May 12, 1886," in *Unity*, June 5, 1886 The *Unitarian*, edited by J. T. Sunderland and Brooke Herford, carried in its May, 1886, issue an article entitled "A New Disaster to Mr. Janson's Church—Help Needed."

59. Lyttle, *Freedom Moves West*, 185.

60. Janson to Rasmus B. Anderson, May 28, 1886.

61. Lyttle, *Freedom Moves West*, 186.

62. Lyttle, *Freedom Moves West*, 186–88.

63. John Halverson, "Historical Review of the Norwegian Evangelical Lutheran Synod in America," in *History of the Scandinavians in the United States*, 1:194 (Minneapolis, 1893).

CHAPTER VI

1. The book was first published, under the title *En ung pige* (A Young Girl) in Copenhagen in 1887. In 1889 it came out in Minneapolis with the title *En saloonkeepers datter*. The information that Mathilde Ilstrup was the model for the heroine was given the author by Eilev Janson in Seattle in 1959.

2. It has been difficult to find information about Christian Haug. In the article, "Kristofer Janson i Amerika," in *Verdens Gang* (Kristiania), January 22, 1885—presumably written by Hamsun—Haug is spoken of as an unusually capable president of Janson's congregation, a man who could manage affairs with great diligence and care when Janson was gone. He was said to have come from Kristiania. The Minneapolis city directory of 1884–85 lists him as a clerk at the Goodfellow and Eastman store. His address is given as 2419 Nicollet Avenue, the Janson residence. The 1886–87 directory gives his address as 713 First Avenue South. After 1887, one finds no mention of him in either *Saamanden* or the newspapers. Neither Amandus Norman nor Skørdalsvold makes any mention of him.

3. Janson, *Hvad jeg har oplevet*, 229. In *Mira*, Drude's autobiographical novel, the heroine turns to writing to assuage loneliness. Drude in publishing this book used the pseudonym Judith Keller.

4. With the women's liberation movement in full swing, the Jansons would find plenty of support today. In *The Feminine Mystique*, 351 (New York, 1963), Betty Friedan has described the life of the young housewife with children and a home in suburbia. She has no money problems and is never called upon to exert any great physical effort, but her days are given over to the service of her home and children, being filled with such trivia as driving children to school and to the Little League baseball practice or the Bluebirds, stacking dishwashers, putting loads in washers and dryers, waxing, polishing, and vacuuming her house, shopping at the supermarket, attending P.T.A. committee meetings—her day so packed that she never has

more than a fifteen-minute interval that is unencumbered. Calling this the "problem that has no name," Ms. Friedan says these women have no "identity"; they get their guidelines from TV commercials. They contrast with Lucy Stone and her colleagues, most of whom fulfilled themselves as women and developed their talents as persons. Betty Friedan feels that this "anatomy is destiny" philosophy has had disastrous consequences both for the women and for their children.

5. Judith Keller, pseud., *Mira*, 13 (Copenhagen, 1897).

6. Information suppplied by Eilev Janson in March, 1959.

7. Janson, "Den Femtende Wisconsin," in *Normænd i Amerika* (Copenhagen, 1887). In a note to Rasmus B. Anderson, Dr. Knut Hoegh, a physician who practiced in La Crosse, Wisconsin, and later in Minneapolis, disparaged Janson's *Normænd i Amerika*, saying that the author put a great tax on one's credence by including such fanciful episodes as the Fifteenth Wisconsin singing Bjørnson's songs as they marched along. The doctor wrote, "It occurs to me that Kristofer has a special talent for misunderstanding the ordinary Norwegian-American." Hoegh to Rasmus B. Anderson, January 14, 1888, in the Anderson Papers.

8. Most of Norman's letters to Janson have been lost, with the exception of the few Janson published in *Saamanden*. Some of those from Janson to Norman have been printed in *Mere Lys* for April–July, 1918. *Mere Lys* was the quarterly Norman published in Hanska, Minnesota. The eleven letters range in time from 1885 to 1893. The one in which Janson suggests that Norman become his student is dated August 9, 1886.

9. John A. Kouwenhoven, *Adventures of America, 1857–1900*, 200 (New York, 1948).

10. Hopkins, *The Rise of the Social Gospel in American Protestantism, 1865–1915*, 99.

11. Norman Foerster and Robert Falk, "The Rise of Radicalism," in *American Poetry and Prose*, 665 (Boston, 1960).

12. Hopkins, *The Rise of the Social Gospel in American Protestantism*, 79.

13. Hopkins, *The Rise of the Social Gospel in American Protestantism*, 68–69.

14. Solon J. Buck, *The Agrarian Crusade*, 120–22 (New York, 1921); John D. Hicks, "The People's Party in Minnesota," in *Minnesota History Bulletin*, 5:531–60 (November, 1924); Hicks, *The Populist Revolt*, 58–61 (Minneapolis, 1931).

15. The meeting was held September 20, 1886; *Budstikken*, September 7, 14, 1886. Janson's Norwegian colleague in the Unitarian ministry, H. Tambs Lyche, wrote an impassioned plea for the Haymarket anarchists which appeared in *Unity* on December 4, 1886, and was entitled "Socialists and Anarchists." He had been among them, he wrote, and knew they were not bad men, however mistaken they may have been in their ideas. They were earnestly trying to improve man's lot, Lyche continued, saying they were tolerant,

kind, and willing to listen to arguments against their position. More than forty years later, the editor of the fiftieth anniversary issue of *Unity* (March 5, 1928) was to call attention to H. Tambs Lyche's "Socialists and Anarchists," saying that perhaps the bravest of all *Unity*'s battles for justice had been the stand it took "during the mad days of the Haymarket Riots and preceding the hanging of the anarchists in November of the following year."

16. *Budstikken*, November 3, 1886.

17. Morris Hillquit, *History of Socialism in the United States,* 253 (New York, 1903).

18. Havelock Ellis, "Eleanor Marx," in the *Adelphi*, 2:37–38 (London, October, 1935). The account quoted from Eleanor Marx Aveling differs in detail from the version Janson has given in his autobiography of his differences with Ibsen. Ibsen did not regain his composure quite so readily. Janson says that, in the evening, after the chair-throwing episode, he and Ibsen went for a walk in Rome, arm in arm, and that Ibsen invited Janson to have a cup of chocolate in a cafe. Possibly in telling of this to Eleanor Marx and her husband, Janson telescoped the ending so that the word "chocolate" was misinterpreted as meaning candy. Ibsen and Janson seem to have had several arguments over *landsmaal*, with Janson, of course, defending the peasant vernacular. It may have been these discussions to which Ibsen was alluding when he wrote to the actor who was the first to play "Hjalmar Ekdal" in *The Wild Duck* that, while he was writing the part, he kept thinking of Kristofer Janson who, Ibsen declared, was never so charming as when he was talking utter nonsense.

19. *Budstikken*, October 20, 1886.

20. *Budstikken*, October 13, 1886. The Norwegian title of the sermon was "Spiritisme og ortodoksisme, fornuftens invendinger."

21. Janson, *Hvad jeg har oplevet*, 233.

22. *Mere Lys*, April–July, 1920.

23. Benjamin O. Flower, *Progressive Men, Women, and Movements of the Past Twenty-Five Years*, 188 (Boston, 1914).

24. Janson to Amandus Norman, October 5, 1886; *Mere Lys*, April–July, 1918.

25. *Christian Register*, December 9, 1886.

26. Isaac Atwater, ed., *History of Minneapolis, Minnesota*, 227 (New York, 1893).

27. *Folkebladet*, February 2, 1887.

28. *Budstikken*, February 16, 1887.

29. The sermon, "Helten fra Nasaret," was announced in *Budstikken* on December 22, 1886. Janson included it in his *Lys og frihed*, 37–43 (Minneapolis, 1892).

30. James Dombrowski, *The Early Days of Christian Socialism in America*, 48 (New York, 1936); Hopkins, *The Rise of the Social Gospel in Amer-*

ican Protestantism, 60–61; Richard Hofstadter, *Social Darwinism in American Thought*, 110–11 (Boston, 1955).

31. Hopkins, *The Rise of the Social Gospel in American Protestantism*, 61.

32. Hopkins, *The Rise of the Social Gospel in American Protestantism*, 82–83.

33. Dombrowski, *The Early Days of Christian Socialism in America*, 103.

34. The lecture, "Den gjøende hund," was published in *Social Demokraten* in Kristiania on March 19, 1887. No printed version in an American newspaper or magazine has been found.

35. *Budstikken*, January 13, 20, 26, March 16, April 13, 27, May 4, 11, 23, 27, 1887.

36. Borghild Lee, the daughter of Mrs. Laura Frisvold Lee, gave this information to the author in Seattle in March, 1959.

37. Mrs. Dina Kolderup to the author, February 4, 1959; Drude Janson to Mrs. Rasmus B. Anderson, April 14, 1887, in the Anderson Papers.

38. Andreas Ueland to Rasmus B. Anderson, December 4, 1887.

39. *Budstikken*, December 6, 1887.

40. Janson to Bjørnson, June 1, 1888.

41. Janson, *Hvad jeg har oplevet*, 222.

42. *Budstikken*, April 13, 20, 27, May 18, 25, 1887.

43. *Minneapolis Evening Journal*, May 2, 1887.

44. *Budstikken*, May 4, June 15, 1887.

45. *Budstikken*, June 29, July 13, 20, 1887.

46. Hjalmar Hjorth Boyesen, "The New School of Norwegian Literature," in the *Critic*, 7:225 (May 7, 1887).

47. *Folkebladet*, May 4, 1887.

48. Nils Michelet to Rasmus B. Anderson, April 3, 1887; *Budstikken*, April 27, 1887.

49. *Budstikken*, May 18, 1887.

50. *Budstikken*, June 29, 1887.

51. Lyttle, *Freedom Moves West*, 189–90.

52. Lyttle, *Freedom Moves West*, 191.

53. *Saamanden* (Minneapolis), April, 1891.

54. *Christian Register*, June 23, 1887; *Budstikken*, June 8, 1887.

55. Drude Janson to Mrs. Rasmus B. Anderson, May 26, 1887.

56. Drude Janson to the Bjørnsons, September 15, 1887.

57. Drude Janson to Mrs. Rasmus B. Anderson, November 30, 1887.

58. *Budstikken*, July 20, 1887.

59. *Christian Register*, September 29, 1887.

CHAPTER VII

1. George Batchelor, "In the North-West," in the *Christian Register*, October 27, 1887.

2. *Mere Lys*, April–July, 1919; article from *Scandia*.

3. Janson to Bjørnson, December 19, 1888.

4. *Saamanden,* February, 1888, March 1888. At the time Drude's article was written, Kimball's courage seemed to have triumphed. However, the ten-vote margin did not allow him much leeway. In the issue of the magazine for October, 1888, one finds that Kimball resigned eleven months after he had delivered his daring sermon.

5. *Budstikken,* October 5, 1887. Janson also contributed "Et kvinde-korstog," which dealt with the women's crusade for temperance in America. It ran in *Nylænde* (Kristiania) in August and September, 1887. Drude was a frequent contributor to *Nylænde,* the organ of the Norsk Kvindesagforening (Norwegian Women's Suffrage Association) and as such the counterpart of the *Women's Journal* in America. In the February 1, 1887, issue, she had an article on how well women's suffrage was working in Washington Territory; for the March 15, 1887, issue, she wrote a eulogistic piece on Mrs. Abby Kelley Foster, whose death had taken place shortly before. Laura Wold, also of Minneapolis, contributed to the May, 1887, issue. It is interesting to note that *Nylænde* sometimes carried articles about Annie Jenness-Miller, the American advocate of reform in women's dress. According to Mrs. Kolderup, Drude was a dedicated disciple of Mrs. Jenness-Miller. In May, 1892, the latter lectured in Minneapolis, and her name now and then turns up in *Saamanden.*

6. A year later, Janson was to preach a sermon on divorce. Still maintaining that couples that could not get along should be able to be legally separated on that ground, he was very much opposed to successive divorces and remarriages. To circumvent this practice, he would prohibit a second marriage, arguing that this rule would cause people to be more thoughtful before entering into marriage in the first place. See *Folkebladet,* October 26, 1887.

7. *Folkebladet,* December 4, 1887.

8. *Budstikken,* April 11, 1888.

9. *Budstikken,* May 9, 1888.

10. *Budstikken,* May 9, 1888.

11. *Saamanden,* September, 1888.

12. *Budstikken,* December 6, 1887, February 15, March 11, April 4, 1888.

13. Einar Skavlan, *Knut Hamsun,* 118 (Oslo, 1929).

14. *Budstikken,* March 12, 1888. Janson's funeral eulogy of Frits Gjellerup, "Ved en anarchists baare" (At an Anarchist's Bier), appeared in *Saamanden,* November, 1891.

15. *Budstikken,* January 25, 1888. Eilev Janson described the stealing of the pigeons to the author on August 18, 1959, in some detail. "When you speak of my home on Nicollet Avenue and my pigeons, it brings back very fond memories. I remember well the incident when the thieves broke into the barn and stole the pigeons. But you do not know the sequel of how I found the thieves. In their eagerness to get away, they left their dog in the hayloft.

I put a leash on him, and the dog took me right to their home, where I found the pigeons in a crate hidden under their bed."

16. *Budstikken*, February 15, 1888.

17. *Budstikken*, February 29, 1888.

18. *Budstikken*, April 25, 1888.

19. *Budstikken*, February 1, 15, 29, March 11, 18, 1888.

20. Skavlan, *Knut Hamsun*, 119–20.

21. *Budstikken*, January 25, 1888.

22. Janson to Amandus Norman, January 2, 1888; *Mere Lys*, April–July, 1918.

23. *Budstikken*, February 8, 1888; Janson, *Hvad jeg har oplevet*, 220–21.

24. *Fædrelandet og Emigranten*, February 29, 1888.

25. *Budstikken*, March 28, 1888.

26. Knut Hamsun, *Fra det moderne Amerikas aandsliv* (American Cultural Life) (Copenhagen, 1889).

27. The *Christian Register* for May 10, 1888, reported that the Minnesota Conference had met at Sioux Falls, South Dakota, on April 26. Janson had spoken on the outlook for missionary work among the Scandinavians in Minnesota, Dakota, Michigan, Missouri, and Kansas, saying that what was needed was "stirring, enthusiastic men, familiar with Western life who were willing to make some personal sacrifice." Janson was to report the event in *Saamanden*, May, 1888, also mentioning the need for more workers. He wrote that the best spirit pervaded the conference, filling all with great hope for the future and for strengthening the feeling of brotherhood. At the conference, a new Unitarian church was dedicated, the result of the tireless work of Carrie Bartletts, the minister.

28. *Budstikken*, May 9, 1888.

29. Janson to Bjørnson, June 1, 1888. It was common for both the Janson children and the Behr girls to take part in church activities. On April 5, 1959, Mrs. Kolderup wrote: "We [the Janson girls, her sister Agnes, and she] helped to act in the plays and in all the bazaars in Nazareth Church basement. We took tickets at his lectures and loved to help in all the many doings to gather money for the church." In an article in the *Western Viking* (Seattle) on November 30, 1962, she wrote of taking part in a Holberg comedy, saying that her sister Agnes was "Jeronimus" and she had been "the witty Pernille." Presumably the play was Holberg's *Julestuen* (The Christmas Party). Arne sometimes took part, but the two older boys do not seem to have done so. Eilev Janson has said that they were also somewhat remiss about attending Saturday school.

30. Janson to Bjørnson, June 1, 1888. At the time Janson wrote this letter, he had carried accounts of Knapp's missionary venture in Japan in *Saamanden* for October, November, December, 1887, and February, 1888. A long article adapted from the writings of Keshub Chunder Sen, a deceased leader

of the Brahmo Somaj sect in India, had appeared in the January, 1888, *Saamanden*.

31. Drude Janson to Mrs. Rasmus B. Anderson, June 9, 1888, in the Anderson Papers.

32. *Budstikken*, June 6, 1888.

33. This information was given the author by Eilev Janson in Seattle, March, 1959. Janson mentions Eilev's being in British Columbia in his letter of August, 1888, to Norman; *Mere Lys*, April–July, 1918. Later, Janson was proud of Eilev's derring-do and mentioned it in letters to Bjørnson on December 19, 1888, August 8, September 16, 1889, and January 22, 1890.

34. *Paa begge sider havet* (Kristiania and Copenhagen, 1890); *Et arbeidsdyr* (Minneapolis, 1889). "Potterville og Perryville" is included in *Paa begge sider havet*.

35. Leo Tolstoy, *A Confession and What I Believe*, tr. by Aylmer Maude (Oxford, 1941). After the publication of *The Kreutzer Sonata*, Janson's enthusiasm for Tolstoy cooled. In response to a reader's inquiry, he wrote in *Saamanden*, August, 1891, that he disliked much of Tolstoy's later work, especially *The Kreutzer Sonata* in which he found the Russian to have a sick exaggeration bordering on fanaticism.

36. Janson, *Ægteskab og skilsmisse* (Copenhagen, 1895).

37. Arthur M. Schlesinger mentions the popularity of Mrs. Ward's novel as evidence that such conflicts were part of the religious unrest of the last quarter of the nineteenth century. See "A Critical Period in American Religion," in *Proceedings of the Massachusetts Historical Society*, 523–47 (Boston, 1935). Two other novels dealing with the same theme, Cecelia Wooley's *Love and Theology* and Margaret Deland's *John Ward, Preacher*, came out the same year and also were widely read.

38. *Saamanden*, January, 1889.

39. Janson to Norman, August 25, 1888; *Mere Lys*, April–July, 1918.

40. *Diderich Menschenskræk* is the name of one of Holberg's plays. Possibly a scene or an act of this play was performed—or it may have furnished material for a monologuist. The bazaar was an eight-day affair, lasting from Monday to Monday. On four evenings, theatrical performances were given: an act of Holberg's *Jacob von Tybo*, a scene from Janson's *Vore besteforældre*, "Oberst Lutken lærer sin tjenere at danse minuet," "Peter Tramps hjemkomst," and "Ole Fets betragtninger"—the last two works by Janson. Tableaux were Dybbøl's "Siege" and "David and Goliath." *Illustreret Ugeblad* gave an account of the program. The other Minneapolis papers concentrated more on the results of the many contests.

41. Janson, *Hvad jeg har oplevet*, 217; Hansen, *My Minneapolis*, 103.

42. *Illustreret Ugeblad* (Minneapolis), October 4, 1888.

43. *Saamanden*, November, 1888.

44. *Budstikken*, October 24, 1888; *Normanna* (Minneapolis), October 27, 1888.

45. Janson to Bjørnson, December 19, 1888.

46. Janson to Bjørnson, December 19, 1888.

47. John D. Hicks, *The Populist Revolt*, 154 (Minneapolis, 1931).

48. *Saamanden*, December, 1888.

49. Henrik Cavling, "Kirkelige forhold," in *Verdens Gang* (Kristiania), December 3, 1888.

50. Knut Hamsun, "Kristofer Janson," in *Ny Jord* (Copenhagen), July–December, 1888.

51. Tore Hamsun, *Knut Hamsun som han var*, 55 (Oslo, 1956).

52. Janson, *Hvad jeg har oplevet*, 225–26.

53. Dombrowski, *The Early Days of Christian Socialism in America*, 104.

54. *Saamanden*, January, 1888.

55. Louis F. Post, *The Prophet of San Francisco*, 91 (New York, 1930).

56. Frank Luther Mott, *A History of American Magazines*, 4:178 (Cambridge, Massachusetts, 1957).

57. Gregory Weinstein, *The Ardent Eighties*, 95 (New York, 1928).

58. B. O. Flower, *Progressive Men, Women, and Movements in the Past Twenty-Five Years*, 173–74 (Boston, 1914).

59. The rabbi mentions that the sentence in chapter eighteen of *Josephus' Antiquities* concerning Jesus came to be judged by authorities as of later insertion and therefore apocryphal. He states that the correspondence of Origen—the Christian scholar of the third century—with Celsus shows that Origen knew nothing of that sentence. The series "Messianske forventninger" appeared in *Saamanden*, November and December, 1888, January and February, 1889.

60. Janson to Bjørnson, December 19, 1888; *Saamanden*, December 19, 1888. For "questioner's standpoint," Janson used the expression "spørsmaaltegnets standpunkt."

CHAPTER VIII

1. The masthead for *Saamanden* for March, 1889, gives Janson's address as 1419 Ninth Street South, whereas all previous issues had carried 2419 Nicollet Avenue.

2. *Illustreret Ugeblad* (Minneapolis), February 28, 1889.

3. In his December 19, 1888, letter to Bjørnson, Janson wrote that he had sold his Nicollet Avenue property and now had the chance to obtain a "princely house." Some indication of its size may be obtained from the use it was put to after the Jansons had sold it. It became the first building to house the Swedish Hospital. Alfred Söderström, in his *Minneapolis minnen*, 259 (Minneapolis, 1899), said it could accommodate thirty patients. For all its elegance, the house does not appear to have been a particularly comfortable place in which to live, largely, it seems, because it was so expensive to keep up. In one of her articles in the *Western Viking* in 1963, Mrs. Kolderup told of the winter she spent in the new house, when her mother was

called to Chicago because of the illness of another daughter. Mrs. Kolderup wrote: "We sat and froze—all winter. . . . Coal was expensive and Aunt Drude had to stretch money far."

4. *Illustreret Ugeblad*, January 17, 31, 1889; *Minneapolis Sunday Tribune*, February 3, 1889; *The North* (Minneapolis), August 21, 1889.

5. *Budstikken*, November 11, 1888; *Normanna* (Minneapolis), November 24, 1888.

6. *Illustreret Ugeblad*, February 21, 1889.

7. *Budstikken*, December 19, 1888.

8. Hamsun's comment that American churches contained "polished people" had also been made by others. In 1886, Washington Gladden is reported to have said that the reason laborers did not attend church was that they could not dress well enough to appear in so stylish a place and that they felt a resentment against their employers. In *The Ancient Lowly*, C. Osborn Ward arraigned "the gilded pulpit" for its neglect of the laborers whose toil supplied its luxuries. Terence V. Powderly, Grand Master Workman of the Knights of Labor, said that, if the Sermon on the Mount were preached without reference to its author, the minister would be warned not to repeat the "ravings of a utopiast." See Hopkins, *The Rise of the Social Gospel in American Protestantism*, 83–85.

9. Hamsun, *Fra det moderne Amerikas aandsliv* (Copenhagen, 1889). This volume has been competently translated by Barbara Gordon Morgridge, *The Cultural Life of Modern America* (Cambridge, Massachusetts, 1969).

10. *Budstikken*, June 26, July 4, 10, 17, 1889.

11. *Budstikken*, July 31, 1889.

12. *Budstikken*, July 31, 1889.

13. *Budstikken*, August 14, 1889.

14. *Budstikken*, August 21, 28, 1889.

15. *Budstikken*, February 20, 1889.

16. *Vikingen* (Madison, Wisconsin), March 19, May 4, 1889.

17. *Illustreret Ugeblad*, April 11, 1889.

18. *Illustreret Ugeblad*, June 20, 1889.

19. Janson to Bjørnson, August 8, 1889; report of the secretary of the Western Unitarian Conference, in Chicago, May 14–16, 1889, in *Unity*, June 1, 8, 1889; *Saamanden*, August, 1889.

20. Details of Eilev Janson's homecoming were related by him to the author in Seattle in March, 1959. Janson speaks of his sons' ambitions in his August 8, 1889, letter to Bjørnson; Drude's description of Eilev is found in her letter to Bjørnson of October 6, 1891.

21. *Mere Lys*, April–July, 1920. Although Janson devoted a long chapter in his autobiography to his years as a minister in America, he mentions none of his associates with the exception of the Kolstad family and Otto Nilsby of Underwood. He characterized Nilsby as a "young, gifted farmer . . . who

was an earnest supporter and helped me with *Saamanden*"; Janson, *Hvad jeg har oplevet*, 215.

22. *Unity*, June 1, 8, 22, 1889.

23. *Saamanden*, May, 1889.

24. For Pentecost's theological views, see *Saamanden*, September, 1888, and July, 1889.

25. *Unity*, March 2, 1889.

26. *Saamanden*, March, July, 1889.

27. This is the original which Janson translated for *Saamanden*'s issue of June, 1889. It is quoted from Dombrowski, *The Early Days of Christian Socialism in America*, 99–100.

28. In *Social Darwinism in American Thought*, 114–15 (Boston, 1955), Richard Hofstadter says of Gronlund: "Now all but forgotten, Gronlund's writings were once widely read by intellectuals interested in socialism who seem to have found satisfaction in his occasional religious phraseology, his moderate tone, his air of theoretical authority."

29. Janson to Jenkin Lloyd Jones, August 8, 1889, in the Jones Papers.

30. Janson to Bjørnson, August 8, 1889.

31. *Saamanden*, September, 1889; *The North*, September 18, 1889.

32. Kristofer and Drude Janson to Bjørnson, September 16, 1889.

33. *The North*, August 21, 1889.

34. Janson's article, "Den norske kunstforening," appeared in *Budstikken*, May 15, 1889. *The North*'s comment was published in the issue of July 3, 1889.

35. Janson, " 'Looking Backward' av Edw. Bellamy," in *Saamanden*, September, 1889. Ordinarily, book reviews were in a column headed "Litera-turanmeldelse" (Book Reviews), but this particular one was placed in the "Arbeidersagen" (Labor Issues) column.

36. *Saamanden*, September, 1889.

37. Janson, "Din brøders blod raaber til mig fra jorden," in *Lys og frihed*, 405–11 (Minneapolis, 1892).

38. *Saamanden*, September, 1889. Janson drew this excerpt from *Unity*, to which H. Tambs Lyche was a frequent contributor. During 1889 alone, he published "A Liberal Liberal Church," "Opportunism," "Robert Elsmere Continued," "Boabdil," "The Prophetic Vision and Opportunism," and "Story Telling in Sunday School."

39. J. B. Silcox, "Kirken og de sociale reformer," in *Saamanden*, October, 1889.

40. Janson to Bjørnson, January 22, 1890.

41. *The North*, October 23, 1889.

42. The fair featured a scene from Hostrup's *Gjenboerne* (The Neighbors) and several tableaux. In addition, several readings or declamations of a humorous nature were given: a lecture on the love of a bachelor, "An Amusing Piece from Mark Twain," and one of Mrs. Caudle's lectures. On

various nights, music was furnished by Drude's niece, Agnes Behr, the Nord-mændenes Sangforening, and Miss Nelson, who played a Hardanger fiddle. *Illustreret Ugeblad*, October 17, November 7, 1889. In its October 23, 1889, issue, *The North* commented: "The entertaining nature of Mr. Janson's fairs is so well known to the public that further recommendation is superfluous." It reported on the success of the fair on October 30, and the tribute to Mrs. Janson, Haug, and Hasberg appeared on November 6, 1889.

43. Janson revealed this information in *Saamanden* in its issue of November, 1889.

44. Janson to Bjørnson, January 22, 1890.

45. Janson, *Bag gardinet* (Minneapolis, 1889).

46. *Budstikken*, February 12, 1890.

47. Andreas Ueland to Rasmus B. Anderson, December 4, 1887, in the Anderson Papers.

48. *Budstikken*, February 19, 1890.

49. In a letter to the author, January 19, 1961, Mrs. Kolderup wrote that her father had been Johan Beer, the son of a wealthy man in Flekkefjord. As a result of Beer's financial irresponsibility, Mrs. Beer (the name became Behr in America) started a pensionat in Kristiania. When her husband's creditors hounded her, she left Norway with Kirsten, a daughter, for Chicago, where another daughter was married, leaving the other girls, Agnes and Dina, with their grandfather at Fana Prestegaard. After the Jansons were established in Minneapolis, she moved to the city and sent for Agnes and Dina. In Minneapolis she made her living by having boarders and by catering. On October 16, 1889, shortly before *Bag gardinet* was published, she advertised in *Budstikken*, saying that she was available for catering public or private parties in both Minneapolis and St. Paul, having at one time managed a pensionat in Kristiania.

50. Janson to Bjørnson, January 22, 1890.

51. The first installment of Janson's translation of Crooker's *Jesus Brought Back* is found in *Saamanden*, January, 1890. His sermon, "Hvorledes skal vi forsone vort samfund med Gud?", appeared in the same issue.

52. *Saamanden*, January, 1890.

53. *Saamanden*, January, 1890.

54. *Saamanden*, February, 1890.

55. *Saamanden*, February, 1890.

56. *Saamanden*, December, 1889.

57. *Saamanden*, February, 1890.

58. *The North*, August 27, 1890.

59. *Current Literature* (New York), February, 1890.

60. *Unity*, February 15, March 11, 1890.

61. *Folkebladet*, March 26, 1890.

62. Janson to Bjørnson, March 31, 1890.

63. *Budstikken*, April 10, 1889.

64. *The North*, April 9, 1890.

65. *Budstikken*, August 6, 1890.

66. On August 1, 1959, Mrs. Kolderup wrote of Mrs. Kate Buffington Davis: "She was the follower of Annie Besant and converted D. J. [Drude Janson] to Theosophy by her great influence over D. J." In 1959, Eilev Janson spoke of his mother's great interest in Theosophy.

67. *Saamanden*, April, 1890.

68. Martin Ridge, *Ignatius Donnelly*, 273 (Chicago, 1965).

69. *Saamanden*, June, July, 1890.

70. Ridge, *Ignatius Donnelly*, 273.

71. Items concerning the Farmers' Alliance appeared in *Saamanden* in the issues of April, June, July, and August, 1890.

72. Janson, "Markus Thrane," in *Saamanden*, June, 1890.

CHAPTER IX

1. *Halleluja-pige* was a term Norwegians at the time commonly applied to Salvation Army women who took part in street meetings. *Hjernekikker* seems to imply that a person always ready to be the confidant of all comers may not (as seems to be implied in Janson's case) be aware of what he neglects in his own household.

2. Drude Janson to Bjørnson, May 22, 1890.

3. At the time Mrs. Stoep told this, she said: "I am not going to tell you the man's name. His family is still living in Minneapolis, and they are very fine people." Janson's words, as she quoted them, were: "Det er sorgelig han skulde gjøre det, men saa godt et menneske som han i grunden var!" According to Mrs. Stoep, Janson's faith was justified. The man came back and the money was repaid. He had heard of a place where he might find work, and, as Mrs. Stoep said, times were hard. In recalling the incident, she said of Janson, "If I had got nothing else from him, that would have been enough."

4. Information given by Eilev Janson; Drude Janson to Bjørnson, October 6, 1891. "Den ideale og den virkelige Kristus," Drude Janson's translation of James Freeman Clarke's "The Ideal and the Actual Christ," appeared in *Saamanden* in April, 1891.

5. Michael Bryan, *Dictionary of Painters and Engravers*, 5:283 (Port Washington, New York, 1964).

6. *Saamanden*, July, 1890.

7. H. H. Boyesen to Rasmus B. Anderson, July [?], 1890, in the Anderson Papers.

8. This information was supplied by Gundersen's daughter, Mrs. Gudrun Rom, in a letter to the author dated June 1, 1960.

9. Mrs. Rom has said that her father once told her Matthew Arnold's *Literature and Dogma* had influenced him so greatly that he considered his reading the book one of the turning points in his life. He later named his son for the British writer.

10. Oscar Gundersen, "Kristofer Janson," in *Minneapolis Søndag Tidende*, August 17, 1890.

11. Kristofer Janson, "Norsemen in the United States," in *Cosmopolitan*, October, 1890.

12. Janson, "Norsemen in the United States."

13. Janson, "Norsemen in the United States." The *Unitarian* for November, 1890, in its review of the article quoted the two paragraphs given here, commenting that Janson had written an interesting account in which he gave "a graphic picture of his countrymen as sticklers for orthodoxy and controversialists." In an annotated bibliography, in O. N. Nelson's *History of Scandinavians and Successful Scandinavians in the United States,* vol. 1, 273, the editor says: "The author makes some assertions which hardly coincide with actual facts; yet his discussion is valuable, both from a literary and a historical standpoint."

14. Henry Steele Commager, *The American Mind*, 75 (New Haven, 1950).

15. *The North*, December 14, 1892. Mrs. Davis is also described as a leader in the city. "Sympathetic, broad, and with nerves strung to a high tension, the mind of this gifted lady has naturally taken a humanitarian bent." Because of her delicate health, the article went on, Mrs. Davis could not be in the forefront of all philanthropic movements in the city but must restrict herself principally to "strictly literary and intellectual phases of the activity so striking in the case of Minneapolis womanhood of late." In spite of Mrs. Davis' devotion "to various 'isms' in latter day's thought," she is described as levelheaded and practical so that "her advice is eagerly sought and highly valued."

16. Mrs. Davis was later mentioned in the October, 1891, issue of *Saamanden* in which Janson commended her for her article in the *Universalist Monthly* on child labor. She had written that a child's right to a free childhood should not be open to discussion in a Christian society. She reported that the 1880 census had shown the number of day workers under 15 to be 1,118,000. Since then, she said, the percentage of children under that age had increased 20 per cent while the number of child workers had gone up 50 per cent. Janson, who had drawn this excerpt from the *Minneapolis Tribune*, described Mrs. Davis as a lady who was well known as a leader in the city's educated and philanthropic circles.

17. *The North*, April 9, 1890.

18. Janson to Johannes J. Skørdalsvold, August 16, 1890. The letter is in the possession of the Skurdalsvold family in Minneapolis. Janson's topic for discussion on September 29, 1890, was "Why Has the Alliance Party Been Organized?" See the *Minneapolis Søndag Tidende*, September 28, 1890.

19. In the October, 1890, issue of *Saamanden,* Janson used five and a half columns in the Labor Issues section to advance the claims of the Alliance party.

20. John D. Hicks, *The Populist Revolt*, 181; Martin Ridge, *Ignatius Donnelly*, 276. In December, 1890, Ignatius Donnelly became president of the Minnesota Farmers' Alliance. In April, 1889, his novel *Caesar's Column* had been published under the pseudonym Edmund Boisgilbert, the publishers as much as indicating that this was not the author's real name. Although major newspapers and periodicals ignored it, the book from the first had a brisk sale, and gradually farm and labor papers took note of it. After the election of 1890, it became known that Donnelly was the author, and this played a part in his winning the presidency of the state Alliance. In the June, 1890, *Saamanden*, Janson (without knowing the author's identity) had given the book an enthusiastic review. The novel, a projection into the year 1988, was written as a series of letters describing the experiences of a young man as he traveled in the United States. Although the book predicted many technological wonders and was replete with hairbreadth escapes, disguised heroes, and the like, it pictured a depraved society with the rich in control and the working class in poverty and ended with a bloody revolution, more violent than any that had preceded it. In his review, Janson translated a long excerpt from "A Twentieth Century Sermon," the book's most famous chapter.

21. *Budstikken*, October 1, 1890.

22. The Danz Orchestra was at the time the most prestigious in Minneapolis. It was the precursor of the Minneapolis Symphony Orchestra, now the Minnesota Orchestra. The letter is included in the Unity Church Papers at the Minnesota Historical Society.

23. *Saamanden*, October, 1890.

24. *Saamanden*, November, 1890.

25. *Saamanden*, December, 1890.

26. Janson refers to Daniel Douglas Home (1833–86). Colin Wilson has described Home as "perhaps the most remarkable and convincing medium who has so far appeared." See *The Occult*, 462 (New York, 1971).

27. Janson, "Hvem er Guds engle?", in *Lys og frihed*, 433–42.

28. Benjamin O. Flower, *Progressive Men, Women, and Movements in the Past Twenty-Five Years*, 187 (Boston, 1914).

29. Janson, "General Booth og frelsesarmeen," in *Saamanden*, November, 1890; "Kjættere og kjætteri" (af Robert Ingersoll, oversat af Otto Nilsby), January, 1891; "Lidt om de ethiske foreninger" (af H. S. Rikstad), February, 1891.

30. Janson, "St. Josephs søstre i Kristiania," July, 1891; "Epiktet," March, 1891; "Muhammed I," April, 1891; "Muhammed II," May, 1891. The articles on Epictetus and Mohammed were part of Janson's series, "Jesu aandelige brødre," which he began in the April, 1889, issue of *Saamanden* and continued at intervals through the next five years, publishing the last in the July, 1894, issue. All in all, there are eighteen articles dealing with ten spiritual leaders: Buddha, Confucius, Lao-Tse, Epictetus, Mohammed, Nanak (the founder of Sikhism), Origen, Marcus Aurelius, George Fox, and

John Wesley. With the exception of the one on Lao-Tse, which was written by H. Tambs Lyche, all were prepared by Janson. The first four dealt with Buddha and may have been the outgrowth of the paper Janson delivered before the Liberal Ministers' Association in January, 1887, the one that drew censure from Sven Oftedal. Buddha was given longer treatment than any of the others, although three articles dealt with Mohammed and two each with Epictetus, Origen, and Marcus Aurelius.

31. Janson, "The Scandinavian Mission," in the *Christian Register*, December 4, 1890.

32. *Budstikken*, December 24, 1890.

33. John Halvorson, "Historical Review of the Norwegian Evangelical Lutheran Synod in America," 193–95, and Knut Gjerset (with revision by F. A. Schmidt), "Historical Review of the United Norwegian Lutheran Church in America," 233–39. Both articles are in Nelson, *History of Scandinavians and Successful Scandinavians in the United States*. See also Andreas Helland, *Georg Sverdrup*, 143–64, and E. Clifford Nelson and Eugene Fevold, *The Lutheran Church among Norwegian-Americans*, 2:40–45.

34. *The North*, April 22, 1891.

35. *Budstikken*, March 25, 1891.

36. Janson to F. A. Schmidt, March 31, 1891. The letter is in the archives of the Norwegian-American Historical Association. In the letter, Janson says it had been decided that three persons would represent each side at the next meeting. The name of the third individual on the Liberal side was never reported.

37. Janson, "Efterdønninger af diskussionen om bibelens inspiration," in *Saamanden*, May, 1891.

38. The bill is in the Minnesota State Archives, in the capitol, St. Paul.

39. *The North*, July 1, 9, 1890. Henrik Cavling, *Fra Amerika*, 2:318–19 (Copenhagen, 1897). Mrs. Stub had edited a collection, *Songs of the North*, in 1894 and intended to follow it with another volume but was prevented from doing so because of illness. Mrs. Dina Kolderup had vivid memories of Mrs. Stub, as indicated in a letter dated February 4, 1959. In one of her articles for the *Western Viking* in Seattle, Mrs. Kolderup wrote of Mrs. Stub as a talented artist who should never have married a Lutheran minister and who was certainly too young to be the stepmother of two half-grown boys.

40. *The North*, March 25, 1891; Drude Janson to Bjørnson, October 6, 1891.

41. *Saamanden*, May, 1891. The first stanza of the poem reads:

> Femti Aar—saaret af Verdens Harm,
> Femti Aar—baaret af Faderens Arm,
> Femti Aar—varmet af Kjærligheds Glød,
> Femti Aar—løftet af Sorg og Nød.

42. *Saamanden*, May, 1891.

43. *The North*, May 12, 1891.

44. Janson, *Hvad jeg har oplevet*, 227–28.

45. *Saamanden*, July, 1891.

46. Apparently Janson drew ideas from a letter of one of *Saamanden's* readers to portray Peter's experiences with the schoolmaster in *Sara*. He had included the letter in an article, "Which Is the Better Educator, Kindness or Punishment?" in *Saamanden*, February, 1889. The circumstances described in the letter are virtually identical to those in the novel.

47. Kristofer Janson, *Sara* (Copenhagen, 1891).

48. Janson, *To arbeider foredrag* (Minneapolis, 1891). On page 3, he gives the sources of his material.

49. Janson, "Hvorfor er vort nuværende sociale system uholdbart?" in *To arbeider foredrag*, 3–22.

50. Janson, "Har vi et bedre system at sætte istedetfor det gamle?" in *To arbeider foredrag*, 23–46.

51. *The North*, September 16, 23, 1891. The "real incident" which sets off the plot of the novel was recorded by Janson in *Amerikanske forholde*, the volume made up of lectures he delivered in Norway after his first visit to America in 1879–80.

52. Janson, *Du er kjød af mit kjød* (Kristiania, 1895).

CHAPTER X

1. The original was written in Kristiania and was dated February 1, 1895.

2. *The North*, October 21, November 11, 17, 1891.

3. *The North*, October 21, 1891. Janson's St. Paul congregation shifted its meetings from Unity Church to Garfield Hall at 774 Arcade Street some time between late September and October 21, the latter date being the first time the paper gave the changed address. The inquiry concerning married teachers appeared in *The North*, September 16, 1891.

4. The Western superintendent (secretary) at the time was the Reverend T. B. Forbush. Possibly Janson found him as picayunish and difficult as Drude reported, but certainly his public utterances never indicated anything but enthusiasm for Janson. Volume 5 of *Saamanden* contains several references to Forbush from which one would gather that the superintendent was a witty, rather expansive man.

5. Drude Janson to Bjørnson, October 6, 1891.

6. *Saamanden*, November, 1891.

7. *Saamanden*, September, 1891.

8. Ivar Langland's letter, appearing in *Saamanden* in October, 1891, aroused considerable interest. See letters of "N. N." of Washburn, Wisconsin, in *Saamanden*, December, 1891, and March, 1892. See also *Saamanden* for April and August, 1892.

9. *Saamanden*, September, 1891.

10. Drude Janson to Bjørnson, January 24, 1896.

11. Anderson, *Life Story*, 302.

12. *The North,* December 9, 1891.

13. *The North,* December 16, 1891.

14. Norwegian biographical sources spell Louise's last name as Bentzen, but it appears that she had anglicized it to Benson while she was in America. That is how she is listed in the Minneapolis city directory. In his *Life Story,* Rasmus B. Anderson has called her "Miss Benson," and J. J. Skørdalsvold has also used that spelling. The time of her coming into the Janson household has been estimated from a letter written by Agnes Behr, dated January 12, 1892, in which she says that the Jansons were very much taken with Louise, as if to imply that her being there and what she said were still something of a novelty. Norwegian sources give Louise Bentzen's birth as January 22, 1861, although an article in *Protestantisk Tidende* (Copenhagen) for 1947 gives her birth year as 1866. The letter from Agnes Behr was given to the author by Mrs. Kolderup to whom it had been addressed. Ingeborg Janson's comments are from a letter to Ragna Alten, dated July 14, 1934. This letter is in the possession of the family of Professor Didrik Arup Seip in Norway; Professor Einar Haugen furnished the author with a copy.

15. *The North,* January 6, 1892; Janson to Bjørnson, March 22, 1892. Janson's "Bjørnstjerne Bjørnson" was the first in the lecture series; Mrs. Esther McDowell of Seattle has supplied the author with a copy of the program.

16. Agnes Behr shifts back and forth from Norwegian to English. The letter was given to the author by Mrs. Dina Behr Kolderup.

17. In the original, Agnes began in English and finished in Norwegian.

18. Janson's account of the conditions he encountered on the west coast and the installation of John L. Ericksen are in *Saamanden,* February, 1892.

19. *The North,* March 16, 1892; *Saamanden,* March, 1892.

20. The young man had written to protest Janson's having said that the poor often brought on their own misfortunes. Actually he had misinterpreted an article in *Saamanden* in which Janson had pointed out that drunkenness and other excesses could cause poverty. The letter and Janson's reply appeared in *Saamanden,* May, 1892.

21. Janson to Bjørnson, March 22, 1892.

22. *The North,* March 13, 27, 1892. Mrs. Dina Behr Kolderup has said that Janson composed an English text, not for one of Madden's compositions, but for *Legende,* the work of the Polish composer Wieniawski. She remembered having heard it at one of the Jansons' musicales. In a letter of August 1, 1959, she described the experience: "When Claude M. played Wieniawski's Legende to which K. J. had composed such a beautiful descriptive poem in which the young lovers drove through the snow-covered steppes of Russia and then the darkness came with terrific snow blinding the way and suddenly the troika with the lovers was hurled down in a deep ravine!" For Mrs. Kolderup this was one of many such experiences she enjoyed at the Jansons. Apparently on this occasion she was fifteen rather than twelve, for she was

born in 1876, and the Jansons did not meet Madden until the spring of 1891. Edvard Grieg composed music for Janson's "Mellom rosor" and that is what is heard in concert today.

23. Ingeborg Janson to Ragna Alten, July 14, 1934.

24. Drude Janson to Bjørnson, January 24, 1896.

25. *The North,* April 6, 1892.

26. *Saamanden,* May, 1892.

27. *The North,* March 9, 1892.

28. *The North,* April 27, 1892.

29. *The North,* May 11, 1892.

30. *The North,* May 18, 1892.

31. Lundeberg had also referred to Janson as a "fanatical Spiritualist," an expression that drew a protest from Dr. M. L. Julihn of Washington, D. C., in the June 8, 1892, issue of *The North.* Julihn did not know Janson, but he objected to the use of the word "fanatical." He declared that he was a Spiritualist himself, having become convinced after a thorough investigation.

32. *Saamanden,* September, 1892.

33. Janson believed in the immanence of God, but he did not consider himself a pantheist. In *Saamanden,* February, 1891, he responded to a charge that he was perilously close to it. He replied that a great difference existed between his views and those of a pantheist, who believed that the spirit of God pervaded all nature but felt this spirit to be a blind force. To Janson, all life emanated from a God who is a conscious, intelligent being.

34. *Unity,* June 23, September 29, 1892; the *Christian Register,* September 29, 1892.

35. In Janson's account of Skaptason's congregation, he erroneously gives the location of Gimli as British Columbia rather than Manitoba. See *Saamanden,* June, 1892.

36. Throughout the Janson story, one comes upon the idea that Norwegian Unitarianism must, of necessity, be different from that of the Americans, containing more emotion and less intellectualization. Writing in *Unity* on August 27, 1887, H. Tambs Lyche heralded the coming of *Saamanden,* saying: "If you will not grossly misunderstand me, we do need something a little *softer,* a little more tender-hearted, 'sentimental'; we *do* have some 'weak' spots in our hearts which *must* be touched or our allegiance is but partial,—then we need something a little more of the 'glory-shouting' kind, and something which will 'go to the hands and muscles' as well as to the head and heart. We have our peculiar needs and sentiments and even our peculiar 'heads.' And Unitarianism is able to fit them all by a little national transmutation." [Italics are in the original.]

37. *The North,* June 22, 1892.

CHAPTER XI

1. Judith Keller, pseud., *Mira: Et livsløb* (Copenhagen, 1897); Drude

Janson to the Bjørnsons, January 29, 1896; Drude to Bjørnson, February 10, 1896 [?]; Drude to Karoline Bjørnson, April 7, 1896.

2. The story of this incident was related to the author by Minnie Running at Hanska in the spring of 1962.

3. In a letter dated April 9, 1959, Eilev Janson wrote: "I told you about mother's affair with Claude Madden and how father accepted it with understanding and tolerance. When it was over and he met Louise, he felt his ties and obligation to mother were over. . . . I loved mother and had the highest regard for her integrity and understanding. But, in spite of that, you can readily understand there might be a slight jealousy, seeing that Louise usurped mother's position in father's life. This might easily be reflected in her writing of *Mira*. The same happened with all the children with the exception of myself. They resented Louise's intrusion into their lives and this caused distrust and dislike of Louise."

4. Peder Ydstie to Torkel Oftelie of Fergus Fall, n.d. It is estimated that this letter was written in the spring of 1894. Mrs. Eilev Janson has said that Ivar's sympathies were with his mother. Certainly one can understand the young man's consternation over his parents' domestic difficulties, wholly aside from his own emotional involvement. Unlike Eilev, he wanted to practice medicine in Minneapolis.

5. *Saamanden*, October, 1892.

6. *Saamanden*, August, 1892.

7. *Budstikken*, March 15, 1893.

8. *Saamanden*, December, 1891. Gundersen's "Til Kristofer Janson" first described Jesus as the man who had preached brotherly love but whose teachings had since been obscured by dogma. By bringing that gospel to the light and living it, Janson was truly the interpreter of Jesus. The last stanza, in translation, reads:

> For what you fought and what you won,
> For what you loosened and you bound,
> For all you heretofore have touched,
> And first and last for deed and word,
> For brotherhood upon the earth,
> My thanks, my warmest thanks!

Concerning Janson's remarks on the pessimism revealed in *Stemningsbilleder*, one can see that Gundersen's private life was such as to give him sobering thoughts. While still in Norway, he became engaged to a girl who worked in a Methodist publishing plant, and it was the girl's savings that financed his migration to America in 1882. As soon as he had established himself in Chicago, he sent for his fiancée and they were married. His wife found work as a printer on *Skandinaven*. A year later their daughter, Gudrun, was born. When the child was six, the mother died suddenly. Gundersen kept their rooms, boarding the child during the day with a family living in the same building. Evenings were spent with his little daughter, Gundersen reserving his own study and writing for the hours after she was in bed. His daughter, the late Mrs. Gudrun Rom, has said that later, while she was a student at the University of Chicago, she received special commendation for a theme she wrote on her father's heroic and successful efforts to give her a happy childhood.

9. *The North*, September 14, 21, 1892.

10. Janson, "Concerning Spiritualism: Its Significance and Dangers" and "Have We Been on Earth Before, and Shall We Return Again?" in *Fire foredrag*, 169–207, 208–48 (Copenhagen, 1894).

11. *Saamanden*, October, 1892.

12. *Saamanden*, February, 1892. The excerpt here is taken from Donnelly's original, reproduced in Ridge, *Ignatius Donnelly*, 295–96.

13. Janson was not alone in his fascination with Donnelly's preamble. Hicks, in *The Populist Revolt*, 235, quotes Jerry Simpson, a prominent Alliance leader from Kansas, as calling the work "one of the most vigorous and at the same time most classic productions of modern literature."

14. *Saamanden*, August, September, 1892.

15. Ridge, *Ignatius Donnelly*, 301; Janson, "How Should a Christian Vote in the Coming Election?", in *Saamanden*, October, 1892.

16. Hicks, *The Populist Revolt*, 267.

17. Hicks, *The Populist Revolt*, 261.

18. Hicks, *The Populist Revolt*, 258; Ridge, *Ignatius Donnelly*, 301.

19. Eilev Janson supplied the information concerning his going to Astoria, Oregon, to practice medicine. *The North* reported his departure from Minneapolis on November 9, 1892.

20. *The North*, December 21, 1892.

21. The previous month Hjalmar H. Boyesen had lectured on Ibsen in Minneapolis. *The North* quoted him as saying that Ibsen "lives in a realm of keen analytical thought, possessing a boldness of conception and execution unknown in any other writer." Boyesen was further reported to have said that Ibsen was devoid of philanthropic tastes and feelings, having a temperament that would be insufferable in a less distinguished person.

22. *The North*, February 1, 1893.

23. Janson's resignation from Nazareth Church was reported in *The North* on March 15, 1893.

24. The report that Janson had been granted a year's leave of absence from Nazareth Church appeared in *The North* on April 12, 1893. "Off to Europe" was printed on April 19.

25. *Mere Lys*, April–July, 1918.

26. *Unity*, July 13, 1893.

27. *The North*, June 21, 1893.

28. *Mere Lys*, April–July, 1918.

29. *Saamanden*, September, 1893.

30. Janson, *Jesus-sangene* (Minneapolis, 1893).

31. *The North*, September 6, 1893; *Saamanden*, September, 1893. Norman's ordination was reported in six lines, contrasting with the account of Janson's farewell reception which followed in more than three columns.

32. *Saamanden*, September, 1893.

33. Although Janson was primarily advertising *Jesus-sangene*, which had just come out, he urged people to get *Lys og frihed* and reminded them that the seventh volume of *Saamanden* was beginning. If every subscriber would get an additional one, *Saamanden* could continue in spite of the many who were remiss in their payment. See *Saamanden*, September, 1893. Three months later, in the December, 1893, issue of *Saamanden*, Meyer made his report.

34. "Ombord," "Brev til *Saamanden*," and "Ogsaa, et brev," in *Saamanden*, November, 1893. Janson's review of *Brogede blade* had appeared in the August, 1893, issue of the magazine.

35. *Saamanden*, December, 1893.

36. "Brev til *Saamanden*," in *Saamanden*, May, 1894.

37. *Saamanden*, August, 1894.

38. The quotations are taken from the letter of Drude Janson to Bjørnson dated January 29, 1896.

39. Drude's explanation to Bjørnson is in her letter of January 29, 1896.

40. Janson to Bjørnson, February 1, 1895.

41. Drude to Bjørnson, n.d. Apparently the letter was written some time between Christmas, 1895, and January 24, 1896.

42. Drude to Bjørnson, January 24, 29, 1896. One section of *Mira* contains a diary kept by the heroine. In Drude's novel, Ernestine Helsing is described as follows: "More and more her real nature protrudes. She makes no attempt at disguise before the children and me when Alf is not present. . . . Something sinister can suddenly mark her madonna expression. It is as if animal claws came forth from under her white garment."

43. Drude to Bjørnson, February 10, 1896[?].

44. Janson to Bjørnson, February 20, 1896.

45. Drude to Karoline Bjørnson, April 7, 1896.

46. Janson to Bjørnson, September 23, 1896.

47. *Norsk biografisk leksikon*, 6:593 (Oslo, 1934).

48. *Aschehougs konversasjons leksikon*, 9:402 (Oslo, 1948).

49. Judith Keller, *Mira*.

CHAPTER XII

1. *Evangelisk Luthersk Kirketidende*, April 21, May 19, 1894.

2. The manuscript of "The Free Christian Church of Minneapolis" by Skørdalsvold was given to the author by Mrs. P. J. Hanson, wife of a former minister of Nora Free Christian Church, Hanska, Minnesota.

3. Anderson, *Life Story*, 302.

4. O. N. Nelson, *History of the Scandinavians and Successful Scandinavians in the United States* (second revised edition, 1969), 1:419.

5. Janson, *Hvad jeg har oplevet*, 267–69.

6. L. Stavnheim, "Amandus Norman," in *Mere Lys*, January, 1932. This issue of the magazine was a memorial to Norman, who died on November 14, 1931.

7. Lyttle, *Freedom Moves West*, 220.

8. Ole Jorgensen, "Speech at the Laying of the Cornerstone of the Nora Church Parsonage, June 24, 1906" (Hanska, 1906). On this occasion, Jorgensen said: "We should remember with gratitude the material assistance and moral encouragement we have received from the American Unitarian Association, which seems to take a special interest in our behalf. It is always a good thing to be in good company, and as long as we keep in close touch with the New England people, we are, as Bjørnson says, in the best society in the world."

9. Information on Amandus Norman's career has been supplied by Julia Becken, his foster daughter. Dr. Eliot is quoted from "The Community Mourns the Death of Dr. Amandus Norman," in *Mere Lys*, January, 1932. Carl W. Schevenius, pastor emeritus of Asbury Methodist Church, Minneapolis, who once visited Norman, was greatly impressed by his library.

10. Janson's letter to Ouren was printed in *Mere Lys*, January, 1918.

11. *Minneapolis Tidende*, March 7, 1918. Stavnheim's address was reprinted in *Mere Lys*, April–July, 1918.

12. The letters were printed in *Mere Lys*, Hage's on the inside cover in January, 1918, and Baumann's in the April–July, 1918, issue. The clergyman for whom the Sons of Norway in 1912 erected a memorial was M. Falk Gjertsen.

13. *Mere Lys*, April–July, 1918.

14. *Mere Lys*, April–July, 1918. This account was reprinted from *Scandia*.

15. *Scandia*, March 2, 1918.

16. Amandus Norman, "Kristofer Janson: As Man, Poet, and Religious Reformer." The address was printed in Unitarian Historical Society, *Proceedings*, 2(Part2):25–27 (Boston, 1932).

17. Norman, "Kristofer Janson: As Man, Poet, and Religious Reformer."

18. Frederick M. Eliot, "Hanska Celebration Gives Proof of the Power and Glory of Unitarianism," in *Christian Register*, September 24, 1931; George F. Patterson, "A Half-Century at Hanska," in *Christian Register*, October 8, 1931.

19. The researches of Alfred Russel Wallace coincided with those of Darwin.

20. Arthur Koestler, "Echoes of the Mind," in *Esquire*, August, 1972.

21. J. B. Rhine, "Spiritualism," in *The ESP Reader,* 12 (New York, 1969).

22. Norman, "Kristofer Janson: As Man, Poet, and Religious Reformer."

A Selected
Bibliography

I. JANSON'S PUBLISHED WORKS RELATED TO HIS YEARS IN AMERICA

A. Books

Den bergtekne. Hamar, Norway, 1876.
The Spellbound Fiddler. Tr. by Auber Forestier (Aubertine Woodward), with an introduction by Rasmus B. Anderson. Chicago, 1880. Second edition, Chicago, 1883.
Amerikanske forholde. Copenhagen, 1881.
Vore besteforældre. Copenhagen, 1881.
Salme og sange for kirke og hjem. Minneapolis, 1883.
Helvedes børn. Chicago, 1884.
Præriens saga. Chicago, 1885.
The Children of Hell. Chicago, 1885.
Wives, Submit Yourselves unto Your Husbands. Chicago, 1886.
Har ortodoksien ret? En række undersøgelser. Minneapolis, 1886.
Nordmænd i Amerika. Copenhagen, 1887.
Et arbeidsdyr. Minneapolis, 1889.
Bag gardinet. Minneapolis, 1889.
Fra begge sider havet. Kristiania, 1890.
Sara. Copenhagen, 1891.
Lys og frihed. Minneapolis, 1892.
Jesus-sangene. Minneapolis, 1893.
Fire foredrag. Copenhagen, 1894.
Ægteskap og skilsmisse: Fire foredrag. Copenhagen, 1895.
Du er kjød af mit kjød. Copenhagen, 1895.
Hvad jeg har oplevet. Kristiania, 1913.

B. Pamphlets

Den norske synode. Minneapolis, 1882.
Sande og falske liberale. Minneapolis, 1883.
Vogter eder for de falske profeter. Minneapolis, 1883.
Skal vi bede til Gud og, i saa fald, hvad skal vi bede om? Minneapolis, 1884.
Jødegud og Kristengud. Minneapolis, 1884. Tr. into Icelandic by Birni Pjeturssyni, Winnipeg, 1887.
De ortodokses og de liberales glæde evangelium. Minneapolis, 1884. Tr. into Icelandic by Birni Pjeturssyni, Winnipeg, 1887.

Kristofer Janson in America

Ortodoksiens modsigelser. Minneapolis, 1885. Tr. into Icelandic by Birni Pjeturssyni, Winnipeg, 1887.
Om bibelen. Minneapolis, 1885.
Svar paa spørgsmaal af en farmergut. Minneapolis, 1887.
Den gjøende hund. Minneapolis, 1887.
Om naadevalget. Minneapolis, 1888.
Hvad de 12 apostle lærte. Minneapolis, 1888.
Var Jesus en kristen? Minneapolis, 1889.
Hvad vil unitarismen? Minneapolis, 1893 [?].
To arbeider foredrag. Minneapolis, 1891.

C. Representative Articles

"A Norse Prose Idyl," in *Dial* (Chicago), November, 1881.
"Religion among the Scandinavians in America," in *Unity* (Chicago), December 1, 1881.
"Kristofer Jansons program," in *Budstikken* (Minneapolis), December 13, 1881.
"The Scandinavians in America," in *Christian Register* (Boston), June 1, 15, 22, 1882.
"Fra Amerika," in *Nyt Tidsskrift* (Kristiania), November, 1882.
"Report from Kristofer Janson," in *Unity*, January 16, 1883.
"Quarterly Report," in *Word and Work* (Boston), June–August, 1883.
"Atmospheric Negations or Truth Tried Through Tornadoes," in *Unity*, August 1, 1883.
"Struck by a Cyclone," in *Christian Register*, August 2, 1883.
"The Scandinavian Mission in Minneapolis," in *Unity*, January 16, 1884.
"Bishop Grundtvig and the Peasant High School," in *Scandinavia* (Chicago), April–May, 1884.
"Our Ancestors," in *Scandinavia*, June, 1884.
"Among the Scandinavians," in *Christian Register*, October 1, 1885.
"The Scandinavian Mission," in *Christian Register*, December 10, 1885.
"Lidt om amerikanske kvinder," in *Framat* (Göteborg), No. 24, 1886.
"A Twice-Told Tale," in *Christian Register*, April 22, 1886.
"How Legends Grow," in *Unitarian* (Chicago), May, 1886.
"The Daisy," in *Christian Register*, June 17, 1886.
"Christmas Customs of Norway," in *Christian Register*, December 16, 1886.
"Brev om bohemeliteraturen," in *Kvinder og Samfundet* (Copenhagen), 1887.
"En kvinde-korstog," in *Nylænde* (Kristiania), August 15, September 1, 15, 1887.
"The Scandinavian Work," in *Christian Register*, September 29, 1887.
"Old Synnove," in *Christian Register*, July 12, 1888.
"Birte," in *Christian Register*, July 19, 1888.
"Sand kvindelighed," in *Hvad Vi Vil* (Copenhagen), May, 1889.

"En gammel jomfru," in *Nordstjernen* (Copenhagen), October, 1889.
"Norsemen in the United States," in *Cosmopolitan*, October, 1890.
"The Scandinavian Mission," in *Christian Register*, December 4, 1890.
"Religious Work with and for Foreigners," in *Unity*, July 13, 1893.

D Periodical

Saamanden, a monthly published in Minneapolis for seven years, from September, 1887, through August, 1894.

II. DISCUSSIONS OF JANSON AND HIS WORK

A By His Contemporaries

H. H. Boyesen, "Kristofer Janson and the Reform of the Norwegian Language," in *North American Review*, October, 1882.
Egil Elda, "Kristofer Janson og den nationale bevægelse i Norge," in *Budstikken*, November 5, 11, 1879.
"En tale om den rene lære," in *Evangelisk Luthersk Kirketidende* (Decorah, Iowa), April 30, 1880.
"Kristofer Janson igjen," in *Folkebladet* (Minneapolis), September 22, 1881.
"Report of Board of Directors' Meeting, American Unitarian Association, November 21," in *Christian Register*, November 24, 1881.
"A New Prophet in Israel," in *Christian Register*, December 1, 1881.
"Kristofer Janson," in *Unity*, December 1, 1881.
Rasmus B. Anderson, "Unitarierne," in *Budstikken*, December 20, 1881.
"Kristofer Jansons program for hans mission i Amerika," in *Folkebladet*, December 22, 1881.
"Ordination of Kristofer Janson," in *Unitarian Review and Religious Magazine* (Boston), January, 1882.
H. H. Boyesen, "Letter to the Critic," in *The Critic* (New York), January 14, 1882.
"Kr. Jansons kirkelige program," in *Evangelisk Luthersk Kirketidende*, March 3, 1882.
"Western Conference Meeting in Cleveland, Ohio, May 4–9, 1882," in *Christian Register*, May 11, 1882, *Unity*, May 16, 1882.
"Struck by a Cyclone," in *Christian Register*, August 3, 1883.
"Advarsel til det luterske kirkefolk," in *Evangelisk Luthersk Kirketidende*, January 16, 1884.
J. J. Julson, "Lidt om pastor K. Jansons seneste optræden her i Chicago," in *Skandinaven* (Chicago), March 25, 1884.
Knut Hamsund, "Hr. dr. Julson," in *Skandinaven*, April 23, 1884.
"A Pathetic Story," in *Minneapolis Evening Tribune*, December 10, 1884.

Kristofer Janson in America

O. J. Rollevson, "A Protest," in *Minneapolis Evening Journal*, January 3, 1885.

"Overtro og vantro," in *Folkebladet*, April 21, 1886.

"We Are Orthodox," in *Minneapolis Evening Journal*, May 3, 1886.

"The Ruined Church," in *Christian Register*, May 13, 1886.

"A New Disaster to Mr. Janson's Church—Help Needed," in *Unitarian* (Chicago), May, 1886.

"Mr. Janson's Appeal," "The Scandinavian Jeremiah," and "A Heraldic View," in *Christian Register*, May 13, 1886.

"Tornadoes and What They Teach," in *Unitarian,* May, 1886.

H. H. Boyesen, "The New School of Norwegian Literature," in *The Critic,* May 7, 1887.

George Batchelor, "In the North-West," in *Christian Register*, October 27, 1887.

Knut Hamsun, "Kristofer Janson," in *Ny Jord* (Copenhagen), July–December, 1888.

Henrik Cavling, "Kirkelige forhold" in *Verdens Gang* (Kristiania), December 3, 1888.

Oscar Gundersen, "Kristofer Janson," in *Minneapolis Søndag Tidende*, August 17, 1890.

"Kristofer Janson and the Scandinavian-American," in *Unitarian*, November, 1890.

Axel Lundeberg, "Kristofer Janson and His Work," in *The North* (Minneapolis), April 2, 7, May 11, 18, June 22, 1892.

A. Grinager, "Smaatræk fra Kristofer Jansons virksomhed i Minneapolis," in *Scandia* (Chicago), February 16, March 2, 1918.

U. H. Lindelie, "Nogle erindringer og betragtninger," in *Decorah-Posten* (Decorah, Iowa), May 31, 1935.

Amandus Norman, "Kristofer Janson: As Man, Poet, and Religious Reformer," The Unitarian Historical Society, *Proceedings*, Vol. 2, Part 2 (Boston), 1932.

B   By Newspapers

Skandinaven, 1879–84.

Norden (Chicago), 1879–81.

Fædrelandet og Emigranten (La Crosse, Wisconsin), 1879–86; Minneapolis, 1886–89.

Budstikken, 1879–92.

Decorah-Posten, 1879–92.

Folkebladet, 1879–90.

Albert Lea Posten (Albert Lea, Minnesota), 1883.

Minneapolis Morning Tribune, 1885, 1889, 1890, 1891.

Minneapolis Evening Journal, 1884–87.

Illustreret Ugeblad (Minneapolis), 1888–89.
Fergus Falls Ugeblad (Fergus Falls, Minnesota), 1888.
The North, 1889–93.
Vikingen (Madison, Wisconsin), 1889.
Normanna (Minneapolis), 1888.
Minneapolis Søndag Tidende, 1890.

C. By Church Periodicals and Records

Unitarian Review and Religious Magazine, 1882.
Christian Register, 1881–93.
Unity, 1881–93.
Unitarian, 1886–89.
Evangelisk Luthersk Kirketidende, 1880, 1882, 1884, 1885, 1894.
*Minutes of the Twenty-Eighth Annual Meeting of the Western Unitarian
    Conference, May 4, 1882.* Filed in Abraham Lincoln Center, Chicago.
    Unitarian Historical Society, *Proceedings*, Vol. 2, Part 2, Boston, 1932.

D. By Correspondence

From the late Dr. Eilev Janson of Seattle, Washington, October 17, 1958,
    to June 18, 1961.
From the late Mrs. Thomas H. (Dina Behr) Kolderup, January 26, 1959,
    to August 31, 1965.
From the late Fru Signe Forchhammer of Copenhagen, August 26, 1959,
    January 7, 1960.
From the late Mrs. Gudrun Gundersen Rom, June 1, 1960, to June 25, 1960.
From Mrs. Elinor Janson Hudson, 1965 to 1973.

III. BACKGROUND MATERIAL

A. Books

Rasmus B. Anderson, *Life Story of Rasmus B. Anderson*. Assisted by Albert
    O. Barton. Madison, Wisconsin, 1915.
Aschehougs konversajons leksikon. Oslo, 1948.
Isaac Atwater, ed., *History of Minneapolis, Minnesota*. New York, 1893.
William D. P. Bliss, ed., *Encyclopedia of Social Reform*. New York, 1908.
Georg Brandes, *Levned II: Et tiaar*. Copenhagen, 1907.
Gustav Brosing, *Det gamle Bergen*. Bergen, 1955.
Michael Bryan, *Dictionary of Painters and Engravers*. New York, 1964.
Solon J. Buck, *The Agrarian Crusade*. New Haven, 1921.
Henrik Cavling, *Fra Amerika*, Vol. 2. Copenhagen, 1897.
Henry Steele Commager, *The American Mind*. New Haven, 1950.

Kristofer Janson in America

James Dombrowski, *The Early Days of Christian Socialism in America*. New York, 1936.

Benjamin O. Flower, *Progressive Men, Women and Movements of the Past Twenty-Five Years*. Boston, 1914.

Betty Friedan, *The Feminine Mystique*. New York, 1965.

Knut Gjerset, *History of the Norwegian People*, Vol. 2. New York, 1915.

J. B. Halvorsen, *Norsk forfatter leksikon 1814–1880*. Kristiania, 1892.

Carl G. O. Hansen, *My Minneapolis*. Minneapolis, 1956.

Andreas Helland, *Georg Sverdrup*. Minneapolis, 1947.

John D. Hicks, *The Populist Revolt*. Minneapolis, 1931.

Morris Hillquit, *History of Socialism in the United States*. New York, 1903.

Richard Hofstadter, *Social Darwinism in American Thought*. Boston, 1955.

Charles Howard Hopkins, *The Rise of the Social Gospel in American Protestantism, 1865–1915*, revised edition. New Haven, 1940.

Halvdan Koht, *Bjørnstjerne Bjørnson: Kamp Liv II*. Oslo, 1932.

John A. Kouwenhoven, *Adventures of America, 1857–1900*. New York, 1938.

Laurence M. Larson, *The Changing West and Other Essays*. Northfield, Minnesota, 1935.

Arthur H. Lyttle, *Freedom Moves West*. Boston, 1952.

Albert Nelson Marquis, ed., *The Book of Minnesotans: A Biographical Dictionary of Living Men in the State of Minnesota*. Chicago, 1907.

Olav S. Midttun, *Bjørnstjerne Bjørnson og folkehøyskolen*. Oslo, 1954.

Frank Luther Mott, *A History of American Magazines*. Cambridge, Massachusetts, 1957.

E. Clifford Nelson and Eugene F. Fevold, *The Lutherans among Norwegian-Americans*. 2 vols. Minneapolis, 1960.

O. N. Nelson, *History of the Scandinavians and Successful Scandinavians in the United States*. 2 vols. Minneapolis, 1893; second revised edition, 1969.

Norsk biografisk leksikon. Oslo, 1934.

Olaf M. Norlie, *History of the Norwegian People in America*. Minneapolis, 1925.

Bessie Louise Pierce, *A History of Chicago*. New York, 1957.

Louis F. Post, *The Prophet of San Francisco*. New York, 1930.

Martin Ridge, *Ignatius Donnelly: The Portrait of a Politician*. Chicago, 1962.

J. Magnus Rohne, *Norwegian-American Lutheranism up to 1872*. New York, 1926.

Marion D. Shutter, *Reverend James Harvey Tuttle, D. D.: A Memoir*. Minneapolis, 1905.

Einar Skavlan, *Knut Hamsun*. Oslo, 1929.

Alfred Söderström, *Minneapolis minnen*, Minneapolis, 1899.

Leo Tolstoy, *A Confession and What I Believe*. Tr. by Aylmer Maude. Oxford, 1941.

Tribune Handbook of Minneapolis. Minneapolis, 1884.
Gregory Weinstein, *The Ardent Eighties.* New York, 1928.
Colin Wilson, *The Occult.* New York, 1971.
Johannes B. Wist, *Norsk-amerikanernes festskrift.* Decorah, Iowa, 1914.

B. Articles

Olav Aasmundstad, "Kristofer Janson—Minne fraa samvære med ham," in *Syn og Segn*, Oslo, 1911.
Frederick M. Eliot, "Hanska Celebration Gives Proof of the Power and Glory of Unitarianism," in *Christian Register*, September 24, 1931.
Frederick M. Eliot, "The Community Mourns the Death of Dr. Amandus Norman," in *Mere Lys* (Hanska, Minnesota), January, 1932.
Illit Grøndahl and Ola Raknes, "Henrik Wergeland," in *Chapters in Norwegian Literature*, London, 1923.
Ivar Handagard, "Kristofer Janson," in *Syn og Segn*, Oslo, 1925.
John Halvorson, "Historical Review of the Norwegian Evangelical Lutheran Synod in America," in *History of the Scandinavians and Successful Scandinavians in the United States*, Vol. 1, 1893.
John D. Hicks, "The Peoples Party in Minnesota," in *Minnesota History Bulletin*, St. Paul, November, 1924.
Ole Jorgensen, "Speech at the Laying of the Cornerstone of Nora Church Parsonage, June 24, 1906," in *Nora fri-kristne menighed* (Hanska, Minnesota), 1906.
Arthur Koestler, "Echoes of the Mind," in *Esquire*, August, 1972.
George F. Patterson, "A Half-Century at Hanska," in *Christian Register*, October 8, 1931.
Arthur M. Schlesinger, "A Critical Period in American Religion," Massachusetts Historical Society, *Proceedings*, Boston, 1935.
L. Stavnheim, "Amandus Norman," in *Mere Lys*, January, 1932.
Olaf B. Viig, "Kristofer Janson," in *Syn og Segn*, Oslo, 1918.

C. Newspapers and Periodicals

Chicago Tribune, April 8, October 10, 18, 1879.
Freeborn County Standard, Freeborn, Minnesota, May 5, 1881.
Minneapolis Journal, January 28, February 5, 1880.
The Housekeeper (Minneapolis), September 15, 1892.

IV. MANUSCRIPTS

The Rasmus B. Anderson Papers in the Wisconsin State Historical Society in Madison. These include the letters of Kristofer and Drude Janson, Hjalmar H. Boyesen, Andreas Ueland, Aubertine Woodward, Eric L.

Petersen, Nils Michelet, and Dr. Knut Hoegh to Anderson. They also contain the letters and notes of Drude Janson to Mrs. Karina Anderson.

The Jones Papers in the library of Meadville Theological School of Lombard College in Chicago, Illinois. They include the letters of Kristofer Janson and Henry M. Simmons to Jenkin Lloyd Jones.

The Bjørnstjerne Bjørnson Papers are in the University Library in Oslo, Norway. They include the letters of both Kristofer and Drude Janson to Bjørnstjerne and Karoline Bjørnson.

The letters of Knut Hamsun to Erik Skram are to be found in Tore Hamsun's *Knut Hamsun som han var*, Oslo, 1956.

The letters of Kristofer Janson to Amandus Norman were printed in *Mere Lys* (Hanska, Minnesota) in April–July, 1918.

Kristofer Janson's letter to Aubertine Woodward of January 8, 1888, is in the Aubertine Woodward Moore Papers at the Wisconsin State Historical Society.

The letters of Anne Romundstad to her fiance, Johannes J. Skørdalsvold, dated October 28, 1888, and April 28, 1889, are in the possession of the Skurdalsvold family in Minneapolis.

Kristofer Janson's letter to Johannes J. Skørdalsvold, dated August 16, 1890, is in the possession of the Skurdalsvold family.

Kristofer Janson's letter to Professor F. A. Schmidt, dated March 31, 1891, is in the archives of the Norwegian-American Historical Association.

Kristofer Janson's letter of November 28, 1890, to the trustees of Unity Church of St. Paul is in the Unity Church Papers in the Minnesota Historical Society, St. Paul.

The letter of Agnes Behr to her sister, Dina, dated January 2, 1892, was given to the author by the late Mrs. Dina Behr Kolderup.

An excerpt from the letter of Ingeborg Janson to Ragna Alten was given to the author by Professor Einar Haugen. It was then in the possession of Professor Didrik Arup Seip, Holmsbo, Norway.

The letter of Peder Ydstie to Torkel Oftelie, dated "the 28th" is in the archives of the Norwegian-American Historical Association.

"The Free Christian Church of Minneapolis by Skørdalsvold," a typewritten manuscript, was given the author by Mrs. P. J. Hansen, the wife of a pastor of the Nora Free Christian Church of Hanska, Minnesota.

"H. F. No. 222, A Bill for an Act to Prescribe the Punishment of Murder in the First Degree," introduced by H. P. Bjorge on February 2, 1891, is to be found in the Minnesota State Archives, St. Paul.

Index